Projective Identification

In this book Elizabeth Spillius and Edna O'Shaughnessy explore the development of the concept of projective identification, which had important antecedents in the work of Freud and others, but was given a specific name and definition by Melanie Klein. They describe Klein's published and unpublished views on the topic, and then consider the way the concept has been variously described, evolved, accepted, rejected and modified by analysts of different schools of thought and in various locations – Britain, Western Europe, North America and Latin America.

The authors believe that this unusually widespread interest in a particular concept and its varied 'fate' has occurred not only because of beliefs about its clinical usefulness in the psychoanalytic setting but also because projective identification is a universal aspect of human interaction and communication.

Projective Identification: The Fate of a Concept will appeal to any psychoanalyst or psychotherapist who uses the ideas of transference and counter-transference, as well as to academics wanting further insight into the evolution of this concept as it moves between different cultures and countries.

Elizabeth Spillius studied general psychology at the University of Toronto (1945), social anthropology at the University of Chicago, The London School of Economics and The Tavistock Institute of Human Relations (1945–1957) and psychoanalysis at the Institute of Psychoanalysis in London (1956 to the present). Her main writings have been *Family and Social Network* (1957, writing as Elizabeth Bott), *Tongan Society at the Time of Captain Cook's Visits* (1982), *Melanie Klein Today* (1988) and *Encounters with Melanie Klein* (2007). She is the Hon Archivist of the Melanie Klein Trust.

Edna O'Shaughnessy came to psychoanalysis from philosophy she trained first as a Child Psychotherapist at the Tavistock Clinic in the 1950s, and then in the 1960s, she trained at the British Psychoanalytical Society, of which she is a training and supervising analyst and also a child analyst. Her many published papers are written from both a clinical and a conceptual perspective.

THE NEW LIBRARY OF PSYCHOANALYSIS
General Editor: Alessandra Lemma

The New Library of Psychoanalysis was launched in 1987 in association with the Institute of Psychoanalysis, London. It took over from the International Psychoanalytical Library which published many of the early translations of the works of Freud and the writings of most of the leading British and Continental psychoanalysts.

The purpose of the New Library of Psychoanalysis is to facilitate a greater and more widespread appreciation of psychoanalysis and to provide a forum for increasing mutual understanding between psychoanalysts and those working in other disciplines such as the social sciences, medicine, philosophy, history, linguistics, literature and the arts. It aims to represent different trends both in British psychoanalysis and in psychoanalysis generally. The New Library of Psychoanalysis is well placed to make available to the English-speaking world psychoanalytic writings from other European countries and to increase the interchange of ideas between British and American psychoanalysts. Through the *Teaching Series*, the New Library of Psychoanalysis now also publishes books that provide comprehensive, yet accessible, overviews of selected subject areas aimed at those studying psychoanalysis and related fields such as the social sciences, philosophy, literature and the arts.

The Institute, together with the British Psychoanalytical Society, runs a low-fee psychoanalytic clinic, organizes lectures and scientific events concerned with psychoanalysis and publishes the *International Journal of Psychoanalysis*. It runs a training course in psychoanalysis which leads to membership of the International Psychoanalytical Association – the body which preserves internationally agreed standards of training, of professional entry, and of professional ethics and practice for psychoanalysis as initiated and developed by Sigmund Freud. Distinguished members of the Institute have included Michael Balint, Wilfred Bion, Ronald Fairbairn, Anna Freud, Ernest Jones, Melanie Klein, John Rickman and Donald Winnicott.

Previous general editors have included David Tuckett, who played a very active role in the establishment of the New Library. He was followed as general editor by Elizabeth Bott Spillius, who was in turn followed by Susan Budd and then by Dana Birksted-Breen.

Current Members of the Advisory Board include Liz Allison, Giovanna di Ceglie, Rosemary Davies and Richard Rusbridger.

Previous Members of the Advisory Board include Christopher Bollas, Ronald Britton, Catalina Bronstein, Donald Campbell, Sara Flanders, Stephen Grosz, John Keene, Eglé Laufer, Alessandra Lemma, Juliet Mitchell, Michael Parsons, Rosine Jozef Perelberg, Mary Target and David Taylor.

The current General Editor of the New Library of Psychoanalysis is Alessandra Lemma, but this book was initiated and edited by Dana Birksted-Breen, former General Editor.

ALSO IN THIS SERIES

Projected Shadows: Psychoanalytic Reflections on the Representation of Loss in European Cinema Edited by Andrea Sabbadini

Encounters with Melanie Klein: Selected Papers of Elizabeth Spillius Elizabeth Spillius. Edited by Priscilla Roth and Richard Rusbridger

Constructions and the Analytic Field: History, Scenes and Destiny Domenico Chianese

Yesterday, Today and Tomorrow Hanna Segal. Edited by Nicola Abel-Hirsch

Psychoanalysis Comparable and Incomparable: The Evolution of a Method to Describe and Compare Psychoanalytic Approaches David Tuckett, Roberto Basile, Dana Birksted-Breen, Tomas Böhm, Paul Denis, Antonino Ferro, Helmut Hinz, Arne Jemstedt, Paola Mariotti and Johan Schubert

Time, Space and Phantasy Rosine Jozef Perelberg

Rediscovering Psychoanalysis: Thinking and Dreaming, Learning and Forgetting Thomas H. Ogden

Mind Works: Technique and Creativity in Psychoanalysis Antonino Ferro

Doubt, Conviction and the Analytic Process: Selected Papers of Michael Feldman Michael Feldman. Edited by Betty Joseph

Melanie Klein in Berlin: Her First Psychoanalysis of Children Claudia Frank. Edited by Elizabeth Spillius

The Psychotic Wavelength: A Psychoanalytic Perspective for Psychiatry Richard Lucas

Betweenity: A Discussion of the Concept of Borderline Judy Gammelgaard

The Intimate Room: Theory and Technique of the Analytic Field Giuseppe Civitarese

Bion Today Edited by Chris Mawson

Secret Passages: The Theory and Technique of Interpsychic Relations Stefano Bolognini

Intersubjective Processes and the Unconscious: An Integration of Freudian, Kleinian and Bionian Perspectives Lawrence J. Brown

Seeing and Being Seen: Emerging from a Psychic Retreat John Steiner

Avoiding Emotions, Living Emotions Antonino Ferro

TITLES IN THE NEW LIBRARY OF PSYCHOANALYSIS TEACHING SERIES

Reading Freud: A Chronological Exploration of Freud's Writings Jean-Michel Quinodoz

Listening to Hanna Segal: Her Contribution to Psychoanalysis Jean-Michel Quinodoz

Reading French Psychoanalysis Edited by Dana Birksted-Breen, Sara Flanders and Alain Gibeault

Reading Winnicott Edited by Lesley Caldwell and Angela Joyce

THE NEW LIBRARY OF PSYCHOANALYSIS

General Editor Alessandra Lemma

Projective Identification
The Fate of a Concept

Edited by
Elizabeth Spillius and
Edna O'Shaughnessy

LONDON AND NEW YORK

First published 2012
by Routledge
27 Church Road, Hove, East Sussex, BN3 2FA

Simultaneously published in the USA and Canada
by Routledge
711 Third Avenue, New York, NY 10017

Routledge is an imprint of the Taylor & Francis Group, an Informa Business

British Library Cataloguing in Publication Data
A catalogue record for this book is available from the British Library

Library of Congress Cataloging-in-Publication Data
Projective identification: the fate of a concept / Edited by Elizabeth
Spillius and Edna O'Shaughnessy.
  p.; cm.
Includes bibliographical references and index.
ISBN 978–0–415–60528–1 (hbk) — ISBN 978–0–415–60529–8 (pbk)
1. Projective identification. 2. Klein, Melanie, 1882–1960.
3. Psychoanalysis—History. I. Spillius, Elizabeth Bott,
1924– editor. II. O'Shaughnessy, Edna, editor.
  [DNLM: 1. Klein, Melanie, 1882–1960. 2. Projection. 3. History, 20th
Century. 4. Identification (Psychology) 5. Psychoanalytic Theory—history.
WM 193.5.P7]
  RC455.4.P76P76 2011
  616.89'17—dc22   2010050600

ISBN: 978–0–415–60528–1 (hbk)
ISBN: 978–0–415–60529–8 (pbk)

Typeset in Bembo
by RefineCatch Limited, Bungay, Suffolk
Paperback cover design by Sandra Heath

Printed and bound in Great Britain by CPI Antony Rowe, Chippenham, Wiltshire

Contents

Contents

Contents

Contributors

Melanie Klein was born in Vienna in 1882 and had brief analyses with Sandor Ferenczi in Budapest and with Karl Abraham in Berlin. In 1925 she was invited by Ernest Jones to give lectures in England and in 1926 to settle in this country, where she gradually gained adherents and developed new psychoanalytic ideas, although she strongly asserted her loyalty to the work of Freud and Abraham. She died in England in 1960. She is usually credited with introducing the concept of projective identification, although other analysts mentioned it in passing before her.

Wilfred Bion further developed Klein's and his own seminal ideas, especially, in the case of projective identification, in distinguishing between psychotic and normal modes of projective identification.

Herbert Rosenfeld was born in Germany but came to Britain in the 1930s where he was analysed by Melanie Klein and became well known particularly for his innovative work in understanding psychotic patients. In the paper reprinted in this book, he helpfully describes several different types of projective identification in psychotic patients.

Betty Joseph has been awarded the Mary Sigourney award for outstanding contributions to psychoanalysis. She is renowned for her interest in psychoanalytic technique, and in particular for her understanding of the expression of projective identification in the analyst–patient relationship.

Michael Feldman was born in South Africa but studied psycho-analysis in Britain and is especially interested in the technique of analysing analyst–patient relationships, including the expression of forms of projective identification.

Ignes Sodré was born in Brazil but came to England and began her study of psychoanalysis when quite young. She has been particularly interested in psychoanalytic technique, including the interpretation of projective identification, and she is also especially interested in the relation between psychoanalysis and literature.

Joseph Sandler was originally from South Africa and came to Britain when quite young where he became a member of the Contemporary Freudian 'group' of British analysts. He was also interested in Kleinian ideas, especially projective identification. Many Kleinians have adopted Sandler's ideas about the 'actualisation' of unconscious phantasies and beliefs, an important aspect of projective identification.

Helmut Hinz together with Elizabeth Spillius, Jorge Canestri, and Jean-Michel Quinodoz gave papers on projective identification at the 2002 Congress of the European Federation of Psychoanalysis in Prague. Dr Hinz is a member of the German Psychoanalytical Association (DPV) and practices in Tübingen. The paper he gave at the Prague Congress on projective identification is reprinted in this book.

Jorge Canestri is a member of the Italian Psychoanalytic Association and is also an overseas member of the Argentine Psychoanalytic Association. The paper he gave at the Prague Congress in 2002 is reprinted in this book.

Jean–Michel Quinodoz is a member of the Swiss Psychoanalytical Society and practices psychoanalysis mainly in Cologny, Geneva. His paper in this book is a reworked version of the paper he gave at the Prague Congress.

Roy Schafer is a member of the American Psychoanalytic Association. He practises mainly in New York, although he lectures and teaches more widely. He has contributed an original paper on American views on projective identification to this book.

Arthur Malin is a member of the American Psychoanalytical Association and of the Los Angeles Institute and Society for Psychoanalytic Studies. In 1966 he and James Grotstein were the first American analysts to write a paper specifically on projective identification; that paper is reprinted in this book.

James Grotstein is a member of the American Psychoanalytic Association and of the Psychoanalytic Centre of California. He and Arthur Malin wrote the first main paper on projective identification in the United States.

Thomas Ogden is a member of the American Psychoanalytic Association, the Psychoanalytic Institute of Northern California and the Psychoanalytic Centre of California. He wrote one of the early (1979) and influential American papers on projective identification, which is reproduced in this book.

Albert Mason originally studied psychoanalysis in England and emigrated to Los Angeles in 1967. He is now a member of the Psychoanalytic Centre of California, the American Psychoanalytic Association and the British Psycho-Analytical Society. His original contribution to this book gives numerous clinical descriptions of patients' expressions of projective identification.

Luiz Meyer practices psychoanalysis in São Paulo, Brazil and introduces the contributions to the description of the use of the concept of projective identification in Latin America.

Gustavo Jarast of the Argentinian Psychoanalytic Association describes the development of the concept of projective identification in Argentina.

Marina Massi of the Brazilian Society of Psychoanalysis of São Paulo describes the historical development of psychoanalysis in Brazil, its many complications because of the multiplicity of psychoanalytic centres, and the many views on the concept of projective identification.

Juan Francisco Jordan-Moore is a member of the Chilean Psychoanalytic Association and practices in Santiago. He describes the critical reception of the concept of projective identification in Chile, with particular attention to attempts by Chilean authors to develop an intersubjective or bi-personal field theory that would enable a fuller account of the complexity of the phenomena involved.

Acknowledgements

Elizabeth Spillius and Edna O'shaughnessy wish to express their thanks, first, to all the authors whose contributions make up this volume. Second, we are grateful to the Melanie Klein Trust both for their general encouragement and also for their financial help which enabled us to employ Sophie Boswell and Jessica Brighty, our first two Editorial Assistants, and later to seek the help of Elizabeth Allison who saw the book through to its conclusion with meticulous editing and energy. Our thanks are also due to John Churcher for valuable assistance, to Richard Rusbridger for helpful advice throughout, to Dana Birksted-Breen as Editor of the New Library, and to the three anonymous readers of our earlier manuscript.

Permissions acknowledgements

Chapter 2 is based on: M. Klein, 'Notes on some schizoid mechanisms'. *International Journal of Psychoanalysis*, 27: 99–110, 1946. © Institute of Psychoanalysis, London, UK. Material reprinted with permission.

Chapter 4 is based on: W.R. Bion, 'Attacks on linking'. *International Journal of Psychoanalysis*, 40: 308–315, 1959. © Institute of Psychoanalysis, London, UK. Material reprinted with permission.

Chapter 5 is based on: H.A. Rosenfeld, 'Contribution to the psychopathology of psychotic states: The importance of projective identification in the ego structure and object relations of the psychotic patient. In P. Doucet and C. Laurin (Eds.), *Problems of Psychosis, Vol. I.*, pp. 115–128. The Hague: Excerpta Medica. Material reprinted with permission.

Chapter 7 is based on: M. Feldman, 'Projective identification: the analyst's involvement'. *International Journal of Psychoanalysis*, 78: 227–241, 1997. © Institute of Psychoanalysis, London, UK. Material reprinted with permission.

Chapter 11 is based on: H. Hinz, 'Projective identification: The fate of the concept in Germany'. *European Psychoanalytical Federation Bulletin*, 56, 2002.

Chapter 12 is based on: J. Canestri, 'Projective identification: The fate of the concept in Italy and Spain'. *European Psychoanalytical Federation Bulletin*, 56, 2002.

Chapter 16 is based on: A. Malin and J.S. Grotstein, 'Projective identification in the therapeutic process'. *International Journal of Psychoanalysis*, 47: 26–31, 1966. © Institute of Psychoanalysis, London, UK. Material reprinted with permission.

Chapter 17 is based on: T. Ogden, 'On projective identification'. *International Journal of Psychoanalysis*, 60: 357–373, 1979. © Institute of Psychoanalysis, London, UK. Material reprinted with permission.

Foreword

Elizabeth Spillius and Edna O'Shaughnessy

When the term 'projective identification' was introduced into the language of psychoanalysis in 1946, there already existed a rich though unsystematised harvest of knowledge about identification. Freud himself had described the primary identifications of the ego with its objects, and also how some identifications can divide or impoverish the ego, e.g., hysterical, multiple and group identifications, while others, like the narcissistic identifications with the object in melancholia, alter the ego in complex morbid ways, and further-more, how the identifications that form the super-ego and the ego ideal structure the mind and cause the ego anxiety through their judgments of guilt and demands, even as they enrich the personality with ideals. In *The Language of Psychoanalysis* Laplanche and Pontalis wrote that in 'Freud's work the concept of identification comes little by little to have the central importance which makes it, not simply one psychical mechanism among others, but the operation itself whereby the human subject is constituted' (Laplanche and Pontalis, 1973, p. 206).

Abraham and Ferenczi also contributed to the notion of identifica-tion, and Anna Freud noted a defence mechanism of identification with the aggressor. But it was Melanie Klein who extended the concept in a far-reaching way. She conceived of identification as creating a whole inner world from the beginning of life, through introjection and projection, so that the ego has, as she expressed it, 'an orientation outwards and inwards' with 'a constant fluctuation between internal and external objects and situations' (Klein, 1945,

p. 409). And then in 1946 in 'Notes on some schizoid mechanisms' she described another form of identification, *projective* identification (in contradistinction to *introjective* identification), a defence mechanism used by the early ego in states of anxiety when, in an omnipotent phantasy, it splits off and projects parts of itself into the object with consequent identifications for ego and object that structure their ensuing relations (Klein, 1946).

Klein's concept of projective identification has aroused an unusual degree of interest among psychoanalysts, both because of its hypothesised role in early normal and abnormal development, and more especially for its illumination of the ways in which communication happens between patient and analyst. Among Kleinian analysts it became a major area of development. Among analysts of other schools it has been adopted for essential or occasional use, and also redefined, disputed and rejected from a variety of perspectives.

A concept is linked many times over – to the phenomena that give it meaning, to other concepts in the language in which it has its place, and to its users who over time develop, enlarge, restrict and even change its meaning. All these have added to the complex, sometimes confusing or even contradictory uses of the term 'projective identification'.

In this book we have several aims: to return to the origins of the concept in the published and unpublished archival writings of Melanie Klein; to try to understand the complexities of the concept itself; to chart its further Kleinian development and also its evolution in other places and other psychoanalytic orientations; to note the grounds for its rejection; and overall, to explore the conceptual and clinical problems that accompany the further evolution and migration of a concept from one psychoanalytic theory to another. All of these endeavours have been much assisted by contributions from colleagues in Britain, Europe, and North and South America.

Introducing *The Language of Psychoanalysis* by Laplanche and Pontalis, Daniel Lagache wrote '*words, like ideas (and together with ideas,) are not merely created – they have a fate*' (Laplanche and Pontalis, 1973, p. viii, our italics). What may be seen in this volume about the creation and the fate of the concept of projective identification, might, we think, in some measure, apply to other significant psychoanalytic concepts.

PART ONE

Melanie Klein's work

The emergence of Klein's idea of projective identification in her published and unpublished work

Elizabeth Spillius

Introduction

I will first describe something of the history of the term 'projective identification' followed by discussion of Klein's own ideas about it in the two published versions of her paper 'Notes on some schizoid mechanisms' (Klein, 1946, 1952a) and in her 1955 paper 'On identification'. Then I will discuss two sets of unpublished entries on the concept of projective identification in the Melanie Klein Archive.

History of the concept

Although Melanie Klein was the originator of the definition and usage of the concept of projective identification as we know it today, she was not the first person to use the actual term. It was first used by Edoardo Weiss, in 1925 in a paper called 'Über eine noch unbeschriebene Phase der Entwicklung zur heterosexuellen Liebe' in the context of explaining sexual object choice (Weiss, 1925). Klein refers to Weiss's paper in *The Psycho-Analysis of Children* (Klein, 1932b, p. 250, n. 2) where she explains Weiss's understanding of sexual object choice, using the term 'projection' in her explanation but not discussing his use of the term 'projective identification' (see also Massidda, 1999 and Steiner, 1999).

There was another precursor to Klein's use of the term projective identification. In 1945, a year before Klein published her first version of 'Notes on some schizoid mechanisms', Marjorie Brierley mentions projective identification in a paper called 'Further notes on the implications of psycho-analysis: Metapsychology and personology', in which she says

> projective identification of ego-ideal with outer object, human or abstract, would appear to be a feature of the economy of all fanatics [. . .] the pedestrian everyday charity that begins at home, as distinct from fanatical devotion of ultra-personal interests, may depend upon projective identification with a fairly well-libidinized operative self.
>
> (Brierley, 1945, p. 96)

Brierley mentions projective identification again in a second paper in 1947. Brierley and Klein do not refer to each other's work, but it looks as if considerable thinking and discussion about introjection, projection and identification was going on among British analysts in the 1940s and that projective identification was not so much a special focus as part of this general discussion.

Klein's published views on projective identification

Klein first mentions the idea of projective identification in her paper 'Notes on some schizoid mechanisms' in 1946 but at first only in passing. In the original version of 'Notes on some schizoid mechanisms', which was published in the *International Journal of Psycho-Analysis* in 1946, Klein describes the process of projective identification as follows:

> Together with these harmful excrements, expelled in hatred, split off parts of the ego are also projected on to the mother or, as I would rather call it, into the mother. These excrements and bad parts of the self are meant not only to injure the object but also to control it and take possession of it. Insofar as the mother comes to contain the bad parts of the self, she is not felt to be a separate individual but is felt to be the bad self.
>
> Much of the hatred against parts of the self is now directed towards the mother. This leads to a particular kind of identifica-

tion which establishes the prototype of an aggressive object relation.

(Klein, 1946, p. 102)

In the next paragraph Klein adds:

> It is, however, not only the bad parts of the self which are expelled and projected, but also good parts of the self. Excrements then have the significance of gifts; and parts of the ego which, together with excrements, are expelled and projected into the other person represent the good, i.e. the loving parts of the self.
>
> (Klein, 1946, p. 102)

In essence these paragraphs are a definition of projective identification, but the concept is not mentioned by name. The actual name 'projective identification' is mentioned not as part of this definition but only in a passing comment two pages later where Klein says, 'I have referred to the weakening and impoverishment of the ego resulting from excessive splitting and projective identification' (Klein, 1946, p. 104);[1] this is the only mention of the concept of projective identification by name in the 1946 version of the paper. It was not until the 1952 version of 'Notes on some schizoid mechanisms' that Klein added the crucial sentence 'I suggest for these processes the term "projective identification" ' to the defining paragraphs quoted above.

Somewhat confusingly, it has become customary for this 1952 version of the paper to be cited as '1946' in the Kleinian literature. It is the 1952 version that is reprinted in Chapter 2 in the present book.

The 1952 version of the paper differs from the 1946 version not only in including the term 'projective identification' in the definition but also in other respects. There are two new paragraphs, one of which is devoted to projective identification, and there is some rearranging of the order of other paragraphs. There are also thirteen new footnotes, notably one to Paula Heimann thanking her for her

---

1 I am grateful to Riccardo Steiner for pointing out that Klein uses the term 'projective identification' in the 1946 version of her paper even though it is not part of her definition of the concept.

'stimulating suggestions' about Klein's paper, one to Ferenczi (1930) on fragmentation, two to Rosenfeld, especially to his papers on depersonalisation (Rosenfeld, 1947) and on male homosexuality and paranoia (Rosenfeld, 1949), and one to an unpublished paper on paranoid attitudes by Joan Riviere which I have been unable to track down (Riviere, unpublished).

According to Hanna Segal (personal communication) the term 'projective identification' was suggested to Klein by her colleague (and patient) Roger Money-Kyrle. Segal also said that Klein did not like the term 'projective identification' and she added that Klein thought of the term in the context of comparing projection with introjection. In the case of introjection, once an object has been taken in several things may happen to it: it may exist inside the subject as an internal object, good or bad; the subject may unconsciously identify with this internal object or with an aspect of it; or both processes may occur, that is, the internal object may be recognised as separate from oneself but it may also be identified with. Klein, according to Segal, thought of projective identification as a parallel process to introjective identification, meaning that projective identification was only one of several possible outcomes of projection, although Klein does not describe what these other outcomes might be.

After 1952 Klein makes comparatively few mentions of projective identification except of course for her paper 'On identification' in 1955 in which identification is the central theme (Klein, 1955). But this paper is an analysis not of a patient but of a character in a novel who projects his whole self into various other people in order to acquire their identity. The idea of this sort of projective identification is still used, but nowadays the concept is more frequently used to describe the projection of aspects of the individual's self into other objects.

Apart from this 1955 paper, the most frequent mentions of projective identification come in 1957 in *Envy and Gratitude* where Klein notes the projective character of envy and the contribution envy makes to difficulties in making the basic and primal split between good and bad experiences and feelings, this split being essential for the development of integration of the ego. Envy leads to attacks on the good object which take the form of projection of bad parts of the self into the good object, resulting in confusion between the good and the bad self, between good and bad aspects of the object, and between self and object.

Klein's unpublished notes on projective identification in the Melanie Klein Archive[2]

If one were to know about Klein's views on projective identification only from her published work, one would conclude that she did not think the concept was very important, for she published comparatively little about it. Once one explores the Klein Archive, however, one finds much more material on the topic, both in the form of theoretical thoughts and in clinical illustration. One file of particular importance, B98, dates from 1946/1947 when Klein was working on her important paper 'Notes on some schizoid mechanisms' (1946), which she always refers to in the Archive as 'my splitting paper', never as 'my projective identification paper'. The file B98 consists of excerpts of clinical material, sporadic notes and some longer theoretical thoughts especially on splitting and projective identification. Other relevant material occurs in parts of file D17, which probably dates from the late 1950s and includes both theory and clinical illustration. The comments on projective identification in file D17 are scattered here and there throughout the file.

James Gammill (1989), whose work with a three-year-old child was supervised by Klein in the late 1950s, has told me that she talked to him in considerable detail about the way his patient was using projective identification. Thus, although Klein published so little about projective identification, it was important in the thoughts she was formulating and using in her supervisions in the late 1950s.

2 The Melanie Klein Archive was given to the Wellcome Library for the History of Medicine by the Melanie Klein Trust in 1984 and has been catalogued by their excellent archivists. The part of the Archive with which I am mainly concerned has been divided into B, C, and D files. B files consist of Klein's clinical notes on patients. C files consist of her papers, published and unpublished. D files consist of her notes on theory and various other matters. In quoting from the Archive I have made minor corrections of spelling but I indicate other changes or comments by putting them within square brackets [ ]. When Klein herself puts brackets in her text, I use rounded brackets ( ). All files are prefaced by PP/KLE followed by the letter and number of the file. In most files the pages are not numbered consecutively so that I have not been able to cite page numbers.

The notes of file PP/KLE, B98, 'Patients' material: theoretical thoughts'

This file of 106 pages dates from 1946 and 1947, the year before and just after the time when Klein's 1946 version of 'Notes on some schizoid mechanisms' was first published. Some pages give theoretical formulations, some give clinical material; some are generalisations about several patients; some give the material of a single patient. The pages are not at all systematically arranged and they seem to have been hastily written or perhaps dictated; almost all are typed. One gets the impression that for this file Klein put down or dictated examples and thoughts on splitting, identification, projection and introjection spontaneously as they occurred to her. Because file B98 file is so long it will not be reproduced in the present book, but I will quote from it in some detail.

Although this material of B98 is interesting in itself, it is not of very much help in showing how Klein arrived at the novel formulations of her 1946 'splitting' paper. It seems to me that there is a huge conceptual leap from the notes of B98 to the paper, which describes her formulation of the paranoid-schizoid position for the first time. In addition, only one of the clinical examples given in the published paper is to be found in B98; nor could I find the clinical examples of the paper in any other part of the Archive. I think it likely that the clinical material and theoretical thoughts of B98 formed a general background for Klein's thinking rather than a specific source of inspiration for the new ideas of 'Notes on some schizoid mechanisms'.

There are certain themes that Klein repeatedly refers to in the notes of B98.

The first theme is that good as well as bad aspects of the self are involved in projective identification. Klein also states this view in her paper 'Notes on some schizoid mechanisms', although she puts less stress on it than she does in the Archive notes, and most of the literature since Klein's work has stressed the projection of bad aspects rather than good. Klein gives several examples of the projection of good aspects of the subject's self, as for example in the case of Patient H, who projected good aspects of himself into one person and bad aspects into another, his analyst:

June 25th, 1946
Patient H felt particular gratification in a situation which could have stirred his jealousy and envy through comparison with

somebody but in fact was only felt to be gratifying. The enviable object – Mrs. X – not only represented an ally in what was felt to be a good cause which she had particularly well dealt with (that is where envy would have come in); but as a good aspect of H himself. It appeared that he felt that he had put everything good he possessed into her. That is how she came to represent himself. During this hour he had a strange feeling of being quite estranged from himself and could not account for that. He had been very satisfied with progress in analysis and insight gained, and was struggling to maintain an exclusively friendly and grateful relation to me. I could show him that the satisfaction led to an increased greedy wish to get more, and that he was trying to prevent his greed because he felt that he would enter my mind violently to rob me. The interpretation was that he was putting into myself all his valueless products, representing faeces and urine, and in this process taking such full possession of me when his products had also come to represent himself. At this moment he said, 'I would wish to get out' with quite a strong physical feeling of breathlessness and oppression. The interpretation being that he would like to withdraw himself out of me which was followed by physical relief. Now we could connect the feeling of strangeness to himself, depersonalisation, with the feeling that he had been inside me, and getting himself out of me had felt that he had left so much of his personality inside me that he was estranged to what he took back. On the other hand, his identification with Mrs. X was based on the feeling that he had put his good things into her and therefore could enjoy without rivalry or envy her accomplishments.

(Klein Archive, PP/KLE, B98)

Klein's second main theme in the notes of B98 is that projection and introjection go together. She says, for example:

To Schizoid paper
Chapter Note (to p.18)
Projective identification is the basis for many anxiety situations of a paranoid nature. Since projection and introjection operate simultaneously, paranoid anxieties focus on persecution within the self and within the object which the self has forcefully entered. The attempts to control an external object by entering it give rise to the fear of being controlled and persecuted by this object. The subject

9

may be unable to withdraw from this object; it is kept imprisoned and subjugated by the object. Once part of the ego, or the whole ego, might be felt to have got lost for ever etc. (I have described formerly, in *The Psycho-Analysis of Children*, such fears as being not only at the bottom of paranoid anxiety but also as a cause for disturbances in the male's sexuality – impotence – and as a basis for claustrophobia.) In addition, the re-introjection of this object, which now represents a combination of a persecutory object and the bad self, reinforces inner persecution. The accumulations of anxiety situations of this nature – particularly the fact that the ego is, as it were, caught between external and internal anxieties – is one of the basic features in paranoia. (Cf. chapter on 'Notes on some schizoid mechanisms' also H. Rosenfeld's paper 'Analysis of a Schizophrenic state with Depersonalization', IJPA Vol. XXVIII, 1947, and Joan Riviere's paper. [Title? Published?])

(Klein Archive, PP/KLE, B98)

She puts it more concisely in another entry:

To Theoretical Reflections
Vampire like sucking. In the first sucking of sadistic character you do not only suck out but you put yourself in. Projective identification already there as a complementary process to earliest greedy introjection of the breast.

I believe that persecutory fear of a greedily introjected object – and later the guilt regarding this – contributes to projection and projective identification.

(Klein Archive, PP/KLE, B98)

Klein also gives a specific example, once again from Patient 'H'.

September 20, 1946
To Splitting paper
Extension into the body, and loneliness derived from the fear of destruction of the object from which one is parting – this has been explained as the fear of loss of the object because of one's own sadistic desires against it. Now in one case, 'H' [this phrase and the letter 'H' are crossed out] I have found that panic connected with the fear of parting or being left alone derived from the feeling that one part of himself remained in me and that he could not

withdraw that before going. The interpretation was that the great grievance and hatred to which parting and being left alone gave rise made the part of himself left inside me particularly vicious. I was therefore not only [left, but left] in great danger. But the feeling of being weakened by such an important part of himself being in me increased the feeling of dependence and anxiety. Correspondingly we found in the same hour again the feeling of bits inside. The interpretation was that to this destruction wrought on me by one part of himself acting so ferociously inside me corresponded a similar state of me as an internal object inside him. This internal 'me' was also a source of great persecution and danger to him, as for that matter I was as an external object when I was treated by his being in me in that way. Both relations – me inside him and him inside me – were connected with a feeling of narcissistic withdrawal, loss of feelings, incapacity of re-establishing the relation to me and to others. Also between these situations on the one hand of being overwhelmed by an internal me or containing a destroyed internal me, and the situation described before (the external one) – there was hardly anything of his personality left. The remaining of feeling and an increased condition of the ego as a consequence of such interpretations [was] strengthened.

(Klein Archive, PP/KLE, B98)

A third major theme in the material of the B98 file is that a person's sense of his own identity is built up around the internalised good object. If this internalisation is not secure, the person resorts to intensive but 'unselective' introjection and to equally intensive and piecemeal projections of aspects of the self. This is how Klein puts it:

One way of formulating the focus which the good internal object provides: the ego builds it up [this probably means 'builds itself up' – EBS] from the identifications. Round the primary good objects cluster the parts of the self which are then as it were held together by this strong identification. If it is not strong enough, the great need of more and more identifications, anybody is taken in, and the connection between this and the unselective throwing out again and dispersing again.

(Klein Archive, PP/KLE, B98)

11

Klein describes the process in an example from a patient whom she calls 'J'.

April 13, 1946

Patient J.: An hour which is characterised by greed and frustration coming up in connection with the holidays. During that hour he refers to a decision to be made, on which he would wish to have my advice because I have common sense and sound judgement. At one point he mentions a friend, X, who suspects his relative who keeps house for him of taking the cream off the milk. He relates that to his relation with me, wishing to be first in order to get the cream of the milk, but then the people following would be deprived, about which he both triumphs and is sorry. Rivals. Then he speaks of X as being delusional on that point. K interprets that at each of these points he was identified, or rather represented by the relative who steals the cream, the rival who is being deprived, the neglected child, the friend who is delusional, which is in contrast to the other fact where the cream is in fact in his mind taken away from the milk. He then adds: 'There must be another part there who watches all that and tries to be common sense.'

K interprets four split off aspects which seem incompatible with one another. At this moment – though very impressed at the beginning with the interpretation, there is great difficulty in following and understanding what I just said. K interprets that this difficulty arises from the thought processes being as split as these different aspects are. Also that his common sense aspect is in identification with me who was common sense at the beginning of the hour; that round this identification, which is also part of himself, he is trying to bring together the split off aspects.

(Klein Archive, PP/KLE, B98)

Klein also touches on this matter of the origin of a weak and divided sense of identity in the description of two sessions with Patient 'H' in October, 1946. In the first session (which I will not report in full) Klein had interpreted that H was suffering from a lack of emotion and that this was a defence. In the next session H had recovered his capacity to feel. In fact he felt very anxious and feared a kind of explosion in which he would blow up into bits, or be blown up. Then he had a vision of a monkey, an unemotional monkey, sitting and eating banana after banana. This was almost immediately followed by another vision of a very wild monkey tearing and breaking everything up.

Klein interpreted that the senseless force he was anxious about was his own impulse, one part of himself destroying and disintegrating him.

> Following this hour, H had a very striking experience. Somebody rang him and he seemed interested in what he was told but found it difficult to follow. In the conversation he tried to bring together two points of this special topic and could not find them. He felt himself talking round about. He was left with an increasing state of anxiety. This conversation did not in fact contain anything which on the surface one would say needed to stir anxiety in him. Later on he suddenly felt that the very fact that he could not bring things together during this conversation, and that his own thoughts had become confused, had roused anxiety in him. He suddenly saw the monkey in front of him, and now he had torn all his thoughts and words to bits.
>
> In the analysis we found that in this conversation he had suddenly become identified with the person who had been mentioned in the telephone talk, with the person who telephoned and with himself in a specially unpleasant situation because the person referred to was an ill person, and anxiety of illness had been stirred strongly through the recent material. All these quick projective identifications related to the analytic work of the last few sessions and increased the feeling of being in bits and being unable to integrate himself. He had been persons A, B, C, D, during this conversation and now he was exposed again to this terrible force represented through the tearing monkey who, as he suddenly felt, tore his thoughts and words to bits.
>
> All these mechanisms were found in somebody who seems quite normal, just someone who tells things in a rather slow, deliberate way, a type one often meets.
>
> (Klein Archive, PP/KLE, B98)

Finally, Klein describes a different sort of patient, a man who is not uncertain about his identity, but is worried about the way he controls women by projective identification.

Patient 'M'
October 12, 1946
The influence the projective identifications have on sexual inter-course are seen quite clearly in somebody whose analysis has not been carried to any length yet. His fear of influencing and moulding the women he is interested in such a way that they are greatly changed and become really like himself. He saw with dismay that a girl he likes and who likes him had changed her style of dressing in the way in which he sometimes likes women to be dressed and he called this 'the thin edge of the wedge'. In the same hour he told me that he does not like this influence at all and is strongly trying to prevent it in present relations. He speaks with great concern about an earlier relation in which this seemed to be one of the factors which made the girl too fond, too dependent on him and finished unsatisfactorily because he cannot bear too great dependence in the woman. Somebody said that he is apt to choose people (in working conditions) who are so receptive to his ideas that they will make a perfect staff. In referring to this influence he said: 'They become really too much like myself and [I] don't want to see so much of myself about.' The sexual relations too were obviously impeded and influenced by these fears. All relationships, but particularly with women, were affected. He does not seem to feel having such powers over men.

Conclusion: The penis being used as a controlling object, as an object to be split off, and then the mechanism of splitting is very active. Not only faeces are split off, but parts of the body which are entering the body and controlling it. Now the penis is then felt to remain inside in a controlling, guiding, etc. way. That too must have a bearing on difficulties in potency, because if it is too much a sent out part of oneself it impedes the capacity.

(Klein Archive, PP/KLE, B98)

Klein also notes that the projection of goodness may deplete the self. She says:

NOTE
The importance of projection and putting out things from the self also in the service of goodness has its effect on the process of depersonalisation. The goodness put out of the self into the other person, and then trying to get it back – a hardly recognisable

14

part of the self. One of the important factors in overdoing this process – the intensity of these processes has already to do with fear and guilt. Here also enters the sacrificial attitude – to take over the badness and suffering from the other object in order that it should remain perfect and unharmed.

(Klein Archive, PP/KLE, B98)

I have quoted these excerpts from the B98 part of the Klein Archive to give an idea of the complexity of the way Klein used the idea of projective identification and of the multiplicity of motives for it. Her brief account of projective identification in 'Notes on some schizoid mechanisms' does not do justice to the variability of patients' projective identifications and the complexity of the relations between projective and introjective identifications. Klein's examples give an idea of the richness and flexibility of her use of her concept, although she does not try to describe this in a systematic way either in her notes or in her publications.

Summary of the main themes of B98 in 1946 and 1947

First, good as well as bad aspects of the self may be projected and identified with.

Second, projection and introjection usually go together.

Third, if there is no strong and stable internalisation of a good internal object around which identifications can cluster, the ego cannot be satisfactorily built up and introjective and projective identifications will be not only complex but also fragmented, unselective and unstable.

The fourth theme is closely related to the third: the ego is likely to be weakened by loss of good and bad parts of the self through excessive projection.

Klein's unpublished notes on projective identification in 1958: Klein Archive, PP/KLE, D17, entitled 'Klein: Technique. New Notes on Technique'

The file D17 covers many topics. It consists of 99 'frames' (meaning pages) of which 11 are devoted to projective identification. One

15

page of these notes is dated 1958 and it seems likely that the other pages may date from the same time. (The 11 pages of D17 that are devoted to projective identification have been printed in Spillius, 2007, pp. 121–126.)

On the first frame (799) of these 1958 notes on projective identification, Klein states in handwriting: 'To be used in a paper on projective identification'. I did not find any such paper in the Archive, but it looks as if by this time, 1958, the term 'projective identification' was worth writing about in its own right. It had apparently acquired an identity of its own and was no longer thought of mainly in the context of general discussions of introjection, projection and identification.

In these unpublished notes from D17, Klein states several views on projective identification.

First, she distinguishes between **projection** and **projective identification** as two steps in the same process. In the first step, which she calls 'projection', something of oneself that is very unpleasant or something that one feels one does not deserve to have is attributed to somebody else. In the second step, which is 'projective identification', this something, good or bad, is split off from the self and put into the object. The two steps, she says, 'need not be simultaneously experienced, though they very often are' (Klein Archive, PP/KLE, D17, frames 802, 840).

I have not found this distinction useful – in fact I find it difficult to see how the second step is really different from the first – and so far as I can see, none of Klein's colleagues has adopted her distinction.

Second, Klein thinks it is **essential for the analyst to project himself into the patient** in order to understand him, and that it is also essential that the analyst should introject the patient. She says:

> Only is [if] the analyst can project himself into the analysand will he be able to understand him deeply enough [. . .] A conclusion from what I am saying would be that an optimum in identification with the patient, both by introjection and projection, is essential for a deeper understanding with the patient, together with a capacity to regain one's own self and ego sufficiently not to be misled by the identification.
>
> (Klein Archive, PP/KLE, D17, frame 804)

Third, as in her published paper (1946, 1952a) Klein stresses that **good as well as bad parts of the self may be projected** into the object (D17, frame 801). There may be several motives for projecting bad aspects of oneself or for making 'bad' penetrations into the object: to get rid of something bad in oneself; greedily to control or rob the object; or to satisfy one's aggressive curiosity (D17, frame 805). The motive she cites for projecting good aspects of oneself is that one feels one does not deserve to have such aspects.

Fourth, Klein says nothing about **countertransference** in these notes of 1958, but we know from notes in other parts of the Archive that Klein did not agree with the idea that the analyst's countertrans-ference could be a useful source of information about the patient (Klein Archive, C72, frames 695–724). This is partly because, like Freud (1910), she defines countertransference as a sign of pathology in the analyst. She does imply, however, in the notes on projective identification in the D17 part of the Archive that the analyst is bound to have a distinct emotional reaction to the patient, and she says explicitly that the analyst may be somewhat anxious both about projecting himself into the patient and about the patient's projecting himself into the analyst (D17, frames 805–806). 'But again,' she adds, 'if the analyst possesses the strength of ego and the other qualities to which I referred earlier, the anxiety of the patient projecting himself into him will not disturb him, and he can then analyse the projection of the patient' (D17, frame 806). She seems to assume that the analyst's emotional reaction needs to be overcome because it will interfere with his capacity to think analytically.

Fifth, I believe that Klein assumes throughout these notes, although she does not explicitly say so, that **projective identification takes the form of an unconscious phantasy**, and I assume that she thought this was also true of introjective identification.

Finally, Klein briefly describes **a clinical session** in which she shows how she analyses a particular instance of projective identifica-tion (Klein Archive, D17, frames 802–803). Because she gives so little published clinical illustration of her ideas about projective identification, I will quote her example here.

In this connection, I wish again to stress the necessity to go step by step according to the emotions, anxieties, etc. activated in the patient, and not to run ahead because the analyst knows already what is behind that. I have an example of this point. The analysand

speaks in an early session of his analysis of some experience in . . .
during the War. They had been warned that there were man-
eating tigers about, but they had not met any. Previous to that, his
suspicions of me, very much stimulated by remarks made [by
others] about me, had come up and had led to his distrust of his
mother. His mother was supposed to have said, as an aunt reported
to him, that, being in very bad circumstances, if she were starving, she would eat her son. Though Mr [X] actually knew quite
well that that was not what she meant, he had never forgotten
this remark, and it had come up in his suspicions of me, together
with his suspicions of my possessiveness, dangerousness, etc. I first
analysed these suspicions and linked them with his suspicions of his
mother, who had actually not been able to give him enough food
at a certain period in his life, and linked these with the man-eating
tiger he had mentioned, his fear that she would eat him and that
she was starving him for bad and dangerous reasons. [He] went on
about his stay in . . . and said that they had never actually met a
man-eating tiger, but had met a bear, and then added laughingly
that the bear did not eat them they ate the bear. My interpretations
were then fully supported, that it was his wish to eat his mother's
breast and that led to his suspicion that his mother was devouring
him. At that moment [he] felt that the plants on my desk actually
belonged to him, corrected this in the next moment, but found
that this was a confirmation of what I said, because he had appro-
priated something that belonged to me.

> (Klein Archive, D17, frames 802–3; this example is also
> cited in Spillius, 2007, pp. 110–111)

It is worth noting here that Klein does not use her distinction
between projection and projective identification in this brief account.
It seems clear that she assumed that projection and projective identification were occurring simultaneously in this instance.

As I discuss in Part Two of this book, some of these points have
been worked on and developed by several of Klein's British Kleinian
colleagues. Some are no longer adhered to, and some are used by
some colleagues but not by others.

This introduction to Klein's published and unpublished work on
the topic of projective identification is here followed by reprinting of
the 1952 version of Klein's 'Notes on some schizoid mechanisms'.

—————————— 2 ——————————

Notes on some schizoid mechanisms[3]

Melanie Klein

Introduction

The present paper is concerned with the importance of early para-noid and schizoid anxieties and mechanisms. I have given much thought to this subject for a number of years, even before clarifying my views on the depressive processes in infancy. In the course of working out my concept of the infantile depressive position, however, the problems of the phase preceding it again forced themselves on my attention. I now wish to formulate some hypotheses at which I have arrived regarding the earlier anxieties and mechanisms.[4]

The hypotheses I shall put forward, which relate to very early stages of development, are derived by inference from material gained in the analyses of adults and children, and some of these hypotheses seem to tally with observations familiar in psychiatric work. To substantiate my contentions would require an accumulation of detailed case mate-rial for which there is no room in the framework of this paper, and I hope in further contributions to fill this gap.

---

3 [Original footnote to 1952 version: This paper was read before the British Psycho-Analytical Society on December 4, 1946, and has been left unchanged and then published, apart from a few slight alterations (in particular the addition of one paragraph and some footnotes).] Editors' note: this chapter reproduces the text of Klein, M. (1952a). Notes on some schizoid mechanisms. In *Envy and Gratitude and Other Works 1947–1963*. London: Hogarth Press (1975), pp. 1–24.

4 Before completing this paper I discussed its main aspects with Paula Heimann and am much indebted to her for stimulating suggestions in working out and formulating a number of the concepts presented here.

At the outset it will be useful to summarize briefly the conclusions regarding the earliest phases of development which I have already put forward.[5]

In early infancy anxieties characteristic of psychosis arise which drive the ego to develop specific defence-mechanisms. In this period the fixation-points for all psychotic disorders are to be found. This hypothesis led some people to believe that I regarded all infants as psychotic; but I have already dealt sufficiently with this misunderstanding on other occasions. The psychotic anxieties, mechanisms and ego-defences of infancy have a profound influence on development in all its aspects, including the development of the ego, superego and object-relations.

I have often expressed my view that object-relations exist from the beginning of life, the first object being the mother's breast which to the child becomes split into a good (gratifying) and bad (frustrating) breast; this splitting results in a severance of love and hate. I have further suggested that the relation to the first object implies its introjection and projection, and thus from the beginning object-relations are moulded by an interaction between introjection and projection, between internal and external objects and situations. These processes participate in the building up of the ego and superego and prepare the ground for the onset of the Oedipus complex in the second half of the first year.

From the beginning the destructive impulse is turned against the object and is first expressed in phantasied oral-sadistic attacks on the mother's breast, which soon develop into onslaughts on her body by all sadistic means. The persecutory fears arising from the infant's oral-sadistic impulses to rob the mother's body of its good contents, and from the anal-sadistic impulses to put his excrements into her (including the desire to enter her body in order to control her from within) are of great importance for the development of paranoia and schizophrenia.

I enumerated various typical defences of the early ego, such as the mechanisms of splitting the object and the impulses, idealization, denial of inner and outer reality and the stifling of emotions. I also mentioned various anxiety-contents, including the fear of being poisoned and devoured. Most of these phenomena – prevalent in the

---

5 Cf. my *Psycho-Analysis of Children* (1932), and 'A Contribution to the Psychogenesis of Manic-Depressive States' (1935).

first few months of life – are found in the later symptomatic picture of schizophrenia.

This early period (first described as the 'persecutory phase') I later termed 'paranoid position',[6] and held that it precedes the depressive position. If persecutory fears are very strong, and for this reason (among others) the infant cannot work through the paranoid–schizoid position, the working through of the depressive position is in turn impeded. This failure may lead to a regressive reinforcing of persecutory fears and strengthen the fixation-points for severe psychoses (that is to say, the group of schizophrenias). Another outcome of serious difficulties arising during the period of the depressive position may be manic–depressive disorders in later life. I also concluded that in less severe disturbances of development the same factors strongly influence the choice of neurosis.

While I assumed that the outcome of the depressive position depends on the working through of the preceding phase, I nevertheless attributed to the depressive position a central role in the child's early development. For with the introjection of the object as a whole the infant's object-relation alters fundamentally. The synthesis between the loved and hated aspects of the complete object gives rise to feelings of mourning and guilt which imply vital advances in the infant's emotional and intellectual life. This is also a crucial juncture for the choice of neurosis or psychosis. To all these conclusions I still adhere.

Some notes on Fairbairn's recent papers

In a number of recent papers,[7] W. R. D. Fairbairn has given much attention to the subject-matter with which I am now dealing. I therefore find it helpful to clarify some essential points of agreement and disagreement between us. It will be seen that some of the conclusions

---

6 When this paper was first published in 1946, I was using my term 'paranoid position' synonymously with W. R. D. Fairbairn's 'schizoid position'. On further deliberation I decided to combine Fairbairn's term with mine and throughout the present book [*Developments in Psycho-Analysis* (Klein et al., 1952), in which this paper was first published] I am using the expression 'paranoid-schizoid position'.

7 Cf. 'A Revised Psychopathology of the Psychoses and Neuroses', 'Endopsychic Structure Considered in Terms of Object-Relationships' and 'Object-Relationships and Dynamic Structure'.

which I shall present in this paper are in line with Fairbairn's conclusions, while others differ fundamentally. Fairbairn's approach was largely from the angle of ego-development in relation to objects, while mine was predominantly from the angle of anxieties and their vicissitudes. He called the earliest phase the 'schizoid position': he stated that it forms part of normal development and is the basis for adult schizoid and schizophrenic illness. I agree with this contention and consider his description of developmental schizoid phenomena as significant and revealing, and of great value for our understanding of schizoid behaviour and of schizophrenia. I also think that Fairbairn's view that the group of schizoid or schizophrenic disorders is much wider than has been acknowledged is correct and important; and the particular emphasis he laid on the inherent relation between hysteria and schizophrenia deserves full attention. His term 'schizoid position' would be appropriate if it is understood to cover both persecutory fear and schizoid mechanisms.

I disagree – to mention first the most basic issues – with his revision of the theory of mental structure and instincts. I also disagree with his view that to begin with only the bad object is internalized – a view which seems to me to contribute to the important differences between us regarding the development of object-relations as well as of ego-development. For I hold that the introjected good breast forms a vital part of the ego, exerts from the beginning a fundamental influence on the process of ego-development and affects both ego-structure and object-relations. I also differ from Fairbairn's view that 'the great problem of the schizoid individual is how to love without destroying by love, whereas the great problem of the depressive individual is how to love without destroying by hate'.[8] This conclusion is in line not only with his rejecting Freud's concept of primary instincts but also with his underrating the role which aggression and hatred play from the beginning of life. As a result of this approach, he does not give enough weight to the importance of early anxiety and conflict and their dynamic effects on development.

Certain problems of the early ego

In the following discussion I shall single out one aspect of ego-development and I shall deliberately not attempt to link it with the

8   Cf. 'A Revised Psychopathology' (1941).

problems of ego-development as a whole. Nor can I here touch on the relation of the ego to the id and super-ego.

So far, we know little about the structure of the early ego. Some of the recent suggestions on this point have not convinced me: I have particularly in mind Glover's concept of ego nuclei and Fairbairn's theory of a central ego and two subsidiary egos. More helpful in my view is Winnicott's emphasis on the unintegration of the early ego.[9] I would also say that the early ego largely lacks cohesion, and a tendency towards integration alternates with a tendency towards disintegration, a falling into bits.[10] I believe that these fluctuations are characteristic of the first few months of life.

We are, I think, justified in assuming that some of the functions which we know from the later ego are there at the beginning. Prominent amongst these functions is that of dealing with anxiety. I hold that anxiety arises from the operation of the death instinct within the organism, is felt as fear of annihilation (death) and takes the form of fear of persecution. The fear of the destructive impulse seems to attach itself at once to an object – or rather it is experienced as the fear of an uncontrollable overpowering object. Other important sources of primary anxiety are the trauma of birth (separation anxiety) and frustration of bodily needs; and these experiences too are from the beginning felt as being caused by objects. Even if these objects are felt to be external, they become through introjection internal persecutors and thus reinforce the fear of the destructive impulse within.

The vital need to deal with anxiety forces the early ego to develop fundamental mechanisms and defences. The destructive impulse is partly projected outwards (deflection of the death instinct) and, I think, attaches itself to the first external object, the mother's breast. As Freud has pointed out, the remaining portion of the destructive impulse is to some extent bound by the libido within the organism.

---

9 Cf. D. W. Winnicott, 'Primitive Emotional Development' (1945). In this paper Winnicott also described the pathological outcome of states of unintegration, for instance the case of a woman patient who could not distinguish between her twin sister and herself.

10 The greater or lesser cohesiveness of the ego at the beginning of postnatal life should be considered in connection with the greater or lesser capacity of the ego to tolerate anxiety which, as I have previously contended (*Psycho-Analysis of Children*, particularly p. 49), is a constitutional factor.

However, neither of these processes entirely fulfils its purpose, and therefore the anxiety of being destroyed from within remains active. It seems to me in keeping with the lack of cohesiveness that under the pressure of this threat the ego tends to fall to pieces.[11] This falling to pieces appears to underlie states of disintegration in schizophrenics.

The question arises whether some active splitting processes within the ego may not occur even at a very early stage. As we assume, the early ego splits the object and the relation to it in an active way, and this may imply some active splitting of the ego itself. In any case, the result of splitting is a dispersal of the destructive impulse which is felt as the source of danger. I suggest that the primary anxiety of being annihilated by a destructive force within, with the ego's specific response of falling to pieces or splitting itself, may be extremely important in all schizophrenic processes.

Splitting processes in relation to the object

The destructive impulse projected outwards is first experienced as oral aggression. I believe that oral-sadistic impulses towards the mother's breast are active from the beginning of life, though with the onset of teething the cannibalistic impulses increase in strength – a factor stressed by Abraham.

In states of frustration and anxiety the oral-sadistic and cannibalistic desires are reinforced, and then the infant feels that he has taken in the nipple and the breast in bits. Therefore in addition to the divorce between a good and a bad breast in the young infant's phantasy, the frustrating breast – attacked in oral-sadistic phantasies – is felt to be in fragments; the gratifying breast, taken in under the dominance of the sucking libido, is felt to be complete. This first internal good object acts as a focal point in the ego. It counteracts the processes of splitting and dispersal, makes for cohesiveness and integration, and

---

11 Ferenczi in 'Notes and Fragments' (1930) suggests that most likely every living organism reacts to unpleasant stimuli by fragmentation, which might be an expression of the death instinct. Possibly, complicated mechanisms (living organisms) are only kept as an entity through the impact of external conditions. When these conditions become unfavourable the organism falls to pieces.

is instrumental in building up the ego.[12] The infant's feeling of having inside a good and complete breast may, however, be shaken by frustration and anxiety. As a result, the divorce between the good and bad breast may be difficult to maintain, and the infant may feel that the good breast too is in pieces.

I believe that the ego is incapable of splitting the object – internal and external – without a corresponding splitting taking place within the ego. Therefore the phantasies and feelings about the state of the internal object vitally influence the structure of the ego. The more sadism prevails in the process of incorporating the object, and the more the object is felt to be in pieces, the more the ego is in danger of being split in relation to the internalized object fragments.

The processes I have described are, of course, bound up with the infant's phantasy-life; and the anxieties which stimulate the mechanism of splitting are also of a phantastic nature. It is in phantasy that the infant splits the object and the self, but the effect of this phantasy is a very real one, because it leads to feelings and relations (and later on, thought-processes) being in fact cut off from one another.[13]

Splitting in connection with projection and introjection

So far, I have dealt particularly with the mechanism of splitting as one of the earliest ego-mechanisms and defences against anxiety. Introjection and projection are from the beginning of life also used in the service of this primary aim of the ego. Projection, as Freud described, originates from the deflection of the death instinct outwards and in my view it helps the ego to overcome anxiety by ridding it of danger and badness. Introjection of the good object is also used by the ego as a defence against anxiety.

12 D. W. Winnicott (loc. cit.) referred to the same process from another angle: he described how integration and adaptation to reality depend essentially on the infant's experience of the mother's love and care.

13 In the discussion following the reading of this paper, Dr W. C. M. Scott referred to another aspect of splitting. He stressed the importance of the breaks in continuity of experiences, which imply a splitting in time rather than in space. He referred as an instance to the alternation between states of being asleep and states of being awake. I fully agree with his point of view.

Closely connected with projection and introjection are some other mechanisms. Here I am particularly concerned with the connection between splitting, idealization and denial. As regards splitting of the object, we have to remember that in states of gratification love-feelings turn towards the gratifying breast, while in states of frustration hatred and persecutory anxiety attach themselves to the frustrating breast.

Idealization is bound up with the splitting of the object, for the good aspects of the breast are exaggerated as a safeguard against the fear of the persecuting breast. While idealization is thus the corollary of persecutory fear, it also springs from the power of the instinctual desires which aim at unlimited gratification and therefore create the picture of an inexhaustible and always bountiful breast – an ideal breast.

We find an instance of such a cleavage in infantile hallucinatory gratification. The main processes which come into play in idealization are also operative in hallucinatory gratification, namely, splitting of the object and denial both of frustration and of persecution. The frustrating and persecuting object is kept widely apart from the idealized object. However, the bad object is not only kept apart from the good one but its very existence is denied, as is the whole situation of frustration and the bad feelings (pain) to which frustration gives rise. This is bound up with denial of psychic reality. The denial of psychic reality becomes possible only through strong feelings of omnipotence – an essential characteristic of early mentality. Omnipotent denial of the existence of the bad object and of the painful situation is in the unconscious equal to annihilation by the destructive impulse. It is, however, not only a situation and an object that are denied and annihilated – it is an object–relation which suffers this fate; and therefore a part of the ego, from which the feelings towards the object emanate, is denied and annihilated as well.

In hallucinatory gratification, therefore, two interrelated processes take place: the omnipotent conjuring up of the ideal object and situation, and the equally omnipotent annihilation of the bad persecutory object and the painful situation. These processes are based on splitting both the object and the ego.

In passing I would mention that in this early phase splitting, denial and omnipotence play a role similar to that of repression at a later stage of ego-development. In considering the importance of the processes of denial and omnipotence at a stage which is characterized by persecutory fear and schizoid mechanisms, we may remember the delusions of both grandeur and of persecution in schizophrenia.

So far, in dealing with persecutory fear, I have singled out the oral element. However, while the oral libido still has the lead, libidinal and aggressive impulses and phantasies from other sources come to the fore and lead to a confluence of oral, urethral and anal desires, both libidinal and aggressive. Also the attacks on the mother's breast develop into attacks of a similar nature on her body, which comes to be felt as it were as an extension of the breast, even before the mother is conceived of as a complete person. The phantasied onslaughts on the mother follow two main lines: one is the predominantly oral impulse to suck dry, bite up, scoop out and rob the mother's body of its good contents. (I shall discuss the bearing of these impulses on the development of object-relations in connection with introjection.) The other line of attack derives from the anal and urethral impulses and implies expelling dangerous substances (excrements) out of the self and into the mother. Together with these harmful excrements, expelled in hatred, split-off parts of the ego are also projected on to the mother or, as I would rather call it, into the mother.[14] These excrements and bad parts of the self are meant not only to injure but also to control and to take possession of the object. In so far as the mother comes to contain the bad parts of the self, she is not felt to be a separate individual but is felt to be the bad self.

Much of the hatred against parts of the self is now directed towards the mother. This leads to a particular form of identification which establishes the prototype of an aggressive object-relation. I suggest for these processes the term 'projective identification'. When projection is mainly derived from the infant's impulse to harm or to control the mother,[15] he feels her to be a persecutor. In psychotic disorders

14 The description of such primitive processes suffers from a great handicap, for these phantasies arise at a time when the infant has not yet begun to think in words. In this context, for instance, I am using the expression 'to project into another person' because this seems to me the only way of conveying the unconscious process I am trying to describe.

15 M. G. Evans, in a short unpublished communication (read to the British Psycho-Analytical Society, January, 1946), gave some instances of patients in whom the following phenomena were marked: lack of sense of reality, a feeling of being divided and parts of the personality having entered the mother's body in order to rob and control her; as a consequence the mother and other people similarly attacked came to represent the patient. M. G. Evans related these processes to a very primitive stage of development.

this identification of an object with the hated parts of the self contributes to the intensity of the hatred directed against other people. As far as the ego is concerned the excessive splitting off and expelling into the outer world of parts of itself considerably weaken it. For the aggressive component of feelings and of the personality is intimately bound up in the mind with power, potency, strength, knowledge and many other desired qualities.

It is, however, not only the bad parts of the self which are expelled and projected, but also good parts of the self. Excrements then have the significance of gifts; and parts of the ego which, together with excrements, are expelled and projected into the other person represent the good, i.e. the loving parts of the self. The identification based on this type of projection again vitally influences object-relations. The projection of good feelings and good parts of the self into the mother is essential for the infant's ability to develop good object-relations and to integrate his ego. However, if this projective process is carried out excessively, good parts of the personality are felt to be lost, and in this way the mother becomes the ego-ideal; this process too results in weakening and impoverishing the ego. Very soon such processes extend to other people,[16] and the result may be an over-strong dependence on these external representatives of one's own good parts. Another consequence is a fear that the capacity to love has been lost because the loved object is felt to be loved predominantly as a representative of the self.

The processes of splitting off parts of the self and projecting them into objects are thus of vital importance for normal development as well as for abnormal object-relations.

The effect of introjection on object-relations is equally important. The introjection of the good object, first of all the mother's breast, is a precondition for normal development. I have already described that it comes to form a focal point in the ego and makes for cohesiveness of the ego. One characteristic feature of the earliest relation to the good object – internal and external – is the tendency to idealize it. In

---

16 W. C. M. Scott in an unpublished paper, read to the British Psycho-Analytical Society a few years ago, described three interconnected features which he came upon in a schizophrenic patient: a strong disturbance of her sense of reality, her feeling that the world round her was a cemetery, and the mechanism of putting all good parts of herself into another person – Greta Garbo – who came to stand for the patient.

states of frustration or increased anxiety, the infant is driven to take flight to his internal idealized object as a means of escaping from persecutors. From this mechanism various serious disturbances may result: when persecutory fear is too strong, the flight to the idealized object becomes excessive, and this severely hampers ego-development and disturbs object-relations. As a result the ego may be felt to be entirely subservient to and dependent on the internal object – only a shell for it. With an unassimilated idealized object there goes a feeling that the ego has no life and no value of its own.[17]

I would suggest that the condition of flight to the unassimilated idealized object necessitates further splitting processes within the ego. For parts of the ego attempt to unite with the ideal object, while other parts strive to deal with the internal persecutors.

The various ways of splitting the ego and internal objects result in the feeling that the ego is in bits. This feeling amounts to a state of disintegration. In normal development, the states of disintegration which the infant experiences are transitory. Among other factors, gratification by the external good object[18] again and again helps to break through these schizoid states. The infant's capacity to overcome temporary schizoid states is in keeping with the strong elasticity and resilience of the infantile mind. If states of splitting and therefore of disintegration, which the ego is unable to overcome, occur too frequently and go on for too long, then in my view they must be regarded as a sign of schizophrenic illness in the infant, and some indications of such illness may already be seen in the first few

---

17 Cf. 'A Contribution to the Problem of Sublimation and its Relation to the Processes of Internalization' (1942) where Paula Heimann described a condition in which the internal objects act as foreign bodies embedded in the self. Whilst this is more obvious with regard to the bad objects, it is true even for the good ones, if the ego is compulsively subordinated to their preservation. When the ego serves its good internal objects excessively, they are felt as a source of danger to the self and come close to exerting a persecuting influence. Paula Heimann introduced the concept of the assimilation of the internal objects and applied it specifically to sublimation. As regards ego-development, she pointed out that such assimilation is essential for the successful exercise of ego-functions and for the achievement of independence.

18 Looked at in this light, the mother's love and understanding of the infant can be seen as the infant's greatest stand-by in overcoming states of disintegration and anxieties of a psychotic nature.

months of life. In adult patients, states of depersonalization and of schizophrenic dissociation seem to be a regression to these infantile states of disintegration.[19]

In my experience, excessive persecutory fears and schizoid mechanisms in early infancy may have a detrimental effect on intellectual development in its initial stages. Certain forms of mental deficiency would therefore have to be regarded as belonging to the group of schizophrenias. Accordingly, in considering mental deficiency in children at any age one should keep in mind the possibility of schizophrenic illness in early infancy.

I have so far described some effects of excessive introjection and projection on object-relations. I am not attempting to investigate here in any detail the various factors which in some cases make for a predominance of introjective and in other cases for a predominance of projective processes. As regards normal personality, it may be said that the course of ego-development and object-relations depends on the degree to which an optimal balance between introjection and projection in the early stages of development can be achieved. This in turn has a bearing on the integration of the ego and the assimilation of internal objects. Even if the balance is disturbed and one or the other of these processes is excessive, there is some interaction between introjection and projection. For instance the projection of a predominantly hostile inner world which is ruled by persecutory fears leads to the introjection – a taking-back – of a hostile external world; and vice versa, the introjection of a distorted and hostile external world reinforces the projection of a hostile inner world.

Another aspect of projective processes, as we have seen, concerns the forceful entry into the object and control of the object by parts of the self. As a consequence, introjection may then be felt as a forceful entry from the outside into the inside, in retribution for violent

---

19 Herbert Rosenfeld, in 'Analysis of a Schizophrenic State with Depersonalization' (1947), has presented case-material to illustrate how the splitting mechanisms which are bound up with projective identification were responsible both for a schizophrenic state and depersonalization. In his paper 'A Note on the Psychopathology of Confusional States in Chronic Schizophrenias' (1950) he also pointed out that a confusional state comes about if the subject loses the capacity to differentiate between good and bad objects, between aggressive and libidinal impulses, and so on. He suggested that in such states of confusion splitting mechanisms are frequently reinforced for defensive purposes.

projection. This may lead to the fear that not only the body but also the mind is controlled by other people in a hostile way. As a result there may be a severe disturbance in introjecting good objects – a disturbance which would impede all ego-functions as well as sexual development and might lead to an excessive withdrawal to the inner world. This withdrawal is, however, caused not only by the fear of introjecting a dangerous external world but also by the fear of internal persecutors and an ensuing flight to the idealized internal object.

I have referred to the weakening and impoverishment of the ego resulting from excessive splitting and projective identification. This weakened ego, however, becomes also incapable of assimilating its internal objects, and this leads to the feeling that it is ruled by them. Again, such a weakened ego feels incapable of taking back into itself the parts which it projected into the external world. These various disturbances in the interplay between projection and introjection, which imply excessive splitting of the ego, have a detrimental effect on the relation to the inner and outer world and seem to be at the root of some forms of schizophrenia.

Projective identification is the basis of many anxiety-situations, of which I shall mention a few. The phantasy of forcefully entering the object gives rise to anxieties relating to the dangers threatening the subject from within the object. For instance, the impulses to control an object from within it stir up the fear of being controlled and persecuted inside it. By introjecting and re-introjecting the forcefully entered object, the subject's feelings of inner persecution are strongly reinforced; all the more since the re-introjected object is felt to contain the dangerous aspects of the self. The accumulation of anxieties of this nature, in which the ego is, as it were, caught between a variety of external and internal persecution-situations, is a basic element in paranoia.[20]

20 Herbert Rosenfeld, in 'Analysis of a Schizophrenic State with Depersonalization' and 'Remarks on the Relation of Male Homosexuality to Paranoia' (1949), discussed the clinical importance of those paranoid anxieties which are connected with projective iden-tification in psychotic patients. In the two schizophrenic cases he described, it became evident that the patients were dominated by the fear that the analyst was trying to force himself into the patient. When these fears were analysed in the transference-situation, improvement could take place. Rosenfeld has further connected projective identification (and the corresponding persecutory fears) with female sexual frigidity on the one hand and on the other with the frequent combination of homosexuality and paranoia in men.

I have previously described[21] the infant's phantasies of attacking and sadistically entering the mother's body as giving rise to various anxiety-situations (particularly the fear of being imprisoned and persecuted within her) which are at the bottom of paranoia. I also showed that the fear of being imprisoned (and especially of the penis being attacked) inside the mother is an important factor in later disturbances of male potency (impotence) and also underlines claustrophobia.[22]

Schizoid object–relations

To summarize now some of the disturbed object-relations which are found in schizoid personalities: the violent splitting of the self and excessive projection have the effect that the person towards whom this process is directed is felt as a persecutor. Since the destructive and hated part of the self which is split off and projected is felt as a danger to the loved object and therefore gives rise to guilt, this process of projection in some ways also implies a deflection of guilt from the self on to the other person. Guilt has, however, not been done away with, and the deflected guilt is felt as an unconscious responsibility for the people who have become representatives of the aggressive part of the self.

Another typical feature of schizoid object-relations is their narcissistic nature which derives from the infantile introjective and projective processes. For, as I suggested earlier, when the ego–ideal is projected

---

21 *Psycho-Analysis of Children*, Chapter 8, particularly p. 131, and Chapter 12, particularly p. 242.

22 Joan Riviere, in an unpublished paper 'Paranoid Attitudes seen in Everyday Life and in Analysis' (read before the British Psycho-Analytical Society in 1948), reported a great deal of clinical material in which projective identification became apparent. Unconscious phantasies of forcing the whole self into the inside of the object (to obtain control and possession) led, through the fear of retaliation, to a variety of persecutory anxieties such as claustrophobia, or to such common phobias as of burglars, spiders, invasion in wartime. These fears are connected with the unconscious 'catastrophic' phantasies of being dismembered, disembowelled, torn to pieces and of total internal disruption of the body and personality and loss of identity – fears which are an elaboration of the fear of annihilation (death) and have the effect of reinforcing the mechanisms of splitting and the process of ego-disintegration as found in psychotics.

into another person, this person becomes predominantly loved and admired because he contains the good parts of the self. Similarly, the relation to another person on the basis of projecting bad parts of the self into him is of a narcissistic nature, because in this case as well the object strongly represents one part of the self. Both these types of a narcissistic relation to an object often show strong obsessional features. The impulse to control other people is, as we know, an essential element in obsessional neurosis. The need to control others can to some extent be explained by a deflected drive to control parts of the self. When these parts have been projected excessively into another person, they can only be controlled by controlling the other person. One root of obsessional mechanisms may thus be found in the particular identification which results from infantile projective processes. This connection may also throw some light on the obsessional element which so often enters into the tendency for reparation. For it is not only an object about whom guilt is experienced but also parts of the self which the subject is driven to repair or restore.

All these factors may lead to a compulsive tie to certain objects or – another outcome – to a shrinking from people in order to prevent both a destructive intrusion into them and the danger of retaliation by them. The fear of such dangers may show itself in various negative attitudes in object-relations. For instance, one of my patients told me that he dislikes people who are too much influenced by him, for they seem to become too much like himself and therefore he gets tired of them.

Another characteristic of schizoid object-relations is a marked artificiality and lack of spontaneity. Side by side with this goes a severe disturbance of the feeling of the self or, as I would put it, of the relation to the self. This relation, too, appears to be artificial. In other words, psychic reality and the relation to external reality are equally disturbed.

The projection of split-off parts of the self into another person essentially influences object-relations, emotional life and the personality as a whole. To illustrate this contention I will select as an instance two universal phenomena which are interlinked: the feeling of loneliness and fear of parting. We know that one source of the depressive feelings accompanying parting from people can be found in the fear of the destruction of the object by the aggressive impulses directed against it. But it is more specifically the splitting and projective processes which underlie this fear. If aggressive elements in relation to the object are predominant and strongly aroused by the frustration of parting, the individual feels that the split-off components of his self, projected into the object, control this object in an aggressive and destructive way. At the same time the internal object is felt to be in the same danger of destruction as the external one in whom one part of the self is felt to be left. The result is an excessive weakening of the ego, a feeling that there is nothing to sustain it, and a corresponding feeling of loneliness. While this description applies to neurotic individuals, I think that in some degree it is a general phenomenon.

One need hardly elaborate the fact that some other features of schizoid object-relations, which I described earlier, can also be found in minor degrees and in a less striking form in normal people – for instance shyness, lack of spontaneity or, on the other hand, a particularly intense interest in people.

In similar ways normal disturbances in thought-processes link up with the developmental paranoid-schizoid position. For all of us are liable at times to a momentary impairment of logical thinking which amounts to thoughts and associations being cut off from one another and situations being split off from one another; in fact, the ego is temporarily split.

The depressive position in relation to the paranoid-schizoid position

I now wish to consider further steps in the infant's development. So far I have described the anxieties, mechanisms and defences which are characteristic of the first few months of life. With the introjection of the complete object in about the second quarter of the first year marked steps in integration are made. This implies important changes in the relation to objects. The loved and hated aspects of the mother are no longer felt to be so widely separated, and the result is an increased fear of loss, states akin to mourning and a strong feeling of guilt, because the aggressive impulses are felt to be directed against the loved object. The depressive position has come to the fore. The very experience of depressive feelings in turn has the effect of further integrating the ego, because it makes for an increased understanding of psychic reality and better perception of the external world, as well as for a greater synthesis between inner and external situations.

The drive to make reparation, which comes to the fore at this stage, can be regarded as a consequence of greater insight into psychic reality and of growing synthesis, for it shows a more realistic response to the feelings of grief, guilt and fear of loss resulting from the aggression against the loved object. Since the drive to repair or protect the injured object paves the way for more satisfactory object-relations and sublimations, it in turn increases synthesis and contributes to the integration of the ego.

During the second half of the first year the infant makes some fundamental steps towards working through the depressive position. However, schizoid mechanisms still remain in force, though in a modified form and to a lesser degree, and early anxiety-situations are again and again experienced in the process of modification. The working through of the persecutory and depressive positions extends over the first few years of childhood and plays an essential part in the infantile neurosis. In the course of this process, anxieties lose in strength; objects become both less idealized and less terrifying, and the ego becomes more unified. All this is interconnected with the growing perception of reality and adaptation to it.

If development during the paranoid-schizoid position has not proceeded normally and the infant cannot – for internal or external reasons – cope with the impact of depressive anxieties a vicious circle arises. For if persecutory fear, and correspondingly schizoid mechanisms, are too strong, the ego is not capable of working through the depressive position. This forces the ego to regress to the paranoid-schizoid position and reinforces the earlier persecutory fears and schizoid phenomena. Thus the basis is established for various forms of schizophrenia in later life; for when such a regression occurs, not only are the fixation-points in the schizoid position reinforced, but there is a danger of greater states of disintegration setting in. Another outcome may be the strengthening of depressive features.

External experiences are, of course, of great importance in these developments. For instance, in the case of a patient who showed depressive and schizoid features, the analysis brought up with great vividness his early experiences in babyhood, to such an extent that in some sessions physical sensations in the throat or digestive organs occurred. The patient had been weaned suddenly at four months of age because his mother fell ill. In addition, he did not see his mother for four weeks. When she returned, she found the child greatly changed. He had been a lively baby, interested in his surroundings, and he seemed to have lost this interest. He had become apathetic. He had accepted the substitute food fairly easily and in fact never refused food. But he did not thrive on it any more, lost weight and had a good deal of digestive trouble. It was only at the end of the first year, when other food was introduced, that he again made good physical progress.

Much light was thrown in the analysis on the influence these experiences had on his whole development. His outlook and attitudes in adult life were based on the patterns established in this early stage. For instance, we found again and again a tendency to be influenced by other people in an unselective way – in fact to take in greedily whatever was offered – together with great distrust during the process of introjection. This process was constantly disturbed by anxieties from various sources, which also contributed to an increase of greed.

Taking the material of this analysis as a whole, I came to the conclusion that at the time when the sudden loss of the breast and of the mother occurred, the patient had already to some extent established a relation to a complete good object. He had no doubt already entered the depressive position but could not work through it successfully and the paranoid-schizoid position became regressively reinforced. This expressed itself in the 'apathy' which followed a period when the child had already shown a lively interest in his surroundings. The fact that he had reached the depressive position and had introjected a complete object showed in many ways in his personality. He had actually a strong capacity for love and a great longing for a good and complete object. A characteristic feature of his personality was the desire to love people and trust them, unconsciously to regain and build up again the good and complete breast which he had once possessed and lost.

Connection between schizoid and manic–depressive phenomena

Some fluctuations between the paranoid–schizoid and the depressive positions always occur and are part of normal development. No clear division between the two stages of development can therefore be drawn; moreover, modification is a gradual process and the phenomena of the two positions remain for some time to some extent intermingled and interacting. In abnormal development this interaction influences, I think, the clinical picture both of some forms of schizophrenia and of manic-depressive disorders.

To illustrate this connection I shall briefly refer to some case-material. I do not intend to present a case-history here and am therefore only selecting some parts of material relevant to my topic. The patient I have in mind was a pronounced manic-depressive case (diagnosed as such by more than one psychiatrist) with all the characteristics of that disorder: there was the alternation between depressive and manic states, strong suicidal tendencies leading repeatedly to suicidal attempts, and various other characteristic manic and depressive features. In the course of her analysis a stage was reached in which a real and great improvement was achieved. Not only did the cycle stop but there were fundamental changes in her personality and her object-relations. Productivity on various lines developed, as well as actual feelings of happiness (not of a manic type). Then, partly owing to external circumstances, another phase set in. During this last phase, which continued for several months, the patient co-operated in the analysis in a particular way. She came regularly to the analytic sessions, associated fairly freely, reported dreams and provided material for the analysis. There was, however, no emotional response to my interpretations and a good deal of contempt of them. There was very seldom any conscious confirmation of what I suggested. Yet the material by which she responded to the interpretations reflected their unconscious effect. The powerful resistance shown at this stage seemed to come from one part of the personality only, while at the same time another part responded to the analytic work. It was not only that parts of her personality did not co-operate with me; they did not seem to co-operate with each other, and at the time the analysis was unable to help the patient to achieve synthesis. During this stage she decided to bring the analysis to an end. External circumstances contributed strongly to this decision and she fixed a date for the last session.

On that particular date she reported the following dream: there was a blind man who was very worried about being blind; but he seemed to comfort himself by touching the patient's dress and finding out how it was fastened. The dress in the dream reminded her of one of her frocks which was buttoned high up to the throat. The patient gave two further associations to this dream. She said, with some resistance, that the blind man was herself; and when referring to the dress fastened up to the throat, she remarked that she had again gone into her 'hide'. I suggested to the patient that she unconsciously expressed in the dream that she was blind to her own difficulties, and that her decisions with regard to the analysis as well as to various circumstances in her life were not in accordance with her unconscious knowledge. This was also shown by her admitting that she had gone into her 'hide', meaning by it that she was shutting herself off, an attitude well known to her from previous stages in her analysis. Thus the unconscious insight, and even some co-operation on the conscious level (recognition that she was the blind man and that she had gone into her 'hide'), derived from isolated parts of her personality only. Actually, the interpretation of this dream did not produce any effect and did not alter the patient's decision to bring the analysis to an end in that particular hour.[23]

The nature of certain difficulties encountered in this analysis as well as in others had revealed itself more clearly in the last few months before the patient broke off the treatment. It was the mixture of schizoid and manic-depressive features which determined the nature of her illness. For at times throughout her analysis – even in the early stage when depressive and manic states were at their height – depressive and schizoid mechanisms sometimes appeared simultaneously. There were, for instance, hours when the patient was obviously deeply depressed, full of self-reproaches and feelings of unworthiness; tears were running down her cheeks and her gestures expressed despair; and yet she said, when I interpreted these emotions, that she did not feel them at all. Whereupon she reproached herself for having no feelings at all, for being completely empty. In such sessions there was also a flight of ideas, the thoughts seemed to be broken up, and their expression was disjointed.

Following the interpretation of the unconscious reasons under-lying such states, there were sometimes sessions in which the emotions and depressive anxieties came out fully, and at such times thoughts and speech were much more coherent.

This close connection between depressive and schizoid phenomena appeared, though in different forms, throughout her analysis but became very pronounced during the last stage preceding the break just described.

I have already referred to the developmental connection between the paranoid-schizoid and depressive positions. The question now

23 I may mention that the analysis was resumed after a break.

arises whether this developmental connection is the basis for the mixture of these features in manic-depressive disorders and, as I would suggest, in schizophrenic disorders as well. If this tentative hypothesis could be proved, the conclusion would be that the groups of schizophrenic and manic-depressive disorders are more closely connected developmentally with one another than has been assumed. This would also account for the cases in which, I believe, the differential diagnosis between melancholia and schizophrenia is exceedingly difficult. I should be grateful if further light could be thrown on my hypothesis by colleagues who have had ample material for psychiatric observation.

Some schizoid defences

It is generally agreed that schizoid patients are more difficult to analyse than manic-depressive types. Their withdrawn, unemotional attitude, the narcissistic elements in their object-relations (to which I referred earlier), a kind of detached hostility which pervades the whole relation to the analyst create a very difficult type of resistance. I believe that it is largely the splitting processes which account for the patient's failure in contact with the analyst and for his lack of response to the analyst's interpretations. The patient himself feels estranged and far away, and this feeling corresponds to the analyst's impression that considerable parts of the patient's personality and of his emotions are not available. Patients with schizoid features may say: 'I hear what you are saying. You may be right, but it has no meaning for me.' Or again they say they feel they are not there. The expression 'no meaning' in such cases does not imply an active rejection of the interpretation but suggests that parts of the personality and of the emotions are split off. These patients can, therefore, not deal with the interpretation; they can neither accept it nor reject it.

I shall illustrate the processes underlying such states by a piece of material taken from the analysis of a man patient. The session I have in mind started with the patient's telling me that he felt anxiety and did not know why. He then made comparisons with people more successful and fortunate than himself. These remarks also had a reference to me. Very strong feelings of frustration, envy and grievance came to the fore. When I interpreted – to give here again only the gist of my interpretations – that these feelings were directed against the analyst and that he wanted to destroy me, his mood changed abruptly. The tone of his voice became flat, he spoke in a slow, expressionless way, and he said that he felt detached from the whole situation. He added that my interpretation seemed correct, but that it did not matter. In fact, he no longer had any wishes, and nothing was worth bothering about.

My next interpretations centred on the causes for this change of mood. I suggested that at the moment of my interpretation the danger of destroying me had become very real to him and the immediate consequence was the fear of losing me. Instead of feeling guilt and depression, which at certain stages of his analysis followed such interpretations, he now attempted to deal with these dangers by a particular method of splitting. As we know, under the pressure of ambivalence, conflict and guilt, the patient often splits the figure of the analyst; then the analyst may at certain moments be loved, at other moments hated. Or the relations to the analyst may be split in such a way that he remains the good (or bad) figure while somebody else becomes the opposite figure. But this was not the kind of splitting which occurred in this particular instance. The patient split off those parts of himself, i.e. of his ego which he felt to be dangerous and hostile towards the analyst. He turned his destructive impulses from his object towards his ego, with the result that parts of his ego temporarily went out of existence. In unconscious phantasy this amounted to annihilation of part of his personality. The particular mechanism of turning the destructive impulse against one part of his personality, and the ensuing dispersal of emotions, kept his anxiety in a latent state.

My interpretation of these processes had the effect of again altering the patient's mood. He became emotional, said he felt like crying, was depressed, but felt more integrated; then he also expressed a feeling of hunger.[24]

24 The feeling of hunger indicated that the process of introjection had been set going again under the dominance of the libido. While to my first interpretation of his fear of destroying me by his aggression he had responded at once with the violent splitting off and annihilation of parts of his personality, he now experienced more fully the emotions of grief, guilt and fear of loss, as well as some relief of these depressive anxieties. The relief of anxiety resulted in the analyst again coming to stand for a good object which he could trust. Therefore the desire to introject me as a good object could come to the fore. If he could build up again the good breast inside himself, he would strengthen and integrate his ego, would be less afraid of his destructive impulses; in fact he could then preserve himself and the analyst.

The violent splitting off and destroying of one part of the personality under the pressure of anxiety and guilt is in my experience an important schizoid mechanism. To refer briefly to another instance: a woman patient had dreamed that she had to deal with a wicked girl child who was determined to murder somebody. The patient tried to influence or control the child and to extort a confession from her which would have been to the child's benefit; but she was unsuccessful. I also entered into the dream and the patient felt that I might help her in dealing with the child. Then the patient strung up the child on a tree in order to frighten her and also prevent her from doing harm. When the patient was about to pull the rope and kill the child, she woke. During this part of the dream the analyst was also present but again remained inactive.

I shall give here only the essence of the conclusions I arrived at from the analysis of this dream. In the dream the patient's personality was split into two parts: the wicked and uncontrollable child on the one hand, and on the other hand the person who tried to influence and control her. The child, of course, stood also for various figures in the past, but in this context she mainly represented one part of the patient's self. Another conclusion was that the analyst was the person whom the child was going to murder; and my role in the dream was partly to prevent this murder from taking place. Killing the child – to which the patient had to resort – represented the annihilation of one part of her personality.

The question arises how the schizoid mechanism of annihilating part of the self connects with repression which, as we know, is directed against dangerous impulses. This, however, is a problem with which I cannot deal here.

Changes of mood, of course, do not always appear as dramatically within a session as in the first instance I have given in this section. But I have repeatedly found that advances in synthesis are brought about by interpretations of the specific causes for splitting. Such interpretations must deal in detail with the transference-situation at that moment, including of course the connection with the past, and must contain a reference to the details of the anxiety-situations which drive the ego to regress to schizoid mechanisms. The synthesis resulting from interpretations on these lines goes along with depression and anxieties of various kinds. Gradually such waves of depression – followed by greater integration – lead to a lessening of schizoid phenomena and also to fundamental changes in object-relations.

41

Latent anxiety in schizoid patients

I have already referred to the lack of emotion which makes schizoid patients unresponsive. This is accompanied by an absence of anxiety. An important support for the analytic work is therefore lacking. For with other types of patients who have strong manifest and latent anxiety, the relief of anxiety derived from analytic interpretation becomes an experience which furthers their capacity to co-operate in the analysis.

This lack of anxiety in schizoid patients is only apparent. For the schizoid mechanisms imply a dispersal of emotions including anxiety, but these dispersed elements still exist in the patient. Such patients have a certain form of latent anxiety; it is kept latent by the particular method of dispersal. The feeling of being disintegrated, of being unable to experience emotions, of losing one's objects, is in fact the equivalent of anxiety. This becomes clearer when advances in synthesis have been made. The great relief which a patient then experiences derives from a feeling that his inner and outer worlds have not only come more together but back to life again. At such moments it appears in retrospect that when emotions were lacking, relations were vague and uncertain and parts of the personality were felt to be lost, everything seemed to be dead. All this is the equivalent of anxiety of a very serious nature. This anxiety, kept latent by dispersal, is to some extent experienced all along, but its form differs from the latent anxiety which we can recognize in other types of cases.

Interpretations which tend towards synthesizing the split in the self, including the dispersal of emotions, make it possible for the anxiety gradually to be experienced as such, though for long stretches we may in fact only be able to bring the ideational contents together but not to elicit the emotions of anxiety.

I have also found that interpretations of schizoid states make particular demands on our capacity to put the interpretations in an intellectually clear form in which the links between the conscious, pre-conscious and unconscious are established. This is, of course, always one of our aims, but it is of special importance at times when the patient's emotions are not available and we seem to address ourselves only to his intellect, however much broken up.

It is possible that the few hints I have given may to some extent apply as well to the technique of analysing schizophrenic patients.

Summary of conclusions

I will now summarize some of the conclusions presented in this paper. One of my main points was the suggestion that in the first few months of life anxiety is predominantly experienced as fear of persecution and that this contributes to certain mechanisms and defences which are significant for the paranoid-schizoid position. Outstanding among these defences are the mechanisms of splitting internal and external objects, emotions and the ego. These mechanisms and defences are part of normal development and at the same time form the basis for later schizophrenic illness. I described the processes underlying identification by projection as a combination of splitting off parts of the self and projecting them on to another person, and some of the effects this identification has on normal and schizoid object-relations. The onset of the depressive position is the juncture at which by regression schizoid mechanisms may be reinforced. I also suggested a close connection between the manic-depressive and schizoid disorders, based on the interaction between the infantile paranoid-schizoid and depressive positions.

Appendix

Freud's analysis of the Schreber case[25] contains a wealth of material which is very relevant to my topic but from which I shall here draw only a few conclusions.

Schreber described vividly the splitting of the soul of his physician Flechsig (his loved and persecuting figure). The 'Flechsig soul' at one time introduced the system of 'soul divisions', splitting into as many as forty to sixty sub-divisions. These souls having multiplied till they became a 'nuisance', God made a raid on them and as a result the Flechsig soul survived in 'only one or two shapes'. Another point which Schreber mentions is that the fragments of the Flechsig soul slowly lost both their intelligence and their power.

One of the conclusions Freud arrived at in his analysis of this case was that the persecutor was split into God and Flechsig, and

---

25 'Psycho-Analytic Notes upon an Autobiographical Account of a Case of Paranoia (Dementia Paranoides)' (S.E. 12).

also that God and Flechsig represented the patient's father and brother. In discussing the various forms of Schreber's delusion of the destruction of the world, Freud states: 'In any case the end of the world was the consequence of the conflict which had broken out between him, Schreber, and Flechsig, or, according to the aetiology adopted in the second phase of his delusion, of the indissoluble bond which had been formed between him and God. . . .' (Loc. cit., p. 69).

I would suggest, in keeping with the hypotheses outlined in the present chapter, that the division of the Flechsig soul into many souls was not only a splitting of the object but also a projection of Schreber's feeling that his ego was split. I shall here only mention the connection of such splitting processes with processess of introjection. The conclusion suggests itself that God and Flechsig also represented parts of Schreber's self. The conflict between Schreber and Flechsig, to which Freud attributed a vital role in the world–destruction delusion, found expression in the raid by God on the Flechsig souls. In my view this raid represents the annihilation by one part of the self of the other parts – which, as I contend, is a schizoid mechanism. The anxieties and phantasies about inner destruction and ego–disintegration bound up with this mechanism are projected on to the external world and underlie the delusions of its destruction.

Regarding the processes which are at the bottom of the paranoic 'world catastrophe', Freud arrived at the following conclusions: 'The patient has withdrawn from the people in his environment and from the external world generally the libidinal cathexis which he has hitherto directed on to them. Thus everything has become indifferent and irrelevant to him, and has to be explained by means of a secondary rationalization as being "miracled up, cursorily improvised". The end of the world is the projection of this internal catastrophe; for his subjective world has come to an end since he has withdrawn his love from it.' (Loc. cit., p. 70.) This explanation specifically concerns the disturbance in object–libido and the ensuing breakdown in relation to people and to the external world. But a little further on Freud considered another aspect of these disturbances. He said: 'We can no more dismiss the possibility that disturbances of the libido may react upon the egoistic cathexes than we can overlook the *converse possibility – namely, that a secondary or induced disturbance of the libidinal processes may result from abnormal changes in the ego. Indeed it is probable that processes of this kind constitute the distinctive characteristic of psychoses' (my italics).* It is particularly the possibility expressed in the last two sentences which provides the link between Freud's explanation of the 'world catastrophe' and my hypothesis. 'Abnormal changes in the ego' derive, as I have suggested in this chapter, from excessive splitting processes in the early ego. These processes are inextricably linked with instinctual development, and with the anxieties to which instinctual desires give rise. In the light of Freud's later theory of the life and death instincts, which replaced the concept of the egoistic and sexual instincts, disturbances in the distribution of the libido presuppose a defusion between the destructive impulse and the libido. The mechanism of one part of the ego annihilating other parts which, I suggest, underlies 'world catastrophe' phantasy (the raid by God on the Flechsig souls) implies a preponderance of the destructive impulse over the libido. Any disturbance in the distribution of the narcissistic libido is in turn bound up with the relation to introjected objects which (according to my work) from the beginning come to form part of the ego. The interaction between narcissistic libido and object-libido corresponds thus to the interaction between the relation to introjected and external objects. If the ego and the internalized objects are felt to be in bits, an internal catastrophe is experienced by the infant which both extends to the external world and is projected on to it. Such anxiety-states relating to an internal catastrophe arise, according to the hypothesis discussed in the present chapter, during the period of the infantile paranoid–schizoid position and form the basis for later schizophrenia. In Freud's view the dispositional fixation to dementia praecox is found in a very early stage of development. Referring to dementia praecox, which Freud distinguished from paranoia, he said: 'The dispositional point of fixation must therefore be situated further back than in paranoia, and must lie somewhere at the beginning of the course of development from auto-erotism to object-love.' (Loc. cit., p. 77.)

I wish to draw one more conclusion from Freud's analysis of the Schreber case. I suggest that the raid, which ended in the Flechsig souls being reduced to one or two, was part of the attempt towards recovery. For the raid was to undo, or, one may say, heal the split in the ego by annihilating the split-off parts of the ego. As a result only one or two of the souls were left which, as we may assume, were meant to regain their intelligence and their power. This attempt towards recovery, however, was effected by very destructive means used by the ego against itself and its projected objects.

Freud's approach to the problems of schizophrenia and paranoia has proved of fundamental importance. His Schreber paper (and here we also have to remember Abraham's paper[26] quoted by Freud) opened up the possibility of understanding psychosis and the processes underlying it.

26 'The Psycho-Sexual Differences between Hysteria and Dementia Praecox' (1908).

PART TWO

Some British Kleinian developments

3

Developments by British Kleinian analysts[27]

Elizabeth Spillius

I believe that nowadays most Kleinian analysts would agree with Klein herself in thinking that although projective identification is important, it is not the most central and distinctively Kleinian concept. Pride of place is reserved for the comprehensive ideas of the paranoid–schizoid and depressive positions. Indeed, the term 'projective identification' was first defined by Klein in her paper 'Notes on some schizoid mechanisms' (1946), which is her definitive statement of the paranoid–schizoid position.

Nevertheless many papers by contemporary Kleinian British analysts use the idea of projective identification clinically and a somewhat smaller number of papers have been specifically devoted to conceptual discussion of the concept (the main discussions occur in Bell, 2001; Bion, 1959; Britton, 1998b; Feldman, 1992, 1994, 1997; Hinshelwood, 1991; Joseph, 1987; Rosenfeld, 1964b, 1971, 1983; Segal, 1964; Sodré, 2004; see particularly Edna O'Shaughnessy's Chapter 9 in the present book; Spillius, 1992). In addition there have been unpublished contributions by Ruth Riesenberg Malcolm, Hanna Segal, Edith Hargreaves, Priscilla Roth, Robin Anderson and Edna O'Shaughnessy. There have also been two conferences on the topic of projective identification, one

---

27 It is not possible to give a precise definition of a 'British Kleinian analyst'. In general usage it means an analyst whose training analyst has been a Kleinian. However, a few analysts in all three British psychoanalytic groups, the Kleinians, the Independents and the Contemporary Freudians, have changed their affiliation after qualification in one group to that of one of the other groups. A few British analysts prefer to identify themselves as 'non-aligned'.

organised by Joseph Sandler in Jerusalem in 1984 (Sandler, 1987b) and one on 'Understanding Projective Identification: Clinical Advances' held at University College London in October 1995.

Klein's original delineation of the concept of projective identification has of course been central to later developments in Britain, and she probably conveyed some of the ideas she describes in the Archive to her patients, colleagues and students. But in spite of Klein's influence the ideas of contemporary Kleinian analysts differ from hers in several respects.

The first change from Klein's view is that all Kleinian analysts now assume that the analyst's countertransference, using that term in its broadest sense, is at least in part a response to the patient's projective identification and can be a useful source of information about the patient.

The second trend is that contemporary Kleinian analysts now follow Bion (1959) in making a distinction between normal and pathological projective identification, although until recently most papers have focused primarily on the pathological aspects.

A third trend is that contemporary Kleinian analysts do not make a point of distinguishing between projection and projective identification as Klein tried to do in her unpublished 1958 notes in the D17 part of the Klein Archive, as I have described in Part One of this book.

A fourth trend consists of distinctions between various sub-types of projective identification within the general category (Britton, 1998b, pp. 5–6; Spillius, 1988a, pp. 81–86).

A fifth trend is a recent but growing recognition that there has been a tendency to think of projective identification as 'bad' and introjective identification as 'good', whereas it is likely to be more useful to recognise both 'concrete' and 'symbolic' forms of phantasy and thought in both types of identification (Sodré, 2004). This recognition has been accompanied by a tendency to look at the movements between processes of projective and introjective identification.

The relation between projective identification and countertransference

Even before Klein's death several authors, among them Heimann (1950), Racker (1953; 1957; 1958b) and Money-Kyrle (1956), were writing about the use of countertransference as a source of information about the patient. This view has become the most accepted and ubiquitous of the trends I have described above. It is one of the few ways in which current contemporary Kleinian thinking and technique differ from that of Klein herself.

In her seminal paper on countertransference **Paula Heimann** (1950) clearly thinks of countertransference as a response to what the patient communicates to the analyst. She says: 'From the point of view I am stressing, the analyst's countertransference is not only part and parcel of the analytic relationship, but it is the patient's *creation*, it is a part of the patient's personality' (Heimann, 1950, p. 83, italics in original). The 'patient's *creation*' sounds very much as if Heimann is thinking here of what Klein and later Kleinian analysts would think of as the patient's projective identification, but Heimann does not use this term, and indeed she thinks of projective identification differently, saying, for example:

> many instances of so-called 'projective identification' should be defined as the reactivation in the patient of his infantile experiences with his rejecting and intruding mother [. . .] 'Projective identification' occurs as a counter-transference phenomenon, when the analyst fails in his perceptive functions, so that, instead of recognizing in good time the character of the transference, he on his part unconsciously introjects his patient who at this point acts from an identification with his rejecting and intruding mother, re-enacting his own experiences in a reversal of roles.
>
> (Heimann, 1966, pp. 224 and 230, footnote 1)

Thus Heimann's use of the term 'projective identification' is noticeably different from the usage of Klein and that of Klein's later Kleinian colleagues.

Among Klein's later colleagues the relation between the patient's projective identification and the analyst's countertransference is partly a matter of definition. When **Wilfred Bion**, for example, uses the actual word 'countertransference' he often means it in the sense used by Freud (1910) and Klein as an expression, largely unconscious, of the analyst's pathology (see, for example, Bion, 1962a, p. 24; 1963, p. 8). At the same time it is clear from his papers, especially 'Attacks on linking' (Bion, 1959, that he uses his own emotional response as a source of information about the patient. In the wider definition of countertransference used by Heimann and Racker this sort of response would be called countertransference. Bion describes this sort of response in 1955 in his paper 'Group dynamics: a review' (Bion, 1955a) and here, somewhat uncharacteristically, he actually uses the word 'countertransference' to describe the analyst's response to the patient's projective identification:

> Now the experience of counter-transference appears to me to have quite a distinct quality which should enable the analyst to differentiate the occasion when he is the object of a projective identification from the occasion when he is not. The analyst feels he is being manipulated so as to be playing a part, no matter how difficult to recognize, in somebody's [*sic*] else's phantasy – or he would do if it were not for what in recollection I can only call a temporary loss of insight, a sense of experiencing strong feelings and at the same time a belief that their existence is adequately justified by the objective situation without recourse to recondite explanation of their causation.
>
> (Bion, 1955a, p. 446)

I take this to mean that the emotions the analyst experiences are aroused at least in part by projections from the patient (or the group) although the analyst is likely to feel that the emotions are largely of his own making.

In 'Language and the schizophrenic', Bion (1955b) describes a similar process with a psychotic patient, saying that his interpretations depended on his use of Klein's theory of projective identification first to illuminate his countertransference, then to frame his interpretation. He describes how in a session with a psychotic patient Bion at first felt a growing fear that the patient would attack him. He interpreted that the patient was pushing into his (Bion's) insides the patient's fear that he would murder Bion. After this interpretation the tension lessened, but the patient clenched his fists. Bion then interpreted that the patient had taken the fear back into himself and was now afraid that he would make a murderous attack. He goes on to say:

> This mode of procedure is open to grave theoretical objections and I think they should be faced [. . .] I think there are signs that as experience accumulates it may be possible to detect and present facts which exist, but at present elude clinical acumen; they become observable, at second hand, through the pressure they exert to

produce what I am aware of as counter-transference. I would not have it thought that I advocate this use of counter-transference as a final solution; rather it is an expedient to which we must resort until something better presents itself.

(Bion, 1955b, pp. 224–225)

Roger Money-Kyrle describes a similar process of using the analyst's countertransference as a way of understanding the patient.

How exactly a patient does succeed in imposing a phantasy and its corresponding affect upon his analyst in order to deny it in himself is a most interesting problem [. . .] In the analytic situation, a peculiarity of communications of this kind is that, at first sight, they do not seem as if they had been made by the patient at all. The analyst experiences the affect as being his own response to something. The effort involved is in differentiating the patient's contribution from his own.

(Money-Kyrle, 1956, p. 342, footnote 10)

In *An Introduction to the Work of Melanie Klein* in 1964, **Hanna Segal** seems to do what Bion describes as 'resorting to countertransference until something better presents itself' (Segal, 1964). She describes projective identification as an ongoing part of clinical work, includes a description of the defensive uses of projective identification and refers to the withdrawal of projective identifications as an important aspect of reparation (Segal, 1964, see especially pp. 14–17 and 63–67).

All Kleinian analysts now agree that countertransference in the form of the analyst's feelings in response to a patient's projective identification may be a useful source of information about the patient, provided, of course, that the analyst is well-trained and reasonably sensitive. The work of Bion, Segal and Joseph has been influential in producing this change, but it has also involved a general change in the definition of countertransference. Most British analysts have adopted the wider definition of countertransference advocated by Paula Heimann (1950) and others rather than the narrower definition of Freud and Klein. This change in the definition of countertransference has meant that projective identification is now sometimes considered to be interpersonal as well as intrapersonal, depending on whether some sort of pressure is put on the object to conform to the subject's phantasy.

53

Normal and pathological forms of projective identification

In his influential paper 'Attacks on linking' (Bion, 1959, reprinted in Chapter 4 of this book), **Bion** makes an important distinction between normal and pathological forms of projective identification. In his view projective identification is an early and very important form of non-verbal communication. He says: 'I shall suppose that there is a normal degree of projective identification, without defining the limits within which normality lies, and that associated with introjective identification this is the foundation on which normal development rests' (Bion, 1967, p. 103).

In 'Attacks on linking' Bion then describes several fascinating but obscure clinical episodes of communication between patient and analyst in which something pathological had apparently happened that had damaged the patient's capacity for verbal communication. Bion goes on to say that an infant is dependent on the receptiveness of the object, typically his mother, to accept projections and to act in such a way that the messages of the projections are understood and appropriately responded to. If the object fails to receive the projections the infant will very probably increase his projective efforts, an escalation which is likely to be repeated later in the individual's analysis. Bion describes the process as follows:

> In the analysis a complex situation may be observed. The patient feels he is being allowed an opportunity of which he had hitherto been cheated; the poignancy of his deprivation is thereby rendered the more acute and so are the feelings of resentment at the deprivation. Gratitude for the opportunity co-exists with hostility to the analyst as the person who will not understand and refuses the patient the use of the only method of communication by which he feels he can make himself understood. Thus the link between patient and analyst, or infant and breast, is the mechanism of projective identification.
>
> (Bion, 1967, pp. 104–105)

But the object's imperviousness to projection is not the only form of attack on the link between infant and object. The infant or later the patient may be so envious of the object that he too attacks the link by assuming that the object's capacity to receive is a greedy attempt to take in the patient's projections in order to destroy them. Between the subject's envy and the object's unreceptiveness the links are damaged, communication is disrupted, curiosity is dulled and a destructive superego is likely to be installed.

In later papers Bion goes on to develop further the idea of the subject's projective identification and the object's response, particularly in his model of the process of containment (Bion, 1962a, 1963, 1965, 1970).

Herbert Rosenfeld, Betty Joseph and others have reiterated Bion's distinction between normal and pathological projective identification. Their descriptions of projective identification, however, have tended to focus on its pathological aspects.

Herbert Rosenfeld has made several important contributions to the understanding of projective identification. In 1947 he describes how his depersonalised patient used projective identification to protect herself and to control others (Rosenfeld, 1947). In 1952 he describes the intrusiveness of a patient's use of projective identification to control his analyst (Rosenfeld, 1952a). In a paper on narcissism in 1964 he draws attention to the fact that identifications by projection and by introjection usually occur at the same time (Rosenfeld, 1964b). In omnipotent identification, which, he says, may occur by both introjection and by projection, the boundary between self and object is denied.

> Identification is an important factor in narcissistic object relations. It may take place by introjection or by projection. When the object is omnipotently incorporated, the self becomes so identified with the incorporated object that all separate identity or any boundary between self and object is denied. In projective identification parts of the self omnipotently enter an object, for example the mother, to take over certain qualities which would be experienced as desirable, and therefore claim to be the object or part-object. Identification by introjection and by projection usually occur simultaneously.
>
> In narcissistic object relations defences against any recognition of separateness between self and object play a predominant part.
>
> (Rosenfeld, 1964b, pp. 170–171)

In a paper of 1971 Rosenfeld makes an important addition to the understanding of projective identification, particularly in the case of psychotic patients (Rosenfeld, 1971, reprinted in Chapter 5 of this book). He emphasises the splitting of the patient's mind that is involved in the projective identification of parts of the mind into an object. He develops a differentiation of several general motives for projective identification: communication, which is based on the normal non-verbal communication between infant and mother; ridding the self of unwanted aspects, which leads to a denial of psychic reality; to control the mind and body of the other, the other being the analyst in the analytic situation; to get rid of awareness of separ-ateness and envy; as a special form, particularly in the case of psychotic patients, of parasitism which involves the patient having an uncon-scious phantasy of virtually living inside the mind of the object. Rosenfeld further elaborates his ideas about these motives and their clinical expression in a later paper called 'Primitive object relations and mechanisms' (Rosenfeld, 1983) and in his book *Impasse and Interpretation* (Rosenfeld, 1987a).

Betty Joseph gives a very clear clinical demonstration of her use of the concept of projective identification in 'Projective identifica-tion: some clinical aspects' (Joseph, 1987, reprinted in Chapter 6 of this book), a paper given at the conference on projective identifica-tion at the University of Jerusalem in 1985.

Three features are distinctive of this paper. First, like Rosenfeld and unlike Klein, Joseph focuses in this paper almost exclusively on the aggressive and negative aspects of projective identification: getting rid of unwanted parts of the self; dominating and controlling the object; avoiding feelings of separateness; taking over the capacities of the object; invading the object in order to damage or destroy it. She mentions the communicative functions of projective identification described by Bion and Rosenfeld but adds that projective identifica-tion is by its nature a form of communication even when communi-cation is not its aim. Second, she emphasises the importance of the patient's defensive efforts to use projective identification to maintain his psychic equilibrium, illustrating the effect of such defensive efforts in the case of a psychotic child, an adult patient 'more or less stuck in the paranoid-schizoid position', and finally in a patient beginning to move towards the depressive position. The third feature of Joseph's paper is her perceptiveness in understanding the effect of her patient's projections on her own emotional state, making it possible for her to understand not only her patients' emotional states but also their use of projective identification to maintain their equilibrium. Unlike Klein, who thought the analyst should overcome the emotional effect of the patient's projection, Joseph uses that emotional effect as a central basis of her understanding.

Ruth Riesenberg Malcolm (1970) describes a perverse phantasy by means of which a patient attempted to get rid of disturbing parts of herself by projective identification, leading to a vicious circle of projection and forceful re-entry.

Robert Hinshelwood (1991) gives a comprehensive account of the definitions and uses of the concept of projective identification not only by Klein and her contemporary Kleinian colleagues but also by American analysts, most of whom, he says, have taken the concept out of its framework in Kleinian theory. He concludes his extensive discussion by saying, 'There appears to be no consensus on the value of the term "projective identification" outside the Kleinian conceptual framework' (Hinshelwood, 1991, p. 204).

Michael Feldman in his paper 'Projective identification: the analyst's involvement' (Feldman, 1997, reprinted in Chapter 7 of this book) shows in detail how patients may use projective identification in a way that impinges on the analyst's thinking, feeling and actions in such a fashion that he is drawn into some form of mutual enactment with the patient, an enactment which is essential for the fulfilment of the patient's unconscious aims.

Projection and projective identification

Although, as I described in Part One, Klein made a distinction – in my view a rather unclear distinction – between projection and projective identification in her unpublished notes of 1958, contemporary Kleinian analysts have not followed her usage in this respect. The usual though tacit attitude of present Kleinian analysts is that there is no really clear distinction, especially no clear distinction in clinical work, between projection and projective identification.

Segal (personal communication) says that Klein viewed 'projection' as the mental mechanism and 'projective identification' as the particular unconscious phantasy expressing it. Bell (2001) also mentions this distinction. Neither Segal nor Bell nor any other British Kleinian analyst distinguishes between projection and projective identification in their own clinical work, although such a distinction has become important to many American analysts (see Chapter 15, 'A brief review of projective identification in American psychoanalytic literature').

Varieties of projective identification

I have suggested (Spillius, 1988a, pp. 81–86) that it might be best to use the idea of projective identification as a general 'umbrella' concept covering a wide variety of specific types of projective identification, although it may also be useful to use particular adjectives to distinguish specific sub-types within the general category. I suggested the term 'evocatory' to describe the sort of projective identification in which a patient's unconscious phantasy is accompanied by behaviours unconsciously designed to evoke a specific sort of response from the object.

Ronald Britton has made a useful distinction between 'attributive' projective identification, in which some aspect of the subject is attributed to the object, and 'acquisitive' projective identification in which the projective phantasy concerns an idea of entering the object to acquire some attribute that the object is thought to possess (Britton, 1998b, pp. 5–6). Britton's idea of acquisitive projective identification describes a process similar to Bollas's idea of 'extractive introjection' (Bollas, 1987, pp. 157–169), indicating the close relation between projective and introjective processes. Most phantasies involving projective identification include elements of both attribution and of acquisition, just as most phantasies of psychic interaction involve both phantasies of projection and of introjection.

Concrete and symbolic thinking in both projective and introjective identification

In her paper 'Who's who? Notes on pathological identification', **Ignes Sodré** makes another valuable addition to the understanding of processes of identification (Sodré, 2004, reprinted in Chapter 8 of this book). She reminds the reader of Rosenfeld's 1964 paper described above in which he says that omnipotent identification, whether by projection or by introjection, obliterates the boundary between self and object:

Even though 'projective identification' is used to describe normal as well as pathological processes, I think that we tend to think of projective processes as more pathological than introjective ones.

(Sodré, 2004, p. 57)

Sodré argues that introjective processes and introjective identification can be just as pathological as projective identification. The pathological element in identification is not, she says, whether it is projective or introjective; it is whether the identification is concrete or symbolic. Sodré makes clear, I think, why we have tended to describe certain identificatory processes as 'projective' when it might have been more useful to have described them as projective identification followed by introjective identification. If the identification is thought to involve 'bad' attributes, we tend to think of it as 'projective'; if it involves 'good' attributes, we tend to think of it as 'introjective'. Sodré illustrates her thesis with her own clinical material but I think it can also be applied to other instances.

For example, in Klein's example of Fabian, the hero of Julian Green's novel *If I Were You* (Klein, 1955), Fabian's behaviour could be regarded as an instance of acquisitive projective identification followed by introjection. Fabian projects himself into other people, according to Klein's analysis, but could also be seen as taking the resulting amalgam of Fabian plus other person back into himself to the point of not knowing who was who.

In describing what he terms the 'identificate' **Leslie Sohn** (1985) describes the way certain narcissistic patients project themselves into the object to take possession of its desirable qualities, an instance of what Britton calls 'acquisitive' projective identification. Sohn describes this entirely as a projective process, although I think one might view it as projection followed by introjection of the desired self/other identificate which is then claimed to be oneself.

With the work of Bion, Rosenfeld, Joseph, Britton, Feldman, Sohn, Sodré and many other Kleinian analysts, I believe that the ideas of projection and introjection have become more clearly defined but also more interconnected with one another to create a coherent approach to the analysis of episodes of intrapsychic and interpersonal interaction. Normality and pathology have come to be regarded not as resting on whether identification is projective or introjective, but rather on the motive and content of the identifications.

Conclusion

The work of British contemporary Kleinian analysts has added several dimensions to Klein's original discussion of projective identification. The analyst's countertransference, using that term in its widest sense, can be a useful source of information about the patient. This change has contributed to the process of regarding projective identification as an interpersonal as well as an intrapersonal process.

Bion's distinction between normal and pathological aspects of projective identification (Bion, 1959, reprinted in Chapter 4 of this book) is now generally accepted, as are the motives described by Rosenfeld (1971) as characteristic of projective identification: communication; control of the other; avoidance of envy; parasitism.

I have described the possible usefulness of describing sub-types of projective identification such as my suggested 'evocative' and 'non-evocative' and Britton's 'attributive' and 'acquisitive' projective identification. Although this chapter has been chiefly concerned with the usage and developments in the use of the concept of projective identification by Kleinian analysts, it should be noted that some Kleinian analysts have been influenced by Sandler's concept of 'actualization' as expressed in two of his papers in 1976 (Sandler, 1976a; 1976b).

Finally, there has been a general tendency to focus on the pathological aspects of projective identification, but this has been corrected, especially clearly shown in the work of Ignes Sodré (2004, reprinted in Chapter 8 of this book), by emphasis on the presence of both constructive and pathological aspects in both projective and introjective identifications. There has also been a gradual recognition that projection and introjection 'operate simultaneously', as Klein put it, a process further stressed by Rosenfeld (1964b). Further, I think that these simultaneous processes occur in both (or perhaps all) members of an interaction, a process which gives psychic and social interchanges immense complexity and variability.

4

Attacks on linking[28]

W. R. Bion

In previous papers (Bion, 1957a) I have had occasion, in talking of the psychotic part of the personality, to speak of the destructive attacks which the patient makes on anything which is felt to have the function of linking one object with another. It is my intention in this paper to show the significance of this form of destructive attack in the production of some symptoms met with in borderline psychosis.

The prototype for all the links of which I wish to speak is the primitive breast or penis. The paper presupposes familiarity with Melanie Klein's descriptions of the infant's fantasies of sadistic attacks upon the breast (Klein, 1935), of the infant's splitting of its objects, of projective identification, which is the name she gives to the mechanism by which parts of the personality are split off and projected into external objects, and finally her views on early stages of the Oedipus complex (Klein, 1928). I shall discuss phantasied attacks on the breast as the prototype of all attacks on objects that serve as a link and projective identification as the mechanism employed by the psyche to dispose of the ego fragments produced by its destructiveness.

I shall first describe clinical manifestations in an order dictated not by the chronology of their appearance in the consulting room, but by the need for making the exposition of my thesis as clear as I can. I shall follow this by material selected to demonstrate the order which these mechanisms assume when their relationship to each other is

---

28 This paper was read before the British Psycho-Analytical Society on 20 October 1957. First published in 1959 in the *International Journal of Psycho-Analysis, 40*, 308–315.

determined by the dynamics of the analytic situation. I shall conclude with theoretical observations on the material presented. The examples are drawn from the analysis of two patients and are taken from an advanced stage of their analyses. To preserve anonymity I shall not distinguish between the patients and shall introduce distortions of fact which I hope do not impair the accuracy of the analytic description.

Observation of the patient's disposition to attack the link between two objects is simplified because the analyst has to establish a link with the patient and does this by verbal communication and his equipment of psycho-analytical experience. Upon this the creative relationship depends and therefore we should be able to see attacks being made upon it.

I am not concerned with typical resistance to interpretations, but with expanding references which I made in my paper on 'The Differentiation of the Psychotic from the Non-psychotic Part of the Personality' (Bion, 1957a) to the destructive attacks on verbal thought itself.

Clinical examples

I shall now describe occasions which afforded me an opportunity to give the patient an interpretation, which at that point he could understand, of conduct designed to destroy whatever it was that linked two objects together.

These are the examples:

i. I had reason to give the patient an interpretation making explicit his feelings of affection and his expression of them to his mother for her ability to cope with a refractory child. The patient attempted to express his agreement with me, but although he needed to say only a few words his expression of them was interrupted by a very pronounced stammer which had the effect of spreading out his remark over a period of as much as a minute and a half. The actual sounds emitted bore resemblance to gasping for breath; gaspings were interspersed with gurgling sounds as if he were immersed in water. I drew his attention to these sounds and he agreed that they were peculiar and himself suggested the descriptions I have just given.

ii. The patient complained that he could not sleep. Showing signs of fear, he said, 'It can't go on like this'. Disjointed remarks gave the impression that he felt superficially that some catastrophe would occur, perhaps akin to insanity, if he could not get more sleep. Referring to material in the previous session I suggested that he feared he would dream if he were to sleep. He denied this and said he could not think because he was wet. I reminded him of his use of the term 'wet' as an expression of contempt for somebody he regarded as feeble and sentimental. He disagreed and indicated that the state to which he referred was the exact opposite. From what I knew of this patient I felt that his correction at this point was valid and that somehow the wetness referred to an expression of hatred and envy such as he associated with urinary attacks on an object. I therefore said that in addition to the superficial fear which he had expressed he was afraid of sleep because for him it was the same thing as the oozing away of his mind itself. Further associations showed that he felt that good interpretations from me were so consistently and minutely split up by him that they became mental urine which then seeped uncontrollably away. Sleep was therefore inseparable from unconsciousness, which was itself identical with a state of mindlessness which could not be repaired. He said, 'I am dry now'. I replied that he felt he was awake and capable of thought, but that this good state was only precariously maintained.

iii. In this session the patient had produced material stimulated by the preceding week–end break. His awareness of such external stimuli had become demonstrable at a comparatively recent stage of the analysis. Previously it was a matter for conjecture how much he was capable of appreciating reality. I knew that he had contact with reality because he came for analysis by himself, but that fact could hardly be deduced from his behaviour in the sessions. When I interpreted some associations as evidence that he felt he had been and still was witnessing an intercourse between two people, he reacted as if he had received a violent blow. I was not then able to say just where he had experienced the assault and even in retrospect I have no clear impression. It would seem logical to suppose that the shock had been administered by my interpretation and that therefore the blow came from without, but my impression is that he felt it as delivered from within; the patient often experienced what he described as a stabbing attack from inside. He sat up and stared intently into space. I said that he seemed to be seeing something. He replied that he could not see what he saw. I was able from previous experience to interpret that he felt he was 'seeing' an invisible object and subsequent experience convinced me that in the two patients on whose analysis I am depending for material for this paper, events occurred in which the patient experienced invisible-visual hallucinations. I shall give my reasons later for supposing that in this and the previous example similar mechanisms were at work.

iv. In the first twenty minutes of the session the patient made three isolated remarks which had no significance for me. He then said that it seemed that a girl he had met was understanding. This was followed at once by a violent, convulsive movement which he affected to ignore. It appeared to be identical with the kind of stabbing attack I mentioned in the last example. I tried to draw his attention to the movement, but he ignored my intervention as he ignored the attack. He then said that the room was filled with a blue haze. A little later he remarked that the haze had gone, but said he was depressed. I interpreted that he felt understood by me. This was an agreeable experience, but the pleasant feeling of being understood had been instantly destroyed and ejected. I reminded him that we had recently witnessed his use of the word 'blue' as a compact description of vituperative sexual conversation. If my interpretation was correct, and subsequent events suggested that it was, it meant that the experience of being understood had been split up, converted into particles of sexual abuse and ejected. Up to this point I felt that the interpretation approximated closely to his experience. Later interpretations, that the disappearance of the haze was due to reintrojection and conversion into depression, seemed to have less reality for the patient, although later events were compatible with its being correct.

v. The session, like the one in my last example, began with three or four statements of fact such as that it was hot, that his train was crowded, and that it was Wednesday; this occupied thirty minutes. An impression that he was trying to retain contact with reality was confirmed when he followed up by saying that he feared a breakdown. A little later he said I would not understand him. I interpreted that he felt I was bad and would not take in what he wanted to put into me. I interpreted in these terms deliberately because he had shown in the previous session that he felt that my interpretations were an attempt to eject feelings that he wished to deposit in me. His response to my interpretation was to say that he felt there were two probability clouds in the room. I interpreted that he was trying to get rid of the feeling that my badness was a fact. I said it meant that he needed to know whether I was really bad or whether I was some bad thing which had come from inside him. Although the point was not at the moment of central significance I though the patient was attempting to decide whether he was hallucinated or not. This recurrent anxiety in his analysis was associated with his fear that envy and hatred of a capacity for understanding was leading him to take in a good, understanding object to destroy and eject it – a procedure which had often led to persecution by the destroyed and ejected object. Whether my refusal to understand was a reality or hallucination was important only because it determined what painful experiences were to be expected next.

vi. Half the session passed in silence; the patient then announced that a piece of iron had fallen on the floor. Thereafter he made a series of convulsive movements in silence as if he felt he was being physically assaulted from within. I said he could not establish contact with me because of his fear of what was going on inside him. He confirmed this by saying that he felt he was being murdered. He did not know what he would do without the analysis as it made him better. I said that he felt so envious of himself and of me for being able to work together to make him feel better that he took the pair of us into him as a dead piece of iron and a dead floor that came together not to give him life but to murder him. He became very anxious and said he could not go on. I said that he felt he could not go on because he was either dead, or alive and so envious that he had to stop good analysis. There was a marked decrease of anxiety, but the remainder of the session was taken up by isolated statements of fact which again seemed to be an attempt to preserve contact with external reality as a method of denial of his phantasies.

Features common to the above illustrations

These episodes have been chosen by me because the dominant theme in each was the destructive attack on a link. In the first the attack was expressed in a stammer which was designed to prevent the patient from using language as a bond between him and me. In the second sleep was felt by him to be identical with projective identification that proceeded unaffected by any possible attempt at control by him. Sleep for him meant that his mind, minutely fragmented, flowed out in an attacking stream of particles.

The examples I give here throw light on schizophrenic dreaming. The psychotic patient appears to have no dreams, or at least not to report any, until comparatively late in the analysis. My impression now is that this apparently dreamless period is a phenomenon analogous to the invisible-visual hallucination. That is to say, that the dreams consist of material so minutely fragmented that they are devoid of any visual component. When dreams are experienced which the patient can report because visual objects have been experienced by him in the course of the dream, he seems to regard these objects as bearing much the same relationship to the invisible objects of the previous phase as faeces seem to him to bear to urine. The objects appearing in experiences which we call dreams are regarded by the patient as solid and are, as such, contrasted with the contents of the dreams which were a continuum of minute, invisible fragments.

At the time of the session the main theme was not an attack on the link but the consequences of such an attack, previously made, in leaving him bereft of a state of mind necessary for the establishment of a satisfying relationship between him and his bed. Though it did not appear in the session I report, uncontrollable projective identification, which was what sleep meant to him, was thought to be a destructive attack on the state of mind of the coupling parents. There was therefore a double anxiety; one arising from his fear that he was being rendered mindless, the other from his fear that he was unable to control his hostile attacks, his mind providing the ammunition, on the state of mind that was the link between the parental pair. Sleep and sleeplessness were alike inacceptable.

In the third example in which I described visual hallucinations of invisible objects, we witness one form in which the actual attack on the sexual pair is delivered. My interpretation, as far as I could judge, was felt by him as if it were his own visual sense of a parental intercourse; this visual impression is minutely fragmented and ejected at once in particles so minute that they are the invisible components of a continuum. The total procedure has served the purpose of forestalling an experience of feelings of envy for the parental state of mind by the instantaneous expression of envy in a destructive act. I shall have more to say of this implicit hatred of emotion and the need to avoid awareness of it.

In my fourth example, the report of the understanding girl and the haze, my understanding and his agreeable state of mind have been felt as a link between us which could give rise to a creative act. The link had been regarded with hate and transformed into a hostile and destructive sexuality rendering the patient-analyst couple sterile.

In my fifth example, of the two probability clouds, a capacity for understanding is the link which is being attacked, but the interest lies in the fact that the object making the destructive attacks is alien to the patient. Furthermore, the destroyer is making an attack on projective identification which is felt by the patient to be a method of communication. In so far as my supposed attack on his methods of communication is felt as possibly secondary to his envious attacks on me, he does not dissociate himself from feelings of guilt and responsibility. A further point is the appearance of judgement, which Freud regards as an essential feature of the dominance of the reality principle, among the ejected parts of the patient's personality. The fact that there were two probability clouds remained unexplained at the time, but in subsequent sessions I had material which led me to suppose that what had originally been an attempt to separate good from bad survived in the existence of two objects, but they were now similar in that each was a mixture of good and bad. Taking into consideration material from later sessions, I can draw conclusions which were not possible at the time; his capacity for judgment, which had been split up and destroyed with the rest of his ego and then ejected, was felt by him to be similar to other bizarre objects of the kind which I have described in my paper on 'The Differentiation of the Psychotic from the Non-Psychotic parts of the Personality'. These ejected particles were feared because of the treatment he had accorded them. He felt that the alienated judgment – the probability clouds – indicated that I was probably bad. His suspicion that the probability clouds were persecutory and hostile led him to doubt the value of the guidance they afforded him. They might supply him with a correct assessment or a deliberately false one, such as that a fact was an hallucination or vice versa; or would give rise to what, from a psychiatric point of view, we would call delusions. The probability clouds themselves had some qualities of a primitive breast and were felt to be enigmatic and intimidating.

In my sixth illustration, the report that a piece of iron had fallen on the floor, I had no occasion for interpreting an aspect of the material with which the patient had by this time become familiar (I should perhaps say that experience had taught me that there were times when I assumed the patient's familiarity with some aspect of a situation with which we were dealing, only to discover that, in spite of the work that had been done upon it, he had forgotten it). The familiar point that I did not interpret, but which is significant for the understanding of this episode, is that the patient's envy of the parental couple had been evaded by his substitution of himself and myself for the parents. The evasion failed, for the envy and hatred were now directed against him and me. The couple engaged in a creative act are felt to be sharing an enviable, emotional experience; he, being identified also with the excluded party, has a painful, emotional experience as well. On many occasions the patient, partly through experiences of the kind which I describe in this episode, and partly for reasons on which I shall enlarge later, had a hatred of emotion, and therefore, by a short extension, of life itself. This hatred contributes to the murderous attack on that which links the pair, on the pair itself and on the object generated by the pair. In the episode I am describing, the patient is suffering the consequences of his early attacks on the state of mind that forms the link between the creative pair and his identification with both the hateful and creative states of mind.

In this and the preceding illustration there are elements that suggest the formation of a hostile persecutory object, or agglomeration of objects, which expresses its hostility in a manner which is of great importance in producing the predominance of psychotic mechanisms in a patient; the characteristics with which I have already invested the agglomeration of persecutory objects have the quality of a primitive, and even murderous, superego.

Curiosity, arrogance and stupidity

In the paper I presented at the International Congress of 1957 (Bion, 1957b) I suggested that Freud's analogy of an archaeological investigation with a psycho-analysis was helpful if it were considered that we were exposing evidence not so much of a primitive civilization as of a primitive disaster. The value of the analogy is lessened because in the analysis we are confronted not so much with a static situation that permits leisurely study, but with a catastrophe that remains at one and the same moment actively vital and yet incapable of resolution into quiescence. This lack of progress in any direction must be attributed in part to the destruction of a capacity for curiosity and the consequent inability to learn, but before I go into this I must say something about a matter that plays hardly any part in the illustrations I have given.

Attacks on the link originate in what Melanie Klein calls the paranoid-schizoid phase. This period is dominated by part-object relationships (Klein, 1948). If it is borne in mind that the patient has a part-object relationship with himself as well as with objects not himself, it contributes to the understanding of phrases such as 'it seems' which are commonly employed by the deeply disturbed patient on occasions when a less disturbed patient might say 'I think' or 'I believe'. When he says 'it seems' he is often referring to a feeling – an 'it seems' feeling – which is a part of his psyche and yet is not observed as part of a whole object. The conception of the part-object as analogous to an anatomical structure, encouraged by the patient's employment of concrete images as units of thought, is misleading because the part-object relationship is not with the anatomical structures only but with function, not with anatomy but with physiology, not with the breast but with feeding, poisoning, loving, hating. This contributes to the impression of a disaster that is dynamic and not static. The problem that has to be solved on this early, yet superficial, level must be stated in adult terms by the question, 'What is something?' and not the question 'Why is something?' because 'why' has, through guilt, been split off. Problems, the solution of which depends upon an awareness of causation, cannot therefore be stated, let alone solved. This produces a situation in which the patient appears to have no problems except those posed by the existence of analyst and patient. His preoccupation is with what is this or that function, of which he is aware though unable to grasp the totality of which the function is a part. It follows that there is never any question why the patient or the analyst is there, or why something is said or done or felt, nor can there be any question of attempting to alter the causes of some state of mind. . . . Since 'what?' can never be answered without 'how?' or 'why?' further difficulties arise. I shall leave this on one side to consider the mechanisms employed by the infant to solve the problem 'what?' when it is felt in relation to a part-object relationship with a function.

Denial of normal degrees of projective identification

I employ the term 'link' because I wish to discuss the patient's relationship with a function rather than with the object that subserves a function; my concern is not only with the breast, or penis, or verbal thought, but with their function of providing the link between two objects.

In her 'Notes on Some Schizoid Mechanisms' (Klein, 1946) Melanie Klein speaks of the importance of an excessive employment of splitting and projective identification in the production of a very disturbed personality. She also speaks of 'the introjection of the good object, first of all the mother's breast' as a 'precondition for normal development'. I shall suppose that there is a normal degree of projective identification, without defining the limits within which normality lies, and that associated with introjective identification this is the foundation on which normal development rests.

This impression derives partly from a feature in a patient's analysis which was difficult to interpret because it did not appear to be sufficiently obtrusive at any moment for an interpretation to be supported by convincing evidence. Throughout the analysis the patient resorted to projective identification with a persistence suggesting it was a mechanism of which he had never been able sufficiently to avail himself; the analysis afforded him an opportunity for the exercise of a mechanism of which he had been cheated. I did not have to rely on this impression alone. There were sessions which led me to suppose that the patient felt there was some object that denied him the use of projective identification. In the illustrations I have given, particularly in the first, the stammer, and the fourth, the understanding girl and the blue haze, there are elements which indicate that the patient felt that parts of his personality that he wished to repose in me were refused entry by me, but there had been associations prior to this which led me to this view.

When the patient strove to rid himself of fears of death which were felt to be too powerful for his personality to contain he split off his fears and put them into me, the idea apparently being that if they were allowed to repose there long enough they would undergo modification by my psyche and could then be safely reintrojected. On the occasion I have in mind the patient had felt, probably for reasons similar to those I give in my fifth illustration, the probability clouds, that I evacuated them so quickly that the feelings were not modified, but had become more painful.

Associations from a period in the analysis earlier than that from which these illustrations have been drawn showed an increasing intensity of emotions in the patient. This originated in what he felt was my refusal to accept parts of his personality. Consequently he strove to force them into me with increased desperation and violence. His behaviour, isolated from the context of the analysis, might have appeared to be an expression of primary aggression. The more violent his phantasies of projective identification, the more frightened he became of me. There were sessions in which such behaviour expressed unprovoked aggression, but I quote this series because it shows the patient in a different light, his violence a reaction to what he felt was my hostile defensiveness. The analytic situation built up in my mind a sense of witnessing an extremely early scene. I felt that the patient had experienced in infancy a mother who dutifully responded to the infant's emotional displays. The dutiful response had in it an element of impatient 'I don't know what's the matter with the child.' My deduction was that in order to understand what the child wanted the mother should have treated the infant's cry as more than a demand for her presence. From the infant's point of view she should have taken into her, and thus experienced, the fear that the child was dying. It was this fear that the child could not contain. He strove to split it off together with the part of the person-ality in which it lay and project it into the mother. An understanding mother is able to experience the feeling of dread, that this baby was striving to deal with by projective identification, and yet retain a balanced outlook. This patient had had to deal with a mother who could not tolerate experiencing such feelings and reacted either by denying them ingress, or alternatively by becoming a prey to the anxiety which resulted from introjection of the infant's feelings. The latter reaction must, I think, have been rare: denial was dominant.

To some this reconstruction will appear to be unduly fanciful; to me it does not seem forced and is the reply to any who may object that too much stress is placed on the transference to the exclusion of a proper elucidation of early memories.

In the analysis a complex situation may be observed. The patient feels he is being allowed an opportunity of which he had hitherto been cheated; the poignancy of his deprivation is thereby rendered the more acute and so are the feelings of resentment at the depriva-tion. Gratitude for the opportunity coexists with hostility to the analyst as the person who will not understand and refuses the patient the use of the only method of communication by which he feels he can make himself understood. Thus the link between patient and analyst, or infant and breast, is the mechanism of projective identifi-cation. The destructive attacks upon this link originate in a source external to the patient or infant, namely the analyst or breast. The result is excessive projective identification by the patient and a deterioration of his developmental processes.

I do not put forward this experience as the cause of the patient's disturbance; that finds its main source in the inborn disposition of the infant as I described it in my paper on 'The Differentiation of the Psychotic from the Non-psychotic Part of the Personality' (Bion, 1957a). I regard it as a central feature of the environmental factor in the production of the psychotic personality.

Before I discuss this consequence for the patient's development, I must refer to the inborn characteristics and the part that they play in producing attacks by the infant on all that links him to the breast, namely, primary aggression and envy. The seriousness of these attacks is enhanced if the mother displays the kind of unreceptiveness which I have described, and is diminished, but not abolished, if the mother can introject the infant's feelings and remain balanced (Klein, 1957); the seriousness remains because the psychotic infant is overwhelmed with hatred and envy of the mother's ability to retain a comfortable state of mind although experiencing the infant's feelings. This was clearly brought out by a patient who insisted that I must go through it with him, but was filled with hate when he felt I was able to do so without a breakdown. Here we have another aspect of destructive attacks upon the link, the link being the capacity of the analyst to introject the patient's projective identifications. Attacks on the link, therefore, are synonymous with attacks on the analyst's, and originally the mother's, peace of mind. The capacity to introject is transformed by the patient's envy and hate into greed devouring the patient's psyche; similarly, peace of mind becomes hostile indifference. At this point analytic problems arise through the patient's employment (to destroy the peace of mind that is so much envied) of acting out, delinquent acts and threats of suicide.

Consequences

To review the main features so far: the origin of the disturbance is twofold. On the one hand there is the patient's inborn disposition to excessive destructiveness, hatred, and envy: on the other the environment which, at its worst, denies to the patient the use of the mechanisms of splitting and projective identification. On some occasions the destructive attacks on the link between patient and environment, or between different aspects of the patient's personality, have their origin in the patient; on others, in the mother, although in the latter instance and in psychotic patients, it can never be in the mother alone. The disturbances commence with life itself. The problem that confronts the patient is: What are the objects of which he is aware? These objects, whether internal or external, are in fact part-objects and predominantly, though not exclusively, what we should call functions and not morphological structures. This is obscured because the patient's thinking is conducted by means of concrete objects and therefore tends to produce, in the sophisticated mind of the analyst, an impression that the patient's concern is with the nature of the concrete object. The nature of the functions which excite the patient's curiosity he explores by projective identification. His own feelings, too powerful to be contained within his personality, are amongst these functions. Projective identification makes it possible for him to investigate his own feelings in a personality powerful enough to contain them. Denial of the use of this mechanism, either by the refusal of the mother to serve as a repository for the infant's feelings, or by the hatred and envy of the patient who cannot allow the mother to exercise this function, leads to a destruction of the link between infant and breast and consequently to a severe disorder of the impulse to be curious on which all learning depends. The way is therefore prepared for a severe arrest of development. Furthermore, thanks to a denial of the main method open to the infant for dealing with his too powerful emotions, the conduct of emotional life, in any case a severe problem, becomes intolerable. Feelings of hatred are thereupon directed against all emotions including hate itself, and against external reality which stimulates them. It is a short step from hatred of the emotions to hatred of life itself. As I said in my paper on 'The Differentiation of the Psychotic from the Non-psychotic Part of the Personality' (Bion, 1957a), this hatred results in a resort to projective identification of all the perceptual apparatus including the embryonic thought which forms a link between sense impressions and conscious-ness. The tendency to excessive projective identification when death instincts predominate is thus reinforced.

Superego

The early development of the superego is effected by this kind of mental functioning in a way I must now describe. As I have said, the link between infant and breast depends upon projective identification and a capacity to introject projective identifications. Failure to introject

73

makes the external object appear intrinsically hostile to curiosity and to the method, namely projective identification, by which the infant seeks to satisfy it. Should the breast be felt as fundamentally understanding, it has been transformed by the infant's envy and hate into an object whose devouring greed has as its aim the introjection of the infant's projective identifications in order to destroy them. This can show in the patient's belief that the analyst strives, by understanding the patient, to drive him insane. The result is an object which, when installed in the patient, exercises the function of a severe and ego-destructive superego. This description is not accurate applied to any object in the paranoid-schizoid position because it supposes a whole-object. The threat that such a whole-object impends contributes to the inability, described by Melanie Klein and others (Segal, 1950), of the psychotic patient to face the depressive position and the developments attendant on it. In the paranoid-schizoid phase the bizarre objects composed partially of elements of a persecutory superego which I described in my paper on 'The Differentiation of the Psychotic from the Non-psychotic Part of the Personality' are predominant.

Arrested development

The disturbance of the impulse of curiosity on which all learning depends, and the denial of the mechanism by which it seeks expression, makes normal development impossible. Another feature obtrudes if the course of the analysis is favourable; problems which in sophisticated language are posed by the question 'Why?' cannot be formulated. The patient appears to have no appreciation of causation and will complain of painful states of mind while persisting in courses of action calculated to produce them. Therefore when the appropriate material presents itself the patient must be shown that he has no interest in why he feels as he does. Elucidation of the limited scope of his curiosity issues in the development of a wider range and an incipient preoccupation with causes. This leads to some modification of conduct which otherwise prolongs his distress.

Conclusions

The main conclusions of this paper relate to that state of mind in which the patient's psyche contains an internal object which is opposed to, and destructive of, all links whatsoever from the most primitive (which I have suggested is a normal degree of projective identification) to the most sophisticated forms of verbal communication and the arts.

In this state of mind emotion is hated; it is felt to be too powerful to be contained by the immature psyche, it is felt to link objects and it gives reality to objects which are not self and therefore inimical to primary narcissism.

The internal object which in its origin was an external breast that refused to introject, harbour, and so modify the baneful force of emotion, is felt, paradoxically, to intensify, relative to the strength of the ego, the emotions against which it initiates the attacks. These attacks on the linking function of emotion lead to an over-prominence in the psychotic part of the personality of links which appear to be logical, almost mathematical, but never emotionally reasonable. Consequently the links surviving are perverse, cruel, and sterile.

The external object which is internalized, its nature, and the effect when so established on the methods of communication within the psyche and with the environment, are left for further elaboration later.

5

Contribution to the psychopathology of psychotic states

The importance of projective identification in the ego structure and the object relations of the psychotic patient[29]

Herbert Rosenfeld

Following the suggestion of the organizers of the Symposium that I should discuss the importance of projective identification and ego splitting in the psychopathology of the psychotic patient, I shall attempt to give you a survey of the processes described under the term: 'projective identification'.

I shall first define the meaning of the term 'projective identification' and quote from the work of Melanie Klein, as it was she who developed the concept. Then I shall go on to discuss very briefly the work of two other writers whose use appeared to be related to, but not identical with, Melanie Klein's use of the term.

'Projective identification' relates first of all to a splitting process of the early ego, where either good or bad parts of the self are split off from the ego and are as a further step projected in love or hatred into external objects which leads to fusion and identification of the projected parts of the self with the external objects. There are important paranoid anxieties related to these processes as the objects filled with aggressive parts of the self become persecuting and are experienced by

29 This article was first published in P. Doucet and C. Laurin (Eds.) (1971). *Problems of Psychosis, Volume 1.* The Hague: Excerpta Medica, pp. 115–128.

the patient as threatening to retaliate by forcing themselves and the bad parts of the self which they contain back again into the ego.

In her paper on schizoid mechanisms Melanie Klein (1946) considers first of all the importance of the processes of splitting and denial and omnipotence which during the early phase of development play a role similar to that of repression at a later stage of ego development. She then discusses the early infantile instinctual impulses and suggests that while the 'oral libido still has the lead, libidinal and aggressive impulses and phantasies from other sources come to the fore and lead to a confluence of oral, urethral and anal desires, both libidinal and aggressive'. After discussing the oral libidinal and aggressive impulses directed against the breast and the mother's body, she suggests that:

> the other line of attack derives from the anal and urethral impulses and implies expelling dangerous substances (excrements) out of the self and into the mother. Together with these harmful excrements, expelled in hatred, split off parts of the ego are also projected into the mother. These excrements and bad parts of the self are meant not only to injure but also to control and to take possession of the object. In so far as the mother comes to contain the bad parts of the self, she is not felt to be a separate individual but is felt to be the bad self. Much of the hatred against parts of the self is now directed towards the mother. This leads to a particular form of identification which establishes the prototype of an aggressive object relation. I suggest for these processes the term *projective identification*.

Later on in the same paper Melanie Klein describes that not only bad, but also good parts of the ego are expelled and projected into external objects who become identified with the projected good parts of the self. She regards this identification as vital because it is essential for the infant's ability to develop good object relations. If this process is, however, excessive, good parts of the personality are felt to be lost to the self which results in weakening and impoverishment of the ego. Melanie Klein also emphasizes the aspect of the projective processes which relates to the forceful entry into the object and the persecutory anxieties related to this process which I mentioned before. She also describes how paranoid anxieties related to projective identification disturb introjective processes. 'Introjection is interfered with, as it may be felt as a forceful entry from the outside into the inside in retribution for violent projections'. It will be clear that Melanie Klein gives the name 'projective identification' both to the processes of ego splitting and the 'narcissistic' object relations created by the projection of parts of the self into objects.

I shall now discuss some aspects of the work of Dr Edith Jacobson who describes psychotic identifications in schizophrenic patients identical with the ones I observed and described as 'projective identification'. She also frequently uses the term 'projective identification' in her book *Psychotic Conflict and Reality* (Jacobson, 1967).

In 1954 (Jacobson, 1954) Edith Jacobson discussed the identifications of the delusional schizophrenic patient who may eventually consciously believe himself to be another person. She relates this to early infantile identification mechanisms of a magic nature which lead to 'partial or total blending of the magic self and object images, founded on phantasies or even the temporary belief of being one with or of becoming the object, regardless of reality'. In 1967 she describes these processes in more detail. She discusses 'the psychotic's regression to a narcissistic level, where the weakness of the bound-aries between self and object images gives rise to phantasies, or expe-riences of fusion between these images. These primitive introjective or projective identifications are based on infantile phantasies of incorporation, devouring, invading (forcing oneself into), or being devoured by the object'. She also says 'We can assume that such phantasies, which pre-suppose at least the beginning distinction between self and object, are characteristic of early narcissistic stages of development and that the child's relation to the mother normally begins with the introjective and projective processes'; and that the 'introjective and projective identifications (of the adult patient) depend on the patient's fixation to early narcissistic stages and upon the depth of the narcissistic regression'. In discussing clinical material of the Patient A she described this fear that any affectionate physical contact might bring about experiences of merging, which in turn might lead to a manifest psychotic state. Her views that the introjec-tive and projective identifications observed in the adult patient depend on the fixation to early narcissistic phases where these iden-tifications originate, seem identical with my own views and there is nothing in her clinical and theoretical observations which I have quoted above with which I would disagree. She stresses, however, that she differs from Melanie Klein and my own opinion in so far as she does not believe that the projective identifications of the adult patient observable in the transference or acted out by the patient with objects in his environment are in fact a repetition of the early infantile projective and introjective processes, but are to be understood as a later defensive process, as in her view early processes cannot be observed in the transference. She also disagrees with my analytic technique of verbally interpreting the processes of projective identification when they appear in the transference, which I regard as of central importance in working through psychotic processes in the transference situation.[30]

Margaret Mahler in 1952 described symbiotic infantile psychoses and suggested that the mechanisms employed are introjective and projective ones and their psychotic elaboration (Mahler, 1952). Her ideas seem to be closely related, but nevertheless quite distinct from what I have described as projective identification. She describes the early mother/infant relationship as a phase of object relationship in which the infant behaves and functions as though he and his mother were an omnipotent system (a dual unity with one common boundary, a symbiotic membrane as it were). In 1967 she says, 'the essential feature of symbiosis is hallucinatory or delusional, somatopsychic, omnipotent fusion with the representation of the mother and, in particular, delusion of common boundary of the two actually and physically separate individuals' (Mahler, 1967). She suggests that 'this is the mechanism to which the ego regresses in cases of psychotic disorganization'. In describing the symbiotic infantile psychosis she says that the early mother–infant symbiotic relationship is intense. The mental representation of the mother remains or is regressively fused with that of the self. She describes the panic reactions caused by separations 'which are followed by restitutive productions which serve to maintain or restore the symbiotic parasitic delusion of oneness with the mother or father'. It is clear that Mahler has introjective or projective processes in mind as the mechanisms which

30 When Edith Jacobson describes the defensive nature of the projective identification in her adult psychotic patients she stresses the projection of bad parts of the self into external objects in order to avoid psychotic confusions, in other words she sees the projective identification of the adult psychotic as the attempt to split off and project into a suitable external object those parts of the self which are unacceptable to the adult ego: the external object would then represent the patient's 'bad self'.

produce the symbiotic psychosis. I have, however, found no clear description of these mechanisms in her papers. She seems to see the symbiotic psychosis as a defence against separation anxiety which links up closely with my description of the narcissistic object relation serving a defensive function. The symbiotic processes described by Mahler have some resemblance to the parasitical object relations I shall describe later. Projective identification which includes ego split-ting and projecting of good and bad parts of the self into external objects is not identitical with symbiosis. For projective identification to take place some temporary differentiation of 'me' and 'not me' is essential. Symbiosis, however, is used by Mahler to describe this state of undifferentiation, of fusion with the mother, in which the 'I' is not yet differentiated from the 'not I'.

In my own work with psychotic patients I have encountered a variety of types of object relations and mental mechanisms which are associated with Melanie Klein's description of projective identifica-tion. First of all, it is important to distinguish between two types of projective identification, namely, projective identification used for communication with other objects and projective identification used for ridding the self of unwanted parts.

I shall first discuss projective identification used as a method of communication. Many psychotic patients use projective processes for communication with other people. These projective mechanisms of the psychotic seem to be a distortion or intensification of the normal infantile relationship, which is based on non–verbal communication between infant and mother, in which impulses, parts of the self and anxieties too difficult for the infant to bear are projected into the mother and where the mother is able instinctively to respond by containing the infant's anxiety and alleviating it by her behaviour. This relationship has been stressed particularly by Bion. The psychotic patient who uses this process in the transference may do so consciously but more often unconsciously. He then projects impulses and parts of himself into the analyst in order that the analyst will feel and under-stand his experiences and will be able to contain them so that they lose their frightening or unbearable quality and become meaningful by the analyst being able to put them into words through interpreta-tions. This situation seems to be of fundamental importance for the development of introjective processes and the development of the ego: it makes it possible for the patient to learn to tolerate his own impulses and the analyst's interpretations make his infantile responses and feelings accessible to the more sane self, which can begin to think about the experiences which were previously meaningless and frightening to him. The psychotic patient who projects predominantly for communication is obviously receptive to the analyst's understanding of him, so it is essential that this type of communication should be recognized and interpreted accordingly.

As a second point I want to discuss projective identification used for denial of psychic reality. In this situation the patient splits off parts of his self in addition to impulses and anxieties and projects them into the analyst for the purpose of evacuating and emptying out the disturbing mental content which leads to a denial of psychic reality. As this type of patient primarily wants the analyst to condone the evacuation processes and the denial of his problems, he often reacts to interpretations with violent resentment, as they are experienced as critical and frightening since the patient believes that unwanted, unbearable and meaningless mental content is pushed back into him by the analyst.

Both the processes of communication and evacuation may exist simultaneously or alternatively in our psychotic patients and it is essential to differentiate them clearly in order to keep contact with the patient and make analysis possible.

As a third point I want to discuss a very common transference relationship of the psychotic patient which is aimed at controlling the analyst's body and mind, which seems to be based on a very early infantile type of object relationship.

In analysis, one observes that the patient believes that he has forced himself omnipotently into the analyst, which leads to fusion or confusion with the analyst and anxieties relating to the loss of the self. In this form of projective identification the projection of the mad parts of the self into the analyst often predominates. The analyst is then perceived as having become mad, which arouses extreme anxiety as the patient is afraid that the analyst will retaliate and force the madness back into the patient, depriving him entirely of his sanity. At such times the patient is in danger of disintegration, but detailed interpretations of the relationship between patient and analyst may break through this omnipotent delusional situation and prevent a breakdown.

There is, however, a danger that the verbal communication between patient and analyst may break down at such times as the analyst's interpretations are misunderstood and misinterpreted by the patient and the patient's communications increasingly assume a concrete quality, suggesting that abstract thinking has almost completely broken down. In investigating such situations, I found that omnipotent projective identification interferes with the capacity of verbal and abstract thinking and produces a concreteness of the mental processes which leads to confusion between reality and phantasy. It is also clinically essential for the analyst to realize that the patient who uses excessive projective identification is dominated by concrete thought processes which cause misunderstanding of verbal interpretations, since words and their content are experienced by the patient as concrete, non-symbolic objects. Segal, in her paper 'Some aspects of the analysis of a schizophrenic' (Segal, 1950), points out that the schizophrenic patient loses the capacity to use symbols when the symbol becomes again the equivalent of the original object, which means it is hardly different from it. In her paper 'Notes on symbol formation' (Segal, 1957) she suggests the term 'symbolic equation' for this process: she writes:

> The symbolic equation between the original object and the symbol in the internal and external world is, I think, the basis of the schizophrenic's concrete thinking. This non-differentiation between the thing symbolized and the symbol is part of a disturbance in the relation between the ego and the object. Parts of the ego and internal objects are projected onto an object and identified with it. The differentiation between the self and the object is obscured then; since a part of the ego is confused with the object, the symbol which is a creation and a function of the ego becomes in turn confused with the object which is symbolized.

I believe that the differentiation of the self and object representation is necessary to maintain normal symbol formation which is based on the introjection of objects experienced as separate from the self.[31] It

---

31 Dr Segal (1957) also stresses greater awareness and differentiation of the separateness between the ego and object in normal symbol formation. She thinks that symbolization is closely related to the development of the ego and the objects which occur in the depressive position. She emphasizes 'that symbols are in addition to other factors created in the internal world as a means of restoring, recreating, recapturing and owning again the original object. But in keeping with the increased reality sense, they are now felt as created by the ego and therefore never completely equated with the original object.'

is the excessive projective identification in the psychotic process which obliterates differentiation of self and objects, which causes confusion between reality and phantasy and a regression to concrete thinking due to the loss of the capacity for symbolization and symbolic thinking.[32]

It is, of course, extremely difficult to use verbal interpretations with the psychotic patient when interpretations are misunderstood and misinterpreted. The patient may become extremely frightened, may cover his ears and try to rush out of the consulting room and the analysis is in danger of breaking down. At such times it is necessary to uncover the projective processes used for the purpose of communication between patient and analyst, which will establish some possibility of simple verbal interpretations to explain to the patient and help him to understand the terrifying situation due to the concrete experience. It is essential for the analyst to remember that all three types of projective identification which I have described so far exist simultaneously in the psychotic patient, and one-sided concentration on one process may block the analysis and meaningful communication between patient and analyst.

There is one further aspect of the psychopathology of psychotic patients that is linked with projective identification – that is the importance of primitive aggression, particularly envy, and the use of projective identification to deal with it.

When the psychotic patient living in a state of fusion (projective identification) with the analyst begins to experience himself as a separate person, violent destructive impulses make their appearance.

---

32 The loss of the capacity for abstract and symbolic thinking of the schizophrenic patient, which leads on to very concrete modes of thinking, has been described by many writers such as Vigotsky, Goldstein and others. Harold Searles (1962) in his paper 'The differentiation between concrete and metaphorical thinking in the recovering schizophrenic patient' suggests that the concrete thought disorders depend on the fluidity of the ego boundaries when self and object are not clearly differentiated. In one of his cases he describes 'abundant evidence of massive projection, not only on to human beings around him but also on to trees, animals, buildings and all sorts of inanimate objects'. Only when ego boundaries gradually become firmly established through treatment can figurative or symbolic thinking develop. Searles' observations have a close relationship to my own observation that excessive projective identification, leading to fusion between self and object, always causes loss of the capacity for symbolic and verbal thinking.

His aggressive impulses are sometimes an expression of anger related to separation anxiety, but generally they have a distinctly envious character. As long as the patient regards the analyst's mind and body and his help and understanding as part of his own self he is able to attribute everything that is experienced as valuable in the analysis as being part of his own self, in other words he lives in a state of omnipotent narcissism. As soon as a patient begins to feel separate from the analyst the aggressive reaction appears and particularly clearly so after a valuable interpretation, which shows the analyst's understanding. The patient reacts with feelings of humiliation, complains that he is made to feel small; why should the analyst be able to remind him of something which he needs but which he cannot provide for himself. In his envious anger the patient tries to destroy and spoil the analyst's interpretations by ridiculing or making them meaningless. The analyst may have the distinct experience in his counter transference that he is meant to feel that he is no good and has nothing of value to give to the patient. There are often physical symptoms connected with this state because the patient may feel sick and may actually vomit. This concrete rejection of the analyst's help can often be clearly understood as a rejection of the mother's food[33] and her care for the infant repeated in the analytic transference situation. When the patient had previously made good progress in the treatment this 'negative therapeutic reaction' is often quite violent, as if he wants to spoil and devalue everything he had previously received, disregarding the often suicidal danger of such a reaction. Many patients experience this violent envy directed against the good qualities of the analyst as quite insane and illogical and as the inner saner part of the patient experiences these envious reactions as unbearable and unacceptable, many defences against this primitive envy are created.

One of these defences relates to the splitting off and projection of the envious part of the self into an external object, which then becomes the envious part of the patient. This kind of defensive projective identification follows the model of Melanie Klein's

---

33 It is of course important to differentiate between a patient's rejection of the analyst's bad handling or misunderstanding, which would repeat a bad feeding situation from the envious aggression of the child which occurs in a good setting. The latter is not only difficult for the primitive ego of the child to tolerate but creates a particularly difficult problem for any loving and caring mother.

description of the splitting off and projection of bad parts of the self, which I quoted in the beginning of this paper.

Another defence against envy relates to omnipotent phantasies of the patient of entering the admired and envied object and in this way insisting that he is the object by taking over its role. When total projective identification has taken place with an envied object envy is entirely denied, but immediately reappears when the self and object become separate again. In my paper 'On the psychopathology of narcissism' (Rosenfeld, 1964b) I stressed that:

> projective identification was part of an early narcissistic relationship to the mother, where recognition of separateness between self and object is denied. Awareness of separation would lead to feelings of dependence on an object and therefore to anxiety (see Mahler, 1967). In addition, dependence stimulates envy when the goodness of the object is recognized. The omnipotent narcissistic object relations, particularly omnipotent projective identification, obviate both the aggressive feelings caused by frustration and any awareness of envy.

I believe that in the psychotic patient projective identification is more often a defence against excessive envy, which is closely bound up with the patient's narcissism, rather than a defence against separation anxiety. In my paper 'Object relations of an acute schizophrenic patient in the transference situation' (Rosenfeld, 1964a) I tried to trace the origin of the envious projective identification in schizophrenia. I suggested:

> If too much resentment and envy dominates the infant's relation to the mother, normal projective identification becomes more and more controlling and can take on omnipotent delusional tones. For example, the infant who in phantasy enters the mother's body driven by envy and omnipotence, takes over the role of the mother, or breast, and deludes himself that he is the mother or breast. This mechanism plays an important role in mania and hypomania, but in schizophrenia it occurs in a very exaggerated form.

Finally, I want to draw attention to two similar types of object relations: a parasitical and a delusional one. In the parasitical object relation the psychotic patient in analysis maintains a belief that he is living entirely inside an object – the analyst – and behaves like a parasite living on the capacities of the analyst, who is expected to function as his ego. Severe parasitism may be regarded as a state of total projective identification. It is, however, not just a defensive state to deny envy or separation but is also an expression of aggression, particularly envy. It is the combination of defence and acting out of the aggression which makes the parasitic state a particularly difficult therapeutic problem.

The parasitic patient relies entirely on the analyst, often making him responsible for his entire life. He generally behaves in an extremely passive, silent and sluggish manner, demanding everything and giving nothing in return. This state can be extremely chronic and the analytic work with such patients is often minimal. One of my depressed patients described himself as a baby, which was like a stone heavily pressing into my couch and into me. He felt he was making it impossible for me either to carry him or to look after him and he feared that the only thing that I could possibly do was to expel him, if I could not stand him any longer. However, he was terrified that he could not survive being left. He not only felt that he had a very paralysing effect on the analysis but that he was paralysed and inert himself. Only very occasionally was it possible to get in touch with the intense feelings either of hostility or overwhelming pain and depression bound up with this process. There was no joy when the analyst was felt to be helpful and alive, as it only increased the patient's awareness of the contrast between himself and the analyst and at times produced a desire to frustrate him, and with this he returned to the *status quo* of inertia, which was felt to be unpleasant but preferred to any of the intense feelings of pain, anger, envy or jealousy which might fleetingly be experienced. As I suggested before, extreme parasitism is partly a defence against separation anxiety, envy or jealousy, but it often seems to be a defence against any emotion which might be experienced as painful. I often have the impression that patients, like the one I described, who experience themselves as dead and are often experienced by the analyst as so inactive that they might as well be dead, use their analyst's aliveness as a means of survival. However, the latent hostility prevents the patient from getting more than minimal help or satisfaction from the analysis. In the more active forms of parasitism the insidious hostility dominates the picture and is much more apparent.

Dr Bion in his book *Transformations* (Bion, 1965) describes a more active case of parasitism. He emphasizes that such patients are particularly unrewarding. The essential feature is simultaneous stimulation and frustration of hope and work that is fruitless, except for discrediting analyst and patient. The destructive activity is balanced by enough success to deny the patient fulfilment of his destructiveness. 'The helpful summary of such a case is described as 'chronic murder of patient and analyst' or 'an instance of parasitism': the patient draws on the love, or benevolence of the host to extract knowledge and power which enables him to poison the association and destroy the indulgence on which he depends for his existence.

It is important to differentiate the very chronic forms of parasitism from the massive intrusion and projective identification into the analyst which resembles parasitism but is of shorter duration and responds more easily to interpretations. It occurs at times when separation threatens or when jealousy or envy is violently stimulated in the transference or in outside life. Meltzer (1967) describes a primitive form of possessive jealousy which plays an important role in perpetuating massive projective identification of a peculiar withdrawn, sleepy sort.

The other form of living entirely inside an object occurs in severely deluded schizophrenic patients who seem to experience themselves as living in an unreal world, which is highly delusional but nevertheless has qualities of a structure which suggests that this hallucinatory world represents the inside of an object, probably the mother. The patient may be withdrawn, preoccupied with hallucinations, in the analysis occasionally projecting the hallucinatory experience on to the analyst, which leads to mis-identifying him and others with his delusional experience. Sometimes the patient may describe himself as living in a world, or object, which separates him entirely from the outside world and the analyst is experienced as a contraption, an actor or a machine and the world becomes extremely unreal. The living inside the delusional object seems to be definitely in opposition to relating to the outside world, which would imply depending on a real object. This delusional world or object seems to be dominated by an omnipotent and sometimes omniscient part of the self, which creates the notion that within the delusional object there is complete painlessness and freedom to indulge in any whim. It also appears that the self within the delusional object exerts a powerful suggestive and seductive influence on saner parts of the personality in order to persuade or force them to withdraw from reality and to join the delusional omnipotent world. Clinically, the patient may hear a voice making propaganda for living inside the mad world by idealizing it and praising its virtue by offering a complete satisfaction and instant cure to the patient. This persuasion or propaganda to get inside the delusional world implies clinically the constant stimulus to all parts of the self to use omnipotent projective identification (forcing the self inside the object) as the only possible method to solve all problems. This situation leads to constant acting out with external objects which are used for projective identification. When, however, projective identification becomes directed towards the delusional object, the saner parts of the self may become trapped or imprisoned within this object and physical and mental paralysis amounting to catatonia may result.

The psychoanalytic treatment of the processes related to projective identification in the psychotic patient

As this paper deals primarily with the psychopathology of psychotic states, I can only briefly discuss my psychoanalytic technique in dealing with psychotic patients to emphasize my contention that the investigation of the psychopathology of the psychotic and the therapeutic approach are closely interlinked.

In treating psychotic states it is absolutely essential to differentiate those parts of the self which exist almost exclusively in a state of projective identification with external objects, or internal ones such as the delusional object I described above and the saner parts of the patient which are less dominated by projective identification and have formed some separate existence from objects. These saner parts may be remnants of the adult personality, but often they represent more normal non–omnipotent infantile parts of the self, which during analysis are attempting to form a dependent relationship to the analyst representing the feeding mother. As the saner parts of the self are in danger of submitting to the persuasion of the delusional self to withdraw into the more psychotic parts of the personality, and to get entangled in it, the former need very careful attention in analysis to help them to differentiate the analyst as an external object from the seductive voice of the omnipotent parts of the self related to the internal delusional object, which can assume any identity for the purpose of keeping up the domination of the whole self. As there is always a conflict, amounting sometimes to a violent struggle, between the psychotic and saner parts of the personality, the nature of this conflict has also to be clearly understood in order to make it possible to work through the psychotic state by means of analysis. For example, the structure and the intentions of the psychotic parts of the patient, which are highly narcissistically organized, have to be brought fully into the open by means of interpretations, as they are opposed to any part of the self which wants to form a relationship to reality and to the analyst who attempts to help the ego to move towards growth and development. The interpretations have also to expose the extent and the method used by the psychotic narcissistic parts of the personality in attempting to dominate, entangle and to paralyse the saner parts of the self. It is important to remember that it is only the sane dependent parts of the self separate from the analyst that can use introjective processes uncontaminated by the concreteness caused by the omnipotent projective identifications; the capacity for memory and growth of the ego depends on these normal introjective processes. When the dependent non–psychotic parts of the personality become stronger, as the result of analysis, violent negative therapeutic reactions usually occur as the psychotic narcissistic parts of the patient oppose any progress and change of the *status quo*, a problem which I recently discussed in detail in a paper on 'The Negative Therapeutic Reaction' (Rosenfeld, 1969).

Case presentation

I shall now bring some case material of a schizophrenic patient in order to illustrate some aspects of projective identification and ego splitting.

Patient A

Had been diagnosed several years ago as schizophrenic, when he had an acute psychotic breakdown which was characterized by over-whelming panic, confusion and fears of complete disintegration. He did not hallucinate during the acute phase, nor are the delusional aspects of the psychosis dominant at the present time, but he is unable to work or to maintain a close relationship with men or women in the outside world. He had been treated by another analyst for several years before starting analysis with me more than a year ago. The previous analyst in his report to me emphasized the patient's tendency to slip into a state of projective identification with the analyst at the beginning of each session leading to the patient's becoming confused and unable to speak in an audible and understandable way. The analyst interpreted to the patient that he expected him, the analyst, to understand him even if he could not talk or think, since he believed himself to be inside the analyst; as a result of such interpretations he generally started to speak more distinctly. During the analysis with me there were further improvements and he felt at times more separate, so that the saner parts of his self were able to form to some extent a dependent relationship to me. However, from time to time, particularly after he had made some progress, or when there were long separations, he fell back to a parasitical relationship of living inside me (projective identification), which led to states of confusion, inability to think and talk, claustrophobia and paranoid anxieties of being trapped by me. When envy was aroused through experiences in the real world, for example when he met a man who was successful in his relationship with women or in his work, after a short conscious experience of envy A would frequently become identified with him. This was followed by severe anxieties of losing his identity and feelings of being trapped, rather than leading to the delusion that he was the envied man or that he was able to function in the outside world similarly to the man with whom projective identification and confusion had taken place.

Last year, in the autumn, I had to interrupt the patient's analysis for a fortnight which disturbed him considerably. Consciously, he seemed unconcerned about my going away which I had of course discussed with him several months before. However, two weeks before the interruption he became acutely anxious and confused and for a day he feared that he would have another breakdown and have to go into hospital. The disturbance started with the patient's complaint that he could not drag himself away from the television screen where he was watching the Olympic games. He felt forced, almost against his will to look at it until late at night. He complained that he was drawn into the hot climate of Mexico which made him feel that being there would make him well. He was also compelled to look at the athletes, or wrestlers and weightlifters and felt he was, or ought to be, one of them. He asked me questions: Why have I to be an athlete? Why can't I be myself? He felt that this looking at television was like an addiction which he could not stop and which exhausted and drained him. At times he felt so strongly 'pulled inside the television' that he felt claustrophobic and had difficulty in breathing. Afterwards during the night he felt compelled to get up and see whether the taps of the washbasin in his flat were closed and whether the stoppers in the basin were blocking up the drainage. He was terrified that both his bath and the basin might overflow and eventually he confessed that he was afraid of being drowned and suffocated. I interpreted to him that after he felt that he was making progress and feeling separate from me he was suddenly overcome with impatience and envy of me and other men who were able to move about and were active. I suggested that it was the envious part which drove him into the identification with other men and myself in order to take over their strength and potency, and in this way the omnipotent part of himself could make him believe that he could be mature and healthy instantly. He agreed with the interpretation without any difficulty and started to speak very fast: he said he knew all this and was quite aware of it, but he also knew that this belief was quite false and that it was a delusion and he was angry at having to listen to a voice in him which was very persuasive and stimulated him to take over the mind and body of other people. I also interpreted to him that I thought that the threatening separation was stimulating his wish to be suddenly grown up and independent in order not to have to cope with the anxieties of being separate from me. He then told me that he was falling every night into a very deep sleep from which he could not easily awake in the morning and so he had arrived late for his session. He compared the feeling of being pulled into the television screen, which seemed to have become identified with the delusional object, to being pulled into this deep sleep. He now spoke fairly fluently and more distinctly and conveyed that he felt now more separate from me. He said he felt disgusted with himself for being a parasite and he also complained that the television experience and his bed were draining his life out of him, so that he had a strong impulse to smash both; he was glad that he had been able to control this in reality. I acknowledged his own observation that his looking at television and being pulled into a deep sleep were experienced by him as parasitical experiences where he felt he was getting into other objects. I pointed out that he felt angry with that part of himself which stimulated him to get inside external objects, the athletes representing me as a successful man who was travelling abroad during the break, and also into internal objects which were represented by his bed. I stressed that at first he felt he probably could

91

control and possess these objects entirely when he got inside them, but very soon he felt enclosed and trapped and persecuted, which roused his wish to destroy the bed and the television screen which had turned into persecuting objects. I thought that his fear of being trapped and his anger related also to the analysis and the analyst. The patient's obsessions about the stoppers of the basin were also related to his fear of being trapped and drowned. It seemed that he had constantly to find out whether after his intrusion into objects he was trapped and was in danger of drowning and suffocating inside, or whether there was a hole through which he could escape.

Simultaneously with the projective identification related to the delusional television experience, the patient was violently pulled into relations to prostitutes. He explained to me that there was a part of him which persuaded him whenever he felt lonely or anxious that he needed to have a lovely big prostitute for nourishment and this would make him well. During the session he assured me that he realized the falsity of the voice, but in fact he very rarely could resist. He felt he wanted to get inside the prostitutes in an excited way in order to devour them, but after intercourse he felt sick and disgusted and convinced that he had now acquired syphilis of the stomach. The patient, during this session, many times asserted that he knew quite well the difference between reality and the delusional persuasion and he also knew what was wrong. But it was clear to me that in spite of this knowledge he was again and again put temporarily into a deluded state by a psychotic omnipotent and omniscient part of him which succeeded in seducing and overpowering the saner part of his personality and induced him to deal with all his difficulties and problems, including his envy, by projective identification. During the session, the saner part of the patient seemed to receive help and support from the analyst's interpretations, but he felt humiliated and angry that he could not resist the domination and persuasion of the psychotic part when he was left on his own. In attempting to examine the reason for listening so readily to the internal voice, I found that he was promised cure, freedom from anxiety and from dependence on myself. I was then able to interpret that the separation made him more aware of feeling small and dependent on me, which was humiliating and painful and increased his envy of me. By omnipotently intruding into me, he could delude himself that from one moment to the next he became grown up and completely all right and could manage without me.

I shall now briefly describe the relationship between ego splitting, projective identification and the persecutory anxieties related to these processes in this patient. On the following session he reported that he felt much better, but in the middle of the session he became very silent and then admitted with shame that he had been intensely anti-semitic some time ago for a period of over six months. He had regarded the Jews as degraded people who were only out to exploit others in order to extract money from them in a ruthless way. He hated exploiters and wanted to attack and smash them for it. I interpreted that while he was aware that this happened in the past, he now felt awful towards me because after yesterday's session he had got rid of the greedy parasitical exploiting part of his self but had pushed it into me. He felt now that I had become his greedy exploiting self and this made him feel intensely suspicious about me. He replied that he feared that I must now hate and despise him, and that the only thing which he could do was to destroy himself or this hated part of himself. I interpreted his fear of my retaliation because when he saw me as a greedy, exploiting Jew he attacked and despised me, and feared that I would hate him because he believed I could not bear that he had pushed his own greedy self into me, not only as an attack but because he could not bear it himself and wanted to get rid of it. I suggested that it was when he felt that I could not accept his bad and hated self that he attacked himself so violently. In fact, the greatest anxiety during this session was related to violent attacks that were directed against his bad self which built up to a crescendo, so that he feared he would tear himself to pieces. He calmed down considerably after the interpretations.

The next session showed progress in relation to the splitting processes, followed in subsequent sessions by some experience of depression. In the beginning of the session the patient reported that he had some difficulty in getting up, but he was glad that he remembered a dream. In this dream he was observing a group of Olympic runners in a race on the television screen. Suddenly he saw a number of people crowding in on to the track and interfering with the race. He got violently angry with them and wanted to kill them for interfering and deliberately getting in the way of the runners. He reported that he had been looking at the television screen for only a short time the night before and had been thinking about the last session in which he had been afraid of damaging himself when he tried to cut off and destroy bad parts of himself. He now was determined to face up to whatever was going on in him. He had no associations to the dream, apart from the fact that the interfering people looked quite ordinary. I pointed out that in this dream he showed in a very concrete way what he felt he was doing when he was looking at television. The interfering people seemed to be the parts of himself which he experienced as worming their way into the track in Mexico when he was greedily and enviously looking at television. In this dream it was quite clear that people representing him were not competing by running, but were simply trying to interfere with the progress of the race. I was then able to show him another aspect of the extremely concrete form of projection which did not only relate to the Olympic runners but to the analyst. I interpreted that he felt when the analysis was making good progress he experienced my interpretations and thoughts as something which he was watching with admiration and envy, like the athletes on television. He felt that the envious parts of himself actually could worm their way into my brain and interfere with the quickness of my thinking. In the dream he was attempting to face up to the recognition that these parts of himself actually existed and he wanted to control and stop them. I also related this process to the patient's complaints that his own thought processes were often interfered with and I related this to an identification with the analyst's mind which he often enviously attacked. Actually, the patient's co-operation during the last week had been very positive, which had led to considerable unblocking of his mind, so that a great number of his projective identifications and splitting processes had shown themselves clearly in the analysis and could be related to the transference situation. In the dream he had actually succeeded in what he announced he tried to do, namely, to face up to the processes by bringing them into the transference rather than attempting to destroy and get rid of them by splitting and projection. This also enabled him to face up to his acute fear of damaging both his objects and his self through his projective identifications. My interpretations seemed to diminish his anxiety about having completely destroyed me and my brain so that I could be experienced as helpful and undamaged, and for certain periods I was introjected as good and undamaged, a process leading gradually to a strengthening of the ego. One of the difficulties of working through such situations in the analysis is the tendency to endless repetition, in spite of the patient's understanding that very useful analytic work is being done. It is important in dealing with patients and processes of this kind to accept that much of the repetition is inevitable. The acceptance by the analyst of the patient's processes being re-enacted in the transference helps the patient to feel that the self, which is constantly split off and projected into the analyst, is acceptable and not so damaging as feared.

I want now to describe briefly a short depressive spell in the patient's illness which throws some light on his internal anxieties related to damage to objects and his self. A few days after the session I reported before, the patient became increasingly concerned about injuries he believed he had done to other people, but most of all he was horrified about what was going on inside himself. For half an hour he experienced intense anxiety and reported that he was too frightened to look inside himself. Suddenly he saw his brain in a terrible state as if many worms had eaten their way into it. He feared that the damage was irreparable and his brain might fall to pieces. Despairingly he said how could he allow his brain to get into such an awful state! After a pause he suggested that his constant relations to prostitutes had something to do with the state of affairs. I interpreted that he felt that he had forced himself during the last weeks into people such as the prostitutes and the athletes and that he was afraid to see that damage outside. The damage to his brain seemed identical to the damage he feared he had done to external objects. He then began to talk about his brain as a particularly valuable and delicate part of his body which he had neglected and left unprotected. His voice sounded now much warmer and more concerned than ever previously, so I felt it necessary to interpret that his brain was also identified with a particularly valuable important object relationship, namely, the analysis and the analyst which represented the feeding situation to him. This he had usually displaced on to the prostitutes to whom he always went for nourishment. I gave him now detailed interpretations of the intensity of his hunger for me, his inability to wait and I described his impulses and the self which he had experienced as boring himself omnipotently into my brain, which contained for him all the valuable knowledge which he longed to possess. Throughout the hour the patient felt great anxiety and almost unbearable pain because he feared he could not repair the damage. However, he was clearly relieved through the transference interpretations which helped him to differentiate and disentangle the confusion between inside and outside, phantasy and reality. I think it was particularly the interpretations about my brain, which showed him that I could still think and function, which both helped him to understand this very concrete phantasy in relation to his own thought processes and to relieve his anxiety about the damage he feared he had done to me.

In this case material I have tried to illustrate some of the processes of projective identification and ego splitting and the part they play in the psychopathology of psychotic patients.

Summary

'Projective identification' relates first of all to a splitting process of the early ego, where either good or bad parts of the self are split off from the ego and are as a further step projected in love or hatred into external objects, which leads to fusion and identification of the projected parts of the self with the external objects. There are important paranoid anxieties related to these processes as the objects filled with aggressive parts of the self become persecuting and are experienced by the patient as threatening to retaliate by forcing themselves and the bad parts of the self which they contain back again into the ego.

In this paper I have discussed a number of processes related to projective identification which play an important part in psychotic patients. First of all, I am distinguishing between two types of projective identification: the projective identification used by psychotic patients for communication with other objects, which seems to be a distortion or intensification of the normal infantile relationship which is based on non-verbal communication between infant and mother; and secondly, the projective identification used for ridding the self of unwanted parts, which leads to a denial of psychic reality. As a third point I am discussing projective identification representing a very common transference relationship of the psychotic patient which is aimed at controlling the analyst's body and mind, which seems to be based on a very early infantile type of object relationship. My fourth point is projective identification used by the psychotic patient predominantly for defensive purposes to deal with aggressive impulses, particularly envy. The fifth point I am drawing attention to are those object relations of the psychotic patient in analysis where he maintains the belief that he is living entirely inside an object – the analyst – and behaves like a parasite using the capacities of the analyst, who is expected to function as his ego. Severe parasitism may be regarded as a state of total projective identification. I am also discussing the parasitical state which is related to living entirely in a delusional world. Sixthly, I am discussing the *psychoanalytic treatment* of the processes related to projective identification in the psychotic patient. Finally, I present case material of a schizophrenic patient in order to illustrate some aspects of projective identification and ego splitting.

—————————————————— 6 ——————————————————

Projective identification

Some clinical aspects[34]

Betty Joseph

———————————————————————————————————

The concept of projective identification was introduced into analytic thinking by Melanie Klein in 1946. Since then it has been welcomed, argued about, the name disputed, the links with projection pointed out, and so on; but one aspect seems to stand out above the firing line, and that is its considerable clinical value. It is this aspect that I shall mainly concentrate on today, and mainly in relation to the more neurotic patient.

Melanie Klein became aware of projective identification when exploring what she called the paranoid-schizoid position, that is, a constellation of a particular type of object relations, anxieties, and defences against them, typical for the earliest period of the individual's life and, in certain disturbed people, continuing throughout life. This particular position she saw as dominated by the infant's need to ward off anxieties and impulses by splitting both the object, originally the mother, and the self and projecting these split-off parts into an object, which will then be felt to be like, or identified with, these split-off parts, so colouring the infant's perception of the object and its subsequent introjection.

She discussed the manifold aims of different types of projective identification, for example, splitting off and getting rid of unwanted

34 This article was published in J. Sandler (Ed.) (1987). *Projection, Identification, Projective Identification*. London: Karnac Books, pp. 65–76. Published with the permission of International Universities Press Inc., Madison, CT, USA.

parts of the self that cause anxiety or pain; projecting the self or parts of the self into an object to dominate and control it and thus avoid any feelings of being separate; getting into an object to take over its capacities and make them its own; invading in order to damage or destroy the object. Thus the infant, or adult who goes on using such mechanisms powerfully, can avoid any awareness of separateness, dependence, admiration, or its concomitant sense of loss, anger, envy, etc. But it sets up anxieties of a persecutory type, claustro-phobic, panics and the like.

We could say that, from the point of view of the individual who uses such mechanisms strongly, projective identification is a phantasy and yet it can have a powerful effect on the recipient. It does not always do so and when it does we cannot always tell how the effect is brought about, but we cannot doubt its importance. We can see, however, that the concept of projective identification, used in this way, is more object-related, more concrete and covers more aspects than the term projection would ordinarily imply, and it has opened up a whole area of analytic understanding. These various aspects I am going to discuss later, as we see them operating in our clinical work; here I want only to stress two points: first, the omnipotent power of these mechanisms and phantasies; second, how, in so far as they orig-inate in a particular constellation, deeply interlocked, we cannot in our thinking isolate projective identification from the omnipotence, the splitting and the resultant anxieties that go along with it. Indeed, we shall see that they are all part of a balance, rigidly or precariously maintained by the individual, in his own individual way.

As the individual develops, either in normal development or through analytic treatment, these projections lessen, he becomes more able to tolerate his ambivalence, his love and hate and depen-dence on objects, in other words, he moves towards what Melanie Klein described as the depressive position. This process can be helped in infancy if the child has a supportive environment, if the mother is able to tolerate and contain the child's projections, intuitively to understand and stand its feelings. Bion elaborated and extended this aspect of Melanie Klein's work, suggesting the importance of the mother being able to be used as a container by the infant, and linking this with the process of communication in childhood and with the positive use of the counter-transference in analysis. Once the child is better integrated and able to recognize its impulses and feelings as its own, there will be a lessening in the pressure to project, accompanied by an increased concern for the object. In its earliest forms projective identification has no concern for the object, indeed it is often anti-concern, aimed at dominating, irrespective of the cost to the object. As the child moves towards the depressive position, this necessarily alters and, although projective identification is probably never entirely given up, it will no longer involve the complete splitting off and disowning of parts of the self, but will be less absolute, more tempo-rary and more able to be drawn back into the individual's personality – and thus be the basis of empathy.

In this paper I want, first, to consider some further implications of the use of projective identification, and then to discuss and illustrate different aspects of projective identification, first in two patients more or less stuck in the paranoid-schizoid position, and then in a patient beginning to move towards the depressive position.

To begin with: some of the implications, clinical and technical, of the massive use of projective identification as we see it in our work. Sometimes it is used so massively that we get the impression that the patient is; in phantasy, projecting his whole self into his object and may feel trapped or claustrophobic. It is, in any case, a very powerful and effective way of ridding the individual of contact with his own mind; at times the mind can be so weakened or so fragmented by splitting processes or so evacuated by projective identification that the individual appears empty or quasi-psychotic. This I shall show with C, the case of a child. It also has important technical implications; for example, bearing in mind that projective identification is only one aspect of an omnipotent balance established by each individual in his own way, an interpretative attempt on the part of the analyst to locate and give back to the patient missing parts of the self must of necessity be resisted by the total personality, since it is felt to threaten the whole balance and lead to more disturbance. I shall discuss this in case T. Projective identification cannot be seen in isolation.

A further clinical implication that I should like to touch on is about communication. Bion demonstrated how projective identifi-cation can be used as a method of communication by the individual putting, as it were, undigested parts of his experience and inner world into the object, originally the mother, now the analyst, as a way of getting them understood and returned in a more manageable form. But we might add to this that projective identification is, by its very nature, a kind of communication, even in cases where this is not its aim or its intention. By definition projective identification means the putting of parts of the self into an object. If the analyst on the receiving end is really open to what is going on and able to be aware of what he is experiencing, this can be a powerful method of gaining understanding. Indeed, much of our current appreciation of the richness of the notion of counter-transference stems from it. I shall later try to indicate some of the problems this raises, in terms of acting-in, in my discussion of the third case, N.

I want now to give a brief example of a case to illustrate the concreteness of projective identification in the analytic situation, its effectiveness as a method of ridding the child of a whole area of experience and thus keeping some kind of balance, and the effect of such massive projective mechanisms on her state of mind. This is a little girl aged 4, in analytic treatment with Mrs Elizabeth Da Rocha Barros, who was discussing the case with me. The child had only very recently begun treatment, a deeply disturbed and neglected child, whom I shall call C.

A few minutes before the end of a Friday session C said that she was going to make a candle; the analyst explained her wish to take a warm Mrs Barros with her that day at the end of the session and her fear that there would not be enough time, as there were only three minutes left. C started to scream, saying that she would have some spare candles; she then started to stare through the window with a vacant, lost expression. The analyst interpreted that the child needed to make the analyst realize how awful it was to end the session, as well as expressing a wish to take home some warmth from the analyst's words for the weekend. The child screamed: 'Bastard! Take off your clothes and jump outside.' Again the analyst tried to interpret C's feelings about being dropped and sent into the cold. C replied: 'Stop your talking, take off your clothes. You are cold. I'm not cold.' The feeling in the session was extremely moving. Here the words carry the concrete meaning, to the child, of the separation of the weekend – the awful coldness. This she tries to force into the analyst and it is felt to have been concretely achieved. 'You are cold, I am not cold.'

The moments when C looked completely lost and vacant, as in this fragment, were very frequent and were, I think, indicative not only of her serious loss of contact with reality, but of the emptiness, vacantness of her mind and personality when projective identification was operating so powerfully. I think that much of her screaming is also in the nature of her emptying out. The effectiveness of such emptying is striking, as the whole experience of loss and its concomitant emotions is cut out. One can again see here how the term 'projective identification' describes more vividly and fully the processes involved than the more general and frequently used terms, such as 'reversal' or, as I said, 'projection'.

In this example, then, the child's balance is primarily maintained by the projecting out of parts of the self. I want now to give an example of a familiar kind of case to discuss various kinds of projective identification working together to hold a particular narcissistic omnipotent balance. This kind of balance is very firmly structured, extremely difficult to influence analytically and leads to striking persecutory anxieties. It also raises some points about different identificatory processes and problems about the term 'projective identification' itself.

A young teacher, whom I shall call T, came into analysis with difficulties in relationships, but actually with the hope of changing careers and becoming an analyst. His daily material consisted very largely of descriptions of work he had done in helping his pupils, how his colleagues had praised his work, asked him to discuss their work with him, and so on. Little else came into the sessions. He frequently described how one or other of his colleagues felt threatened by him, threatened in the sense of feeling minimized or put in an inferior position by his greater insight and understanding. He was, therefore, uneasy that they felt unfriendly to him at any given moment. (Any idea that his personality might actually put people off did not enter his mind.) It was not difficult to show him certain ideas about myself – for example, that when I did not seem to be encouraging him to give up his career and apply for training as an analyst, he felt that I, being old, felt threatened by this intelligent young person coming forward, and, therefore, would not want him in my professional area.

Clearly, simply to suggest, or interpret, that T was projecting his envy into his objects and then feeling them as identified with this part of himself might be theoretically accurate, but clinically inept and useless; indeed it would just be absorbed into his psychoanalytic armoury. We can see that the projective identification of the envious parts of the self was, as it were, only the end result of one aspect of a highly complex balance which he was keeping. To clarify something of the nature of this balance, it is important to see how T was relating to me in the transference. Usually he spoke of me as a very fine analyst and I was flattered in such ways. Actually he could not take in interpretations meaningfully, he appeared not to listen properly; he would, for example, hear the words partially and then re-interpret them unconsciously, according to some previous theoretical and psychoanalytical knowledge, then give them to himself with this slightly altered and generalized meaning. Frequently, when I interpreted more firmly, he would respond very quickly and argumentatively, as if there were a minor explosion which seemed destined, not only to expel from his mind what I might be going to say, but enter my mind and break up my thinking at that moment.

In this example we have projective identification operating with various different motives and leading to different identificatory processes – but all aimed at maintaining his narcissistic omnipotent balance. First we see the splitting of his objects – I am flattered and kept in his mind as idealized; at such moments the bad or unhelpful aspect of myself is quite split off, even though I don't seem to be achieving much with him; but this latter has to be denied. He projects part of himself into my mind and takes over; he 'knows' what I am going to say and says it himself. At this point, a part of the self is identified with an idealized aspect of myself, which is talking to, interpreting to, an idealized patient part of himself; idealized because it listens to the analyst part of him. We can see what this movement achieves in terms of his balance. It cuts out any real relationship between the patient and myself, between analyst and patient, as mother and child, as a feeding couple. It obviates any separate existence, any relating to me as myself; any relationship in which he takes in directly from me. T was, in fact, earlier in his life slightly anorexic. If I manage for a moment to get through this T explodes, so that his mental digestive system is fragmented, and by this verbal explosion, as I said, T unconsciously tries to enter my mind and break up my thinking, my capacity to feed him. It is important here, as always with projective identification, to distinguish this kind of unconscious entering, invading and breaking up from a conscious aggressive attack. What I am discussing here is how these patients, using projective identification so omnipotently, actually avoid any such feelings as dependence, envy, jealousy, etc.

Once T has in phantasy entered my mind and taken over my interpretations, and my role at that moment, I notice that he has 'added to', 'improved on', 'enriched' my interpretations, and I become the onlooker, who should realize that my interpretations of a few moments ago were not as rich as his are now – and surely I should feel threatened by this young man in my room! Thus the two

103

types of projective identification are working in harmony, the invading of my mind and taking over its contents and the projecting of the potentially dependent, threatened and envious part of the self into me. This is, of course, mirrored in what we hear is going on in his outside world – the fellow students who ask for help and feel threatened by his brilliance – but then he feels persecuted by their potential unfriendliness. So long as the balance holds so effectively, we cannot see what more subtle, sensitive, and important aspects of the personality are being kept split off, or why – we can see that any relationship to a truly separate object is obviated – with all that this may imply.

A great difficulty is, of course, that all insight tends to get drawn into this process; to give a minute example: one Monday, T really seemed to become aware of exactly how he was subtly taking the meaning out of what I was saying and not letting real understanding develop. For a moment he felt relief and then a brief, deep feeling of hatred to me emerged into consciousness. A second later he added quietly that he was thinking how the way that he had been feeling just then towards me, that is, the hatred, must have been how his fellow students had felt towards him on the previous day when he had been talking and explaining things to them! So, immediately that T has a real experience of hating me because I have said something useful, he uses the momentary awareness to speak about the students, and distances himself from the emerging envy and hostility, and the direct receptive contact between the two of us is again lost. What looks like insight is no longer insight but has become a complex projective manoeuvre.

At a period when these problems were very much in the forefront of the analysis, T brought a dream, right at the end of a session. The dream was simply this: T was with the analyst or with a woman, J, or it might have been both, he was excitedly pushing his hand up her knickers into her vagina, thinking that if he could get right in there would be no stopping him. Here, I think under the pressure of the analytic work going on, T's great need and great excitement were to get totally inside the object, with all its implications, including, of course, the annihilation of the analytic situation.

To return to the concept of projective identification; with this patient I have indicated three or four different aspects: attacking the analyst's mind; a kind of total invading, as in the dream fragment I have just quoted; a more partial invading and taking over aspects or capacities of the analyst; and finally putting parts of the self, particularly inferior parts, into the analyst. The latter two are mutually dependent, but lead to different types of identification. In the one, the patient, in taking over, becomes identified with the analyst's idealized capacities; in the other, it is the analyst who becomes identified with the lost, projected, here inferior or envious parts of the patient. I think it is partly because the term is broad and covers many aspects that there has been some unease about the name itself.

I have so far discussed projective identification in two cases caught up in the paranoid–schizoid position, a borderline child and a man in a rigid omnipotent narcissistic state. Now I want to discuss aspects of projective identification as one sees it in a patient moving towards the depressive position. I shall illustrate some points from the case of a man as he was becoming less rigid, more integrated, better able to tolerate what was previously projected, but constantly also pulling back, returning to the use of the earlier projective mechanisms; then I want to show the effect of this on subsequent identifications and the light that it throws on previous identifications. I also want to attempt to forge a link between the nature of the patient's residual use of projective identification and its early infantile counterpart and the relation of this to phobia formation. I bring this material also to discuss briefly the communicative nature of projective identification.

To start with this latter point, as I said earlier, since projective identification, by its very nature means the putting of parts of the self into the object, in the transference we are of necessity on the receiving end of the projections and, therefore, providing we can tune into them, we have an opportunity par excellence to understand them and what is going on. In this sense, it acts as a communication, whatever its motivation, and is the basis for the positive use of countertransference. As I want to describe with this patient, N, it is frequently difficult to clarify whether, at any given moment, projective identification is primarily aimed at communicating a state of mind that cannot be verbalized by the patient or whether it is aimed more at entering and controlling or attacking the analyst, or whether all these elements are active and need consideration.

A patient, N, who had been in analysis many years, had recently married and, after a few weeks, was becoming anxious about his sexual interest and his potency, particularly in view of the fact that his wife was considerably younger. He came on a Monday, saying that he felt that 'the thing' was never really going to get right, 'the sexual thing', yes, they did have sex on Sunday, but somehow he had to force himself and he knew it wasn't quite all right, and his wife noticed this and commented. It was an all-right kind of weekend, just about. He spoke about this a bit more and explained that they went to a place outside London, to a party; they had meant to stay the night in an hotel nearby, but couldn't find anywhere nice enough and came home and so were late. What was being conveyed to me was a quiet, sad discomfort, leading to despair, and I pointed out to N how he was conveying an awful long-term hopelessness and despair, with no hope for the future. He replied to the effect that he supposed that he was feeling left out, and linked this with what had been a rather helpful and vivid session on the Friday, but now, as he made the remark, it was quite dead and flat. When I tried to look at this with him, he agreed, commenting that he supposed he was starting to attack the analysis, etc.

The feeling in the session now was awful; N was making a kind of sense and saying analytic things himself, which could have been right, for example about the Friday, and which one could have picked up, but, since they seemed flat and quite unhelpful to him, what he seemed to me to be doing was putting despair into me, not only about the reality of his marriage and potency, but also about his analysis, as was indicated, for example, by the useless, and by now somewhat irrelevant, comment about being left out. N denied my interpretation about his despair about the progress of the analysis, but in such a way, it seemed to me, as to be encouraging me to make false interpretations and to pick up his pseudo-interpretations as if I believed in them, while knowing that they and we were getting nowhere. He vaguely talked about this, went quiet and said: 'I was listening to your voice, the timbre changes in different voices. W (his wife), being younger, makes more sounds per second, older voices are deeper because they make less sounds per second, etc.' I showed N his great fear that I showed with my voice, rather than through my actual words, that I could not stand the extent of his hopelessness and his doubts about myself, about what we could achieve in the analysis and, therefore, in his life, and that I would cheat and in some way try to encourage. I queried whether he had perhaps felt that, in that session, my voice had changed in order to sound more encouraging and encouraged, rather than contain the despair he was expressing. By this part of the session my patient had got into contact and said with some relief that, if I did do this kind of encouraging, the whole bottom would fall out of the analysis.

First, the nature of the communication, which I could understand primarily through my counter-transference, through the way in which I was being pushed and pulled to feel and to react. We see here the concrete quality of projective identification structuring the counter-transference. It seems that the way N was speaking was not asking me to try to understand the sexual difficulties or unhappiness, but to invade me with despair, while at the same time unconsciously trying to force me to reassure myself that it was all right, that interpretations, now empty of meaning and hollow, were meaningful, and that the analysis at that moment was going ahead satisfactorily. Thus it was not only the despair that N was projecting into me, but his defences against it, a false reassurance and denial, which it was intended I should act out with him. I think that this also suggests a projective identification of an internal figure, probably primarily mother, who was felt to be weak, kind, but unable to stand up to emotion. In the transference (to over-simplify the picture) this figure is projected into me, and I find myself pushed to live it out.

We have here the important issue of teasing out the motivation for this projective identification: was it aimed primarily at communicating something to me; was there a depth of despair that we had not previously sufficiently understood; or was the forcing of despair into me motivated by something different? At this stage, at the end of the session, I did not know and left it open.

I have so much condensed the material here that I cannot convey adequately the atmosphere and to and fro of the session. But towards the end, as I have tried to show, my patient experienced and expressed relief and appreciation of what had been going on. There was a shift in mood and behaviour as my patient started to accept understanding and face the nature of his forcing into me, and he could then experience me as an object that could stand up to his acting in, not get caught into it, but contain it. He could then identify temporarily with a stronger object, and he himself became firmer. I also sensed some feeling of concern about what he had been doing to me and my work – it was not openly acknowledged and expressed but there is some movement towards the depressive position with its real concern and guilt.

To clarify the motivation as well as the effect of this kind of projective identification on subsequent introjective identification, we need to go briefly into the beginning of the next session, when N brought a dream, in which he was on a boat like a ferry boat, on a grey-green sea surrounded by mist; he did not know where they were going.

Then nearby there was another boat which was clearly going down under the water and drowning. He stepped on to this boat as it went down. He did not feel wet or afraid, which was puzzling. Amongst his associations we heard of his wife being very gentle and affectionate, but he added that he himself was concerned; was she behind this really making more demands on him? She, knowing his fondness for steak and kidney pudding, had made him one the night before. It was excellent, but the taste was too strong, which he told her!

Now the interesting thing, I think, was that, on the previous day I had felt rather at sea, as I said, not knowing exactly where we were going, but I was clear that the understanding about the hopelessness and the defences against it was right, and, though I had not thought it out in this way, my belief would have been that the mists would clear as we went on. But what does my patient do with this? He gratuitously steps off this boat (this understanding) on to one that is going down, and he is not afraid! In other words, he prefers to drown in despair rather than clarify it, prefers to see affection as demands, and my decent, well-cooked steak and kidney interpretations as too tasty. At this point, as we worked on it, N could see that the notion of drowning here was actually exciting to him.

Now we can see more about the motivation. It becomes clear that N was not just trying to communicate and get understood something about his despair, important as this element is, but that he was also attacking me and our work, by trying to drag me down by the despair, when there was actually progress. After a session in which he expressed appreciation about my work and capacity to stand up to him, he dreamt of willingly stepping on to a sinking boat, so that either, internally, I collude and go down with him or am forced to watch him go under and my hope is destroyed and I am kept impotent to help. This activity also leads to an introjective identification with an analyst-parent who is felt to be down, joyless and impotent, and this identification contributes considerably to his lack of sexual confidence and potency. Following this period of the analysis, there was real improvement in the symptom.

Naturally these considerations lead one to think about the nature of the patient's internal objects, for example, the weak mother, that I described as being projected into me in the transference. How much is this figure based on N's real experience with his mother, how much did he exploit her weaknesses and thus contribute to building in his inner world a mother, weak, inadequate and on the defensive, as we saw in the transference? In other words, when we talk of an object projected on to the analyst in the transference, we are discussing an internal object that has been structured in part from the child's earlier projective identifications, and the whole process can be seen being revived in the transference.

I want now to digress and look at this material from a slightly different angle, related to the patient's very early history and anxieties. I have shown how N pulls back and goes into an object, in the dream, into the sinking boat, as in the first session he goes into despair, which is then projected into me, rather than his thinking about it. This going into an object, acted out in the session, is, I believe, linked with a more total type of projective identification that I indicated in the sexual dream of T, and referred to briefly at the beginning of this paper, as being connected with phobia formation. At the very primitive end of projective identification is the attempt to get back into an object, to become, as it were, undifferentiated and mindless and thus avoid all pain. Most human beings develop beyond this in early infancy; some of our patients attempt to use projective identification in this way over many years. N, when he came into analysis, came because he had a fetish, a tremendous pull towards getting inside a rubber object which would totally cover, absorb, and excite him. In his early childhood he had nightmares of falling out of a globe into endless space. In the early period of analysis he would have severe panic states when alone in the house, and would be seriously disturbed or lose contact if he had to be away from London on business. At the same time there are minor indications of anxieties about being trapped in a claustrophobic way, for example, at night he would have to keep blankets on the bed loose or throw them off altogether; in intercourse phantasies emerged of his penis being cut off and lost inside the woman's body. As the analysis went on, the fetishistic activities disappeared and real relationships improved, and the projecting of the self into the object could clearly be seen in the transference. He would get absorbed in his own words or ideas or in the sound of my words and my speaking, and the meaning would be unimportant compared with the concrete nature of the experience. This type of absorption into words and sounds, with the analyst, as a person, quite disregarded, is not unlike the kind of process that one sometimes sees in child patients, who come into the playroom, on to the couch, and fall so deeply asleep that they are unable to be woken by interpretations. It is, therefore, interesting to see in N how he has always concretely attempted to get into an object, apparently largely in order to escape from being outside, to become absorbed and free from relating and from thought and mental pain. And yet we know that this is only half the story, since the object he mainly got into was a fetish and highly sexualized. And still in the modern dream of getting into the drowning boat there was masochistic excitement that he tried to pull me into and in this sense it needs to be compared with T. I described how, as his constant invading and taking over was being analysed, we could see in T's sexual dream an attempt totally to get inside me with great excitement. I suspect there is much yet to be teased out about the relation between certain types of massive projective identification of the self and erotization.

Now I want to return to the material that I quoted and to the question of projective identification in patients who are becoming more integrated and nearer to the depressive position. We can see in the case of N, unlike T who is still imprisoned in his own omnipotent, narcissistic structure, that there is now a movement, in the transference, towards more genuine whole object relations. At times he can really appreciate the strong containing qualities of his object; true he will then try to draw me in and drag me down again, but there is now potential conflict about this. The object can be valued and loved, at times he can consciously experience hostility about this, and ambivalence is present. As his loving is freed, he is able to introject and identify with a whole valued and potent object, and the effect on his character and potency is striking. This is a very different quality of identification from that based on forcing despairing parts of the self into an object, which then in his phantasy becomes like a despairing part of himself. It is very different from the type of identification we saw in T, where the patient invaded my mind and took over the split and idealized aspects, leaving the object, myself, denuded and inferior. With N, in the example I have just given, he could experience and value me as a whole, different and properly separate person with my own qualities, and these he could introject and thereby feel strengthened. But we still have a task ahead, to enable N to be truly outside and able to give up the analysis, aware of its meaning to him and yet secure.

Summary

I have tried in this paper to discuss projective identification as we see it operating in our clinical work. I have described various types of projective identification, from the more primitive and massive type to the more empathic and mature. I have discussed how we see alterations in its manifestation as progress is made in treatment and the patient moves towards the depressive position, is better integrated and able to use his objects less omnipotently, relate to them as separate objects and introject them and their qualities more fully and realistically, and thus also to separate from them.

7

Projective identification

The analyst's involvement[35]

Michael Feldman

In Klein's original formulation of the mechanism of projective identification she referred to an unconscious phantasy in which the patient expelled what were usually disturbing contents into another object. This object is partially transformed in the patient's mind as a consequence of the projection, being now possessed of qualities the patient has expelled. In addition to its use as a method of evacuation, Klein suggested that projective identification may fulfil a variety of other unconscious functions for the patient, such as leading to him believing that he possesses the object, or controls it from within. These projective processes usually alternate with introjective ones. Thus the phantasy of forceful entry into the object by parts of the self in order to possess or control the object creates problems with normal introjection, which the patient may find difficult to distinguish from forceful entry from the outside, in retribution for his own violent projections (Klein, 1946, p. 11).

The exploration of these unconscious phantasies has increased our understanding of the functions and defensive needs these primitive mental mechanisms serve for the patient. While the elucidation of these processes has, in the past, often seemed to emphasise the analyst's role as a dispassionate observer, the impingement of the patient's

35 This chapter reproduces the text of Feldman, M. (1997). Projective identification: the analyst's involvement. *International Journal of Psycho-Analysis, 78,* 227–241.

phantasies and actions on the analyst has in fact been recognised from the earliest days of psychoanalysis. Following the early work of Heimann (1950) and Racker (1958a) there has been increasing interest in the systematic investigation of the way in which the patient's phantasies, expressed in gross or subtle, verbal or non-verbal means, may come to influence the analyst's state of mind and behaviour. Fairbairn wrote: 'in a sense, psychoanalytical treatment resolves itself into a struggle on the part of the patient to press-gang his relationship with the analyst into the closed system of the inner world through the agency of transference' (Fairbairn, 1958, p. 385).

We now recognise that while this conscious or unconscious pressure on the analyst may interfere with his functioning, it can also serve as an invaluable source of information concerning the patient's unconscious mental life – his internal object relations in particular. More recently, a number of authors have been concerned to elaborate the concept of countertransference into what is described as an 'interactive' model of psychoanalysis, where the emphasis is on the significance of the analyst's own subjective experiences in his understanding of and his method of responding to his patient. Tuckett (1997) has provided an excellent commentary on some of the interesting work in this area. Building upon the notions of Racker (1958a), Sandler (1976a) and Joseph (1989a), he elaborates a model of the analytic situation in which both the patient and the analyst engage in unconscious enactment, placing more or less subtle pressure on the other to relate to them in terms of a present unconscious phantasy. He makes the point that 'Enactment makes it possible to know in representable and communicable ways about deep unconscious identifications and primitive levels of functioning which could otherwise only be guessed at or discussed at the intellectual level.'

In this paper I want to focus particularly on the nature of the involvement by the analyst that the patient seems to require as an essential component of the defensive use of projective identification. I will suggest that the projection of elements of a phantasised object relationship represents an attempt by the patient to reduce the discrepancy between an archaic object relationship and an alternative object relationship that might be confronting the patient and threatening him. There are times when the analyst is used primarily as the recipient of projections by which he is transformed in the patient's phantasy alone. More commonly, as described above, it seems necessary for the patient that the analyst should become involved in the living out of some aspects of phantasies that reflect his internal object relations.

I hope to illustrate some of the ways in which the patient's use of projective identification exerts subtle and powerful pressure on the analyst to fulfil the patient's unconscious expectations that are embodied in these phantasies. Thus the impingement upon the analyst's thinking, feelings and actions is not an incidental side-effect of the patient's projections, nor necessarily a manifestation of the analyst's own conflicts and anxieties, but seems often to be an essential component in the effective use of projective identification by the patient. Later in the paper, I will consider some of the defensive functions these processes serve. Confronted with such pressure, the analyst may apparently be able to remain comfortable and secure in his role and function, involved in empathic observation and understanding, recognising the forces he is being subjected to, and with some ideas about their origins and purpose. He may, on the other hand, be disturbed by the impingement and transformation in his mental and physical state, becoming sleepy, confused, anxious or elated. Finally, it may become apparent to the analyst that he has unconsciously been drawn into a subtle and complex enactment that did not necessarily disturb him at first, but which can subsequently be recognised as the living out of important elements of the patient's internal object relationships.

We are concerned with a system in which both patient and analyst are dealing with the anxieties and needs aroused in each of them by the phantasies of particular object relationships. The disturbance in either the patient, or the analyst, or both, arises from the discrepancy between the pre-existing phantasies that partly reassure or gratify, and those with which each is confronted in the analytical situation, which are potentially threatening. I am suggesting that this unwelcome discrepancy drives each to deploy either projective mechanisms or some variety of enactment in an attempt to create a greater correspondence between the pre-existing unconscious phantasies and what they experience in the analytic encounter. As I hope to illustrate, part of the analyst's struggle involves the recognition of some of these pressures, and the capacity to tolerate the gap between the gratifying or reassuring phantasies and what he is confronted with in the analytical situation, which includes the unconscious anxieties evoked by the patient's projections.

Rosenfeld (1971) describes a psychotic patient who, when confronted with interpretations he admired, was filled with envy and driven to attack his analyst's functions. In his phantasy, he wormed his way into the analyst's brain, like a parasite, interfering with the quickness of his thinking. This use of projective identification was often accompanied by the patient becoming confused, unable to think or talk properly, with claustrophobic and paranoid anxieties about being trapped in the analyst. Rosenfeld describes the need for the analyst empathically to follow the patient's description of both real and fantasised events, which are often re-enacted by being projected into him. The analyst has to bring together the diffuse, confused or split-up aspects of the patient's pre-thought processes in his own mind so that they gradually make sense and have meaning (Rosenfeld, 1987c, p. 160).

When Rosenfeld was able to interpret the dynamics of the patient's state to him in a clear and detailed way, his anxiety about having completely destroyed the analyst's brain diminished, and the patient was able, with relief, to experience him as helpful and undamaged. When it became possible for the patient to introject this object in a good state, he could, for a while, recover his own capacities for clearer thought and speech.

Bion (1958) gives a complex description of the beginning of a session with a psychotic patient, who gave the analyst a quick glance, paused, stared at the floor near the corner of the room, and then gave a slight shudder. He lay down on the couch, keeping his eye on the same corner of the floor. When he spoke, he said he felt quite empty, and wouldn't be able to make further use of the session. Bion spells out the steps in the process by which the patient first used his eyes for introjection, and then for expulsion, creating a hallucinatory figure that had a threatening quality, accompanied by a sense of internal emptiness. When he made an interpretation along these lines, the patient became calmer and said, 'I have painted a picture'. Bion writes, 'His subsequent silence meant that the material for the analyst's next interpretation was already in my possession' (p. 71). Bion suggested that his task was to consider all the events of the session up to that point, try to bring them together and discern a new pattern in his mind which should be the basis for his next interpretation.

A young man, Mr. A, encountering me for the first time after a holiday break, was initially disconcerted by finding someone new with him in the waiting room, and then came to the view that I might have made a mistake, which would cause me discomfort and embarrassment which I would not be able to face, and he imagined I would send a colleague to deal with the problem. Once he had arrived at this construction, the patient became the calm and confident observer of his muddled analyst. The patient later told me that during my absence he had found himself in a mess, he had lost his watch, and felt he hadn't known what was going on.

I suggested that the patient's experience of confusion and his difficulties over time had become projected, in phantasy, into me. After finding himself briefly discomforted in the waiting room, he 'cured' himself of his disturbing experience, so he became the calm analytic observer, while, in his phantasy, I had to summon help to rescue me from the mistake I had made over my timetable.

These examples illustrate patients' unconscious belief in the effectiveness of a concrete process by which (usually) undesirable and threatening parts of the personality can be split off and projected. The motives for this projection vary, but the involvement of the object as a recipient of this projection is a defining characteristic of projective identification, as is the belief in the transformation of the object by the projection. This transformation may take place in relation to a delusional or hallucinatory object, an absent object or a dream object, but central to our work is the investigation of the process in relation to the analyst in the room with the patient. In the examples quoted, the patients seemed to have no doubt about the effectiveness of the transformation of themselves that accompanied the transformation of the object. I think there was a general assumption, based on previous experience, of the sympathy, understanding and receptivity of the analyst, but it is a feature of the projective processes manifested in these examples that they did not depend on concurrent evidence of the analyst's capacity or willingness to receive the projections.

Indeed, the noteworthy feature of these examples is the contrast between the picture we have of the analyst's actual mental state, and the way in which this is represented in the patient's phantasy. As Bion has pointed out, patients vary in the extent to which they are able to take 'realistic steps' to affect their object by projective identification, and vary in their capacity to recognise and respect the actual properties of the object. Thus with some patients, the omnipotent phantasy is likely to have little counterpart in reality. While Rosenfeld and Bion have made important contributions to our understanding of the impact of the patient's projections on the analyst, in the situations I have quoted, they both convey thoughtful, calm, benign attention, in marked contrast to the phantasy either of a persecutory object, or an analyst whose mind has been invaded and damaged. When Rosenfeld talked to his patient, in a clear, insightful and empathic way, taking the phantasy into account, but clearly demonstrating a state of affairs diametrically opposed to that which obtained in the patient's phantasy, the patient was relieved, and was able to recover some of his lost ego functions.

With my own patient, Mr A, I found myself interested in and concerned about the patient's experience and the properties with which I had temporarily been invested in the patient's mind. I did not actually feel uncertain or confused, and I was confident I was seeing the right patient at the right time. What my patient said did not, on this occasion, discomfort me. The other feature of this brief example is that when I did talk to the patient in a way that conveyed that I was neither confused nor particularly anxious, and gave him the impression that something was being understood, he was able to recall and integrate more of his own experiences. Later in the session he told me that during the holidays he had moved out of his office to a larger, more spacious office on a higher floor. The two people with whom he had shared the old office had been away, and when they returned they complained bitterly about the terrible mess he had left. Mr A said, indignantly, that there might have been a bit of untidiness: he had intended to clear it up, but he had been busy with other things. He went on to suggest that his colleagues were being unreasonable and neurotic, and he gave other examples of their childish behaviour. He began to sound like the confident and superior person in the larger office whom I had encountered at the start of the session.

What I think I had failed to question initially was why I should have felt so comfortable and secure, presented with the material at the start of the first session after a break. I suspect that I was, in part, enacting the object relationship that the patient subsequently made clearer to me. I was the confident, sane and sensible figure in a superior position, dealing with someone into whom almost all the disturbance and confusion had been projected. This projection and the slight enactment it gave rise to failed to disturb me, or even to alert me at the time, since my role as the unruffled observing analyst in the office above was congruent with a version of myself with which I was reasonably comfortable, at least for a while.

Reflecting on this material, what I also failed to recognise initially was the patient's unconscious communication of a bitter complaint about my responsibility for having left him with such a mess during the holiday, defensively claiming that I had intended to do something about it, but largely denying my responsibility for the disorder. As I will illustrate later, we have learnt not only to take notice of our feelings of discomfort as possible reflections of the patient's projective identification, but also to consider situations in which we find ourselves perhaps feeling a little too secure and comfortable, confident about where the pathology lies, and who is responsible for the mess. I think this example illustrates that there is in fact a complex relation between the projection into an object in phantasy (even in the absence of the actual object), and what happens as soon as the patient and analyst encounter one another, when quite subtle, non-omnipotent interactions begin to take place, usually based on unconscious projections into the analyst.

Of course, it is not difficult to see the advantages of projection into a hallucinatory, delusional or absent object. Since it is an omnipotent process, there is no doubt about the object's receptivity, and the consequent transformation (there also seem to be no problems about the corresponding introjection of the object's valuable properties). The patient is not confronted with the contrast between phantasy and reality, which is disturbing, nor with the differences between himself and his object.

What were the factors that allowed the more benign, integrative process, which Rosenfeld describes, to take place, albeit temporarily? How can a patient sometimes tolerate, and indeed feel greatly relieved by, being confronted with an analyst in a state quite discordant with their psychic reality at that moment? Why, on the other hand, do some patients feel driven to use other methods, more subtle or more violent, to involve the analyst through projective identification? While Bion's patient had split off and projected a dangerous persecutory version of the analyst into the hallucinatory object in the corner, he did at least have some conception of benign symbolic communication, which is implied in the belief that it was possible to paint a picture in the mind of a suitably receptive analyst. Other patients either seem to have no belief in this possibility, or cannot tolerate such a configuration. Bion (1959) has vividly described how the infant, confronted with what seems like an impenetrable object, is driven to attempt to project into such an object with more and more force. The early experience of such difficulties with the object's receptivity may drive the patient to involve the analyst in such a way that his mind is actually disturbed, or actually to force him to become compliant or persecutory. It is as if the patient has such doubts about the possibility either of symbolic communication or the object's receptivity to any form of projection that he cannot relent until he has evidence of the impact on the analyst's mind and body. If this consistently fails, confirming an early experience of an unavailable, hateful object, he may give up in despair.

We tend to assume that once the patient has felt understood, in the sense of some important part of him being accepted, he would be relieved by the contrast between the more sane and benign imago of the analyst and the archaic one projected into him (to use Strachey's [1934] terms). We sometimes assume that it is only the operation of the patient's envy that militates against this. However, it often seems that there is a different drive in operation, namely the pressure towards identity, which seems paradoxical and difficult to reconcile with the longing for a better, more constructive experience. It is as if the patient requires the analyst's experience or behaviour to correspond in some measure to his unconscious phantasy, and is unable to tolerate or make use of any discrepancy, however reassuring we might assume that to be. On the contrary, as Sandler and Sandler (Sandler, 1990; Sandler and Sandler, 1978) have pointed out, the patient's attempts to 'actualise' such phantasies can be regarded as a form of wish-fulfilment, serving a reassuring and gratifying function.

Joseph (1987) describes a session in which an analyst interpreted a deprived child's reaction to the imminent end of a Friday session. The analyst interpreted the child's urgent wish to make a candle as an expression of her desire to take a warm object away with her. The child screamed, 'Bastard! Take off your clothes and jump outside'. The analyst tried to interpret the child's feelings about being dropped and sent into the cold, but the child replied, 'Stop your talking, take off your clothes! You are cold. I'm not cold'. While the projection into the representation of the analyst leads to the child saying, 'You are cold. I'm not cold', this will not suffice for the child. Her non-delusional perception of the analyst as being relatively warm and comfortable drives her to try to force the analyst actually to take off her clothes, so that she would indeed be cold, and there would not be the immensely painful and disturbing discrepancy between the internal representation and the figure she encounters in the external world. This dramatic scenario is reproduced in more subtle ways with many of our patients.

I am suggesting this goes beyond and seems to conflict with the need to feel understood, or reassured about the capacity of the object to take in and to 'contain' the projections. The lack of this identity between the internal and external reality may not only stir up envy, or doubts about the object's receptivity, but create an alarming space in which thought and new knowledge and understanding might take place, but which many patients find intolerable.

Incidentally, I am assuming some familiarity with the way in which Rosenfeld and Bion have expanded and deepened our understanding of the use of projective identification as a means of communication and recognised the forceful or even violent use of projective identification in an attempt to get through to an impenetrable, rejecting object. Clinically, of course, the patient's use of more forceful projection may be driven by his experience of the analyst as a non-understanding, non-receptive figure, which the analyst may not perceive.

There have been important developments in our recognition and understanding not just of the ways in which the patient might need to project a feeling of confusion, inadequacy or excitement into the analyst, but the more complex and subtle ways in which the analyst is induced into states of mind, sometimes accompanied by various forms of enactment, which are relevant to the patient's early history, and his current anxieties, defences and desires. I want to consider what functions these interactions serve for the patient, and how he might succeed in involving the analyst. Sometimes the analyst will recognise that there is something slightly alien, disturbing, discordant with a view of himself that he can comfortably tolerate, and we have learnt to consider this state as a result of the patient's projective identification. This recognition can lead us to a better understanding of our own difficulties, as well as the important configurations in the patient's object relationships which are being lived out in the analytic situation. What writers such as Joseph and O'Shaughnessy (1992) have described are the difficulties in easily or quickly recognising the analyst's involvement resulting from the projective identification. On the contrary, the analyst may have the sort of comfortable, benign, dispassionate involvement I described at the beginning of the paper. What sometimes emerges is that this state represents the unconscious convergence of the patient's and the analyst's defensive needs and may militate against real progress.

Money-Kyrle (1956) has described the process taking place in the analyst as follows: 'As the patient speaks, the analyst will, as it were, become introjectively identified with him, and having understood him inside, will re-project him and interpret' (p. 361). When there are particular difficulties in understanding or helping the patient, two factors may contribute to this. Firstly, there is the patient's projection and disowning of unwanted aspects of himself. Secondly, when these projections correspond to aspects of the analyst himself that are unresolved and not understood, he may have difficulty in appropriately re-projecting the patient. If he then 'cannot tolerate the sense of being burdened with the patient as an irreparable or persecuting figure inside him, he is likely to resort to a defensive kind of re-projection that shuts out the patient and creates a further bar to understanding'. He makes the point that for some analysts – for example, those who most crave the reassurance of continuous success – the strain of not being able to understand or help the patient is felt more acutely than others. Money-Kyrle suggests that the extent to which an analyst is emotionally disturbed by periods of non–understanding will probably depend, in the first instance, on another factor: the severity of his own superego. If our superego is predominantly friendly and helpful, we can tolerate our own limitations without undue distress, and, being undisturbed, will be the more likely to regain contact quickly with the patient. But if it is severe, we may become conscious of a sense of failure as the expression of an unconscious persecutory or depressive guilt. Or, as a defence against such feelings, we may blame the patient.

While I find Money-Kyrle's descriptions familiar and convincing, what we have become more aware of is that when the analyst is confronted with the anxieties and strain he describes, he may be unconsciously drawn to diminish them by enacting a complex object relationship with the patient that initially serves to reassure both. I believe this is achieved by the analyst striving to create a closer correspondence between a relatively comfortable or gratifying internal representation of himself and the way in which he experiences and interprets the external situation. Indeed, while I think Money-Kyrle is describing the process by which the analyst disentangles himself from the patient's projection in order to understand and communicate, the re-projection he describes may actually be a form of enactment by which the analyst deals with an uncomfortable version of his relationship with the patient. To return for a moment to Rosenfeld's paper describing his work with the psychotic patient, which I quoted at the beginning:

One of the difficulties of working through such situations in the analysis is the tendency to endless repetition, in spite of [the patient's] understanding that very useful analytic work was being done. It is important in dealing with patients and processes of this kind to accept that much of the repetition is inevitable. The acceptance by the analyst of the patient's processes being re-enacted in the transference helps the patient to feel that the self, which is constantly split off and projected into the analyst, is acceptable and not so damaging as feared.

(Rosenfeld, 1987c, p. 180)

Why does Rosenfeld address his colleagues in this way? I think the point he is making is that unless the analyst recognises the fact of and perhaps even the necessity for the repetition and re-enactment, he may become disheartened, confused or resentful. In other words, far from being able to feel reasonably confident in the representation of himself as a helpful, effective, patient analyst, he might be burdened by an intolerable version of himself that he may then try to deal with very concretely. This could be enacted by the analyst blaming or accusing the patient in a hostile and critical way, entering into a defensive collusive arrangement, or by terminating the treatment in despair.

What I am thus suggesting is that what is projected is not primarily a part of the patient, but a phantasy of an object relationship. It is this that impinges upon the analyst, and may allow him to remain reasonably comfortable, or may disturb him and incline him to enact. This enactment is sometimes congruent with the phantasy that has been projected, so that the analyst becomes a little too compliant or too harsh. On the other hand, the enactment might represent the analyst's attempt at restoring a less disturbing phantasy to the fore (for example, having to distance himself consciously or unconsciously from an impotent or sadistic archaic figure). Finally, we must also be aware that the impulse towards enactment may reflect unresolved aspects of the analyst's own pathological internal object relations.

I believe some of these issues are addressed by O'Shaughnessy (1992) with great clarity and insight. She describes how a patient initially drew her into making denuded, un-disturbing interpretations, and offering what seemed like reasonable links with the patient's history. Thus, it seems, the analyst initially felt reasonably comfortable with her role and functions. After a period of time, however, she became uneasy and dissatisfied with such interpretations, which felt inauthentic, and which did not seem to promote any change. The insight, and work involved in the recognition of something in the patient's limited and over-close relationship with her, and her own denuded functioning with the patient, which needed exploration and thought, led, I believe, to a crucial transformation in the analyst's representation of herself, and consequently in her ability to function. There is a convergence between the internal representation of herself as a thoughtful, reparative figure and the person who has now been able to recognise the degree of acting out that inevitably occurs, and this can be used to further understanding. This shift in internal perspective promotes the change from the situation in which the analyst is unwittingly involved in the enactment of the patient's problems, to the emergence of the potential for containment and transformation by the analyst, reflected in a shift in the style and content of the interpretations.

What O'Shaughnessy was then able to recognise was the function this over-close, secluded and denuded relationship served for the patient. The fact that the patient made a refuge of symmetry and over-closeness suggested that she was afraid of differences and distance between herself and her objects. The placation between analyst and patient was necessary because the patient feared either too intense erotic involvement or violence between them. I assume she had unconsciously evoked corresponding versions of these disturbing phantasies in the analyst's mind, which resulted in her functioning in the way she initially described. O'Shaughnessy describes how, in sessions when acute anxiety threatened, the patient worked to rebuild her refuge, subtly and powerfully controlling the analyst to be over-close and to operate within its limits.

Thus, at the beginning of the analysis, the patient transferred her highly restricted object relations into the analytic situation. She must have communicated with words and non-verbal projections her intense anxieties about a fuller and freer object relationship, with the terrifying erotic and violent phantasies associated with this.

I believe the analyst's anxieties about being experienced both by the patient and herself, in these disturbing and destructive roles, led her to function in the way the patient apparently required. While this may have served as a necessary temporary refuge at the start of the analysis, the analyst subsequently felt uneasy and dissatisfied with her role, and was then able to think about it in a different way.

I think the patient always finds this shift very threatening – it creates an asymmetry, and may arouse envy and hatred, with powerful attempts to restore the status quo ante. This may be successful if the analyst cannot tolerate the uncertainty, anxiety and guilt associated with the emergent phantasies of the relationship as a frightening, disappointing and destructive one, and we sometimes need the internal or external support of colleagues to sustain our belief in what we are attempting to do.

Meltzer describes a somewhat similar dynamic in relation to a group of disturbed patients who use extensive projective identification, which results in a compliant, pseudomature personality:

> the pressure on the analyst to join in the idealization of the pseudo-maturity [is] . . . great, and the underlying threats of psychosis and suicide so covertly communicated . . . the countertransference position is extremely difficult and in every way repeats the dilemma of the parents, who found themselves with a 'model' child, so long as they abstained from being distinctly parental, either in the form of authority, teaching, or opposition to the relatively modest claims for privileges beyond those to which the child's age and accomplishments could reasonably entitle it.
>
> (Meltzer, 1966, pp. 339–340)

The parental figure is thus faced either with the phantasy of being helplessly controlled, or the phantasy of driving the child into madness or suicide.

In the final part of this paper, I should like to illustrate in more detail first the way in which I believe a patient was able to use projection into the internal representation of the analyst (in his absence), to free herself from anxiety, whereas in the subsequent analytic sessions she needed to involve the analyst in different ways. I believe she achieved this through her projection of phantasies of disturbing object relations that were not only reflected in her verbal communications, but also partially enacted by her in the sessions. I suspect that if the analyst is receptive to the patient's projections, the impact of the patient's disturbing unconscious phantasies that concern the nature of his relationship with the patient inevitably touch on the analyst's own anxieties. This may evoke forms of projection and enactment by the analyst, in an attempt at restoring an internal equilibrium, of which the analyst may initially be unaware. The difficult and often painful task for the analyst is to recognise the subtle and complex enactments he is inevitably drawn into with his patient, and to work to find a domain for understanding and thought outside the narrow and repetitive confines unconsciously demanded by the patient, and sometimes by his own anxieties and needs. While the achievement of real psychic change is dependent on this process, it is threatening for the patient and liable to mobilise further defensive procedures.

The patient I want to describe is a single woman, who has been in analysis for several years. She arrived on a Monday morning and after a silence told me she was very involved in something that had occurred on Saturday, and which she hadn't thought about since – not until she was actually here. A friend, who works as a psycho-therapist, told her about a young male supervisee who confessed to her that he had seduced one of his patients. My patient's friend told her not to tell anyone, and as soon as she said that my patient immediately thought of me. My patient proceeded to give some details of the complicated connections between therapists, supervisors and the patient involved. She seemed very concerned about who discussed what with whom, and commented on how incestuous it all seemed. She added that there was something almost sinister about all these people knowing about it. Then, after a silence she said, 'thinking about it here, I was wondering why it should come to my mind here. I feel reasonably calm about it, it doesn't make me want to curl up in horror. I feel sufficiently removed from it, otherwise it would be horrific'.

There was a tense and expectant silence, and I felt aware of a pressure to respond quickly to what she had brought. When I did not do so, she commented that the silence seemed rather ominous.

When, on the Saturday, my patient was confronted with the disturbing image of a therapist's incestuous involvement with his patient, and told not to tell anyone, I was conjured up in her mind, and I believe she projected the knowledge, the anxiety and disturbance into me. It was then not something she had in mind to tell me about – on the contrary, it had become unavailable to her until she actually encountered me on Monday. I suggest we are thus dealing not with ordinary thinking or communication but rather with the omnipotent projection in phantasy not only of mental contents but also of the capacity to think about them. Since the process is an omnipotent one, the patient does not need to use symbolic means of communication. In this case the phantasy involves an object immediately receptive to the patient's projections, and apparently neither disturbed by them, nor changed into something threatening. Involving the object in this way seems to have succeeded in completely freeing the patient of anxiety and discomfort.

When she encountered me at the beginning of the session on Monday, and became aware that in reality I did not have possession of what she had got rid of, she recovered that part of her mind, and its contents, which had in phantasy been projected. She was then driven to use verbal and non-verbal communication in a non-omnipotent way, apparently in order to achieve the same outcome. While telling me about all the incestuous connections between therapists, supervisors and patients, it was striking that my patient wondered why all of this should come into her mind while she was with me, apparently failing to make the link between the story she reported and the phantasies connected with her own relationship with her analyst. I believe that by the combination of conscious and unconscious actions involved in this procedure, the patient was able both to communicate with and to 'nudge' the analyst into thinking about and taking responsibility for the thoughts, phantasies and impulses towards action that threatened her.

The point I wish to emphasise is that the projective mechanisms served several functions. Firstly, they evidently allowed the patient to disavow the disturbing or potentially disturbing responses to what her friend had elicited. Secondly, they involved the analyst in the sense that it was now his function to make the connections, and think about the significance of what she had communicated. Thirdly, I hope to illustrate the way in which they served to draw the analyst into the partial enactment of some of the underlying phantasies that had been elicited, which had to be dealt with by the patient, in spite of the analyst's conscious attempts to avoid such an enactment, and to find a working position with which he could feel reasonably comfortable.

In the session, I was made aware of the obvious role I was expected to play by the palpable pressure to respond quickly to what she had brought, and make some half-expected comment or interpretation. My long experience with this patient suggested that if I had complied, and directly addressed the material she had brought, offering some rather obvious answers to why it should come to her mind in the room with her analyst, there were a limited number of repetitive, and unproductive scenarios.

126

The first, and most common one, involved the patient relaxing and withdrawing, re-enacting with me the procedure that had taken place on Saturday when her friend had spoken to her, making it clear that the difficult and potentially disturbing material was no longer in her possession, but in mine. The second involved a less complete projection, in which the patient retained some contact with what had been projected, but resisted the dangerous prospect of thinking for herself about these issues, insisting that it was my function to do so. The third scenario was one in which my interpretations were themselves concretely experienced as threatening and demanding intrusions. In the session I have described, I was not aware of being disturbed by the contents of the patient's material, but I was troubled and disheartened by the prospect of enacting one of these repetitive and unproductive roles with her. However, when I remained silent for a while, attempting to find a way of understanding and approaching the patient, my silence nevertheless evoked the patient's phantasy of a disturbing archaic object relationship, in which she was involved with a threatening, 'ominous' figure, filled with unspoken, alarming things, potentially intrusive and demanding.

I believe she had partially re-created an important archaic object relationship through the interaction of two powerful factors. Firstly, the phantasised projection into the analyst of some of these archaic qualities and functions. Secondly, by communicating and behaving in the way she had, she was indeed faced with an analyst whose mind was filled with thoughts about what she had told him, who did indeed want something from her, and might make difficult and 'intrusive' demands on her. When these expectations and experiences were coloured by the qualities projected into them, the patient was indeed living out an archaic, familiar object relationship.

In this session, and those that followed, I felt the need to try and find a way of working that I hoped would partially avoid the repetitive interactions I have described. I remained silent at times, trying to understand what was taking place, or made comments on what I thought the patient was doing with me, or expecting of me. I also attempted to get the patient to explore what was making her so uncomfortable, and some of the links between her material, her family history, and the analytical situation that I thought were available to her. I was made aware of the threat my efforts posed to the patient's equilibrium, and her extreme reluctance to allow either of us to escape from familiar interactions that appeared, paradoxically, to be necessary and reassuring for her. I felt subjected to powerful pressure either to allow myself to be used in such a way that I had to take responsibility for the disturbing material that the patient projected, or to enact some elements of the phantasy of a forceful seductive or intrusive relationship. I was thus confronted with painful and unwelcome representations of my role in relation to my patient, and continued to struggle to find an approach that I felt might be more constructive, and with which I could be more comfortable.

There is always the idea that by remaining more silent, or speaking more, understanding the situation in a different way, taking a different tack, one can free oneself from such repetitive and unproductive inter-actions. Sometimes this is manifested in the thought (held by the analyst, or the patient, or both) that if the analyst changed, or were a different kind of analyst, these problems would not arise. Of course, these considerations have to be taken seriously, and will often have some element of truth. However, for much of the time in dealing with my patient, I came to believe that whatever I said or did was liable to be experienced in accordance with the limited, archaic phantasies I have briefly indicated, and that the repetitive living-out of these phantasies in the sessions served important and reassuring functions for the patient. There were brief periods of thoughtful reflection that were a relief to me, as I felt I could regain a sense of my proper function. However, it was evidently painful and difficult for the patient to be anywhere outside the familiar and reassuring enactments, and she would quickly withdraw again, or re-evoke the excited provocative relationship in which, paradoxically, she seemed to feel safer.

For example, after a period of difficult work the patient said, thoughtfully, 'I can see . . . both sides . . . in what has been going on. I can appreciate you want me to . . . look rather more closely at the things that have come up. After all, just putting them out in an extremely cautious way as "ideas" doesn't get me any further'. Her voice then became firmer and more excited: 'At the same time it seems remarkable to me that I'm even prepared to mention these things. In fact I'm amazed. I must feel very confident that I am not going to be pushed into anything more'. Her excitement escalated, and she repeated how extraordinary it was that she had said as much as she had, what a risk she had taken that I would seize on the oppor-tunity. She said that normally her main concern was to avoid saying things if she could foresee some sort of opening she might give me, so she has to make sure this doesn't occur.

Thus, having briefly and uncomfortably acknowledged the existence of an analyst who was actually trying to help her, and the recognition of the defensive processes she was so persistently caught up in, she moved in to a state of erotised excitement that gripped her for much of the rest of the session. The patient thus seemed compulsively driven to involve me in interactions in which she either experienced a tantalising, ominous withholding or exciting demanding sexual intrusion. These were, of course, aspects of the powerful oedipal configuration that had been evoked in her mind by the episode her friend had originally reported to her, and which had important links with her early history.

While it is familiar to us, I find that the recurrent pressure on the analyst to join the patient in the partial enactment of archaic, often disturbed and disturbing object relationships is one of the most interesting and puzzling phenomena we encounter. With my patient, what functions did it serve to involve me not as a helpful benign figure, but a version of a disturbing archaic one? I suspect there are many answers to this. This interaction frees the patient from knowledge of and responsibility for her own impulses and phantasies: she is predominantly a helpless victim. It was very evident in the sessions that it provided her with a degree of gratification and excitement. It may have served as a means of making me recognise and understand aspects of her history, or her inner life, which I had thus far failed to address, although I am uncertain about suggesting this as her motive. What I want to add is the way in which it seems to serve a reassuring function if what is enacted in the external world corresponds in some measure with an object relationship that is unconsciously present. The alternative, when she is confronted with the discrepancy between the two, is painful and threatening.

From the analyst's point of view, I suspect that if he is receptive to the patient's projections, the phantasies of archaic object relationships must inevitably resonate with the analyst's own unconscious needs and anxieties. If these relate too closely to areas of conflict that remain largely unresolved, there are dangers that the analyst will be driven into forms of enactment that either gratify some mutual needs or defend him against such gratification. Hoffman points out:

Because the analyst is human, he is likely to have in his repertoire a blueprint for approximately the emotional response that the patient's transference dictates and that response is likely to be elicited, whether

129

consciously or unconsciously . . . Ideally this response serves as a
key – perhaps the best key the analyst has – to the nature of the
interpersonal scene that the patient is driven by transference to
create.

(Hoffman, 1983, p. 413)

As Joseph (1987, 1988), O'Shaughnessy (1992) and Carpy (1989)
have suggested, we may have to recognise that a degree of enactment
is almost inevitable; part of a continuing process that the analyst can
come to recognise, temporarily extricate himself from, and use to
further his understanding. Indeed, in the clinical situation I have just
described, it seemed important to recognise the pressure towards
enactment within the patient, and the corresponding pressures felt by
the analyst. The recognition of the compulsive and repetitive nature
of these interactions may have important consequences. As Rosenfeld
and O'Shaughnessy have indicated, it may allow the analyst to
recover some sense of his own proper function. This diminishes the
discrepancy between his own phantasies of his role and what is manifested in the analytical situation. If the analyst is also more able to
tolerate whatever discrepancies exist, he will be less driven to use
projective mechanisms and the forms of enactment I have been
describing. In the space thus created, he may be able to think differently about his patient.

In this chapter I have tried to emphasise that what is projected into
the analyst is a phantasy of an object relationship that evokes not only
thoughts and feelings, but also propensities towards action. From the
patient's point of view, the projections represent an attempt to reduce
the discrepancy between the phantasy of some archaic object relationship and what the patient experiences in the analytical situation.
For the analyst too, there are impulses to function in ways that lead
to a greater correspondence with some needed or desired phantasies.
The interaction between the patient's and the analyst's needs may
lead to the repetitive enactment of the painful and disturbing kind
that I have described. It may be very difficult for the analyst to extricate himself (or his patient) from this unproductive situation and
recover his capacity for reflective thought, at least for a while.

As I have indicated, the difficulty is compounded when the projection into the analyst leads to subtle or overt enactments that do not
initially disturb the analyst, but on the contrary constitute a comfortable collusive arrangement, in which the analyst feels his role is

congruent with some internal phantasy. It may be difficult to recognise the defensive function this interaction serves both for the patient and the analyst and the more disturbing unconscious phantasies it defends against.

The analyst's temporary and partial recovery of his capacity for reflective thought rather than action is crucial for the survival of his analytical role. The analyst may not only feel temporarily freed from the tyranny of repetitive enactments and modes of thought himself, but he may believe in the possibility of freeing his patient, in time. However, such moves are likely to provoke pain and disturbance in the patient, who finds the unfamiliar space in which thought can take place frightening and hateful.

8

Who's who?

Notes on pathological identifications[36]

Ignes Sodré

Freud's (1917) discovery, in 'Mourning and melancholia', of the process through which the ego unconsciously identifies with the intro-jected bad object (the rejecting loved object) thus becoming a victim of its own superego, was one of the most important breakthroughs in psychoanalysis: perhaps as important as the discovery of the meaning of dreams and of the Oedipus complex. The idea that when individ-uals feel 'I am the worst person in the world', they may in fact be unconsciously accusing somebody else whose victim they feel they are, but who, through a pathological process of introjection and iden-tification, they have 'become', was indeed a revolutionary one, and one which is still of tremendous clinical importance for us today.

Freud (1917) describes the establishing of what he calls a narcis-sistic identification with the abandoned object in two ways: as a passive taking in of the object – 'thus the shadow of the object fell upon the ego' (p. 249) – and as an active process in which 'the ego wants to incorporate this object into itself, and, in accordance with the oral or cannibalistic phase of libidinal development in which it is, it wants to do so by devouring it' (p. 249). He also describes the ego as being overwhelmed by the object. It would seem then that there

36 This chapter reproduces the text of Sodré, I. (2004). Who's who? Notes on pathological identifications. In E. Hargreaves and A. Varchevker (Eds.), *In Pursuit of Psychic Change: The Betty Joseph Workshop*. London: Brunner-Routledge, pp. 53–68.

is no differentiation between self and object at that point – the intro-jected object occupies the entire ego – except of course that this is not entirely true, since the ego has undergone a 'cleavage' and some of it has now become the 'special agency' that judges it (the ego who has become the object) so harshly. As we know, the superego was subsequently also seen by Freud as the product of introjections. In psychoanalytic theory, introjections leading to identifications with primary objects very soon became linked with normal development; but the kind of identification described in 'Mourning and melancholia' is a massive, pathological one, characterised by an extraordi-nary clinical event: the subject seems to have 'become' the object.

In his paper 'On the psychopathology of narcissism' Rosenfeld (1964b) stated:

> Identification is an important factor in narcissistic object relations. It may take place by introjection or by projection. When the object is omnipotently incorporated, the self becomes so identified with the incorporated object that all separate identity or any boundary between self and object is denied. In projective identifi-cation parts of the self omnipotently enter an object, for example, the mother, to take over certain qualities which would be experi-enced as desirable, and therefore claim to be the object or part-object. Identification by introjection and by projection usually occur simultaneously.
>
> (Rosenfeld, 1964b, p. 170)

This is an extremely clear differentiation between two modes of identification; the first description corresponds to Freud's mechanism in melancholia, the second follows Klein's (1946) discovery of the mechanism of projective identification. But I think it is worth noticing that Freud's description of the more active (cannibalistic) form of incorporation is in fact similar to the description of projec-tive identification. Rosenfeld (1964b) stressed the omnipotent quality of this type of projective identification; Freud had, as we know, pointed out the hidden mania implied in melancholia. It seems to me that some states of massive projective identification are like a manic version of what Freud described as the melancholic's narcissistic identification with the (now externally annihilated) object.

In this chapter I shall focus mainly on the interaction of projections, introjections and manic mechanisms in the creation and perpetuation

133

of those states of pathological identification which are usually described as 'the subject is in massive projective identification with the object', as opposed to states where the subject 'gets rid of something' or 'does something to the object' by the use of projective identification. You will have gathered from my title that I am concerned with exploring extreme shifts in a person's sense of identity. I will bring clinical examples to illustrate both the question of the loss of a sense of identity and the shift into a different identity through the use of excessive introjective and projective identification.

The sense of identity stems simultaneously from the differentiation of the self from its objects and from various identifications with different aspects of the objects. All object relations depend on the capacity to remain oneself while being able to shift temporarily into the other's point of view. Any meaningful interchange between two people involves of necessity an intricate process of projections, introjections and identifications. 'Projective identification' is an umbrella term which includes many different processes involving the operation of both projection and introjection; it is used to describe normal modes of communication as well as extremely pathological manoeuvres and even permanent pathological states which are at the root of some character traits.

One way of differentiating the complex processes involved in the various aspects of what is called 'projective identification' from 'classical' projection is that projective identification takes place in an object relationship and, therefore, necessarily affects both subject and object (in phantasy, but often in external reality too), whereas it should be at least possible, in theory, to conceive of projection as not necessarily related to a specific object into which something is being projected. But having said that, I must confess that I find it difficult to imagine a projection into outer space, or into something inanimate or abstract, without imagining too that whatever has been projected into has become personified in some way.

Projective identification as a defence mechanism has as its primary aim the wish to get rid of a particular experience; I do not think it is true to say that what characterises projective identification is that the subject (the 'projector', as it were) maintains links with the part of the self that is now felt to be inside the 'object, the 'receptor' (see for instance Ogden's [1979] discussion). This may occur, but the hallmark of projective identification – and especially of pathological projective identification – is the wish to sever contact with something that provokes pain, fear, discomfort; the word 'identification' should, in this particular instance, refer to the object's identification (in the subject's mind) with the projected experience, and not to the subject's identification with the object: as Sandler (1987b) clearly pointed out, the self wants to dis-identify with that which is projected.

Projective identification, by definition, affects the sense of self, since it involves getting rid of aspects of the personality through splitting them off and locating them in the object, so that in the subject's phantasy the identities of both subject and object are affected. It also may involve acquiring aspects of the object, in which case the identities are further modified. In her seminal papers where she first discovered and conceptualised projective identification, Klein (1946, 1955) described both archaic processes furthering communication and development (a concept developed and expanded by Bion [1962a] in his theory of the container) and a pathological process leading to loss of contact with the self and aiming at omnipotent control of the object. Massive projective identification with the object implies a phantasy of 'becoming' the object or a particular aspect or version of the object (and here the word identification refers also to the subject's identification with aspects of the object) whereas the object 'becomes' the self, or personifies an unbearable aspect of the self (a process first described by Anna Freud [1936] as 'identification with the aggressor'). I will suggest that such states of pathological identification imply the excessive use not only of violent projections but also of concrete, pathological introjections and that this mode of functioning also relies for its 'success' on the massive use of manic defences.

Excessive use of projective identification can lead, on the one hand, to confusion and loss of a firm sense of self and, on the other, to an extreme rigidity in character, where artificial new boundaries are created between subject and object, but are then tenaciously adhered to. In this case, the new boundaries between what is 'me' and what is 'you' have to be maintained as a fortress against the threat of the return of the split-off projected parts of the self, which results not in confusion but in its extreme opposite, in an absolute certainty which has to be maintained at all costs, to the impoverishment of the personality and serious disturbance in the capacity for object relations. Arrogance as a character trait is, I think, a good example of this state of affairs; it is essentially a state of permanent projective identification with an idealised bad object (I will explain what I mean by this later).

Looking rather schematically into what happens in projective identification, one could say that from the point of view of the 'projector',
a part of the self becomes in phantasy a part of the object through a
complicated manoeuvre which, for the sake of simplicity, we could
temporarily call 'projective dis-identification'; the projector is not
consciously aware of that aspect of the self, since he believes that it
belongs to the object. This process, which happens in unconscious
phantasy, can of course have an effect on the object – the 'receptor'
– in external reality (Sandler describes this as the 'actualisation' of the
projective identification, whereas Spillius uses the term 'evocative').
If this is the case then, from the point of view of the 'receptor', there
is an intrusion of something foreign into the self which causes a partial
– or total – 'forced introjective identification'.

What the outcome of this situation will be will depend on the degree
of intrusiveness and violence of the projection matched up with the
'receptor's' capacity (or lack thereof) to introject and partially identify
with what has been introjected without losing the boundaries of the
self. In other words a helpful 'receptor' should be able to function as a
container (Bion) who can simultaneously experience what it is like to
feel what the other person feels (for instance, a mother who can
empathise with her baby) through introjecting what is being projected
as the experience of an object. This experience is, in the inner world,
incorporated into the picture of the internal object and not into that of
the self. (It is obvious that if a mother felt totally identified with her
distressed baby she would not be able to help the baby. For example,
she has to take in her baby's fear of not surviving and to be able partially,
and temporarily, also to fear for its survival. But if she becomes so
persecuted and overwhelmed by the baby's terrified crying to the point
of feeling, 'I will not survive', then she will 'be' the baby and the baby
will 'be' a persecutor; more like a bad mother to her. This then might
lead to her emotionally abandoning or even attacking the baby.)

The central characteristic of the use of 'projective identification' is
the creation in the subject of a state of mind in which the boundaries
between self and object have shifted. This state can be more or less
flexible, temporary or permanent. The motives for such unconscious
manoeuvres are manifold, from the need to maintain psychic equilibrium and avoid pain, to the more intrusive ones of robbing and
depleting the object. The object's perception of and method of
dealing with what is being projected will also affect the development
of the object relationship that is taking place at that moment.

136

Even though 'projective identification' is used to describe normal as well as pathological processes, I think that we tend to think of projective processes as more pathological than introjective ones. When we think of somebody being identified with somebody else, we tend to think rather loosely of introjective identification as healthier than projective identification. We visualise two very different object relationships: one in which the self receives something from the object, and the other in which there is massive intrusion into the object. And of course emotional development does depend essentially on taking in from our objects and identifying with them. But we can excessively polarise these different modes, seeing one as a peaceful welcoming of the object into the inner world, and the other as the warlike invasion of the object. In fact, as we know, there is pathological introjection as much as pathological projection. Furthermore, projection and introjection are psychic mechanisms based on phantasies which are felt to have the power of concrete actions, and phantasies are totally coloured by affect and motive. If identification is based on the wish to become the object (and therefore to rob the object of its identity), as opposed to the wish to be like the object, therefore allowing the object to continue existing with its identity preserved – then this is pathological and destructive. And although it is important in analysis to investigate the unconscious phantasy manoeuvres used to achieve this taking over of the object – to differentiate what happens through concrete introjection from what happens through intrusive massive projection – the fundamental point is that the integrity of the object has been damaged or destroyed in this process. We are talking here of an 'imperialist' attitude towards the object and in this universe the different phantasies and mechanisms employed are simply tactical manoeuvres to defeat the enemy.

Pathological introjective identification implies a phantasy of concretely taking something in, whereas a normal identification with an internal object presupposes a capacity to introject symbolically while allowing the object to retain its separate identity. The same is true of normal projection, of course: when the ego is functioning in a depressive position mode, symbolic projection into the other's mind – being able to put oneself imaginatively in the other's place – helps us to understand who the other person is.

In his paper 'Remarks on the relation of male homosexuality to paranoia, paranoid anxiety and narcissism' Rosenfeld (1949) uses a very interesting dream from his patient to illustrate the origin of projective identification. I will quote it here because it is such a clear example of two points I want to stress: first, the fact that not only affects and parts of the personality are projected, but also modes of functioning; and second, the role of wholesale, concrete introjection of the object in states of pathological, massive identification.

Rosenfeld describes this patient as consciously afraid that the analyst will become too interested in him; he is therefore often silent when he has thoughts that he thinks are of special interest to the analyst.

> Dream: He saw a famous surgeon operating on a patient, who observed with great admiration the skill displayed by the surgeon, who seemed intensely concentrated on his work. Suddenly the surgeon lost his balance and fell right inside the patient, with whom he got so entangled that he could scarcely manage to free himself. He nearly choked, and only by administering an oxygen apparatus could he manage to revive himself.

Rosenfeld comments that the patient had paranoid fears of being controlled by the analyst from inside and that later on in the analysis he became more aware of his fear of falling inside the analyst and becoming entangled inside him.

This dream is a very striking example of how the whole process of projective identification is itself projected. The surgeon/analyst in the dream relates to the patient via intrusive projective identification: such is his curiosity that he gets concretely inside his patient. What is projected is not only curiosity but also a mode of functioning. You could say that this happens because this is the only mode of relating that the patient knows. This is a patient who thinks very concretely; but the fact that the surgeon 'administers to himself an oxygen apparatus' seems to me to indicate that the patient thinks that the analyst can save his own life – his separate identity – by recovering his capacity to function as an analyst. I think the fact that the word 'apparatus' appears in the dream text, rather than simply 'oxygen', reinforces this idea. I suspect that 'administering an oxygen apparatus' stands for a capacity of the analyst's that the patient has, in phantasy, robbed him of through the projection of his all encompassing infantile curiosity. In the dream this capacity is now available for reintegration into the patient's picture of the analyst. (In the patient's inner world, the analyst 'cures' himself by re-establishing himself as the analyst, with a separate identity and capacities.) This suggests that this patient is therefore capable of conceiving of such a function. I imagine also that this patient has already begun to find out, in his analysis, that massive projective identification is not a great method through which to live one's life! I think this dream is a rather beautiful metaphor for moments when the analyst feels entirely at the mercy of violent projections and then recovers his capacity to function.

I also wanted to use this dream to illustrate something else. What we have here is the patient ending up with the analyst in his belly, as opposed to ending up inside the analyst. He has power over the analyst because the analyst is inside him, not him inside the analyst. In other words, not only has he projected a whole way of functioning into the analyst, but also he has swallowed the analyst: a pathological massive introjection. There is an expression in Portuguese to describe somebody who feels he is superior to everybody else: 'He thinks he's got the king in his belly'. (So, through swallowing the king, he is superior even to the king.) An extremely complex interplay between projections and introjections takes place continuously to perpetuate this peculiar state of affairs, but I think it may be useful when describing states of massive projective identification – 'becoming' the object – to picture not only the patient inside the analyst (following Klein's description of the infantile impulses to invade the mother) but also the patient with the analyst inside (related to phantasies of primitive oral incorporation of the mother). Triumph in this case comes from having swallowed the whole object, thus totally controlling and owning its power and strength. Manic mechanisms are involved in this process by which the self becomes so much bigger than the object and so much more powerful.

I hope to illustrate with the following clinical example the interplay of projective and introjective mechanisms in massive projective identification, as well as the manic flavour of such operations.

Mr A: 'becoming' the idealised bad object

A narcissistic young man comes into the session and looks at me more closely than usual, staring intensely into my eyes in a way that feels uncomfortable, intrusive. He lies on the couch and, with a rather superior tone of voice, tells me that he can clearly see that I must be quite shortsighted, I have that kind of unfocused look in my eyes. It is ridiculous that I do not wear glasses but I am obviously too vain to do so. I say rather hesitantly that perhaps there is a reason why he feels today that I cannot see him properly and I get an absolutely furious, indignant and self-righteous response: I want everything to be his problem, I don't want to admit to my own failures, and I clearly suffer from an inferiority complex about my eyesight. He adds that he has had his eyes tested and has 100 per cent vision.

I think a very complex process of projections, introjections and identifications has occurred to produce this state of affairs and I will now look in detail into what I think may have happened.

Something has obviously taken place that is connected to vision, specifically to do with seeing into the other person. He may have felt misunderstood in the previous session but I am more inclined to think that he felt understood in a way that was threatening to him. My capacity to see inside him made him too anxious, lest insight would threaten his pathological, but desperately needed, psychic equilibrium (Joseph, 1989b) or, perhaps, because he feels envious when he thinks I have better 'eyes' than he – probably both. I do not know what has happened, but I ask you to accept this as a working hypothesis so that this can be used as an example of the kind of process that can take place.

What gives him the absolute certainty that I am shortsighted and pathologically vain (preferring not to see than to wear glasses) is, I suspect, a projection of his fear of insight and of his narcissism. This is one aspect of his use of projective identification whereby I, his object, am now identified with unwanted aspects of himself. From his point of view, though, this could also be described as projective dis–identification, since through this process he loses part of his identity. He has lost contact with his narcissistic hurt, his fear of being inferior and despised, etc.

Another aspect of projective identification, the phantasy of intrusively being able to get inside the object – is illustrated by his omnisciently 'knowing' what is in my mind: he 'knows' that I cannot see properly and he also 'knows' that this makes me feel inferior to him.

There is something else going on though, which I think has to do with pathological introjection rather than projection. How has he acquired these omniscient (100 per cent vision) malevolent eyes and whose eyes are they? I suggest that these were originally my perceptive and therefore threatening analytic eyes, inflated by idealisation. I am shortsighted not only because I now contain the projection of his lack of insight – and his narcissistic inability to see as far as the other person – but also that my eyes that could see into him have been concretely incorporated by him. In this defective, concrete introjection, if he has the 'analyst's eyes', then I obviously do not have them any more. In other words, if we assume that I made some interpretation yesterday that revealed something to him that he had not been able to see before, and by interpreting made him aware that I could 'see' (had good 'eyesight' and was interested in him), he perhaps did not take this in a healthy introjective way which would make it possible for both of us to see, but instead took over my function concretely. He acquired my capacity to describe some aspect of himself or some situation in his internal world, rather than taking in my description of what I thought I was observing in him, so that the interpretation couldn't be used to further his capacity to think about himself. Instead, he became the Me who can see into somebody else's mind.

(In normal identification, I introject your perceptive eyes, they are now felt to be symbolically in my mind and, through identification, I may then be able to see like you see, but you remain the owner of your eyes. And since this is a benign interchange, the relationship remains one of mutual co-operation. In pathological identification, not only do I become the sole possessor of the eyes because of a failure in symbolisation, but also the relationship is now dominated by a struggle for power in which omniscient knowledge acts as a barrier against insight.)

The person who arrives in the consulting room is now an 'analyst' (or rather, a caricature of one) whose primary concern is to look inside the other's mind and reveal what can be seen there to a disturbed 'patient' me, but in a cruel, humiliating way.

This is then what is described as 'being in massive projective identification with' the object. This cruel, self-righteous, omniscient person lying on my couch is my patient in a state of total projective identification with . . . me! A rather distorted (I hope!) version of his analyst. And this is what it feels like to be seen through 'my' eyes, which are now my patient's property: it is to be seen as inferior, vain, blind. If this is what has happened, then the analyst in my patient's mind is definitely a bad object and a very powerful one. I suggest that this particular brand of badness – cruel omniscience – is the product of an idealisation of a hated but also envied capacity of the object. The feared perceptive eyes are certainly a very desirable attribute, which is why they get stolen. No shame or guilt are apparent in this process, only manic triumph.

In other sessions, the process may happen slightly differently. An object with helpful eyes may be temporarily introjected – sometimes he can feel helped by an interpretation and feel some relief at being understood – but then the separation at the end of the session may cause an upsurge of hostility due to the pain of jealousy or envy or to an increase in persecutory anxiety. In his phantasy, if he takes in what I give him he will lose his defences, will become dangerously dependent, etc. (In this case there would be hostile projections into the internal object and the perceptive eyes, now transformed into cruel eyes, have to be stolen as if they were a weapon to be stolen from an enemy.)

Miss B: the loss of parts of the self

I will now bring an example from a patient who can get into massive states of projective identification with a bad object, but who does so much more temporarily. She is a very fragile, borderline young woman, whose identifications shift rather quickly, producing a sense of fragmentation and of loss of a sense of identity (I am very grateful to Richard Rusbridger for allowing me to use his clinical material).

The previous weekend had been extremely distressing for Miss B. Her boyfriend, C, a pop star musician, had been on tour around the country for several weeks and was coming back to visit her. She had been waiting for his arrival in an eager but also rather desperate mood. He arrived in a manic state, very much the star, made absolutely no emotional contact with her, found it intolerable when she started clinging to him, and finally left with his friends for an excited, drunken night out, leaving her behind in a distraught condition. Throughout the following week Miss B was in a very bad state, on the brink of completely falling apart. What follows is a summary of the following Monday session.

She starts talking, hesitating, and in a very croaky voice, 'Last night I just cancelled everything, and went out and got drunk, and had quite a nice time, and at one point felt much better about everything in a drunken way, and kind of went round the place'. She then said, 'It was really strange, because I thought I would do some work, but . . .' and went on to describe meeting several people for drinks in what seemed to be a very excited, possibly dangerous, way which seemed to the analyst to be exactly how she had described her boyfriend's activities in the previous weekend. The narrative was punctuated with comments like, 'I've erased everything from my mind'. At some point in the session she exclaimed, 'I am not afraid of C [the boyfriend] any more!'

It seemed clear to her analyst that her way of 'cancelling every-thing' was via getting into a state of massive projective identification with the manic boyfriend (in the transference a cruel weekend analyst). The patient in the room seemed to have come out of that state, now felt to be in the past, so that she seemed able to listen to his interpretations. But there was an interesting misunderstanding at one point. The narrative about the night's events had started with her explaining that she 'had driven John, a boy I know, home to X' (a place quite far away); it ended with her driving around very late at night, until she was 'flagged down by two chaps' and she had driven one of them 'home'. The analyst asked her if she meant that she had driven the man to his home and she answered, as if it was obvious, that she meant her own home.

The analyst was rather alarmed at this, feeling that his patient had been putting herself through a really dangerous experience, and took this description of the end of her manic night out to mean her acting out an identification with an unfaithful, promiscuous boyfriend/analyst.

Miss B made it clear then that this was not the case at all, that she had recognised a friend, Paul, in the road and that it had been helpful to have him at home, had made it possible for her to sleep. She then explained that 'cancelling everything' had begun as trying to stop a terrible pain in her back, and then it had become exciting to feel so very strong; but at the end of the night she had felt terrible about 'total disengagement'. It became quite clear, then, that for this patient, the state of massive projective identification with a manic bad object starts with 'driving away' to some far away place some part of herself and that she can only come 'home' (to her house, to her own iden-tity, and also to her session) if she takes back inside parts of herself that have been fragmented and spread 'around town', as it were. So whatever actually happened in the previous night in external reality, what we have in the session is a narrative that gives a particular shape and meaning to psychic events.

This patient is on some level able to communicate to her analyst the temporary loss of contact with essential parts of herself that have to be recovered so as to enable her to go 'home', that is to say, to recover some sense of who she is. Her state of projective identification with the manic object is only temporary and threatens her with a loss of her sense of identity. Ultimately she knows that this powerful manic person in the night is not her real self. This is a temporary state, a defence that becomes threatening. I am not suggesting, of course, that this patient is suddenly 'cured' of her need to relate to her object through pathological projective identification. For instance, I suspect that even though she could come to the session and take in her analyst's interpretations, which involves a relationship with a less malevolent object and some awareness of a need to be helped to be more in contact with herself, her dependency still resides partly in this other, more receptive object. She mentioned at some point how much time she spends looking after others and there was a distinct sense in the material that the analyst in the here–and–now of the session is 'flagging her down' with his attention and his comments and that her listening to him is probably coloured by her 'helpfulness' to him. But it is clear that the objects involved in this interchange are in fact kinder and saner, and that she is consciously aware of her need to be 'reconnected' again.

In my patient, Mr A, who was also identified with a manic object, these states are much more inflexible. He is much more solidly identified with the idealised bad object and there is great commitment to keeping things this way. The equilibrium of the personality depends on maintaining this identification, and splitting mechanisms are constantly used to prevent any awareness of weaker, dependent parts. Mr A's pathological identification is more or less permanent and when this equilibrium is threatened his reaction is paranoid. Miss B's projective identification with the object, although extensive, is only temporary. She is much more fragile, her defensive solutions do not last and the state of 'becoming' the object very quickly becomes a threat in itself. It is as if Mr A is in possession of the object, has taken it over; whereas Miss B seems possessed by the manic object. She never entirely loses her awareness that she has been invaded by something alien to her. Or perhaps one could say that she does not idealise the bad object in the same way Mr A does, and her identifications shift. In the presence of her sensitive analyst she is also projectively identified with a helpful parent who picks people up, drives them home, etc.

I will now bring another example from Mr A to illustrate the technical difficulties the analyst may feel confronted with when an object relation that seems very fixed and unchangeable is dominating the transference. I find it useful to refer here to Joseph's careful exploration and development of Klein's concept of transference as a 'total situation'. I think this concept can help us to keep in mind the fact that a whole mode of functioning between two people is being repeated in the situation in the session. (I am of course taking it for granted that, as the analyst, one must always try to differentiate between what is being projected and the effect this has on oneself, which is due at least partly to one's own psychological make-up.)

Mr A, who is by profession a journalist, wrote a novel and sent it to a well-known publisher. He received a letter of rejection from one of the directors of the publishing house (a writer himself). His reaction in the session was one of moral indignation and contempt. It was absolutely clear that this director had been motivated in his action by envy of Mr A's superiority as a novelist. As soon as I took up what I thought was Mr A's terrible hurt and disappointment at this rejection he became enraged with me, clearly feeling that I was trying to project into him feelings that were absolutely not his. I seemed to have become the publisher who was rejecting (refusing to publish, as it were) his point of view. Soon an impasse was created in the session. I felt I had either to accept his version of the situation or I would become entirely identified with the publisher in his mind and not only suffer a barrage of hatred and contempt but also, as the 'enemy', be entirely unable to help my patient. I began to feel more and more trapped in a situation in which I had either to remain silent or agree with what seemed to me a rather mad version of events; that the only conceivable reason for being rejected is that one is far superior to the rejecting person. (As with the 'eyesight' situation in the first example, what seems so disturbing in these states is his certainty about the state of mind of the object.)

It would seem that Mr A has projected his envy of a creative parent who can produce a viable baby into the 'publisher', an aspect of me as a parent whom he sees as wanting to thwart his creativity: possibly of course an internal object created originally by introjecting a disturbed parent. But is this what happens in the session? I did not feel envious of my patient, I felt isolated as if I had lost any hope of ever getting through to him. It was impossible for me to 'publish' my thoughts (for instance, about the pain of being rejected, the defensive nature of his superiority, and his hatred of me as a cruel publisher trying to put him down).

Thinking about the session afterwards, though, I became aware that all the interpretations I could think of were really aiming at changing the situation by reversing it: either his version is published, or my version is. No wonder we didn't get anywhere!

These are really difficult situations to get out of and often only through thinking carefully about it afterwards can one begin to visualise what actually took place, without having to be either victim or aggressor, which is what one undoubtedly is (and not only in the patient's phantasy) when trying to deal with projections by (unconsciously) re-projecting them. What I am talking about is a necessary shift in the analyst to a position from which it would be possible to observe what is happening in the interaction between these two people in the session. From this position it becomes more possible to see who is who and what is the object relationship which is being enacted in the transference. In this case, this could be seen to be one between somebody who is trying to get something through, something that absolutely must be seen to be of value, and somebody else who is impenetrable, unreachable, who says 'No!' to any attempt at communication. (This experience links closely to what I have learned about Mr A's first two years of life, when his mother was severely depressed and withdrawn.)

Mr A's change of identity gives me first-hand experience, as it were, of contact with his internal object. By trying to visualise the total situation, I have some hope of understanding his underlying despair and of finding a way out of the impasse in which we could be trapped into only repeating and not working through.

The plural psychoanalytic scene

Introduction

Elizabeth Spillius and Edna O'Shaughnessy

In Part Three we describe the views held by members of several psychoanalytic schools of thought about the concept of projective identification. Because it is somewhat unusual for a concept to be so widely known as the term 'projective identification' has come to be, we have asked ourselves several questions about how this has come about. What is it about the concept that has aroused such interest? Are there any particular factors that contribute to a receptive attitude towards the adoption of the concept, and what factors mitigate against such receptiveness? Is it possible to 'lift' a concept from one psychoanalytic milieu and use it in another without altering the concept or the receiving psychoanalytic school of thought in the process? We have looked at these questions with the help of colleagues from four psychoanalytic cultures: first, the Contemporary Freudian and Independent members of the British Psychoanalytical Society; second, the views about projective identification held by three schools of thought in Europe – German psychoanalysts, Italian and Spanish psychoanalysts, and French-speaking psychoanalysts; third, we look at the attitude of American psychoanalysts towards the concept; and finally we examine the views of Latin American psychoanalysts.

The British Psychoanalytic Society

9

The views of Contemporary Freudians and Independents about the concept of projective identification

Edna O'Shaughnessy

Some of the reasons and some of the passions for using, or not using, the concept of projective identification are to be found in the history of the British Psychoanalytic Society. After the Controversial Discussions (finely chronicled by King and Steiner, 1991) held during the Second World War, the British Society divided itself into Classical Freudians, later known as the Contemporary Freudians; a Middle group, later called the Independents, and a Klein group, the Kleinians.

This division into three groups had its beginnings in a dispute over child analysis during the 1920s between Anna Freud in Vienna and Melanie Klein in Berlin. The dispute involved issues of transference, unconscious phantasy, the super-ego and the Oedipus Complex. Milton, Polmear and Fabricius (2004) describe how

> Klein was glad to accept Ernest Jones's invitations, first in 1925 to lecture in the British Psychoanalytic Society, and then in 1926 to live in London. Klein was grateful for the warm and generally open-minded reception of the British somewhat distanced as they were from the analytic fray of mainland Europe.
>
> (Milton et al., 2004, p. 64)

They record the terrible circumstances that in 1938 forced Sigmund and Anna Freud to come to London as refugees from the Nazis –

books burned, Freud himself suffering from advanced cancer of the jaw. About the Classical Freudian group they write:

> From 1933 many European refugee analysts were helped to settle in London . . . the emigres closest to Freud and his daughter . . . felt they had to protect the legacy of their mortally ill friend and teacher. For them Klein's ideas were not psychoanalytic at all; she was heretical in an analogous way to Jung or Adler.
>
> (Milton et al., 2004, pp. 64–65)

But 'Klein and close supporters . . . felt deeply that their developments were true to Freud's vision, and were dismayed at the prospect that they might even be expelled from the British Society' (Milton et al., 2004, p. 65). Expulsion would have been a grim reversal of fortune for Melanie Klein, whose ideas had interested British colleagues such as Ernest Jones, Edward Glover (for a time), Ella Sharpe, Marjorie Brierley, and Sylvia Payne. Joan Riviere and Susan Isaacs eventually became Klein's close colleagues, and so for a time did the young Donald Winnicott. All of these analysts were making fresh discoveries. Thus, on one side there was a battle for the scientific right of analysts to make clinical advances and develop new concepts, and, on the other, the Classical Freudians fought for the preservation of psycho-analysis as a heritage that had been cruelly lost in Europe.

Eric Rayner explains in his book *The Independent Mind in British Psychoanalysis* (Rayner, 1990) that 'The majority of the British Society, particularly those who had been its original members, wished to take sides with neither group', and he stresses the Independents' pride in origins that go back to the founding members of the British Society (Rayer, 1990, pp. 2 and 45). In *The British School of Psychoanalysis: The Independent Tradition* (Kohon, 1986) Gregorio Kohon describes how 'a Middle Group was created: the Society remained one, but divided into three separate groups [. . .] It was another characteristic achievement of the British Psychoanalysts, accomplished through their remarkable capacity for compromise' (Kohon, 1986, p. 45).

Once the three groups had formed themselves during the 1940s and 1950s, each tended to see itself in ways that were discordant with how it was seen by the other two, and psychoanalytic questions, sometimes mixed with personal animosities and training and institutional prob-lems, were oppositional and militarised. While both Independents and Kleinians paid special attention to object relations, Independents focused on pathology caused by external objects. From a Kleinian perspective, this was a neglect of inner sources of disturbance. Independents, in their turn, saw Kleinians as over-focused on the inner world, especially on innate destructiveness, and as failing to take into account real life experiences. Both Kohon and Rayner see Independents as ready to add to their own tradition with ideas from Anna Freud and Melanie Klein, and from elsewhere in the world too; Independents prized their variety of orientations as against the more unified approach of the other two groups, particularly the Kleinians. But the other two groups tended to see Independents as relying on a set of too loosely related ideas and seeking an identity through what they were not.

Yet, in this anxious and divided institution, with its mix of facts and shibboleths about its groups and its members, there remained a will to stay together, and, moreover, there came a remarkable flowering of psychoanalytic ideas. Kleinian papers were specially written for the series of Scientific Discussions on Controversial Issues by Susan Isaacs, Paula Heimann and Melanie Klein.[37] Among the Classical Freudians, Anna Freud, Dorothy Burlingham, Willi Hoffer and Edward Glover were all writing papers, as were Ernest Jones, Ella Sharpe, Marjorie Brierley and Sylvia Payne, soon to be followed by Michael Balint, William Gillespie, Donald Winnicott, John Bowlby and John Klauber among the Independents. And Melanie Klein was formulating a new theory of psychic development (see Spillius, Chapter 1 in this book), in which she stated the hypothesis of a depressive position first (Klein, 1935, 1940), following it with an account in 'Notes on some schizoid mechanisms' (Klein, 1946) of an earlier paranoid–schizoid position in the first three months of life. It was in this latter paper, reprinted in Chapter 2 of this book, that Klein introduced the term 'projective identification' as the name of an early defence mechanism of the ego in its struggles with anxiety.[38]

37 These discussions, now generally known as the Controversial Discussions, took place in the British Society from 1941 to 1945, and have been impressively discussed in King and Steiner (1991), where the papers are collected.

38 Though neither refers to the other, it is of particular interest that Majorie Brierley (1945) had used the same term, 'projective identification', in a sense not so different from Klein's the year before; Brierley repeated it in her paper of 1947, though thereafter she did not pursue this line of thought. See Spillius, Chapter 1 in this book. The very first use of the term 'projective identification' would seem to be in 1925 by Weiss, who also took it no further (Weiss 1925). See an interesting exchange of letters between G. B. Massida and R. Steiner on the 'origins of concepts' (Massida, 1999). See also Spillius, Chapter 1 in this book.

Klein's colleagues, Joan Riviere (Unpublished), Herbert Rosenfeld (1947, 1949, 1971) and Hanna Segal (1950), quickly saw how the phenomenon of projective identification might advance the understanding of patients, and Paula Heimann (1950), then still a member of Klein's group, read a much-cited paper 'On countertransference' at the Amsterdam Congress, in which, without using the term 'projective identification', she stated: 'From the point of view I am stressing, the analyst's countertransference is not only part and parcel of the analytic relationship, but it is the patient's *creation*, it is part of the patient's personality', and further, 'The analyst's countertransference is an instrument of research into the patient's unconscious' (Heimann, 1950, pp. 83 and 84, italics in original). However, Melanie Klein herself had misgivings about the idea of countertransference, fearing that the analyst might confuse what he felt for reasons of his own with what his patient felt. As we shall see, the clinical use of countertransference remains a controversial issue.

The decade after the formation of the three groups that preserved the unity of the British Society was full of troubles. Pearl King observes that at that time 'it was painful for those Members and students who became involved in the inter-group tensions' (King and Steiner, 1991, p. 908). It must have been painful for everyone. In 1956 Paula Heimann left Klein's group to join the Independents. Regarding projective identification, she eventually adopted a usage at odds with standard Kleinian usage. 'Projective identification' she wrote 'occurs as a countertransference phenomenon when the analyst fails in his perceptive functions' (Heimann, 1969). Margret Tonnesmann discusses Heimann's changing views in her Editor's Introduction to Heimann's collected papers (Tonnesmann, 1989).

Meanwhile, British Kleinians continued to develop the concept. Rosenfeld explored its intrusive aspects, especially in the psychotic and borderline transference, Segal linked it to her work on symbolic equations and concrete thinking, Money-Kyrle examined its varying roles in countertransference, Bion made it central to his new formulations about the development and failure of communication and thinking; Joseph explored it clinically in transference and countertransference. Projective identification became an integral part of Kleinian theory and technique.

On the world scene in the 1960s and 1970s psychoanalysis was changing. In the USA the school of ego-psychology was beginning to lose its exclusive predominance. Non-medical analysts gained admission to the American Psychoanalytic Association in 1988. The work of Loewald, Kernberg, Schafer and Ogden, influenced by contact with the two British object relations schools of Klein and Winnicott, contributed to a new complex plural scene (see Roy Schafer, Chapter 14 in the present volume). Relational and interpersonal groups were legitimised. Kohut founded the American school of self psychology. In the British Society the groups became less sectarian. Anna Freud (1967), for instance, in a paper 'About losing and being lost', described these phenomena in classical Freudian terms but also mentioned a link to Klein's idea of projective identification. Sandler and Dreher (1996) offer an overview of these events. By the 1980s Wallerstein could ask the question 'One psychoanalysis or many?', and give the answer 'Many' – a 'Many' with relations to the 'One' of clinical practice (Wallerstein, 1988). And with the change to pluralism in the 1970s and 1980s came a growing interest in Kleinian ideas. Martin Miller (Independent) charted the occurrence in journals of the concept of projective identification and found that while it is less frequently referred to in American journals, the trend is the same: from the 1970s on, the term 'projective identification' occurs with increasing frequency in UK and US journals (Martin Miller, personal communication).

In 1984 Joseph Sandler, who at that time held the Chair of Psychoanalysis in Jersualem, organised a conference 'because of the current interest in projective identification'. Speakers were international: Betty Joseph, a London Kleinian (see Chapter 6 in this book), W. W. Meissner and Otto Kernberg from the USA and Rafael Moses from Israel. The conference proceedings were published under the title *Projection, Identification, Projective Identification* (Sandler, 1987b) with Sandler himself adding an important paper on 'The concept of projective identification' (reprinted here in Chapter 10).

Sandler's stated aim was to make projective identification 'comprehensible to those lacking a Kleinian psychoanalytic background' (Sandler, 1987b, p. xi). It is instructive to see how he does this. In a scholarly manner he discusses the wide, and still widening, range of phenomena that the concept is used to refer to, and also its affinities with some Contemporary Freudian thinking: how Anna Freud (1936) in *The Ego and the Mechanisms of Defence* had a similar idea about 'identification with the aggressor' and 'living through another person' as 'a form of altruism' (A. Freud, 1936, pp. 117 and 132). He also links projective identification to his own clinical findings about the wishes of patients to actualise phantasies with their analysts (Sandler, 1976a). He has a struggle with what he calls 'concrete terms' in Mrs Klein's formulations in a way a Kleinian might not have, because for a Kleinian such 'concrete terms' are readily clarified by other Kleinian concepts, like the paranoid-schizoid position, Segal's (1957) differentiation of symbolic equations from symbols, and Rosenfeld's (1952a) notion of intrusions. Sandler writes in 'The concept of projective identification':

> Let me stress, however, that together with the Kleinians, I believe that the processes of projective identification (in the sense in which I can make use of them) play a highly significant part in development and in the clinical psychoanalytic situation. Projective identification has given an added dimension to what we understand by transference, in that transference need not now be regarded simply as a repetition of the past. It can also be a reflection of fantasies about the relation to the analyst created in the present by projective identification and allied mechanisms.
>
> (Sandler, 1987a, p. 20)

I think Sandler's account of the actualisation of role-relationships contributed both to the further understanding of projective identification itself, and also to the success of his aim of making projective identification 'comprehensible to those lacking a Kleinian psychoanalytic background' (Sandler, 1987a, p. xi).

Sandler also addresses another problem, the problem of taking a concept into a different frame of reference. He writes, 'I believe it is mistaken to assume that the idea of projective identification *as a mechanism* is a part of a package which includes a theory of development and which has to be accepted in its entirety' (Sandler, 1987a, p. 19, italics in original). Unless in one gulp Sandler were to become a Kleinian and so lose his identity as a Contemporary Freudian, some conceptual unlinking must be done: the mechanism of projective identification, in Sandler's phrase, needs to be 'fruitfully separated' from its Kleinian theory. How otherwise can an analyst of one persuasion take ideas from another?

Indeed, a willingness to do just this has always been part of the Independent tradition that has allowed them to experiment with concepts. In his book *Freedom to Relate*, Roger Kennedy, an Independent analyst, discusses this issue in a chapter called 'Are psychoanalytic concepts too rigid?' (Kennedy, 1993). He shows how Freud's central concepts had a flexibility of use that could accommodate new discoveries and also how Freud's new uses remained alongside his old. Kennedy writes:

> There is, in fact, a problem about making any psychoanalytic definition: there are so many different analytic assumptions that it is difficult to be certain of making any commonly accepted statement, and opinions on theory and practice differ widely. This could be interpreted as evidence of psychoanalytic chaos, but it may also indicate a rich variety of approaches, or of different 'voices in the psychoanalytic conversation'.
>
> (Kennedy, 1993, p. 34)

And, in fact, Contemporary Freudian and Independent voices have participated in the 'conversation' about projective identification, to different degrees and in different ways. Pearl King (1974), Denis Carpy (1989) and Eric Rayner (1992), all Independents, make reference to projective identification in connection with transference and countertransference. In more extensive contributions, Michael Sinason (1993, 1999) examines its role in psychosis, as does Paul Williams in a book written with Murray Jackson, *Unimaginable Storms* (Jackson and Williams, 1994), and also Brian Martindale, for example, in his paper on 'New discoveries concerning psychoses and their organizational fate' (Martindale, 2001). Michael Brearley, in an unpublished paper, 'The psychoanalyst's neutrality', uses the notion of projective identification for a fresh exploration of the concept of analytic neutrality. In her writings Dana Birksted-Breen has linked the concept to her themes, especially in 'Time and the après-coup' (Birksted-Breen, 2003).

I also made some informal enquiries by email of Independent and Contemporary Freudian colleagues who tend to participate in the exchange of ideas in the British Society. Some did not reply. Those who did, whether by email or in conversation, offered a range of views. A few said they never used the concept, but worked in a different way with their preferred notion of projection. Several others said they had trained in the British tradition and so had been influenced by groups other than their own, and sometimes used projective identification in work with more disturbed patients, or to understand a primitive defence, or in supervision to help a supervisee recognise a countertransference experience. By far the majority of my respondents

159

said they found projective identification an essential concept for clinical work and supervision, and for the understanding of groups and strange psychic phenomena. 'Base my work on it', 'couldn't work without it', 'embedded in my thinking' were frequent phrases. Even so, with only one exception, every respondent, from the most negative to the most enthusiastic, was critical of the Kleinians' clinical use of projective identification – criticisms I come to later.

These replies from colleagues were lively. Many reflected on the concept itself, with illustrations from their clinical experience. They questioned whether 'projective identification' was too wide a term and whether the phenomena it denotes were intrinsically yoked or disparate. They asked: What is the relation of projective identification to its components of splitting, projection and identification? Can there be projection without an object, or projection without identification? Is projective identification both intra-psychic and inter-psychic? Several suggestions were made to limit or to redefine the concept in one way or another, or to introduce some additional new term.

These discussions, many at some length, by Contemporary Freudians and Independents show, as do their books and papers, that there are indeed gains to be had from the 'fruitful separation' of a concept from its home theory. There are also pitfalls. I think we can live with terms having different uses, which, as Roger Kennedy points out, is not untypical of psychoanalysis in either classical or recent more plural times. What is more serious is that misunderstandings of the original concept can occur through the undoing of significant connections with its home theory. One frequent misconception in the answers to my enquiry was that projective identification, as introduced by Klein in 'Notes on some schizoid mechanisms' (Klein, 1946), was essentially an aggressive mechanism. In her paper Klein first describes the ego's projection of hated parts of itself and how after this event 'the hatred of parts of the self is now directed towards the mother.' She continues, 'This leads to a particular form of identification which establishes the prototype of an aggressive object–relation. I suggest for these processes the term "projective identification".' But she goes on to say

It is, however, not only the bad parts of the self which are expelled and projected, but also good parts of the self. Excrements then have the significance of gifts, and parts of the ego which, together with excrements, are expelled and projected into the other person represent the good, i.e. the loving parts of the self [. . .] The projection of good feelings and good parts of the self into the mother is essential for the infant's ability to develop good object–relations and to integrate the ego.

(Klein, 1946, pp. 8–9)

That is to say, classically, 'projective identification' was introduced by Klein to name processes both hostile and loving.

The nature of Klein's overall opus may lend itself to misunderstanding. In her writings of the 1920s and early 1930s, one of her emphases had been on aggressive infantile phantasies of intrusion into the mother, and these form part of the later concept of projective identification. However, by the time she introduced projective identification in 1946 Klein had formulated a new theory of psychic development, at the core of which was the ego's anxiety for the survival of both itself and its objects, and its anxious vicissitudes with love and hate, depression as well as persecution, problems of guilt and reparation as much as aggression (Klein, 1935, 1940). Indeed, immediately preceding her introduction of the concept of projective identification Klein writes of the ego's 'vital need to deal with anxiety' (Klein, 1946, p. 4). As I see it, a common misunderstanding of Klein's concept comes from the omission of the part of her hypothesis which states that *one of the driving forces of projective identification is the ego's need to survive.* And as Elizabeth Spillius describes in Chapter 1, Klein's stress on the projection of good feelings was even more marked in her unpublished notes in the Melanie Klein Archive than in her published paper of 1946.

Respect for the integrity of a theory may contribute to a reluctance to make Sandler's 'fruitful separation'. I think that the coherence of a theory in which terms have interlocking meanings is sometimes a reason in the British Psychoanalytic Society for not using a concept from a group different from one's own. I have long thought that Winnicott's concept of transitional space (Winnicott, 1953) identifies important phenomena. Yet I have never used the idea, because to separate 'transitional space' from Winnicott's theory of development and use it, or its several cognate terms, in a Kleinian context that in some relevant respects is a theory opposite to Winnicott's, would so change the concept as to become a misuse of it. Winnicott's trajectory goes from illusion through transitional space towards object relations, while Klein's developmental path starts with object relations – intermixed with other states of mind. Again, the Contemporary Freudian term 'individuation' captures what happens as the depressive position sets in when projections are withdrawn and objects start to be experienced as whole and separate. But I feel unable to borrow the term and say of the onset of the depressive position that 'self and object become individuated', because the Contemporary Freudian theory of original merging in which individuation has its home is so different from Klein's theory. Canestri (see Chapter 12 in this book) examines some of these conceptual problems in the plural state of psychoanalysis.

Longstanding unresolved scientific differences between the groups are yet other reasons why Contemporary Freudians and Independents might not use the concept of projective identification or use it somewhat differently. Contemporary Freudians and Independents tend to see the early ego as less active than Kleinians do and conceptualise the connections between mother and infant with their own, different ideas. A patient's internalised psychic history could not then be seen by them as repeatable in the same way via communicative projective identifications to an analyst whose countertransference could reveal something of the nature of these fundamental links – the early containments, or failures and projections from objects into infant, or the attacks by object or infant on the communicative links. Balint (1950) and Winnicott (1971) for instance offer other perspectives for clinical practice that are still alive today in the British Society. For a comparison of Contemporary Freudian, Independent and Kleinian views on countertransference, see Hinshelwood (1999). Rather than the notion of projective identification, many Contemporary Freudians and Independents prefer for clinical practice Pearl King's (1978) idea of 'the analyst's total affective response'. The related problem of the analyst disentangling his feelings from those coming to him from the patient is also approached differently. In the Kleinian tradition there are papers by Money-Kyrle (1956), Joseph (1978), Brenman-Pick (1985) and Feldman (1997), while Fonagy (1991) and Parsons (2000) put forward other, distinctive views.

I come now to Contemporary Freudian and Independent criticisms of the Kleinians and projective identification that were made in response to my email enquiry. First, there is the charge of over-use, that Kleinians 'explain' as projective identification all the patient's communications and all the analyst's feelings, both of which, it was often insisted, are made up of many different things that cannot be reduced to one. Second, many respondents contended (sometimes contradicting earlier appreciative remarks) that the concept of projective identification was an aggressive mechanism through which Kleinian analysts over-focused on an assumed innate destructiveness of their patients. And third, a few Contemporary Freudians and Independents thought the concept tempted Kleinians into making interpretations with unwarranted haste in the 'here and now' and furthermore – a view elaborated in print by Pearl King (2004) – that the concept of projective identification is to blame for a thin style of 'me-you' analysing that has become current in the British Society.

The first thing to be said is that a Kleinian analyst, like any other, needs to question himself, his relations to his patient, and his way of conceptualising. And we have also to remember that any concept and any technique can be poorly used. Every orchard has its bad apples. However, while I agree that not all a patient's communications are made by projective identification and that the analyst's countertransference too is formed by many things, I would point out that because of the major and multiple roles of projective identification in Kleinian theory, projective identification is bound to have much Kleinian use. I contest the charge that Kleinians use the concept to over-focus on destructiveness. Nor is it true that projective identification in itself implies a denuded 'me-you', 'you-me' technique of analysis. Klein wrote in 1952: 'It is my experience that in unravelling the details of the transference it is essential to think in terms of *total situations* transferred from the past into the present, as well as of emotions, defences, and object relations' (Klein, 1952b, p. 55, italics in original). She added on the next page:

It is only by linking again and again [. . .] later experiences with earlier ones and *vice versa*, it is only by consistently exploring their interplay that present and past can come together in the patient's mind. This is one aspect of the process of integration.

(Klein, 1952b, p. 56)

Hanna Segal, discussing the curative factors in psychoanalysis, reminds us of how very many there are:

a full interpretation will involve interpreting the patient's feelings, anxieties and defences, taking into account the stimulus in the present and the reliving of the past. It will include the role played by his internal objects and the interplay of phantasy and reality.

(Segal, 1962, p. 212)

She adds: 'though we cannot always make a full interpretation, we aim eventually at completing it' (p. 212). No analyst can address everything at once; each analyst – approaches differ – makes his choice of what is urgent for now and what will have to wait for later.

Pearl King (2004) raises a further issue. 'What has happened to psychoanalysis in the British Society?' she asks

As I understand it the way the phrase 'here and now' is presently used by many people in the Society from all three groups, i.e. many Kleinians, some Contemporary Freudians and some Independents, they use it to refer to the actual relationship in the session and what the analyst thinks the patient is doing to him.

(King, 2004, p. 127)

It seems to me that it is the *doing* involved in projective identification that arouses most unease (see Hinz's excellent discussion in Chapter 11 of this book). That we – whether the 'we' is patient and analyst, individual colleague and individual colleague, or the three groups of the British Society – *that we psychically do things to each other*, as, of course, we *do* to people in our inner and external lives and also to society at large, brings enormous anxiety and guilt. It is not merely that we have thoughts and phantasies about, or exchange words with, our fellow human beings, but, to use Sandler's notion, *actualisations* occur: projections from one psyche intrude into another and affect it – leaving the recipient feeling disturbed, inferior, manipulated into action, wrong, guilty, or anxious. Conversely, projections can also bring relief, or a sense of affirmation or gratitude or pleasure. Bion's theory of thinking and his writings on container-contained formulate the general hypotheses of this area (Bion, 1962b). Over the years Betty Joseph (1989b) has illustrated the anxieties and pressures that lead to 'acting in', the 'doing' in analysis that occurs between patient and analyst, while Michael Feldman (1997) describes the many factors, including unresolved problems in the analyst, that lead to the analyst becoming *actually* involved in 'the complex intrapsychic and interpersonal process which constitutes projective identification' (see Chapter 7 in this book). Indeed, in 1915 Freud commented, 'It is a very remarkable thing that the *Ucs* of

164

one human being can react upon that of another, without passing through the *Cs'* (Freud, 1915b, p. 194). Projective identification gives a name to the way one psyche does things to, and for, another.

Well – where does this leave us after I, a Kleinian, have tried to answer some of the criticisms of Contemporary Freudians and Independents? I suspect it leaves us where we were – in disagreement. Disagreements, especially those between analytic schools, are complex, involving plural theories and concepts, unsettled controversies about development and the causes of pathology, disagreements over analytic technique, plus all the problems of verifying and falsifying competing clinical claims about non-replicable analytic encounters that can be approached in more than one way even from within a single school of analytic thought, though this does not, as David Tuckett has put it, mean 'that anything goes' (Tuckett, 2005). Over many years in the British Society, while some early differences have been settled others have not, and I think this is due to yet another complication: our old group passions.

By tradition, analysts in the British Society belong to the same group as their training analyst. All candidates go through the same training and can choose supervisors from any group. In addition, all students now go to a third consultant, who must have a different theoretical orientation from their first supervisor, for ten consultations on their work with their first patient. We all end with a combination of conscious, and also unconsciously influential, identifications, immediate analytic and supervisory experience, plus further knowledge from case presentations of the work of the other two groups. In this internal admixture are loyalties, hostilities, anxieties and guilts connected with the groups — one's own and the other two. Among things said or emailed to me in response to my enquiries were professions of exasperation with the notion of projective identification, even when the analyst used it himself/herself, along with the charge of Kleinian over-use that I discussed above. One Contemporary Freudian explained: 'Projective identification is the Kleinian flag. That's how non-Kleinians see it.' When projective identification is felt to hoist a group flag, it means our three groups are not yet out of their old battlefield, what Riccardo Steiner (1985) has called 'the political militarization of ideas' where there are winners, losers, triumphs and useless guilts for having analytic ideas.

What can we learn from this account of a local institution, a psychoanalytic village whose neighbours in the 1950s battled over concepts and partly defined their psychoanalytic identity by concepts? The concept of projective identification was born in those times and concepts still matter intensely – and not only for their scientific use. Projective identification is a Kleinian concept, and sometimes it has an emblematic meaning that wakes up memories of antipathies and clashes and opposed group loyalties and identities. Yet times have also changed – perhaps more than we all realise. There is freer thinking about psychoanalytic ideas and clinical experience, and many in the British Society wish to discard habits anchored in procedural memories about groups and historic personages, and younger analysts and students have yet to make their voices – the voices of the future – known.

When a concept like projective identification, because of its intrinsic value, gains a primacy over others we have to worry about how we experience this. We harm ourselves if acceptance of a Kleinian idea is seen as and/or becomes a Kleinian triumph rather than a contribution to a shared Freudian enquiry. Even so, inequality of conceptual achievement, along with a scientific evaluation, brings concerns about losing significant Contemporary Freudian and Independent ideas, and anxieties about the sources of psychoanalytic identity.

We all have to continue to work under the tensions intrinsic to pursuing one approach while colleagues pursue another within the same institution, trying to remember also that analysts from one orientation may gain from and contribute to another. For those with a liking for so doing, there is the chance to engage with the plural aspects of the contemporary psychoanalytic scene, local and world-wide, a formidable enterprise about concepts and the psychic realities named by concepts. As we gain in understanding it is likely there will be more resolution to our rival conceptualisations, though who knows when – or whether – we shall eventually arrive at a universal language for psychoanalysis.

Meanwhile, in the British Society we are still trying to find ourselves; we are again full of troubles as we struggle with our reasons and our passions in a new epoch that has come upon us so untidily.

──────── 10 ────────

The concept of projective identification[39]

Joseph Sandler

The introduction of the concept of projective identification by Melanie Klein in 1946 was set against a rather confused and confusing background of literature on various forms of internalization and externalization – imitation, identification, phantasies of incorporation and many varieties of projection. Projective identification is a broad concept, as the following description by Hanna Segal indicates.

> In projective identification parts of the self and internal objects are split off and projected into the external object, which then becomes possessed by, controlled and identified with the projected parts. Projective identification has manifold aims: it may be directed towards the ideal object to avoid separation, or it may be directed towards the bad object to gain control of the source of danger. Various parts of the self may be projected in order to get rid of them as well as to attack and destroy the object, good parts may be projected to avoid separation or to keep them safe from bad things inside or to improve the external object through a kind of primitive projective reparation. Projective identification starts when the paranoid–schizoid position is first established in relation to the breast, but it persists and very often becomes intensified when the mother is perceived as a whole object and the whole of her body is entered by projective identification.
>
> (Segal, 1973)

39 This chapter reproduces the text of Sandler, J. (1987). The concept of projective identification. *Bulletin of the Anna Freud Centre, 10*, 33–49.

In this context Segal explicitly treats projective identification as a mechanism of defence, but elsewhere she describes it as 'the earliest form of empathy', and as providing 'the basis for the earliest form of symbol-formation' (Segal, 1973). Melanie Klein saw it as a vehicle for distinguishing 'me' from 'not-me' (Klein, 1946). Rosenfeld (1965) has described processes entering into psychotic states and comments that 'Melanie Klein described these primitive object relations and the ego disturbances related to them under the collective name "projective identification".' In the last 35 years, projective identification has become increasingly seen by Kleinian analysts as a central mechanism in countertransference, and in this context Bion's addition of the container-contained model has played a specially important part (Grinberg, Sor, and de Bianchedi, 1977). Ogden (1979, 1982) has emphasized the role of projective identification as the pathway from the intrapsychic to the interpersonal.

It is possible to cite many other ways in which the concept of projective identification has been employed, and it is clear that its 'collective' and necessarily 'elastic' nature must render any precise definition implausible. But it must be equally clear that the term projective identification has carried with it an idea which has proved to be of substantial value to a significant group of analysts. It has become a central Kleinian clinical concept, although it is also used by analysts of other orientations. However, it is a notion which is difficult to discuss from a non-Kleinian perspective. This may be due in part to the fact that those who use the concept tend to speak of it as a single mechanism, while in fact it is one which (like so many others in psychoanalysis) shifts its meaning according to the context in which it is being used. It has as a result acquired a certain mystique, with the unfortunate consequence that it is sometimes either dismissed entirely or thought to be understandable only with special 'inside knowledge'.

This paper refers to some of my own attempts to get to grips with the concept, and I have no doubt that I will be seen by some to have done violence to it. Because my own frame of reference is in significant respects different from that of the Kleinians, it has been necessary to break the concept down in my own mind in order to digest and absorb it. For the sake of convenience I shall present the material which follows under a number of different headings. Like all concepts in psychoanalysis, that of projective identification has undergone a progressive development since its introduction, and it is convenient to separate three stages in this development. These stages are, I believe, conceptually clear-cut, although they overlap considerably, and the ideas of the first and second stages have persisted alongside those of the third.

Some remarks on the background

In the period between the two world wars, and particularly after the mid-twenties, processes of internalization and externalization became increasingly important in psychoanalytic thinking. These processes were particularly evident in psychotic patients, and this led Melanie Klein to construct and elaborate a theory of development in which object relationships were seen as being built up on the basis of such internalizing and externalizing processes. She distinguished the two 'positions' in normal development on the basis of the two major psychotic states in which such processes could be seen most clearly. Although one might disagree with Mrs Klein's theory of development and with the concrete nature of her formulations, in retrospect we can see that she was the analyst who gave the earliest and greatest recognition to projective and identificatory processes in the development of object relationships, and to their operation in the here-and-now of the transference. I believe that it was clinical pressure which prompted this development, and in this context it is interesting to note that Anna Freud has remarked, in her work on the mechanisms of defence (Freud, 1936), that she was prompted to develop her ideas by the need to understand resistances in analysis more fully. In relation to Anna Freud's introduction of a number of new defences in 1936, I have commented elsewhere that

> What Anna Freud did at this time was to introduce a whole class of what might be called object-related defences, which involved reversal of roles or some combination of identification and projection. These are defences in which there is an active interchange between aspects of the self and of the object, the unacceptable aspects of one's own self being dealt with by producing (or attempting to produce) their appearance in the external object. Often, simultaneously, frightening or admired aspects of the object may be taken into the self.
>
> (Sandler, 1983)

169

First stage projective identification

When Melanie Klein introduced the term projective identification in 1946, she said:

> Much of the hatred against parts of the self is now directed towards the mother. This leads to a particular form of identification which establishes the prototype of an aggressive object–relation. I suggest for these processes the term 'projection identification'. When projection is mainly derived from the infant's impulse to harm or to control the mother, he feels her to be a persecutor. In psychotic disorders this identification of an object with the hated parts of the self contributes to the intensity of the hatred directed against other people.
>
> (Klein, 1946)

Although this formulation was put by Mrs Klein in very concrete terms, it can be understood as referring to processes which occur in phantasy processes of change in the mental representation of self and object occurring at various levels of unconscious phantasy. The concreteness of the formulations can be taken to refer to processes imagined as concrete, i.e. involving images of literal incorporation or 'forcing' something into an object. The processes described served the function of being defensive or adaptive in the immediate present, although when they occur in extreme form in infancy they may have harmful effects on later development. Melanie Klein can be taken to be referring here to shifts and displacements within the child's representational world (Sandler and Rosenblatt, 1962). Identification with parts of an object can be regarded as a 'taking into' the self-representation aspects of an object-representation. Projection is then a displacement in the opposite direction, i.e. aspects of the self-representation are shifted to (and made part of) an object-representation. In my view it does not matter very much, in this context, whether we speak, for example, of 'the bad parts of the self' or of 'the hated (or despised) unwanted aspects of the self-representation', as long as we agree that the processes as described by Mrs Klein occur within phantasy life. Moreover, in my view, for conceptual purposes we can separate the idea of projective identification as a mechanism operating in the here-and-now from processes described in the Kleinian theory of early development. I shall touch on this point again later, but I want to emphasize that what is of the greatest importance for me in Mrs Klein's formulation is her description of a mental mechanism or set of mechanisms. For Melanie Klein projective identification involved splitting, which I would understand in this context as a splitting-off of parts of the self-representation or of the object-representation. Projective identification involves projection in that it is an identifying of the object with split-off parts of the self. When the process moves in the opposite direction, i.e. identifying oneself with aspects of the object, Mrs Klein speaks of introjective identification.

I have referred here to first stage projective identification in order to emphasize the point that for Mrs Klein projective identification was a process which occurred in phantasy. Let me put it another way. The real object employed in the process of projective identification is not regarded as being affected – the parts of the self put into the object are put into the phantasy object, the 'internal' object, not the external object. This is borne out by the way in which transference and countertransference are treated in Mrs Klein's writings. Transference reflects infantile object relationships (Klein, 1952b), and is a phantasy about the analyst which needs to be analysed. It is a phantasy which creates a distortion of the patient's perception of the analyst, a distortion based on, among other things, the projective identification which has affected the patient's phantasy about the analyst. Countertransference, in its turn, is scarcely mentioned, and when it is (e.g. in 'Envy and gratitude': Klein, 1957), it is regarded as a hindrance to the analyst's technique.

Second stage projective identification

It was probably inevitable that the concept of projective identification came to be widened soon after its introduction, and I want to touch here on a particular extension of the concept to object relationships in general and to the transference-countertransference relation between patient and analyst in particular. In 1950, Paula Heimann (then very much a Kleinian) drew attention to the positive value of countertransference thoughts and feelings in analysis. She stated, 'The analyst's countertransference is an instrument of research into the patient's unconscious', and remarked 'From the point of view I am stressing, the analyst's countertransference is not only part and parcel of the analytic relationship but it is the patient's creation, it is part of the patient's personality' (Heimann, 1950).

It is of interest that a number of writers made a very similar point at about this time, some linking countertransference specifically with projective identification. Thus Racker, in a series of papers beginning in 1948 (Racker, 1968), connected the analyst's countertransference response to projective identification on the part of the patient. In regard to a case which he was discussing, he said:

> [. . .] the 'projective identification' . . . frequently really obtains its ends − in our case to make the analyst feel guilty, and not only implies (as has been said at times) that 'the patient expects the analyst to feel guilty', or that 'the analyst is meant to be sad and depressed'. The analyst's identification with the object with which the patient identifies him, is, I repeat, the normal countertransference process.

Racker makes a valuable distinction in this context between concordant and complementary identification on the part of the analyst. To put it simply, countertransference based on a concordant identification occurs when the analyst identifies with the patient's own phantasy self-representation of the moment. Countertransference based on a complementary identification occurs when the analyst identifies with the object-representation in the patient's transference phantasy.

Heimann, Racker and others, such as L. Grinberg, 1957 and 1985 (referred to in Grinberg, 1962), made a significant extension of projective identification by bringing it into conjunction with the analyst's identification with the self- or object-representation in the patient's unconscious phantasies, and with the effect of this on the countertransference. The countertransference reaction could then be a possible source of information for the analyst about what was occurring in the patient.

I have called the formulations referred to above second stage projective identification because they represent an extension of Melanie Klein's original propositions, whereas projective identification occurring within the person's phantasy life (reflected in a phantasy distortion of the analyst), can be called first stage projective identification. If either the self or object represented in such unconscious phantasies is identified with by the analyst to a degree sufficient to contribute to the analyst's countertransference, we have a second stage.

Third stage projective identification

In this stage of the development of the concept it is no longer one or other aspect of the unconscious phantasies that is identified with by the analyst. Projective identification is now described as if the externalization of parts of the self or of the internal object occurs directly into the external object. This extension was given its main impetus by work of Bion in the late 1950s and found explicit expression in his concept of the 'container' (Bion, 1962a, 1963). Bion describes the function of the container by presenting what is essentially Melanie Klein's description of projective identification, to which he adds the following (Grinberg et al., 1977):

> One of the consequences of this process is that, by projecting the bad parts (including phantasies and bad feelings) into a good breast (an understanding object), the infant will be able – insofar as his development allows – to reintroject the same parts in a more tolerable form, *once they have been modified by the thought (reverie) of the object. . . .* (my italics).

By no stretch of the imagination can this be understood as occurring in phantasy only, nor is this what Bion intended to imply. What he describes here is a concrete 'putting into the object'. He says:

> An evocation of the bad breast takes place through a realistic projective identification. The mother, with her capacity for reverie, transforms the unpleasant sensations linked to the 'bad breast' and provides relief for the infant who then reintrojects the unmitigated and modified emotional experience, i.e. reintrojects . . . a non-sensual aspect of the mother's love.

Bion's formulations can be related to Winnicott's 'holding' function of the good-enough mother (Winnicott, 1958), and are echoed too in aspects of Ogden's conception (Ogden, 1982). What Bion has proposed in the container-contained metaphor is clearly of great relevance for analytic technique, and I shall return to this projective identification later.

It must be clear that all the theoretical propositions put forward in connection with transference and countertransference apply equally to object relationships outside the analytic situation.

173

Comments

The comments which follow relate to various aspects of the projective identification, and are somewhat disjointed. However, they will give an indication of my own view of projective identification.

1. An integral part of Kleinian theory is that which relates to very early infantile development, and to early object-relations. Later adult functioning is seen as rooted in this particular developmental view. As a consequence, Kleinian formulations regarding adult mental processes tend to use the same concepts as those which are used to describe infantile ones. However, I believe that it is a mistake to assume that the idea of projective identification as a mechanism is part of a 'package' which includes a theory of development and which has to be accepted in its entirety. Nor need we be put off by the concreteness of the metaphors used, for we all use metaphors in our theory (and in our interpretations), and what is important is to be aware that we are using metaphors. Consequently I have no difficulty in absorbing Mrs Klein's description of projective identification (first stage projective identification) into my own frame of reference, in which it can be regarded as a mechanism involving shifts and displacements in mental representation or in phantasy. I would put emphasis on its role as a mechanism for regulating unconscious feeling states and emphasize, too, that this mechanism can be divorced if necessary from the specific phantasy content associated with projective identification by Mrs Klein and her followers. Let me stress, however, that together with the Kleinians, I believe that processes of projective identification (in the sense in which I can make use of them) play a highly significant part in development and in the clinical psychoanalytic situation. Projective identification has given an added dimension to what we understand by transference, in that transference need not now be regarded simply as a repetition of the past. It can also be a reflection of phantasies about the relation to the analyst created in the present by projective identification and allied mechanisms.

2. The element of control of the objects (into which parts of the self have been projected) has been consistently stressed by Kleinian writers on projective identification, and it is an element which is, I believe, central to the concept. What one wants to get rid of in oneself can be disposed of by projective identification, and through controlling the object one can then gain the unconscious illusion that one is controlling the unwanted and projected aspect of the self. The

174

urge to control the object is evident in the process of 'living through another person' – Anna Freud's 'altruistic surrender' (Freud, 1936) can be taken to be a good example of this process. But there is a further aspect of the wish to control the object which is worth stressing. It is a common clinical observation that patients who feel guilty ('attacked by an internal persecutor') may deal with the guilt and gain powerful narcissistic supplies by projecting the guilty ('bad') part of the self on to another, while at the same time identifying (by 'introjective identification') with the persecutor. This provides a double gain, i.e. the gain of identifying with the (usually idealized) part of the superego introject as well as that of getting rid of the 'bad' unwanted part of the self. This gives a powerful motive for control of the object into which the projective identification has taken place (Sandler, 1960).

3. I have made use of the phrase 'into the object' rather than 'on to'. For many years, of course, projection 'into' was Kleinian usage, and non-Kleinians took care to speak of 'projection on to'. However, if we accept that projection is a process that involves self- and object-representations, then we need have no difficulty in accepting the phrase 'into the object'. But this does not mean, in my view, that we have necessarily to accept the idea that projective identification is accompanied by phantasies of entering and invading. However, the idea of 'forcing' an aspect of oneself into the object raises no difficulty because projective identification as a mechanism of defence aims at reducing anxiety, and this is a strong motive for applying force to keep the projected aspect on the other side of the self-object boundary. This force is reflected in the resistance shown by patients to accepting projected aspects of the self back into the self-representation.

4. The role of the self-object boundary is clearly important in projective identification and deserves a few comments. For projective identification to function as a mechanism of defence the existence of a boundary between self and object is essential so that a person can feel dissociated from the split-off parts of the self. In psychotic states it is difficult to maintain representational boundaries so projective identification may be intensified as an attempt to establish the boundaries. If they cannot be satisfactorily established then a state of panic may follow. It is worth noting that although we, as observers, may see the massive use made of projective identification in certain psychotic states, for the psychotic the existence of a persecutor in his phantasies means that he has (perhaps only temporarily) established a self-boundary

175

of sorts. Here I find myself in disagreement with those who tend to see projective identification as a psychotic mechanism only. While it may be massive in psychosis, it is nevertheless ubiquitous; it might also be preferable, in line with this, to speak of pathogenic rather than pathological projective identification.

5. It has been stated (Klein, 1946) that projective identification is a mechanism whereby the boundary between self and object is established in infancy. This notion of projective identification is difficult to reconcile with the requirement of a self-object boundary for successful projective identification. I would suggest that the concept need not be applied to these early differentiating processes, but, if it is, it could be understood as referring to the differentiation of mental representations of self and object in a way which is different from projective identification as a mechanism of defence. What I mean is that we can conceive of attempts at projection and identification (or, perhaps better, identification and dis-identification) occurring as the infant struggles to organize what has been regarded as a state of primary confusion between experiences of self and object, and thereby to gain control over his feeling states. These attempts can be taken to contribute, in their turn, to the gradual establishment of self and object boundaries.

6. If we turn now to second stage projective identification we must immediately be concerned with the relation between a phantasy of the object (the object representation) as modified by projective identification and its effect on a real external person. This is, as has been pointed out by many, most evident in the dimension transference-countertransference. From the point of view of my own frame of reference it is insufficient to say that the internal phantasy object is 'put into' the analyst. Rather, I understand the process in the following way:

(a) A phantasy is created, involving the analyst. Projective identification enters into the creation of the phantasy, which is a wishful one, i.e. it has behind it a pressure towards gratification or fulfilment.

(b) The patient attempts to actualize (Sandler, 1976a) the unconscious wishful transference phantasies, to make them real, to experience them (either overtly or in disguised form) as part of reality. He will do this in numerous ways in the analytic situation, some of which will evoke a countertransference response which can be meaningful to the analyst in the ways described by Heimann, Racker, Grinberg and many others. In a previous paper (Sandler, 1976b), relating to

176

actualization and object relationships, I commented on the wishful phantasy as follows:

> [. . .] it involves a self-representation and object representation, and an interaction between the two. There is a role for both self and object. Thus the child who has a wish to cling has, as part of this wish, a mental representation of clinging to someone else; but he also has, in his wish, a representation of the object responding to his clinging in a particular way. Those role relationships which appear in the transference are representative of the important wishful aspect of the unconscious phantasy life. This is rather different from the idea of a wish consisting of a wishful aim being directed towards the object. A notion of an aim which seeks gratification needs to be amplified by an idea of a wished-for role interaction, with the wished-for or imagined response of the object being as much a part of the wishful phantasy as the activity of the subject in that wish or phantasy . . . it can be said that the patient in analysis attempts to actualise the role relationship inherent in his current dominant unconscious wish or phantasy, and that he will try to do this (usually in a disguised and symbolic way) within the framework of the analytic situation . . . it is not a great step to say that the striving towards actualisation is part of the wish-fulfilling aspect of all object relationships. I do not use the term actualisation here in the same sense as it is used by a number of other psychoanalytic authors, but quite simply in the dictionary sense, that is, as a making actual; a realisation in action or fact.

This quotation relates to the evocation of a response in the analyst which reflects in some way the role of the object in the current wishful phantasy of the patient. This would correspond to Racker's (1968) notion of the analyst's complementary identification with the phantasied object of the active internal object relationship. The concordant identification, on the other hand, can be said to be the analyst's identification with the self-representation involved in the patient's wishful phantasy. However, I want to suggest that countertransference response due to second stage projective identification is always based on identification with a phantasy object, and that when it appears to be identification with aspects of the self-representation, a further intrapsychic step has occurred in the patient's phantasying process, i.e. a further projective identification has taken place into a new phantasy analyst–object which then contains projected aspects of the self.

7. The central contribution to third stage projective identification is that of Wilfred Bion, and the container model is of substantial clinical and theoretical interest. What I understand by it, in my own frame of reference, is the capacity of the caretaking mother to be attentive to and tolerant of the needs, distress, anger as well as the love of the infant, and to convey, increasingly, a reassurance that she can 'contain' these feelings and, at an appropriate time, respond in a considered and relevant way. Through this the infant learns that his distress is not disastrous, and by internalizing the 'containing' function of the mother (through identification or introjection) gains an internal source of strength and well-being. The 'reverie' of the mother is to be distinguished from an immediate 'reflex' response to the child. The latter process does not require the identification with the child's distress in the same way as does the 'reverie' of the 'containing' mother.

As far as the analytic situation is concerned, there is a parallel with the description given for the mother and infant. The analyst as 'container' is, as I see it, the analyst who can tolerate the patient's distress, hostility, love – indeed, all his phantasies and feelings, and who as a consequence of his 'reverie' can return them to the patient in the form of interpretations which will allow the patient to accept as aspects of himself those parts which he had previously considered to be dangerous and threatening, and which had been dealt with defensively, with ensuing cost. What I find unacceptable is the notion that this process is one of projective identification, unless the concept is stretched to extreme limits. We would have to say, for example, that the child's cry of distress is 'put into' the mother by projective identification, and it seems to me that this represents a caricature of the original concept. The 'container' model can, I believe, be fruitfully separated from the developmental theory to which it is attached, as well as from the concept of projective identification (although what the analyst will 'contain' will encompass the patient's transference projections as well as his distress), and has value in its own right. In this regard the following comments (Sandler and Sandler, 1984) are relevant:

> . . . to achieve what we regard as the aim of the analytic work we need to bring the patient to the point where he can tolerate, in a

safer and more friendly fashion, the previously unacceptable aspects of himself. In order to do this he will need to gain insight, in an emotionally convincing manner, not only into the content of his unconscious phantasies, but also into the nature of what, for present purposes, we shall refer to as his 'inner world', i.e. his unconscious relation to his introjects, with whom he had a continual unconscious internal dialogue . . ., his unconscious anxieties and conflicts as well as his methods of resolving such conflicts. This includes, of course, an understanding of his own usual defensive mechanisms and manoeuvres, with particular reference to the projections and externalizations that occur in his unconscious phantasy life – the spectrum of mechanisms that have come to be called projective identification. To the extent that we can achieve our analytic aims we will . . . be able to bring about the reduction of conflict and associated painful affects, and to permit a deflection of what was not previously tolerated near consciousness into conscious or preconscious thought and phantasy . . . it is our task to work with the patient in such a way that as much as possible of the content of what has come close to the surface layers . . . can be made readily available to consciousness. In our work we strive to bring about the liberation of such material through appropriate interpretations, particularly the interpretation of conflict. But because what we have available is the adult form of the relevant unconscious content, in order to anchor the progressive mapping of the patient's inner world and the central and recurring themes in his present unconscious, we have also to reconstruct the patient's past in a relevant way, just as much as we have to make constructions about his current inner world (which is, of course, a direct descendant of the inner world he formed in childhood); and we link the two together.

8. Projective identification has been regarded as the basis for empathy, but a simple statement of this sort does not have a great deal of explanatory power without amplification. I want to suggest that the state of primary confusion between self and object which I referred to earlier in this paper (usually called primary identification) is one which persists in modified form throughout life, and which can provide the basis for the capacity for empathy. Some time ago W. G. Joffe and I put forward the following formulation in a paper on the tendency to persistence (Sandler and Joffe, 1967), and I have

taken the liberty of quoting from it at length because of its relevance to projective identification:

> Identification (we refer here to secondary identification), as a number of authors now see it, involves a change in the self-representation on the model of an object-representation; and projection is the attribution to an object-representation of some aspect of the self-representation. These processes can occur after the boundaries between self- and object-representations have been created; before that, we have the state referred to by Freud as primary identification, 'adualism' by Piaget and primary identity by others. A better term to designate this early state might be 'primary confusion' [. . .] If we apply the idea of persistence to processes of identification and projection in the older child or adult we can postulate that there will always be a momentary persistence of the primary state of confusion, however fleeting, whenever an object is perceived or its representation recalled. What happens then is that the boundaries between self and object become imposed by a definite act of inhibiting and of boundary-setting. It is as if the ego says 'This is I and that is he.' This is a very different idea from that of a static ego boundary or self-boundary which remains once it has been created. What develops [. . .] is the ego function of disidentifying, a mental act of distinguishing between self and object which has to be repeated over and over again; and the function of disidentifying makes use of structures which we can call boundaries.
>
> The persistence of this genetically earlier primary confusion in normal experience is evident when we think of the way in which we move and tense our bodies when we watch ice skaters, or see a Western. We must all surely have had the experience of righting ourselves when we see someone slip or stumble. In these everyday experiences there is a persistence of the primary confusion between self and object; and this may more readily occur in states of relaxation or of intense concentration in which the bringing into play of boundary-setting may temporarily be suspended or delayed. [. . .] The persistence of this genetically early state [. . .] must surely provide the basis for feelings of empathy, for aesthetic appreciation, for forms of transference and countertransference in analysis [. . .] and in connection with what we call secondary identification and projection, we would suggest that the bridge to these processes

is the persisting momentary state of primary confusion or primary identification which occurs before the process of 'sorting out' or 'dis-identifying' occurs. One result of this 'sorting out' may be that aspects of the object-representation are incorporated into the self-representation and vice-versa.

The existence of fleeting primary identifications after infancy can give us a tool for improving our understanding of processes of projective identification, for the notion of persistence allows us to account for the fact that we must, in some way, be aware that what we have projected is our own in order to feel the relief of being rid of it. I would suggest that in all forms of defensive projection there is a constant to-and-fro, an alternation between the momentary state of 'oneness', of primary identification or primary confusion, and the 'sorting out' referred to earlier. This would allow one to feel that what is projected is fleetingly 'mine', but then reassuringly 'not mine'.

I want to end these comments by expressing some concerns which I am sure are shared by others. First, because projective identification is more of a descriptive than an explanatory concept, and because its range of meanings is wide, its use without further elaboration provides a ready pseudo-explanation. Such pseudo-explanations are tempting, and we should be on our guard against them. If projective identification is used as an explanation, its specific meaning in the relevant context should, I think, always be given. Second, because of the close link between the concept of projective identification and our extended understanding of countertransference, it is tempting to see all feelings, phantasies and reactions of the analyst to his patient as being an outcome of what the patient has 'put into' the analyst by means of projective identification.

Unfortunately, the differentiation of what belongs to the patient and what to the analyst is likely to remain with us for some time as a difficult technical problem.

Continental Europe

Introduction

Elizabeth Spillius

The three papers in this section were given at a meeting of the European Psychoanalytical Federation at Prague in 2002. They were part of an attempt to achieve greater clarity about the differences and agreements among European analysts on topics of mutual interest. Eike Wolff, the editor of the journal *Psychoanalysis in Europe*, introduced the topic of projective identification by saying:

> In the last fifteen years, the term 'projective identification' has expanded at an inflationary rate and in some places has thrown concepts such as 'transference' and 'transference neurosis' into the background. Reflection on the various uses of the term in different European countries and analytical schools can strengthen the awareness of the advantages and the dangers involved in extensive habitual use of the concept.

At the conference Elizabeth Spillius briefly introduced the topic, followed by Helmut Hinz, who described the reception of the concept in Germany, Jorge Canestri of the Italian Association, who talked about the fate of the concept in Italy and Spain, and Jean-Michel Quinodoz of the Swiss Society, who described the response of French-speaking psychoanalysts to the concept. All four contributions were published in 2002 in *Psychoanalysis in Europe: Bulletin 56* (Canestri, 2002; Hinz, 2002; J.-M. Quinodoz, 2002a; Spillius, 2002). The papers of Hinz and Canestri are reproduced here, followed by Quinodoz's 2003 version of his paper, somewhat revised for inclusion in the present book.

Projective identification

The fate of the concept in Germany

Helmut Hinz

Reception, positive adoption, critical and aversive voices: German contributions

In order to outline the reception of the concept of projective identi-fication, I began by looking in the index of key words to the psycho-analytic journal *Psyche* to see when this term first started to appear in articles there. It is first mentioned in 1957 with the translation of Melanie Klein's *Envy and Gratitude*, followed in 1960 by Klein's 'Some theoretical conclusions regarding the life of the infant' (Klein, 1952c). These in turn are followed by Betty Joseph's 'Some charac-teristics of the psychopathic personality' (Joseph, 1961), as well as A. Bonnard's 'Pre-body ego types of (pathological) mental func-tioning' (Bonnard, 1961), and J. O. Wisdom's 'A methodological approach to the problem of hysteria' (Wisdom, 1962). The first German contribution to make use of the key term projective identi-fication was published in 1962. It was by Wolfgang Loch and bore the title 'Anmerkungen zur Pathogenese und Metapsychologie einer schizophrenen Psychose' (Loch, 1962). It was followed by H. A. Thorner (1963). In 1963, Bion's *Theory of Thinking* was made available in translation, followed by another contribution by Wolfgang Loch on the subject of identification-introjection.

During the period up to 1992, the term projective identification appeared in a total of 40 articles in the journal *Psyche*. In 1985, R. Zwiebel wrote a report about a conference in Jerusalem organized by Joseph Sandler on the theme 'Projection, Identification and Projective Identification' (Zwiebel, 1985) and, in 1988, a first original work by the same author was published using the term projective identification in the title (Zwiebel, 1988). This paper offers a sound theoretical overview of the concept of projective identification. It was followed in 1989 by a clinical presentation by Hinz with the title: 'Projektive Identifizierung und psychoanalytischer Dialog' (Hinz, 1989).

As early as 1965, Wolfgang Loch was giving projective identification a central place in his lectures because its interpretation could contribute to a 'restructuring of the ego' (Loch, 1965, p. 55) insofar as 'strongly defended material' and 'split-off parts' of the ego are brought into words, and this 'strongly stimulates a new balance' and a 'better foundation of the ego'. In a 1975 lecture, in his apt formulation,

> the analyst gets projected parts of the patient 'put inside himself', and in such a way that he is forced to take up these parts, and then, for example, feels the urge to do something. This suggests that projective identification holds an intrusive potential for action.
>
> (Loch, 2001, p. 127)

The oral transmission of the term, for example through lectures, guest speakers, supervisions, is not easy to trace. In 1995, R. Klüwer assessed the overall situation as follows: 'It is safe to say that Melanie Klein did not have much influence on German psychoanalysis until the end of the eighties and was quite insignificant in the seventies and eighties before that' (Klüwer, 1995, p. 47).

One important reason for the delayed reception of Melanie Klein's research lies in German history. This became the subject of increased reflection in Germany from 1977 after the IPA Members' meeting turned down the German invitation to hold the 1981 IPA Conference in Berlin. Commenting on this episode in her preface to the German edition of the *Complete Works of Melanie Klein*, Ruth Cycon (1995) had the following to say:

> The cruel and destructive psychotic phantasies discovered by Melanie Klein, of chopping up, tearing up, robbing and defecating, of burning (through urine), of poisoning (through excrement), of gassing (through intestinal gases) and the total annihilation of the object that has become absolutely bad, through excessive projection, provoked horror, rejection and hostile defence when

187

described in detail, because they had become a reality in German history. . . . It was unbearable to look this time of destruction and irreparable guilt in the eye, something that only seems possible for us human beings over a longer span of time.

(Cycon, 1995, p. xii)

Although this is a German problem, it is more generally rooted in a refusal to recognize human destructiveness. Reflecting on this difficulty, Freud commented: 'I presume that a strong affective factor is coming into effect in this rejection. Why have we ourselves needed such a long time before we decided to recognize an aggressive instinct?' (Freud, 1933, p. 103). Seventy years later, a strong affective factor is still at work, resulting in continuing widespread rejection of the theory of the death instinct, of destructive narcissism and certain aspects of projective identification (see Frank, 2002).

In Germany, from about 1980, a small, but growing number of analysts began to experience and become aware of a pervasive lack of clinical understanding. Their intense personal wish for better understanding and practice in their day-to-day work with patients led them to London for supervision. They also formed supervision groups in Germany under the direction of psychoanalysts from the Kleinian group. Herbert Rosenfeld headed one of the first of these groups, in Heidelberg, from 1981 to his death at the end of 1986. Other groups followed and individual analysts and smaller groups worked regularly with Kleinians in London. This continuous joint clinical work resulted in a more precise knowledge and refinement of interpretative strategies for dealing with severely disturbed patients and with perverse, addictive and psychotic mechanisms in neurotic patients. In this way, practical experience was gained in working with early anxieties and defence formations, including projective identification. Ruth Cycon, a participant in the supervision group with Rosenfeld and later Feldman, sums it up this way: 'It was above all Herbert Rosenfeld who imparted a new understanding of the transference and countertransference processes and a Kleinian technique that seeks to comprehend everything the patient says, step by step, as expressing the current transference situation' (Cycon, 1995, p. xv). Such experiences had an impact on training analyses and supervisions of candidates. My own psychoanalytic development was shaped by them. In my estimation, the greatest differences between analysts in Germany today lie not so much in theoretical differences, such as their rejection or acceptance of the concept of projective identification, but in their practical firmness in examining countertransference and transference in the analytic situation precisely every step of the way. However, my experience has shown that this microanalysis in *hic et nunc et mecum* is refined and becomes more flexible through the concept of projective identification.

Then, in the 1990s, the discussion came to a head. A number of interesting papers on projective identification began to be published by German authors (Cycon, Beland, Gutwinski-Jeggle, among others). One Frankfurt author's comment on this development seems revealing to me: 'The concept is having a heyday at the moment, and I would even say it is running amok in the psychoanalytic literature. Nearly every author has his or her own idea of this process' (Dornes, 1993, p. 1145). This way of putting it, as almost 'running amok', shows what characterizes the term's reception in Germany: on the one hand, a broad positive reception of the concept, and on the other, the suspicion that it might be a source of dangerous influences.

On the positive reception of the concept

In 1995, Gutwinski-Jeggle summarized the reception of the concept in this way: 'The analytic world could not get around acknowledging Paula Heimann's concept of the countertransference nor Melanie Klein's observations on projective identification' (Gutwinski-Jeggle, 1995, p. 71).

In my opinion, this has to do with the intellectual strength of this Kleinian concept, which condensed a complex clinical experience to one single concept, or even tapped into it for the first time: namely, the experience that intrapsychic and interpersonal processes run in parallel and intersect and influence one another. This understanding of the analytic process is at the level of modern epistemology, which gave us the idea of the observer who is dependent on the observation. These interactions are easier to examine in the analytic situation with the help of an elastic term such as projective identification. The term 'projective identification' proves to be especially useful because it provides a common denominator for the multifarious, often simultaneous functions of this process: the desire to penetrate the object, to control and manipulate it, the perception or illusion of actually being able to do this, taking on the object's characteristics, getting rid

189

of a bad quality by putting it into the object, protecting a good one in the same way (Spillius, 1988b, pp. 83–84).

The concept of projective identification also proved to be useful in enabling analysts to explain intense countertransference feelings and impulses, which compelled one to act, in consequence of a non-verbal, action-based form of communication. Accordingly, in the subsequent period, many distinctions and further developments of the concept were also eagerly seized on and accepted: the important differentiation between normal and pathological projective identification, for example, and/or between a purely communicative and an evacuative function of projective identification. Spillius now speaks in terms of evocatory and non-evocatory, and Britton of attributive and acquisitive forms.

Technical refinements in treatment resulting from the concept of projective identification were also adopted. One example was Segal's suggestion that if an interpretation of the projectively identified object-relations aspects is given too early and is not sufficiently worked through in the countertransference, it may be experienced by the patient as a 'persecutory pushing back' of what had been projected (Segal, 1964, p. 121). Another was Steiner's differentiation between analyst-centred and patient-centred interpretation (J. Steiner, 1993, p. 144). Contributions on technique were also forthcoming in Germany, such as the distinction between 'interpretation of the projective identification' versus 'interpretation from within the projective identification' (Hinz, 1989, p. 616), and the distinction between communicating as conveying an experience and communicating as sharing an experience (Hinz, 1989, p. 611).

My own clinical experience in dealing with the concept of projective identification is shaped by the analysis of a patient in her late twenties with a borderline syndrome. She had a severe object-relations disorder, behaved promiscuously, quickly broke off every relationship she began and had therefore also already had very many initial analytic contacts that failed or never got beyond the initial contact, without being able to begin an analysis. In this analysis, what initially played a key role was that she talked a lot and very fast, but more with the unconscious intention of avoiding understanding. Understanding would have meant the beginning of a relationship and that had to be avoided, because this was connected to evoking the early trauma she had suffered. The analyst was projectively identified with not-understanding, which could thus be brought into a meaningful interpretative context in this way.

When this hurdle was overcome, a great inner unrest came to the fore, which also projectively affected the analyst. Over a long phase of the analysis, the interpretative work consisted in taking the tormenting unrest that the patient created in the analyst as a key message, which the patient was sending without being able to put it into words. Simply stating what the analyst felt and understood as projective identification, initially without making any further causal connection beyond that, led with impressive clarity to first moments of calm in this analysis. All I said, for example, was: 'You're full of agitation, you feel like a bundle of nerves.' I think this is an example of interpretation from within the projective identification.

This example is characterized by an understanding of a long-lasting countertransference experience in terms of projective identification. With a second clinical illustration, I would like to show how counter-transference perceptions of short duration can be used to leave aside the content level of communication in favour of an underlying level of unconscious communication that has greater relevance. A patient spoke so quietly that several words and then the context of what was being said remained incomprehensible. In situations like this it can be extremely helpful to think in terms of a projective iden-tification and to resist the impulse to ask for clarification. Leaving aside the substantive context of the content and taking my hunches about this patient and the current situation into account, I inter-preted that what she probably wanted to tell me more than anything else at the moment was how mysterious her relationship was to her, and she was wondering how she would be able to understand what was going on here. She immediately reacted very defensively and full of cynical self-deprecation: 'I'm an idiot, mentally deranged.' This self-destructiveness is otherwise usually hidden behind superficial friendliness. It is activated when it becomes possible for her to articu-late this level of her search for a relationship and her experience of not-knowing. At this level it is entirely unclear to her whether she is dealing with a helpful or a destructive object.

Critical voices and aversions to the concept

Critics of the concept of projective identification take their cue from Melanie Klein's own ambivalence about her concept. She apparently had doubts about its usefulness and was afraid that it would be misused as an alibi for the analyst's own insufficiencies, because he might downplay the complexity of the analytic relationship and blame his own emotional reactions on the patient without working on them, integrating and converting them further reflexively. Hanna Segal has often described how Melanie Klein once told an analyst: 'You need a little self-analysis' (Gutwinski-Jeggle, 1995, p. 72) because he felt confused and took this to be an expression of confusion in his patient.

This concern about potential misuse of the concept is often coupled with the accusation that Melanie Klein had a mechanistic understanding, that she believed parts of the self are put into the object directly without taking the object's capacity to work on them into account. This is identical with the prejudice or preconceived notion, that Kleinians deny or underestimate the influence of the analyst, the object or external reality, both in the present and genetically.

Accordingly, in Germany there is a widespread opinion that the Kleinian technique is 'highly theory-driven' (Thomä and Kächele, 1985, p. 150), intrusive and that Kleinian technique leads to super-ego intropression and causes the clinical phenomena that are found. These critical opinions, which to some extent are due to weaknesses of early Kleinian work, and to the adoption of an inferior imitation of her theory and technique, easily become solidified into the form of prejudices if they spring from theory that is too quickly received and intellectualized.

In many cases, I think, there is also a fear of the clinical experience that could be gained if these concepts were applied skilfully. Another factor involved in the rejection of the concept is the suspicion that the fuzziness in the concept's definition leads to confusion, directly to countertransference mysticism, to a lack of scientific rigour and to self-isolation in the scientific community. However, it has already been pointed out that the elasticity of a concept has advantages in clinical practice for its clinically flexible usefulness. We should not follow the example of those philosophers who are always cleaning their spectacles in order to see better but never actually looking through them in order to see anything.

Instead, let us recall Max Planck, who illustrated the usefulness and importance of basic concepts that cannot be defined with perfect clarity by demonstrating to his friends while washing dishes how a wine-glass can be polished clean with a dirty tea-cloth. The difficulty of defining projective identification more clearly lies in the high degree of complexity of the processes that it seeks to grasp. It is an attempt to make explicit that an archaic form of communication leads to an interpenetration of the boundaries between two psychic systems (subject and object) for the purpose of building up primarily one of these systems.

A quote from a textbook on psychoanalytic therapy will serve as an illustration of these critical-aversive voices:

> If most of the most important part of the exchange between patient and analyst could be explained according to the model of projective and introjective identifications, then psychoanalysis would have its own and original theory of communication. This would largely be beyond critical examination by other disciplines because in cases of doubt it could always be said by recourse that unconscious processes are involved here.
>
> (Thomä and Kächele, 1985, p. 151)

This seems to suggest that analysts are not allowed to discover anything that others cannot scrutinize with their methods, and that a fruitful concept should not be used because it could be misused.

It is repeatedly contended that the concept of projective identification has been disproved by the results of infant research. This is not borne out on closer examination: infant researchers come to the interesting conclusion that

> psychoanalytic theory so far underestimates the infants, yet on the one hand it tends to overestimate the infant's abilities by deeming it capable of complicated mental operations – such as hallucinatory wish-fulfilment, omnipotent phantasies and projective identification – which it does not even have yet.
>
> (Dornes, 1993, p. 1116)

Many results of infant research provide impressive proof of the infant's abilities for coherent self- and object perception (Dornes, 1993, p. 1129). As I see it, this result confirms an important prerequisite for Kleinian developmental theory: at the beginning is the experience of separateness, not non-separateness or symbiosis. These are already a form of defence if separateness and infantile need for help are felt to be unbearable. Projective identification can then be understood to be an early active mechanism of protection and defence. Winnicott already assumed that there was an alternation of coherence and incoherence and Bion described the ongoing oscillation between the paranoid–schizoid and the depressive position (or between PS–D). Wolfgang Loch assumed that the (more coherent) depressive position might precede the (incoherent) paranoid–schizoid position.

In my view, the controversy regarding projective identification has to do with divergent concepts of representation and symbol. There are those who would not speak in terms of representation and symbol formation until language development starts and elaborated conditions prevail; while others assume that early, archaic coherence-experiences close to the body exist, i.e. precursors of representation and symbol formation. These are stored in the memory as action sequences and interaction patterns between the baby and the person taking care of it (in connection with physical sensations and the care-taking of great bodily needs). Gaddini speaks here in terms of body-phantasy and phantasy in the body. At the same time, image impressions are stored as iconic representations. Under these conditions experiences are inscribed in the memory and rewritten – in other words pre-represented, while not yet represented in the word-memory. It then is possible to imagine that defence processes become operative from the very beginning in moments of excessive strain on the coherence of the child's psyche, such as Gaddini's imitation and projective identification. Infant research appropriately assumes that 'Thought by the pre-symbolic child [is] tied to action and perception, senso–motoric and not symbolic' and that 'Its "object presentation" [is] an object sensation and identical with the sensory perceptions that the object triggers in him' (Dornes, 1993, pp. 1144 and 1143).

At this point, one problem of infant researchers often sets in, namely an epistemological and psychoanalytic naivety. The infant is imagined as being the passive receptacle of sense perceptions. It is forgotten that the infant too can only tap into his world and make perceptions by means of unconscious phantasies that act like pieces of theory.

To conclude my discussion of the concept's rejection by infant researchers, I will once again quote a passage from Dornes that provides a good illustration of the clinical relevance, practicability and modernity of the term projective identification, which is fifty years old:

A depressive infant does not project any depressive phantasies that it does not have, but its physical posture has become sunken, its motor skills and breathing has slowed down, its face is lifeless, its interaction lacking in vitality: (. . .) even adults who are not depressive are infiltrated by this affect and style of interaction. Their interactions slow down, their facial expression becomes less lively, and after a short time they feel exhausted. An unpleasant sensation of the infant has settled on them. It was not 'projected', but communicated via interactional forms of behaviour. The adult cannot evade the communicative affect entirely as in the case of projective identification; it now interacts depressively itself and gives the affect back to the infant.

(Dornes, 1993, p. 1146)

Finally, I would like to mention one more reason for the aversion to the term projective identification which seems important to me. Bion had taken over the concept of projective identification and expanded it to describe a fundamental form of emotional mental exchange and the emergence of the psyche. Projective identification is the decisive communicative bridge between inside and outside, infant and caring person. Projective identification can therefore aptly be referred to as a 'social umbilical cord' (Frank, 2001). Initially, however, the concept was much more narrowly defined. Melanie Klein emphasized the mode of aggressive penetration into the object, taking possession of it, manipulating and controlling it. She spoke of the 'prototype of an aggressive object relation'. By expanding the concept into a fundamental mechanism in the emergence of the psychic apparatus, of thought and thinking, this aspect receded into the background. And yet precisely this violent and perhaps ugly side has great theoretical and clinical importance. This is the case not only when we have to deal with serious pathologies and unbearable mental states that can only be projected. The packaging of the concept in the concept of 'containment' and its popularization contributed further towards making it pleasing. Thus, the ugly but realistic aspects were extracted from the concept. Yet, these are necessary in order to be able to perceive and modify psychic reality in its cruel and deadly aspects. When terms like containment or, fifteen years earlier, holding function became fashionable, these watered down and lost the complexity of the concept of projective identification. In the popularized form of containment there is only successful containing, but no longer any form of failure, which Bion clearly described. The following playful formulation nevertheless captures something true about the story of the reception of projective identification in Germany. There are good and bad Kleinians: Melanie Klein is a bad Kleinian and Bion is a good Kleinian. My personal, only slightly ironic statistic reads as follows: in the Federal Republic of Germany, about 20 per cent are bad Kleinians, and 80 per cent are good Kleinians. Only very few want to be counted among the bad ones.

The action potential in unconscious phantasy, in the transference, and the intrusive action potential of projective identification

Ever since 'Remembering, repeating and working through' (Freud, 1914), analysts have known that the analytic aim of conscious remembering can usually only be achieved via the detour of repeating. The technical knowledge that transference is a form of remembering has also been established. Ideas, experiences and actions emanating from an unconscious object relations experience and fantasy are repeated. Positive and negative feelings, libidinal and aggressive aspirations, fantasies and behaviour patterns – in other words, the totality of an object relationship – are repeated and actualized, which in turn implies an element of action. The concept of countertransference as an emotional–mental and initially unconscious reaction by the analyst to the transference, has also become generally indispensable. Anxiety had to be overcome just to recognize the transference, for the treatment ideal of rapid dissolution of a disorder failed when it came up against the phenomenon of repetition and the transference as resistance to the continuing process of investigation. It took courage to give serious consideration to the phenomenon of countertransference, given the fact that it shattered the scientific ideal of the distanced, contemplative analysis of a phenomenon and the independence of the observation from the observer. Years of psychoanalytic work were required before the fact that transference is not just a hindrance to the analysis, but can also be its ally could be established and accepted. The same is true with regard to the long and hard struggle to gain recognition that the countertransference is an important emotional indicator for and instrument of psychoanalytic investigation and not a failure on the analyst's part, as it were. As we know, Paula Heimann and Heinrich Racker were revolutionary pioneers in this endeavour, while Melanie Klein and the Kleinians were still dragging their feet. And today we know that the counter-transference is 'the best of servants but the worst of masters' (Segal, 1981, p. 86).

This discovery of the interaction and reciprocal dynamics of trans-ference and countertransference was extremely uncomfortable for psychoanalysis, but also extremely interesting. As a consequence, the category of causality was pushed into the background and the cate-gory of reciprocity moved to the fore as a complementary paradigm. This development was further radicalized by the discovery of projec-tive identification, as the concept of projective identification is the description of an interpersonal process which draws the analyst, actively and with pressure, into affirming the patient's unconscious system of perception, thinking and fantasy. The patient's intensive yearning for identity seeks to bring external reality into harmony with their unconscious fantasy (Feldman, 1997; Hinz, 2002b) because if they do not harmonize, this can trigger intense anxiety.

On the internal affinity of transference and projective identification

This unconscious but effective pressure to bring the object relation-ship in line with the unconscious object–relations fantasy comes from an action component and/or action potential that is already inherent in the simple transference. Sandler, Dare, and Holder (1973) had defined the following with regard to the transference:

> that transference need not be restricted to the illusory appercep-tion of another person . . . but can be taken to include the uncon-scious (and often subtle) attempts to manipulate or to provoke situations with others which are a concealed repetition of earlier experiences and relationships (. . .). It is likely that such acceptance or rejection of a transference role is not based on a conscious awareness of what is happening, but rather on uncon-scious cues.
>
> (Sandler et al., 1973, p. 48, quoted by Klüwer, 1995, p. 52)

The intrinsic affinity between transference and projective identifi-cation becomes clear from Sandler's definition of the concept of projective identification in 1984 at the conference in Jerusalem:

197

In our opinion, it is useful to regard projective identification as a mechanism in which undesired aspects of the self (or desired, but unachievable states of the self) are perceived and called forth in another person. This is accompanied by the attempt to control this other person, in order thus to gain the unconscious illusion of control over the externalised aspects of the self. The projected behavior is evoked and induced by means of subtle unconscious pressure and cues . . . and can be seen best in the transference-countertransference situation in the therapy.

(quoted in Zwiebel, 1985, p. 458)

The common features of transference and projective identification seem important to me. They have in common the inherent endeavour to push the other person unconsciously towards a repetition, towards a behaviour, towards a pattern of action or to an action, to manipulate the person subtly, in order to control him. This common basis implies that the concept of projective identification does not describe a special case or an exceptional situation, but rather deepens and refines the concepts of transference and of projection. For those dimensions of the personality in which paranoid-schizoid mechanisms are predominant, in other words, where the symbolization, or representation, of the absent object is damaged, splitting and omnipotence hold sway as defences. Making a sharp distinction between remembering and repeating, or as the case may be, between thinking and action, may be misleading for the analyst's understanding, and this is not only the case in severely disturbed patients. The patterns of action and behaviour in the analytic situation are the concretized forms of thinking and experiencing respectively available in a given case, 'because we basically have to assume that patients bring their customary attitudes and modes of behaviour as a whole into the relationship with the analyst, not just their way of thinking' (Joseph, 2001, p. 135)

An important German contribution in this area was made by Wolfgang Loch, who offered the following formulation in 1965:

Transference and countertransference, are, as we know, 'motivated' forms of behaviour in the sense that they represent object relationships that are driven by or brought about by instinctual drive needs. But this means that the ego, as the executive organ, is under pressure; for in such cases, it works, energetically speaking with motivational cathexes which press for a rapid discharge. (. . .)[40] In the analyst's introspection, the thus instinctually determined interpretations are heralded by their urgent character. One feels virtually forced to give a certain association as an interpretation. If one can analyze this pressing association quickly, it is possible to allow the countertransference motivating it to become conscious and thus put oneself in a position to verbalize a 'constructive' interpretation.

(Loch, 1965, pp. 41–42)

Freud established a system of coordinates for the analyst with his statement:

When I instruct a patient to abandon reflection of any kind and to tell me whatever comes into his head, I will rely firmly on the presumption that he will not be able to abandon the purposive ideas inherent in the treatment and I feel justified in inferring that what seem to be the most innocent and arbitrary things which he tells me are in fact related to his illness. There is another purposive idea of which the patient has no suspicion – one relating to myself.

(Freud, 1900, p. 532)

Between this X-axis and Y-axis lies the field of research of analysis. To the extent that the patient is always talking about his relationship with the doctor, everything that he tells him is

in the sense of the transference at the same time a stimulus for the doctor, in which – unconscious – expectation is brought forth that this partner will react in just the same way as the decisive others (those persons who had a formative influence on him) have done in the past. The fact is, the patient must want this; consequently, he keeps holding on to the illness, indeed he is constantly driven to nip in the bud every attempt to overcome the illness, insofar as he is holding on to the illness, as indeed he must, (. . .) want the

---

40 The counterpart to such 'motivational cathexes' are so-called 'attention cathexes'. Only if the ego works with attention cathexes, that do not have any aims such as specific objects or selectivity . . . is there a guarantee that not inner needs, but real features decisively determine perception and experience.

(Loch, 1965, pp. 41–42)

same manner and attitude [as those] of the persons in which the illness thrived (. . .) In that sense, transference means evoking those conditions which perpetuate the pathological solution.

(Loch, 1965, pp. 39–40)

As already indicated above, the common basis of transference, projection and projective identification has an important source in memory. We can assume that the first traces of memory come from the perception of bodily processes and physical interactions with the caregiver. For analytical investigation and treatment, it is probably important to be able to work not just at the level of the lexical memory and iconic memory, in other words, at the level of memory in words and images, respectively, but also at the level of action-patterns, in other words, to search for the action-memory, which is manifested in the behaviour patterns in the doctor–patient relationship.

It can be assumed that the analyst will not be able to make headway with his patient into areas that are relevant for the genesis of the illness and for its healing process until he recognizes and interprets processual figures and patterns of action, 'process identifications' (Danckwardt, 2001) below the level of the spoken contents. Closely connected to this are recommendations to attend not only to the content of the verbal communication, but also its form, not only to what is being communicated, but also how and what function that which is being communicated presumably has in the current relationship, taking note not only of the verbal communications, but also the gesticular, phonetic, the scenic and the action dialogue (Bion, Loch, Argelander, Klüwer, Joseph, Feldman). Form is sedimented content, psychoanalytically expressed: the form of the message holds a hidden meaning which corresponds to a deeper transference layer, which initially cannot be communicated verbally.

Scenic function of the unconscious and action dialogue: event and interpretation, interaction of unconscious phantasy and behaviour

In 1946, Melanie Klein described the processes to which, according to Elizabeth Spillius, she initially rather casually, then in 1952 definitively, gave the name of 'projective identification'. At the same time, 'split-off parts of the ego are also projected on to the mother or, as I

200

would rather call it, into the mother' (Klein, 1952a, p. 8) In a foot-note to this statement she adds, almost apologetically:

> The description of such primitive processes suffers from a great handicap, for these phantasies arise at a time when the infant has not yet begun to think in words. In this context, for instance, I am using the expression 'to project into another person' because this seems to me the only way of conveying the unconscious process I am trying to describe.

As far as I can tell, this situation remains unchanged, even if develop-mental psychologists use the new term 'interactional communica-tion' instead of projective identification and unconscious phantasy. If the infant researchers then also forget that the infant is not a passive receptacle but creates its environment at the same time in accordance with its inner reality, this would be a setback behind the insights of psychoanalysis.

Therefore, one can agree with Dornes, for example, who makes a case for a theory of the interaction between phantasy and behaviour. Although these processes still cannot be described more precisely or more simply even today, the auxiliary construction that, based on the principle of human similarity, 'analogous and/or complementary affects' can be evoked in the analyst seems helpful to me (Dantlgraber, 1982). Understanding grows from classifying the evoked affects in 'emotionally accented ideational images, in other words, phantasies', i.e. through the integration of a previously 'split-off affect into a meaning context' (Dantlgraber, 1982). What seems important about this is that emotion results from situational interpretation and situa-tional interpretation leads to emotion (Beland, 1992, pp. 63 and 66). Together they form an elementary unit. Early processes of exchange, in other words introjection, projection and projective identification, thus mean that psycho-physical sensitivities, phantasies and affects of the parents and the infant are communicated via interactional processes and mutual assignments of meaning and taken up, understood or misunderstood by the infant and the parents, that is to say, are inter-preted or misinterpreted by them.

My impression is that the current focus of the psychoanalytic discussion has more or less shifted away from projective identifica-tion and towards examining its results. Numerous works on enact-ment, involvement and on the microanalysis of the patient's reactions to an interpretation and the effort to listen to the listening prove this. In this connection, it should also be pointed out that in Germany Alfred Lorenzer had a great deal of influence with the concept of Tiefenhermeneutik (hermeneutics of depth) and the Hermeneutik des Leibes (hermeneutics of the body), as did Hermann Argelander, with his works at the end of the 1960s on the scenic function of the unconscious. And Rolf Klüwer, with his studies on the communicative function of acting out in the analytic situation, apparently independently of the Kleinian research and using different terminology, assigned great importance to the observation of enactments and modes and patterns of behaviour in the doctor–patient relationship. In particular, the works of Argelander had a strong influence in shaping the analytic understanding in Germany, as did the works of Racker on concordant and/or complementary countertransference, which are closely related to the theme of projective identification.

In spite of these developments in the direction of microanalytic research on the situational and actional aspects, on enactment and role adoption, it is important to note with some modesty that even the analyst who works conscientiously and in a modern fashion in this way and observes his countertransference feelings in order to make use of them as a treatment instrument is not immune to the risk of finding only what he already knew was there anyway, in the manner of a subsuming logic. However, the same is also true for all other psychoanalytic means of access. This is why the methodological and utopian guiding principle of evenly suspended attention (disciplined pushing back of theory, memory and wish) is of the utmost importance.

How much development takes place in an analysis also depends essentially on the analyst's person; into which areas he has advanced in his training analysis, what theoretical concepts he favours, what experiences he can take in (cf. Money-Kyrle, 1991): the degree to which the analyst can, for example, think and feel in terms of sharing the responsibility for 'mistakes, misunderstandings and failures' (Steffens, 1999, p. 79). Can he uphold or restore a 'thinking and feeling space' for himself (Gutwinski-Jeggle, 1995, p. 76) under the influence of an intrusive action potential? The concept of projective identification can help in any case to feel complex clinical situations more flexibly and think them through. To give an example: anyone who knows the difference between a projective identification for the purpose of communicating an unspeakable (or inexpressible) experience and a projective identification that has the purpose of getting rid of an unconscious experience, knowing that it depends on his own personal make-up, his own reaction, whether or not projective identification can be turned into a communication (from 'Notes on some schizoid mechanisms') (Spillius, 1990, p. 106) can in a corresponding situation wind up deciding that the patient can, at the moment, under the greatest pressure, do nothing more than get rid of everything and throw it out of himself. Even in this situation, this could still prove to have a value as an acceptable interpretation and secure its status as a verbal communication.

Projective identification

The fate of the concept in Italy and Spain

Jorge Canestri

In order to trace an outline, even though incomplete, of the fate and use of the concept of projective identification in Italian and in Spanish psychoanalysis, I have examined its literature and have benefited from the help of colleagues from these two countries. I am grateful to them, although the responsibility for anything that is missing or inaccurate, and for the general layout of this presentation, obviously falls on me.[41]

Some general premises

Some preliminary statements will be useful to help identify the problem we are dealing with. First, even when we have in mind the study of the evolution of a specific concept, it is necessary first to outline the history of the general evolution of the psychoanalytical theory in each country, and to describe the modalities for training in the psychoanalytical institutes and the general cultural orientation in the society. The acceptance of a particular concept by the psycho-analytical community is the result of many factors: some of them are exquisitely individual, for example training undergone in another

41 I especially thank for their assistance my Italian colleagues Jacqueline Amati Mehler, Stefano Bolognini and Federico Flegenheimer, and my Spanish colleague Luis Martin Cabré.

country; others are more general, for example the theoretical orientation and the traditions of the society. This outline exceeds our present capacity and, in the case of the history of psychoanalysis in Italy, we can rely on some excellent treatises.

Second, regarding the concept itself, there appears to be a certain amount of consensus within the literature around the fact that Melanie Klein, in 1946, proposes a definition of projective identification adhering to that of a typical defence mechanism in the classical sense: it seems to be linked to instinctual problems and reveals the need for the ego to defend itself. In 1955 she extends the process to normality, both in order to account for empathy as well as to consider its functions in normal development. These two meanings would be explored in various Italian and Spanish works on the matter, but the use of the second meaning is predominant. This orientation does not appear to follow the British orientation: an initial study of the psychotic pathologies with a particular focus on the psychopathological role played in them by projective identification; a subsequent analysis of the communication functions in the mother–child and in the analyst–patient relationships.

Third, the initial clarity of Klein's definition, describing a specific and unitary mechanism, becomes progressively obscured. A concept that has become inflated and confused in its clinical and theoretical use (Amati Mehler, 2003) is referred to, and there is a tendency to consider it as 'a general term indicating a certain number of distinct processes that are however correlated, connected to splitting and projection', according to the definition of O'Shaughnessy (1975).

Some epistemological premises

First, from an epistemological point of view, it would be advisable to make some preliminary specifications. Two interpretative positions can be identified from today's theoretical pluralism. One of these states that psychoanalysis has a central indispensable nucleus composed of a small number of fundamental theoretical propositions, to which 'puzzle' solutions are linked in an attempt to solve partial problems. The other position says that we are dealing with diverging and accomplished theories concerning the psychic apparatus. My opinion is that each of the psychoanalytical positions presents a different theoretical picture, both in the sense of a global theory as well as concerning the details of the functioning of the psychic apparatus. Therefore, whoever produces interpretative hypotheses of a phenomenon, does so within a general theoretical framework that can be more or less well characterized and more or less explicit.

Second, the unity of analysis, from an epistemological point of view, is in the theory. The empirical data on which we work are the data of the methodological empirical basis, in other words data that presuppose the use of material or conceptual instruments that in their turn respond to a theory (this is the case with projective identification). A different theory of the instrument (or the use of a different instrument) has an inevitable consequence on the methodological empirical basis, on the method itself and consequently on the theory (this also applies to projective identification).

Third, if we agree with what has been said, we must ask ourselves whether we can use a concept taken from one theory in the context of another theory, without altering it or modifying it into something else, and without the concept in question entering into obvious contradiction with the theory into which it has been imported. I must say that, looking again at the literature on this theme, it is difficult not to conclude that in certain uses the concept of projective identification is rendered unrecognizable and incompatible with its guest theory, as well as making it incoherent. The argument invoked for the use of this concept within theoretical positions that would apparently discourage it, is that the phenomenon described by projective identification exists 'in nature' and can easily be observed in clinical practice. This objection is naive and does not take into consideration what was said above, in other words it confuses the epistemological empirical basis with the methodological one. What we can testify to is a phenomenon that certainly exists: how it is observed, conceived and theorized belongs to a different order of things, to a level of abstraction that is not equivalent to the phenomenal.

Fourth, any hypothesis that tries to describe a mechanism, whether it be defensive or normal, cannot be formulated, discussed and put into practice outside a more general hypothesis about the development of the psychic apparatus. Consciously or not, every hypothesis of this type is embedded in a theory of development and cannot be intrinsically in contradiction with it. The concept of projective identification is incompatible with some psychoanalytical theories that have elaborated hypotheses that differ greatly from the Kleinian ones on psychic development.

The area of research

In Italy there are two psychoanalytical societies, the Italian Psychoanalytical Society (SPI) and the Italian Psychoanalytical Association (AIPsi.), and both have a pluralistic tradition, in other words different theoretical orientations cohabit within the societies and within their training. There are also two societies in Spain, the Spanish Psychoanalytical Society and the Madrid Psychoanalytical Association. As far as I know, the Madrid Association is also pluralistic, while the Spanish Society has a mainly Kleinian tradition. In all that follows it must be borne in mind that, as I live and work in Italy, my knowledge of Italian psychoanalysis is more complete than that of Spanish psychoanalysis, which is accessible to me through personal relationships, presentations of works, visits and supervisions, but mainly due to my knowledge of the Spanish, or in some cases Catalan, literature.

Italy: the first works

In Italy, from the 1960s to the 1980s, psychoanalysis appears to undergo a process of de-provincialization and liberation from previous cultural and political tendencies (Corti, 1983). This is also the period during which the British influence is felt, through its literature as well as through supervisions, seminars and the periodic visits of some of the more well-known British analysts of the Kleinian school: Rosenfeld, Bion, Meltzer, and so on. Concepts from the Kleinian theory appear in the literature and among them we find the concept of projective identification. However, as I mentioned earlier, the importance of this concept is mainly emphasized for its significance and its value in the analyst–patient relationship. This fact explains why – as within the British Society – the concept of projective identification remained intimately linked to that of countertransference, which ended up by finding its rationale in projective identification. This is very clear in some of the pioneering work of two Italian analysts who are also quite well known abroad, S. Manfredi Turilazzi (1974, 1984a, 1984b) and L. Nissim Momigliano (1974, 1984, 1991). The main concern of these two authors seems to be the fact that the continuous use of projective identification on the part of the patient may make the analyst blind. The analyst does not fully understand the countertransference and he suffers manipulations and intrusions without being able to diagnose them or use them therapeutically. An adequate knowledge of projective identification would, on the other hand, enable him to understand the counter-transference more clearly and would favour its containing function. The introjection of the analyst's containing function on the part of the patient would allow for mutative changes.

Another analyst, G. Di Chiara, describes a similar position in a paper published in 1983 and much quoted in Italy (Di Chiara, 1983). The author's reflections are mainly focused on protecting the analyst and the patient from intrusive and parasitic operations. Some important ideas can be found in this work, written ten years after the initial papers of Manfredi and Nissim. First of all, the fact that the author speaks of the protection of the analyst and the patient implies acceptance of L. Grinberg's hypothesis of counterprojective identification (Grinberg, 1962). The analyst who makes a counterprojective identification as a result of the patient's projective identification produces a counter-acting. This phenomenon is not confined to particularly serious situations, but appears to be ubiquitous.

Another difference lies in the fact that the author already speaks of a group of phenomena gathered together under the common denominator of projective identification, and no longer of a single phenomenon. He says: 'It is difficult to find a sufficiently clear definition of projective identification, that is, a definition that includes all the phenomena that are grouped under this denomination'. Di Chiara states that these different phenomena

> have in common a mental operation that originates in a part of the psychic apparatus and terminates either in a part of another psychic apparatus or in another part of the same apparatus in which it originated, producing alterations in the emitting part as well as in the receiving part.
>
> (Di Chiara, 1983, p. 467)

This definition already emphasizes some of the problems that will subsequently be raised; for example, can an operation that terminates in another part of the same apparatus be considered to be projective identification? This question was re-examined only ten years later in a work by J. Amati Mehler. Moreover, Di Chiara (contrary to his predecessors) is sensitive to the possible incompatibility of the simultaneous or alternative use – in terms of projective identification – of the Freudian structural model and of the internal objects model. However, he concludes that the problem is manifest not in clinical practice or in the observed phenomenology, but in the incapacity of the theory to represent the facts, therefore running into the objections that I mentioned earlier: our data are not empirical, but rather empirical methodological; in other words interpreted with a conceptual instrument and through a theory. From this perspective no clinical phenomena exist that are exempt from theory.

A year later, the same author wrote with F. Flegenheimer an accurate historical-critical note about this concept in which they review the main stages in the diffusion of projective identification in the international and Italian psychoanalytical community (Di Chiara and Flegenheimer, 1985). Some of the problems mentioned – a weighing down of the concept that has become too broad, loose and inclusive, its incompatibility with certain theoretical patterns, the divergence of opinions between those who think the concept of projective identification should also include projection, and those who think the contrary, the objections to Grinberg's concept of counterprojective identification, and so on – are already put forward in this note, as they are in the notes that R. Speziale-Bagliacca adds to the Italian publication of Grotstein's book on this subject (Speziale-Bagliacca, 1983). There is a notable omission in the historical-critical note by Di Chiara and Flegenheimer (1985): they do not consider E. Gaddini's contribution on imitation, but this will be taken into account in a work by M. Mancia (1996).

In 1984 Manfredi Turillazzi published a work of which I quote the summary:

This contribution endeavours to fill the gap between our daily clinical work and psychoanalytical language and to rediscover the lost meaning of words which we continue to use. I particularly examine the meaning of the term 'projective identification' and the widening of the gap between its conceptual definition and its clinical use. I think that what we want to describe with this term can be understood only in the context of a psychoanalytical object relations theory and I have attempted to provide a basis for the definition of 'internal object'. In my opinion projective identification, within this framework, is nothing but the externalization through acting of an internal object relation.

(Manfredi Turilazzi, 1984b)

If we compare this summary with her work of 1974 we can see that she no longer concentrates on theory: the phenomenon of projective identification must be understood within an object relations theory, and it is nothing but an externalization through acting. But she also reveals that there is a gap between clinical work and theory, that psychoanalytical language has become babelized, and that the words we use to describe and conceptualize the phenomena are worn out and function as umbrellas sheltering more differences than similarities. This last level of awareness is not dissimilar to that of many other analysts of the international community. On the other hand, there may be doubts about the theoretical decision proposed by the author: is Kleinian theory part of object relations theory? Some analysts would be prepared to uphold the contrary. Are projective identification and externalization synonymous? Here also it is reasonable to have doubts.

Italy, twenty years later

In the following years, during the 1990s, I believe that the concept of projective identification was incorporated into current use and charged with all the ambiguities already mentioned. Analysts use it in the discussion of their clinical cases without – or so it seems to me – making much effort to suggest intersections between apparently incompatible models. At times one has the feeling that the problem of incompatibility is not even noticed or taken into consideration. A specific analysis of the concept is not re-proposed until 1993 by Amati Mehler. I will deal with this work later.

Among the developments during this period I will only mention a paper by A. Ferro (1987), in which we can observe theoretical intersections that will become increasingly frequent in the literature. Ferro wrote a work on the 'Inversion of the flow of projective identifications', a situation in which the projective identification originates in the analyst, 'in three different situations: that of an analyst weighed down by his own anxiety; that of an analyst undergoing intrusion by a particular disturbing patient, and finally that of an analyst performing his normal work' (Ferro, 1987, p. 70), but it is not conceived in terms of counter-projective identification. It is an interesting work, with abundant clinical material illustrating the author's theses that reflect Ogden's observations about the technical errors to be attributed to the analyst's projective identification (Ogden, 1979). Ferro moves within a Kleinian theoretical framework, in a Bionian–Meltzerian version (inversion of alpha function), but he takes into consideration some of Winnicott's contributions, as he will continue to do later. I may add that during the 1990s, in Italy Kleinian theory was mainly defined in Bionian terms.

It goes without saying that many other authors (F. Fornari, L. Generali Clemens and others) and articles could be mentioned, but I have tried to quote only the bare minimum of works, specifically regarding projective identification, that will allow readers who are not familiar with Italian psychoanalytical literature to find their way along the historical pathway that this concept has followed in Italy.

The work by J. Amati Mehler, mentioned above, is in the form of a comment and simultaneously a discussion of Joseph Sandler's contributions on projective identification (Sandler, 1987b). The title of this paper, 'Internalization and externalization processes: projective identification', already suggests a framework for the concept in question: it is interpreted as being part of complex and controversial processes of internalization and externalization that have different characterizations in the different theoretical models. If these psychic events to which projective identification belongs are considered in terms of processes, then they must be inserted into an overall theory of the relationships of outside/inside, subjective/objective, self/other. I will supply an example given by the author: from the Kleinian point of view projective identification is a mechanism whereby self-object boundaries are established in infancy; from Sandler's point of view, for projective identification to function as a mechanism of defence it is necessary to postulate the existence of a boundary between self and object. Therefore, if we want to make a coherent examination of the concept, we are obliged to consider (paraphrasing the author): first, the degree of psychic maturation (and, I would add, the kind of theory we have on it), second, whether the projection that we are describing and conceptualizing is the projection of instinctual drives or other contents, such as representations of the self, representations of whole or part objects, representations of fused parts of the self and of the objects, other aspects of their relation, and so on, third, whether we consider projective identification as a mechanism of defence, or as a physiological phenomenon that contributes towards differentiation between the self and the external world, and represents a normal way of communication both between mother and child and between adults.

Amati Mehler's work is therefore in the form of an examination articulated around each of the concepts that are in one way or another involved in the concept of projective identification, and also around the theoretical frameworks inside which each of them could be inserted. This fact, as well as her own personal theoretical beliefs, leads her to take into consideration E. Gaddini's concept of imitation, which had not found a place in the notes by Di Chiara and Flegenheimer. The concept is internationally known and needs no comment; it is sufficient to say that its insertion in this context is justified to the extent that it describes an operation that differs from that of introjection, that contributes to the identification and appears to be based on omnipotent fantasies connected with primitive perceptions of the modification of the baby's body. I quote Gaddini's concept because it will be included in the last work that I shall mention.

At this point we should recall the statement made by Sandler in the title of a work he wrote: 'On communication from patient to analyst: not everything is projective identification' (Sandler, 1993). This serves as an introduction to the work of M. Mancia (1996). The author says that with the concept of projective identification, Klein (1946) introduced a new scientific paradigm to psychoanalysis, that of the unconscious pre-verbal modalities that operate, also defensively, in the analytical relationship. In this definition he appears to deal with projective identification both as a defence mechanism and as a communicative modality, even though his research seems more oriented towards this latter aspect of the concept. The author proposes a pathway through very different disciplines and developmental theories, 'in the attempt to elaborate an integrated hypothesis on the role of the very early imitations, the representations and the various forms of identification' (Mancia, 1996, p. 226) (among which is projective identification). It is within this framework that Gaddini's imitation – referred to earlier – rightly finds its place, a concept 'neglected and underestimated by psychoanalysis'. Mancia is aware of the implicit risks in the construction of an integrated hypothesis:

> Although I am aware of the difficulty of integrating knowledge deriving from different methods of study, I think it is legitimate to try to elaborate complex hypotheses that take into consideration the relevant phenomena also beyond the different theoretical contexts inside which they are constructed.
>
> (Mancia, 1996, p. 226)

For example, this leads him to confront Piaget's theory of imitation, Meltzoff's genetic imitative competences, Brazelton's primary inter-subjectivity, Trevarthen's proto-conversations, Condon and Sander's auto- and hetero-synchrony, and so on. I think it is easy to see how the problem that I referred to earlier becomes complicated: is it possible and valid to interpret a concept by isolating it from the overall theory from which it originates? Mancia's attempt is in any case part of a group of works that seek to integrate data deriving from different disciplines, and it reflects a definite interest in acquiring a better knowledge of those modalities of communication that previously were only 'obscure'.

Spain: general considerations

I will now try briefly to examine projective identification in Spanish psychoanalysis, although there have been some obstacles for me to overcome. Some of them have already been mentioned; others derive from the scarcity of specific publications, although I have been able to undertake only limited bibliographical research. I mentioned earlier that in order to understand and follow the adoption and development of a concept deriving from a different cultural context to the guest one, it is necessary to investigate the local psychoanalytical history and culture. I think this is also true for Spain, a country that has two different psychoanalytical traditions and that uses two different languages, Spanish and Catalan. As I have already said, the theoretical tradition of the Madrid Association is more pluralistic; the influence of French psychoanalysis has been and is important, also for reasons connected with training (some members of the association trained in Paris). On the other hand, the tradition of the Spanish Society, based in Barcelona, is much closer to Kleinian theory.

In the psychoanalytical history of the Madrid Association, one significant fact from the point of view of our discussion was the arrival of a migratory current from Latin America, specifically from Argentina Uruguay and Peru, that was assimilated by the Association. It is particularly necessary to remember the presence of L. Grinberg, an author mentioned previously – especially in terms of his concept of counterprojective identification – who was of a clearly Kleinian stamp. The presence of Grinberg as a training analyst certainly played a role in encouraging the use of Kleinian concepts in clinical work

213

and in theory. It is obvious that Grinberg's interest in the concepts of projective identification and counterprojective identification has meant that they are now used in the Association's scientific discussions. I have several doubts about the effects that this may have had on the scientific developments in the long term. My impression, confirmed by conversations with colleagues and friends of the Association, but in any case open to discussion, is that with Grinberg's departure from Madrid, the place of Kleinian theory in the theoretical thinking of the Association was progressively weakened. I will not examine the works of this author here as they are very well known and, moreover, it is not entirely legitimate to consider him as a representative of Spanish analysis.

Spain: some relevant works

Research into the *Revista de Psicoanálisis de Madrid* in order to find works specifically dedicated to projective identification has not yielded much information. One paper called 'Sobre identificación proyectiva', published in the *Revista*, is by a Catalan analyst, E. Jiménez, from the Spanish Psychoanalytical Society (Jiménez, 1995). Jiménez describes the origins of the concept of projective identification in Klein's work as a prototype of a sadistic object relationship as well as the basis of empathy. The communicative or evacuative aspect of the operation is connected not only to the contents of the unconscious phantasy, but above all to the level of splitting and omnipotence. There follows an examination of the ideas of the post-Kleinian analysts (British) who broadened and enriched the concept. The novel idea that this author introduces is that of considering Esther Bick's 'adhesive identification' (Bick, 1968) as being a 'second mechanism of narcissistic identification'. Jiménez adheres to Meltzer's dimensional model of the mind, and he particularly refers to the bi-dimensional state, in which anxiety is manifested through the phantasy of breaking through the surfaces. The author emphasizes that in this mental state projective identification cannot exist inasmuch as it needs a three-dimensional space (Bion), but adhesive identification can exist for the interpretation of psychopathological problems such as autism and 'as if' personalities.

Jiménez is fully aware that when a concept such as this is introduced into Kleinian theory, consequences are unavoidable. He says that there are problems connected with the need to redefine certain

Kleinian hypotheses related to the functioning of the very early ego at the dawn of mental life and certain relational concepts, for instance that of primary narcissism. The author's proposal to confront the problem from a Bionian genetic point of view – the passage from bi-dimensionality to tri-dimensionality and from adhesive to projective identification – is accompanied by all the difficulties inherent in the joining together of two patterns that are basically incompatible unless some of the fundamental concepts of one of them, in this case the Kleinian one, are relinquished. From this point of view, the work well exemplifies the conflict that is created if a concept corresponding to one particular schema of development is introduced into another. Contrary to other authors, although he proposes an integrative solution that is difficult to accomplish, Jiménez is aware of the problems that need to be resolved and states that it is necessary to promote greater theoretical rigorousness.

In 1991, in the IPA monograph *On Freud's 'Analysis Terminable and Interminable'*, T. Eskelinen de Folch published an article entitled 'The obstacles to the analytic cure', in which she studies the role of projective identification in provoking forms of alienation of the personality in external reality (Eskelinen de Folch, 1987). These forms constitute a difficulty in the analytic process, a particular form of repetition compulsion linked to concealed nuclei of the personality. The author believes that the concept of projective identification and a detailed knowledge of the various forms that it can take would allow us to recuperate the object relationship which exists behind the more or less severe fragmentation of the self and objects through explorations of the transference. Like others by the same author, this article is generally of a Kleinian stamp, without any concessions to hazardous theoretical intersections.

In the same field of Catalan analysis, I would like to mention a book by A. Pérez-Sánchez, *Análisis terminable* (Pérez-Sánchez, 1997), published in Spanish. Although he does not deal specifically with the subject of projective identification, when speaking about the termination of the analytic process and in the analysis of the case presented, he uses the concept with pertinence and in adherence to Kleinian theory.

I think that this short review, although incomplete, provides evidence of a considerable familiarity with and use of the concept of projective identification in Catalan psychoanalysis coherent with the Kleinian theoretical affiliation of the Spanish Society. It is also possible to observe a greater preoccupation with theoretical coherence, whenever use is to be made of concepts in some way connected to that of projective identification, but deriving from different theoretical patterns.

I will now conclude this very brief incursion into Italian and Spanish psychoanalysis regarding the destiny of the concept of projective identification. Can we make a diagnosis of the present situation and a prognosis for the future? Can we propose some suggestions?

Some provisional conclusions

As far as the present situation is concerned, at least four different ways of conceptualizing and using projective identification can be identified.

First, analysts who are theoretically and clinically Kleinian and who use the concept both in theory and in practice in a way that is not dissimilar to that described by Spillius (1992), both for 'pathological' and for 'ordinary' defensive processes. The description of the sub-types of projective identification varies according to preferences for one Kleinian author or another: evocatory or non-evocatory (Spillius, 1994), attributive or acquisitive (Britton, 1998a), and so on. My impression is that this category is prevalent in the Spanish Society, and more in the minority in the Italian and Madrid Associations.

Second, analysts who integrate the concept in a general theoretical grouping that includes segments of various theories: Freudian-Kleinian when there is a tradition binding them to the French analysis of the past or the present; Kleinian-Bionian-Winnicottian when they are close to British psychoanalysis. I think that this is the majority group and it is in these cases that there is need for reflection about the coherence of the resulting theory and the possible denaturalization of the original concept. Generally speaking, the authors in question do not seem to be too preoccupied with taking these risks into consideration or with averting them.

Third, analysts who, besides favouring concepts stemming from various theories, add to them data and hypotheses from other disciplines that can be used to support or as 'proof' of the validity of the psychoanalytic concepts, or as 'updates' of the theory in general.

Fourth, analysts who are aware of the difficulties deriving from these operations, as well as the difficulties perhaps present in Kleinian theory itself, and who seek to investigate the analysis of the concept and to relate it to an integral theory of the development of the psychic apparatus. This group of analysts – to my mind very much in the minority – postulates the need for greater theoretical rigorousness.

Making a prediction for the future is not easy and would in any case be presumptuous. It is, however, reasonable to hypothesize that the concept of projective identification will continue to be central to clinical practice. If it has been integrated into theoretical models that at first sight seem to be incompatible with those from which it stems, this is also a sure indication of its validity and usefulness both as a theory and in the clinical field. It is likely that these theoretical patch-works will continue, with the addition of interdisciplinary concepts. This might lead to an increase in the babelization of psychoanalytic language and could put its theoretical coherence at risk. The call of certain authors for theoretical rigorousness would therefore seem legitimate.

Bion emphasized the need to identify points of congruence between the different psychoanalytic models, and this is undoubtedly possible and desirable. However, the points of congruence can reveal not only the convergence, but also the divergence, of certain positions within one or more theories. I think that a careful analysis of the differences and the compatibilities can only be of benefit to our discipline.

——————————— 13 ———————————

Projective identification in contemporary French-language psychoanalysis[42]

Jean-Michel Quinodoz

The gradual advance of Kleinian concepts in psychoanalysis as practised in the French-speaking world

A concept considered to be typically Kleinian

Projective identification was described by Klein in 1946. From then on, it has been considered by many analysts to be one of the characteristic concepts of the Kleinian school, a source of admiration for some and an excuse for criticism for others. It has been said that the concept of projective identification is the *pons asinorum* of Kleinian theory, in other words that it is *the* prerequisite for understanding Kleinian thinking, just as Pythagoras's theorem is a key concept in descriptive geometry. René Diatkine would poke gentle fun at those psychoanalysts, Kleinians or not, who used the concept:

> It is easy to measure the degree of Kleinianism of a keynote speaker: just calculate the time that elapses between the beginning of the talk and the first use of the term 'projective identification'. The shorter the time, the more Kleinian the speaker!
>
> (an anecdote told me by Paul Denis)

---

42 Translated by David Alcorn.

This joke is not without its ironic side: it hints at the resistance that Kleinian thinking has encountered in French-speaking countries, and still does, though to a lesser degree than before. In this chapter, I shall explore the importance of the concept of projective identification for contemporary French-language psychoanalysts – focusing on those who belong to the International Psychoanalytical Association – before concluding this overview with a few hypotheses concerning the reasons for such resistance.

A phenomenon often described in clinical terms before being conceptualized

Though it is often labelled as typically Kleinian, the phenomenon that, in 1946, Melanie Klein called projective identification does not in fact belong to Kleinian thinking as such – far from it, indeed, because the idea was already floating around long before Klein conceptualized it. The idea of projection is implicit in Ferenczi's article 'Introjection and transference' (Ferenczi, 1909), and exists in many of Freud's own writings too. Similar phenomena are also described in various psychoanalytic texts dating from the 1920s and 1930s, although the authors do not make any clear distinction between these and projection as such. French-speaking psychoanalysts too have made similar statements in the past. For example, with reference to female homosexuality, R. de Saussure highlighted the partial character of what is projected onto the homosexual's partner, as well as the narcissistic nature of this kind of identification:

> To my mind, homosexual fixation has much more to do with a division of narcissism than with an object-related fixation. [. . .] Such women project outside of themselves either their masculinity or their femininity, and they are attracted to women who are the opposite of themselves. Indeed, their aim is much more to identify with their partner than to love her in an object-related way.
>
> (de Saussure, 1929, p. 70)

In this complex movement, the idea of projective identification highlights the details that come into play in projective and identificatory phenomena.

219

France: a two-stage development

Klein's ideas made only very slow headway in the French-language countries, and in France in particular, where it was a two-stage process. Though her theories on child psychoanalysis were acknowledged in the 1950s, her ideas then fell into relative disuse before resurfacing once again in the 1970s and thereafter continuing to develop right up to the present day.

Back in the 1930s, Jacques Lacan was undoubtedly one of the first psychoanalysts in France to recognize the importance of Klein's thinking. What interested him in particular was her idea of the early stages of the Oedipus complex; this led him to 'refocus the Oedipal question in terms of triangulation, while taking into account the various contributions of the Kleinian school' (Roudinesco and Plon, 1997, p. 746). Later, from the 1950s on, Klein's ideas aroused increasing interest among child psychoanalysts such as René Diatkine and Serge Lebovici. At the same time, Lacan was beginning to criticize Klein's theses, even though he himself had made use of them in constructing some of his own conceptions; Lacan's ambivalent attitude towards Klein was to have a significant impact on many psychoanalysts in French-speaking countries. One particular anecdote is a significant indication of Lacan's attitude towards Klein. In the early 1950s, René Diatkine translated Klein's *The Psycho-Analysis of Children* (Klein, 1932b) into French for the first time. At that time, he was in analysis with Lacan. One day, Lacan asked the enthusiastic young translator to lend him a copy of the translation. Lacan never gave it back to Diatkine, claiming that he had mislaid it. Unfortunately, it was the only copy, and Diatkine's translation was lost for ever. It was only many years later that the book was finally translated, but by someone else.

In France, after a silence that lasted 20 years, renewed interest in Klein's work began with the arrival in Paris of James Gammill in 1969, followed by that of Jean Bégoin and Florence Bégoin-Guignard in 1970. Gammill, an American-born psychoanalyst, was trained in London; his analyst was Paula Heimann, and Melanie Klein was one of his supervisors. Jean Bégoin came from Annecy and was analysed by Marcelle Spira in Geneva, while Florence Bégoin-Guignard had trained in Geneva. These psychoanalysts joined forces with Donald Meltzer, whose ideas were rapidly spreading throughout French psychoanalytic circles, thanks in particular to the publication of his *The Psycho-Analytical Process* (Meltzer, 1967), translated into French by Jean Bégoin and

Florence Bégoin-Guignard. In the years that followed, this initially small group gradually expanded and came to include Geneviève Haag and Didier Houzel (both of whom had supervision in London), as well as Cléopâtre Athanassiou, a pupil of Esther Bick. In addition, Pierre and Claudine Geissmann in Bordeaux were trying to discover how to overcome the difficulties they were having in treating severely psychotic children; they travelled to London on a regular basis between 1982 and 1987 in order to have supervision with Hanna Segal and to attend meetings of the British Psychoanalytical Society. Thus, in France, Kleinian thinking began initially to spread among child and adolescent psychoanalysts, as well as those who treated psychotic patients.

Gradual growth in Switzerland, Belgium and French-speaking Canada

In other French-language countries, Kleinian ideas began to make headway in the 1950s and 1960s. In the French-speaking part of Switzerland, it was Marcelle Spira who initiated the movement; she settled in Geneva in 1956 after leaving Argentina, which was also where she trained (J.-M. Quinodoz, 2002b). During several decades, Spira trained many Swiss and other European psychoanalysts, and had as guest speakers at her seminars Melanie Klein, Betty Joseph and Herbert Rosenfeld, who all contributed to the spread of Kleinian ideas, especially in Geneva, in spite of the strong opposition which that theory encountered. In the 1980s, Hanna Segal conducted a seminar in Geneva which lasted for all of ten years. In Belgium, Kleinian ideas began to make some progress in the 1960s, again among child psychoanalysts in particular, thanks to contacts with neighbouring countries such as the Netherlands. In Canada, French-speaking psychoanalysts learned of Klein's ideas thanks to J-B. Boulanger, who translated Klein's book, *The Psycho-Analysis of Children* (1932), to C. Scott in 1954, and then to Henri Rey who made regular visits to the country in the 1970s.

The main contributions of the French-speaking world

Making projective identification more familiar to the French world

Starting in the 1970s, several French-speaking psychoanalysts who use the concept of projective identification in a Kleinian or

221

post-Kleinian context have published papers, only a few of which have been translated into English.

When we talk of projective identification, Florence Guignard is, for most French-language psychoanalysts, the name that most readily springs to mind. Her many publications (successively as F. Bégoin, F. Bégoin-Guignard and F. Guignard) testify to her commitment to the idea; one such is the interesting exchange of correspondence she had with M. Fain (1984) on the topic of projective identification and hysterical identification. In the course of that discussion, F. Guignard emphasized the stumbling blocks that prevented French-speaking psychoanalysts from having a proper understanding of the notion of projective identification. Most of them, she argued, remained attached to a 'classic Freudian' approach to splitting – i.e., one that related only to splitting of the ego and not to that of the object at the same time. She also pointed out that they had some difficulty in understanding the concept of part-object introjection (Guignard, 1984, p. 521). G. Bayle's controversial point of view on the concept of splitting – according to him, the word 'splitting' designates simply the result of a defensive process, never the defence mechanism itself; in other words, it is not an action that takes place in the mind (Bayle, 1996, pp. 1334–1335) – led Guignard (1996) to put the notion back into its proper conceptual context. It must be noted, all the same, that ideas have gradually evolved since the 1970s and that the term is no longer taboo; anyone who talks nowadays of splitting would not automatically be labelled 'Kleinian', as once was the case.

It may be useful to remind French-language psychoanalysts, who sometimes have their own particular idea of what splitting is all about, that a distinction should be drawn between what Freud called splitting and Melanie Klein's definition of the term (Canestri, 1989). For Freud, splitting of the ego is the result of a denial of some perception of reality, such that the ego finds itself divided – in a passive sort of way, one could say. On the other hand, for Klein and the post-Kleinians, splitting is an active defence mechanism that has many different modalities. In the preface to the French translation of his *Dictionary of Kleinian Thought*, Hinshelwood (2000, p. 3) points out that the English language can make subtle distinctions between different kinds of splitting (splitting up, splitting off, separated off, separated apart, etc.), a possibility that does not exist in French. 'I wonder if the linguistic constraints of the French language, in relation to this fundamental concept (splitting), make Melanie Klein's thinking seem less subtle to the French-speaking reader, leading to less interest in her ideas.'

As for more recent publications, there is the chapter that Guignard devoted to projective identification in her *Épître à l'objet* (Guignard, 1997), in which she reminds the reader that the concept includes a wide spectrum of associated phenomena. Several child and adolescent psychoanalysts refer to the idea of projective identification in their work – A. Anzieu, C. Athanassiou, G. Haag, and D. Houzel. When D. Ribas (1992) emphasizes the absence of projection in infantile autism, he is in fact referring exclusively to adhesive identification, which, as he says, is a more primitive mechanism than projective identification.

Projective identification and projection – in what way are they different?

Alain Gibeault asked this question in his paper 'De la projection et de l'identification projective' ('On projection and projective identification') (Gibeault, 2000a). In that text, he considers whether the concept, as defined by Klein in 1946, simply overlaps that of projection as described by Freud or whether it adds something to Freud's notion. After discussing the various meanings of introjection and projection as processes, Gibeault highlights the difficulty that we encounter when trying to specify the differences between projection and projective identification, given the contradictory positions to which the question gives rise. In his conclusion, Gibeault goes back to Freud's definition of projection: 'an aspect of oneself which, denied or repressed, is then attributed to an external object; in so doing, the subject does not want to rediscover in the other person what has been projected into that person' (Gibeault, 2000a, p. 742).

Contributions from Switzerland, Belgium and Canada

In the French-speaking part of Switzerland, Danielle Quinodoz has published two remarkable papers that deal with projective identification *stricto sensu*. In 'Interpretations in projection' (D. Quinodoz, 1989), she suggests an innovative technical approach:

In a nutshell, this form of interpretation consists in the analyst's lending his voice directly to the part of the patient projected into him. The analyst speaks in the first person, saying aloud what he thinks the projected part of the patient would have told him if it had been able to speak.

(D. Quinodoz, 2002, pp. 112–113)

In *Words that Touch*, D. Quinodoz makes a detailed study of projective identification in the light of clinical examples, emphasizing the notion of projective counter-identification that León Grinberg (1962) introduced. According to D. Quinodoz, the difficulty that French-language psychoanalysts encounter in imagining the idea of *bodily fantasy* leads to a problem with mentally representing the notion of projecting a fantasied part of the ego that involves bodily fantasies; this obstacle, she feels, is linked *inter alia* to the continuing impact of Lacan's ideas – for him, the body could refer only to concrete reality, thereby excluding bodily fantasies from the psychoanalytic field.

As far as my own work is concerned, I have in the main highlighted the phenomena that involve integration, when projective identification weakens and leaves more room for introjection; this occurs both in the experience of 'buoyancy' when separation anxiety is worked through in the psychoanalytic process (J.-M. Quinodoz, 1992), and in the kind of dream that 'turns the page' – dreams that appear to be regressive but in fact have to do with integration (J.-M. Quinodoz, 2001). In French-speaking Switzerland, projective identification is a notion that is used also by child analysts, including those who work with psychotic children (Manzano and Palacio Espasa, 1986), as well as in mother-infant therapies where it is particularly useful for explaining normal and pathological projection (Manzano, Palacio Espasa, and Zilkha, 1999). Contributions from various other analysts also take the idea of projective identification into account, for example the creative and innovative Kleinian perspective suggested by M. Spira (1985).

Projective identification would appear to be a concept that is both well accepted by Belgian psychoanalysts and used by them in their clinical work. The reports drawn up by M. Haber and J. Godfrind-Haber (2002) bear witness to this, as do the various discussions that followed on from their work.

As regards French-speaking Canadian analysts, Kleinian and post-Kleinian conceptions have been further developed, in particular by P. Drapeau and G. da Silva. Recently, L. Brunet and D. Casoni (2001) have tried to 'sort things out in the conceptual Tower of Babel' that is projective identification; they argue that the connection between projective identification and the containing function is particularly helpful as a model for understanding how some analysands use the object in the transference–countertransference relationship. However, projective identification may be used defensively, with the risk that some analysts could attribute to the notion all sorts of meanings, 'some [of which] have resulted in dubious countertransferential "alibis" (Aulagnier 1984), and hence have contributed to the hesitation many psychoanalysts have in referring to the concept' (Brunet and Casoni, 2001, pp. 137–138).

The present–day situation: informal soundings

What do contemporary French-language psychoanalysts think of the concept of projective identification? To what extent do they use it in their clinical practice? To answer these questions, I sought the opinion of some of my analyst colleagues, members of the International Psychoanalytical Association, either in informal discussions with them or through examining what they have written on the subject (J.-M. Quinodoz, 2002a). These soundings enabled me to divide them into four main groups.

Psychoanalysts who refer directly to Kleinian concepts

This first group comprises not only those psychoanalysts who were trained by Kleinians but also those who are receptive to Kleinian thinking without necessarily having had any formal training in that approach. For analysts who belong to this group, the concept is a fundamental contribution to psychoanalytic theory and they make use of it in their clinical work – just as they refer to Kleinian thinking in general as an integral part of their clinical practice. In France, those who belong to this group are, for the most part, psychoanalysts who work with children and adolescents, and with psychotic patients; in other French-language countries, there are some adult psychoanalysts who belong to this group.

225

Psychoanalysts who consider projective identification to be one of many projective phenomena

It becomes obvious when discussing the question with them that, since the early 1980s, many French-language psychoanalysts have shown increasing interest in projective mechanisms as such. Particularly attentive to what is projected into the analyst's mind, they raise issues that have mainly to do with what the analyst does with such projections. For the most part, they tend to speak in terms of the countertransference rather than of projective identification as such.

There is also some considerable variation in the way that these analysts describe the projective phenomenon on which they are focusing; this is more easily detected in their writings than in oral discussions with them.

For example, in his 'The dead mother', André Green (1980) describes clinical phenomena that closely resemble projective identification, yet in that paper he writes only of 'projection', never of 'identification'. In a later paper, Green (1990) introduces the idea of 'foreclosed projection' (*projection forclose*), which he locates somewhere between 'ex-corporation' and 'projection', in order no doubt to underline the distinction he draws between that notion and projective identification. For Racamier, post-Kleinian psychoanalysts use the term 'projective identification' in much too wide a sense; he preferred the term 'projective injection' (*injection projective*) to the one Segal suggested – 'identificatory projection' – because, in his opinion, 'projective injection is carried out at one go and in the original tongue, as it were, directly and proximately' (Racamier, 1992, p. 99). Michel de M'Uzan (1994) calls 'paradoxical thinking' (*pensée paradoxale*) a clinical phenomenon that closely resembles what the analyst may experience in the countertransference when the patient resorts to projective identification. He does not, however, make any reference to splitting, projection or identification; in his view, 'paradoxical thinking' belongs to an inter-subjective space that he calls the 'chimera', one which is neither wholly the analyst's nor wholly the patient's. The psychosomatic school of thought in Paris refers to 'projective reduplication' (*reduplication projective*), a term introduced by C. David and M. de M'Uzan. R. Roussillon describes the type of communication found in the 'narcissistic transference' in terms that would seem to imply, *inter alia*, the idea of splitting:

> A kind of transference 'by reversal' replaces or is added to the 'displacement' transference typical of the transference neurosis; here, the patient, split-off from any possibility of integration and therefore 'in parallel', as it were, makes the analyst experience what proved impossible to experience properly in the patient's own life.
>
> (Roussillon, 1999, p. 14)

A. Eiguer highlights a particularly corrosive attempt to control the object by means of a kind of projection that he calls 'narcissistic induction' (Eiguer, 1989). J-Cl. Rolland (quoted in Smith, 2002) described a session in which he felt overwhelmed by terror as if he were 'identified with a nightmare', so powerful was the impact of his patient's transference. In his view, an 'over-restrictive theory' prevented him from discovering that some clinical experiences force the analyst to participate in the 'action' of the transference, in such a way as to 'embody' the patient's states of anxiety.

It is obvious from what I have just said that practically every one of the psychoanalysts I have mentioned has his own way of putting things. This makes it difficult to decide what differentiates any one concept from the others – and all the more so, indeed, because the analysts concerned rarely refer to similar concepts that have been defined earlier. The resulting impression is one of dispersal and a lack of conceptual unity. In suggesting some new notion, they hardly ever make any reference to the idea of projective identification, though the term is a well-defined one; and when it is referred to, it is often treated as banal, or classed as just one modality of projection among many.

Psychoanalysts who accept only those psychoanalytic concepts established by Freud

This is the third category – the concept of projective identification is not referred to at all by these analysts, because they adhere strictly to Freud's writings. Since projective identification is not one of the concepts specifically described and developed by Freud, it hardly ever rates a mention in their work.

Psychoanalysts who are more or less ambivalent towards Kleinian ideas

Finally, there are some psychoanalysts who are more or less ambivalent towards Kleinian thinking – and, therefore, towards projective identification. Some are quite scathing in their criticism, which, moreover, is often based on prejudice: they unwittingly reveal their lack of true knowledge concerning Kleinian theory (though they *think* they understand it well). Some analysts, for example, are still convinced that Klein spoke only of the mother's role, never of the father's, in the parent–infant relationship – it is as though they had never read Klein's writings. For example, in his article on projective identification, F. Pasche (1982) is convinced that his criticism of projective identification is perfectly justified when he claims that a Kleinian psychoanalyst simply returns the patient's projections without first transforming them and that, as a result, the counter-transference is always 'put to one side' (Pasche, 1982, p. 410). When confirmed analysts speak with apparent authority on such topics, their albeit unreliable statements often go unchallenged among their readers or their audience, who do not check their sources.

On the other hand, the ambivalence of some analysts is tinged with respect. This is the case, for example, of J. Laplanche, who has never disguised his interest in Klein's contributions even though he remains wary of 'Kleinianism', of its 'proselytism', its 'failure to address basic questions' and its 'hegemony' (Laplanche, 1992, p. 215). In expressing his fear of Kleinian attempts at hegemony, Laplanche, in my view, has identified one of the sources of the ambivalence that some analysts feel – fascinated by (and sometimes drawing their inspiration from) Kleinian concepts, they do not want to admit as much.

Projective identification in its own specific context

After this overview that has enabled us to see just how diverse the points of view on the question are, I find it necessary to refocus my ideas and concentrate on the main theme of this essay, i.e. on projective identification and its own specific theoretical and technical context. This brief reminder will then enable me to highlight the convergences and divergences between the various points of view. I should point out, however, that, in making comparisons, I do not intend to give the impression that one point of view is superior to another; my aim is to further our understanding of how the various analysts work and of the genuine differences between them.

Careful attention to the transference–countertransference situation

In order to pinpoint and to analyse the phenomena linked to projective identification, technical considerations are important, because we have to adopt an approach that closely monitors the development of the transference–countertransference situation. The constant and meticulous attention given to the details of what is happening in the transference and countertransference enables us to distinguish between what comes from the patient and what our own contribution is to the continuous to and fro movement of projections and introjections typical of the analytical relationship. This is particularly useful when the emotionality involved is tinged with persecutory aspects, which encourage projection, or depressive elements, which favour insight; these differences in tone must be closely followed. For Klein and Kleinian psychoanalysts, the most appropriate way to obtain this kind of clinical material is to establish a clear and well-defined psychoanalytic setting, in order to analyse the fantasies and affects in a 'global-situation' context and to limit as far as possible any acting-out. From this point of view, the Kleinian approach is a demanding one. That said, I do not believe that following so precisely the *hic et nunc* of what is being experienced in the setting necessarily implies that the psychoanalyst who adopts such a perspective loses sight of the process as a whole.

Bion's contribution is inseparable from that of Klein

W. R. Bion's contribution (Bion, 1962a, 1967) to the concept of projective identification is fundamental in terms of the development of Klein's ideas; if it is isolated from the sources on which it is based, some degree of misunderstanding is only to be expected. As J. Chasseguet-Smirgel (personal communication, 2002) has said, to omit Klein and refer only to Bion is 'an indelicate way of nullifying the line of descent that runs from Klein to Bion'.

Bion's starting point was the pathology of the paranoid-schizoid position. His fundamentally innovative development of Klein's work was the distinction he drew between pathological projective identification and the normal, neurotic form of projective identification that underpins empathy. The difference between paranoid anxiety and depressive position anxiety is also the basis on which Bion developed his theory of the container and the transformation of β-elements into α-elements; the latter are required for symbol formation and for growth, while β-elements can only be evacuated – having no developmental potential, they lead only to concrete thinking (Segal, 1957).

The idea of 'capacity for reverie', the distinction between normal and pathological projective identification and the transformation of β-elements into α-elements throw light on the psychoanalyst's work and help us to understand it better: the patient's projections are taken in, transformed, then returned – they are not simply pushed back into the patient without having been worked through, as some unfounded criticism of projective identification would have us believe. If that were the case, the psychoanalyst would resemble the dysfunctional mother in Bion's description, so incapable of tolerating her infant's projections that she in fact reinforces her child's projective identification and renders it meaningless. Also, the idea of the *mother's* 'capacity for reverie' is often misunderstood as implying a dyadic relationship that excludes the father; that, however, was not Bion's idea. For him, maternal reverie means that the baby and the father are *both* present in the mother's mind. From that point of view, Winnicott, not Bion, was the one who explicitly declared that the containing mother is in a dyadic fusional relationship with her infant.

Convergence and divergence

Increasing communication between different currents of thought in psychoanalysis

As I have pointed out, projective identification is a relatively well-defined concept that covers a wide range of projective phenomena extending from neurosis to psychosis. Moreover, it participates in the differentiation between the more elaborate defence mechanisms linked to repression and the more primitive ones; as such, it is a particularly suitable instrument for the analysis of narcissistic, borderline or psychotic patients.

Over a long period of time, projective identification was felt to belong exclusively to the Kleinian school of thought, but this is no longer entirely the case. Many contemporary psychoanalysts accept the concept and integrate it into their clinical work, just as they do its underlying notions such as denial of psychic reality, splitting, projection and introjection of parts of the self, and the object's identification with the projections received (Sandler, 1987b). This is particularly true of French-language analysts in Switzerland, Belgium and Canada, who are probably much more in contact with various international currents of thought in psychoanalysis than their counterparts in France.

That said, the situation has changed somewhat in France too over the past few decades, as the various articles and papers I mentioned earlier go to show. Many French analysts have told me that they pay very close attention to the transference–countertransference experience and that, in their view, projective identification is a fairly well-recognized concept even though they themselves may prefer to use others. As a result, it is no longer possible to contrast Kleinian and Freudian technique in so radical a manner as de M'Uzan (1994) – he considered the Kleinian approach to be too 'tactical' because it focused to an excessive degree on the details of the transference–countertransference experience and contrasted it with the 'strategic' approach that he claimed was exclusive to the Freudian model.

Nowadays, when psychoanalysts belonging to the French school of thought show interest in patients who are difficult to treat, their perspective is mainly that of 'borderline' cases, and when they refer to the British school, they readily quote Winnicott and Bion, as though to avoid mentioning Klein. Generally speaking, there now seem to be fewer differences between the technique employed by these analysts and that of practitioners – in Italy, Germany or the Scandinavian countries as far as Europe is concerned – who have integrated at least some Kleinian conceptions. I believe that these developments are the result of an increasing exchange of ideas on the international level – especially through symposia such as the one in

Brighton which brought together French and British psychoanalysts; the latter, for example, showed considerable interest in notions that have done much for the originality of the French current of thought in contemporary psychoanalysis.

Significant differences in technique

Narrowing the gap between different schools of thought is a highly positive development, but we must not play down the differences that remain, some of which are particularly relevant to the topic of this paper. It seems to me that it is in the technical approach to the psychoanalytic treatment of neurotic, narcissistic, borderline or psychotic patients that one of these differences is particularly evident.

For some psychoanalysts, the classic analytical technique – with its couch-and-armchair setting – is suited above all to neurotic patients, those who, from the preliminary interviews onwards, show that they can make use of their capacity for symbolic representation in dealing with their intrapsychic conflicts. When there are deficiencies in that capacity, these analysts feel that classic psychoanalytic treatment is not indicated and tend to offer the patient psychoanalytic treatment with each sitting opposite and in full view of the other. According to Gibeault (2000b), this 'face-to-face' approach is a way of avoiding pathological regression and the consequent risk of psychic disorganization or even disintegration.

> Analytic work on the couch is necessarily 'traumatic' because of its suspension of sight and action, for it involves a return to an anxiety about non-representation that has to be negotiated through capacities for topographical and formal regression. Face-to-face analysis restores what was suspended, in this case visual support for the fragility of the ego during a resumption of the psychic functioning that is also a capacity for forming a potential space for play (Winnicott 1971).
>
> (Gibeault, 2000b, p. 383)

This approach is very different from the Kleinian one, which applies equally to neurotic patients and to those who are narcissistic, borderline or psychotic – and perhaps even more so to the latter, if we refer to the clinical examples that are reported in various publications. It is true, of course, that Kleinian psychoanalysts do resort to the facing-each-other technique whenever the patient finds lying on the couch to be unbearable – but when they do so, they maintain the well-defined psychoanalytic setting because they feel that that setting creates the best possible conditions for identifying and analysing the transference–countertransference experience.

These different technical approaches are based on differences in theoretical conceptualisations that I cannot develop here, because these issues go somewhat beyond the scope of this chapter. The broad overview that I have given should, all the same, leave enough space for different shades of opinion – some of which are quite contrasted – to be expressed.

Influences that go far back

How is it that French-language psychoanalysts – and especially those in France itself – have only recently shown any interest in the projective phenomena that occur in the transference–countertransference relationship, as well as in the concept of projective identification and the theoretical and technical context that surrounds these notions?

There is of course a tradition that goes back to the introduction of Freud's ideas into France in the 1920s; at that point, they dealt mainly with the neuroses, since he was still working on their application to depression and the psychoses. However, I think that in spite of disagreement on certain fundamental issues, the ideas that Lacan began to put forward from the 1950s on have influenced and continue to influence psychoanalytic thinking in France and in other French-language regions.

I feel that the 'return to Freud' that Lacan advocated in 1953 focused attention more or less permanently on the neuroses and verbal communication to the detriment of the psychoanalytic approach to more severe pathological states and non-verbal communication. The 'return to Freud' did not concern the whole range of his work, but mainly the period between 1900 and 1905, when his emphasis was on the part played by language, symbolism and condensation in dreams and in jokes. As a result, a considerable amount of Freud's contributions from 1915 on were pushed into the background – and this was when Freud was exploring the possibility of using psychoanalysis to treat depression and the psychoses, thereby opening the way to post-Freudian ideas (J.-M. Quinodoz, 2000). Moreover, Lacan was firmly against making use of the countertransference in the course of an analysis, as F. Duparc (2001) has pointed out; that is why it took several decades for the concept to be accepted into mainstream French psychoanalytic thinking even though it had been introduced in the early 1950s. Among the reasons for rejecting it, Duparc suggests that Lacan considered the countertransference to carry the risk of setting up a mirror relationship that would be dyadic in nature and exclude the presence of any *tiers* or third party. The point of view of those psychoanalysts who belong to the Paris Psychoanalytical Society or the French Psychoanalytical Association has changed over the years as regards the countertransference; the idea has gradually come to be generally accepted, thanks in particular to the work of S. Vidermann, M. Neyraut, P. Aulagnier and J. McDougall. On the other hand, the point of view of those psychoanalysts who belong to the Lacanian school of thought is the same today as it was in Lacan's day: rejecting the countertransference is one of the principles on which their work is based (Widlöcher, 2003). In addition, Lacan felt that, in cases of psychosis, the transference could not be analysed. For Lacan, foreclosure (*forclusion*) is characteristic of the psychoses, but he never indicated, how, in his view, foreclosure could be reversed; as a result, his point of view concerning the treatment of psychosis remained a purely speculative one (Diatkine, 1997).

Lacan's influence made itself felt not only through his theoretical and technical conceptions but also via the fascination his personality evoked. I cannot help thinking that the ambivalent attitude of some analysts towards Kleinian ideas is very similar to that of Lacan himself: there is perhaps a hint here of unconscious transgenerational identification with his personality.

In a recently published book, the psychoanalyst Maria Pierrakos (2003) discusses the transgenerational indentifications that she has identified in post-Lacanian analysts – with whom, indeed, she is very familiar, having for twelve years served as stenotypist at Lacan's *Seminars*. She points out that many of Lacan's followers identify not only with the 'Master's' way of putting things – plays on words, puns and spoonerisms – but also with many aspects of his personality such as his love of paradox and enigmatic statements or his 'disdainful mocking' of anything that had to do with feelings. 'Have they all caught the *Witz*-bug?' she asks. 'What is it that is both hidden by and yet revealed through this desire to astound, to captivate, to hypnotize?' (Pierrakos, 2003, p. 35). She goes on to say that those who were analysed by Lacan and attended his *Seminars* had the impression that Lacan's

> public face, with its cynicism and its coldness, was completely at odds with what they knew of the man himself. That transference, forever unresolved, has kept them irrevocably in slavery, because each of them thought that the entire Janus-like figure was for him or her alone.
>
> (Pierrakos, 2003, p. 38)

A plea for genuine controversy

It is time for me to conclude. To my mind, the concept of projective identification is fundamental to our work as analysts; I was delighted to accept the invitation that Elizabeth Spillius and Edna O'Shaughnessy addressed to me, all the more so since, based in Geneva, I feel close both to the British (and, more specifically, Kleinian) tradition and to the French school of thought. When I focus on projective identification and its use in the psychoanalytic approach to narcissistic, borderline or psychotic patients, it does not mean that I am neglecting the original contributions of the French tradition as regards neurotic patients. On the contrary – I believe that the variety of points of view in contemporary psychoanalytic thinking is a great advantage; but if we are to avoid frittering away the inheritance that Freud left us, we need a genuine debate more than ever. For this to be productive, we have to create favourable conditions for true dialogue, as R. Bernardi (2002, p. 851) noted: 'When this occurs, controversies promote the discipline's development (*i.e. that of psychoanalysis*), even when they fail to reach any consensus'.

SECTION 3

The United States

Introduction

Elizabeth Spillius

The idea of projective identification has aroused considerable interest among American psychoanalysts and psychotherapists, a process that is here described in two papers. The first, by Roy Schafer, is based on his very extensive knowledge of the various schools of thought in American psychoanalysis and their response to the idea of projective identification. The second, by Elizabeth Spillius, briefly reviews some of the considerable body of American psychoanalytic literature on the topic of projective identification. These two expositions are followed by three noteworthy papers. The first, by Arthur Malin and James Grotstein, is one of the earliest American papers on the topic of projective identification. The second, by Thomas Ogden, expounds his views on the topic about a decade later. The third paper, written for the present volume, presents the views of Albert Mason, a British analyst who settled in Los Angeles in the late 1950s, and whose views on the concept express both his British origin and his subsequent clinical experiences of projective identification with American patients.

14

Projective identification in the USA

An overview

Roy Schafer

I do not find a center to the uses of *projective identification* (PI) in the USA. The concept is being used as though it fits into whatever happens to be one's established theory and mode of practice. Variations extend from Grotstein's close adherence to Klein, Bion, and Meltzer to informal or improvisational applications in specific clinical instances. Some are not clearly different from Freud's *projection* or from attribution, imitation, manipulation and persuasion.

I will organize this scattered material around a listing of what I consider the conceptual issues encountered or created by recent authors. Some of these issues are new versions of age–old epistemological controversies.

1 The clinical scene in the USA has featured the rising influence of such object relational thinkers as Klein, Winnicott, Bion, Fairbairn, Ferenczi and Loewald and such interpersonal-relational thinkers as Harry Stack Sullivan, Stephen Mitchell, and Jay Greenberg. This change has been evidenced by widespread attention to the interplay of transference and countertransference. Sometimes, projective identification is implied rather than named in clinical interpretations and discussions.
2 In general, use of the idea tends to be stripped of its specifically Kleinian origin (the same may be said of those counterproductively overshadowed concepts *introjective identification* and *introjection*). My impression is that affiliation anxiety might be playing a

240

part in trendy and selective use of the terminology of projection. Nevertheless, a broad overview of clinical practice suggests that the awareness of projective identification has led to a gain in clinical effectiveness at the expense of conceptual rigor, technical consistency, and professional candor.

3 Judging by citations in texts and reference lists of recent years, Thomas Ogden seems to have been the most influential USA writer on projective identification, though Grotstein remains the most prolific in this regard. Kernberg has also made notable use of the concept. In his early publications Ogden stayed close to Klein and Bion. Like Bion, he emphasized projective identification as both defence and communication, in this way opening himself to somehow having to include in one approach both intrapsychic and interpersonal orientations. Grotstein's recent *projective trans-identification* reaches toward the same goal. However, Ogden's interest in defensive uses of projective identification has declined as he has shifted his focus to intersubjectivity – what he now discusses under 'the third.' Ogden designates projective identification as one aspect of the intersubjective third. The third is a realm of subjective experience and discourse that comes into being uniquely between each analyst-analysand pair; in addition to the two individual subjectivities, the third is a source of words, feelings, desires, mental states, and fantasies, and it must be taken into account as *a* or *the* crucial sign of a genuine analytic process. I do not think Ogden has so much integrated the intrapsychic and interpersonal orientations – they may be irreconcilable – as linked them verbally and applied them eclectically in his clinical work. His prominence in this area suggests that many students and readers find his approach quite helpful. However, it can be argued that in this way he is reinforcing widespread use of eclectic tendencies while perpetuating theoretical disarray.

4 *Intersubjectivity* is being used, especially by those in the relational school, as a sufficient basis for disestablishing the analyst's expertise in interpreting the interplay of transference and countertransferences. Now, it is to be as though two transferences are interacting on 'a level playing field' (in the words of Owen Renik). On this understanding, it remains for the two participants to 'negotiate' the nature of the conflicts or desires being expressed in the clinical interaction, if necessary with some personal disclosure provided by the analyst.

In the published illustrations of this approach, I do not find much, if any, convincing evidence of any traditional analytic sort that this leveling move has had the desired egalitarian result. The evidence provided usually cites behavioral change assessed at face value while setting aside patient exploration of unconscious fantasies about would-be egalitarianism. The end result is a mix of interpersonal and relational presuppositions and practices and modified, often 'wild,' premature or superficial attempts at interpretation. The context is defined in terms of enactments within simultaneous interpersonal and intersubjective realities.

5 The interest in projective identification as communication has led some analysts to make prominent use of Bion's idea of containment. Together, these two concepts are being employed in several new lines of study in an old research area: infant and child development. Outstanding in this development are neuropsychological imaging studies and studies of attunement and attachment. Some of these studies use rapid photographic sequences of mother-child interactions. However, *projective identification* is not often featured in these contexts. It is, of course, linked to Kleinian propositions based on Freud's speculatively introduced ideas about Life and Death Instincts and to the assumed influence of unconscious phantasies so early in development as to seem inborn. Neither of these propositions fit readily into current neuro-cognitive-developmental contexts that deny the possibility of self-object differentiation sufficient to accommodate Klein's formulations. Consequently, the concept tends to be condemned, avoided or disavowed on scientific grounds. I believe contemporary review, clarification and perhaps reformulation of Klein's propositions and their origins and place in clinical practice might protect *projective identification* from being explicitly barred from general psychoanalytic discourse.

The developments just summarized entail a major shift of emphasis in thinking about projective identification: the prime assumption in this regard being that human relatedness itself could not take place in its absence. Thus, Ogden emphasizes that the projective identification, containment and reverie in the third represent a 'self-curative' 'reaching out.' I take him to be positing a primary need to be understood and contained by others, to be in their thoughts and their modes of response; also, in the case of psychic damage, a need for others to 'be these' in a new, safer and better way. To my mind, Ogden is developing another way of thinking about Loewald's 'new object' and 'ego core held in trust' as well as contemporary Kleinian formulations concerning latent phantasies of, and hopes for, the good object relationships that might emerge from entering the depressive position. All of which brings us back to Freud's propositions concerning expressions of a Life Instinct aimed toward unity and survival.

The new focus on adaptation can also be found in clinical psychological research, for instance in the work on *adaptive projective identification* by Blatt and associates.

6 Three major sources of diverse usage and confusion regarding projective identification remain to be mentioned.

(a) In the USA, the reference to identification is often understood to mean a two-step process, the first being projection and the second, identification with the changed object. A model for this view can be found in Freud's theory of superego formation: the boy identifies with the projectively exaggerated, threatening and vengeful father. As I understand Klein's concept, it involves only one step: unconscious identification is implied whenever parts of the self are intruded into the object.

(b) There exists a common disinclination to think of projection *into* the object. In effect, this disinclination implies balking at the interpretation of unconscious, concrete phantasies of substantial, bodily substantial parts of the self and the object. I believe the preference for projection *on to* the object representation is also based on a perhaps unrecognized vestige of Freud's theories of distributions of cathexes on the model of electrical charges.

(c) Some clinicians are troubled by the relatively large number of features and uses of projective identification: defensive; protective of good parts of the self; a way to control others or to merge with them; an aspect of idealization; a prerequisite of human communication; crucial in empathizing; and so on. The concept's definitions have varied accordingly, and led to the objection that *projective identification* covers too much territory. It loses meaning by meaning too much. This objection is, I would say, based on analysts' impatience with their having to practice contextual thinking and engage in close listening to phenomenological accounts of subjective experience. In principle, there is no reason why a series of aims cannot be served by one mechanism or process. Meanings vary; today's analysts are beyond routine interpretations; analytic work is more challenging and interesting than ever.

There is one final thought I consider it necessary to introduce before concluding this sketch of recent developments surrounding *projective identification* in the USA: Whatever the benefits of the increasing focus on communication, intersubjectivity, and interpersonal relatedness and adaptation, they are offset by the shift of emphasis away from the intrapsychic, endogenous, destructive, and from conflict in the internal world.

These emphases have, however, established the value of conceptualizing *projective identification* in psychic functioning. Future efforts to strike a balance in this regard will be a source of unending controversy. The history of ideas shows this to be so.

A brief review of projective identification in American psychoanalytic literature

Elizabeth Spillius

In this chapter I attempt to illustrate some of the general themes described by Roy Schafer (in Chapter 14) in his helpful overview of the work of American psychoanalysts on the concept of projective identification. The chapter is based partly on general reading and partly on information provided by Psychoanalytic Electronic Publishing ('PEP' CD-Rom).[43] My brief survey suggests that although the interest of American psychoanalysts in the idea of projective identification began slowly, by the 1970s it had begun to quicken and by the 1990s nearly four times as many American as British authors were writing about the topic.

This surge of interest in projective identification coincided with increasing American interest in British object–relations theory, especially in the work of Winnicott, Fairbairn, Klein and Bion, and with the growth in American analysis of various sorts of relational, inter-personal and intersubjective approaches to the relationship between analyst and patient. At first, interest in projective identification was focused on the term itself – its meaning and possible usefulness or lack of usefulness. As time has gone on – it is now more than forty-five years since Malin and Grotstein wrote what I believe was the first American paper on projective identification – it seems to me

---

43 I am grateful to Professor David Tuckett for assistance in using the PEP CD-Rom in locating relevant papers concerning projective identification in 2003 and again in 2008.

that the analysts and therapists who have been using the idea have been taking it more for granted. They tend to mention the term in the course of discussing other clinical or conceptual problems; sometimes they do not mention the term explicitly, although they seem to be using the idea. Perhaps this is a sign that the idea of projective identification has gradually come to be more accepted.

The European contributors to the present book have suggested that when a new psychoanalytic concept is adopted into a different psychoanalytic tradition it is likely not to fit very well, leading sometimes to changes in the concept, sometimes to changes in the recipient tradition. The process of evaluation of a new and unfamiliar concept by members of another psychoanalytic tradition tends to be accompanied by much attention to definition, especially at first. This has certainly been the case in the United States, where there has been a great deal of discussion about what projective identification really is and how it should be defined, which has only recently begun to decline.

Most though by no means all of the American authors who write about the concept of projective identification describe the differences between Klein's and Bion's usages, usually by saying that Klein's usage is intrapsychic whereas Bion's is interpersonal, or intrapsychic *and* interpersonal (Bion, 1959; Klein, 1946, 1955). Most authors do not mention Bion's distinction between normal and pathological projective identification or his discussion of the processes that tend to lead to pathological projective identification (Bion, 1959). Only the American analyst Judith Mitrani, and to some extent Grotstein and Ogden, stress Bion's emphasis on projective identification as a normal mode of communication between infant and mother, with the accompanying assumption that it is a normal mode of communication between adults as well (Mitrani, 2001).

Very few American authors mention the work of Rosenfeld on projective identification (Rosenfeld, 1971, 1987b) and the few who include Rosenfeld are usually those who have worked with very disturbed patients. But Rosenfeld's most important paper on projective identification (Rosenfeld, 1971), reprinted in Chapter 5 in the present book, is not cited in the American literature, perhaps because it was first published in an obscure book. This paper by Rosenfeld includes a comprehensive statement about the various motives for projective identification (see Chapter 5) a topic which, surprisingly, is not usually systematically described or discussed in the American literature.

246

A feature that has been much discussed in the American literature is whether or not there is a difference between projection and projective identification. Grotstein is apparently the only American analyst who explicitly follows the current but usually tacit British usage in stating that it is not useful to make such a distinction (Malin and Grotstein, 1966). Virtually all other American authors say or imply that in 'projection' the projector loses contact with what he has projected into the other person, whereas in 'projective identification' the link is (unconsciously) maintained. Some American authors define projection as 'intrapersonal' and projective identification as 'interpersonal' (e.g. Gilhooley, 1998). Often it is also pointed out that in the case of projective identification the projector uses some sort of evocative behaviour designed to get the recipient of the projection to experience feelings appropriate to the content of the projection. This distinction is very similar to, perhaps the same as the distinction I have made between 'evocative' and 'non-evocative' projective identification (Spillius, 1988b, pp. 81–86). The difference, however, is that I describe both the evocative and non-evocative varieties as projective identification, whereas in American usage the tendency is to describe the non-evocative type as 'projection' and the evocative type as 'projective identification' (see, for example, Garfinkle, 2005). In any case I think that these two types are much more difficult to distinguish in practice than in theory.

Another difference between American and British usage is that most British Kleinian analysts tend to use or at least to be aware of the distinction that Ronald Britton has made between what he calls 'attributive' and 'acquisitive' projective identification (Britton, 1998a), whereas these terms and the distinction they describe are seldom used in the American literature, although Stanley Rosenman's idea of 'assaultive' projective identification describes a very much intensified form of what Britton describes as 'acquisitive' projective identification (Rosenman, 2003). Both Britton's and Rosenman's terms are similar to Donald Meltzer's idea of 'intrusive' projective identification (Meltzer, 1967, p. xi).

Another theme in connection with projective identification is its link to the concepts of transference and countertransference. The analyst's response to the patient's projective identification is a central preoccupation for many American authors; indeed, James Grotstein says: 'American interest in projective identification was largely due, in my considered opinion and experience, to the rapid growth in interest in countertransference phenomena, and this was due in turn to the increased interest in the treatment of borderlines' (James Grotstein, personal communication, 2005). Most American authors who write about countertransference as a response to projective identification now appear to be using the term 'countertransference' in the widened sense suggested by Paula Heimann (1950) and others. As Glen Gabbard points out, the idea of projective identification in its interpersonal dimension, together with the idea of countertransference enactment, has been an important aspect of what he calls 'the emerging common ground' in which countertransference is gradually coming to be conceived as a joint creation by analyst and patient (Gabbard, 1995).

In discussing the connection between projective identification and countertransference, several American authors mention the work of León Grinberg (1962), especially his idea of 'projective counter-identification'. But, with the exception of Otto Kernberg (1989, p. 80), the authors who cite Grinberg usually alter his definition to mean the way the analyst responds to the patient's projective identification, a countertransference response, using that term in its broadest sense. That is not, however, what Grinberg meant. It is perhaps what he should have meant, but not what he actually meant. In his view projective identification is not a countertransference response, for he defines countertransference as involving the analyst's psychopathology. He thinks that projective counter-identification is the patient's fault, so to speak. The patient has projected something into the analyst with such force that *any* analyst would be compelled to identify with the projection. I think that this definition limits the term's usefulness, for there is no way of being sure that all analysts would react to a particular case of projective identification in the same way, a point also made by J.S. Finell (1986). It is perhaps for this reason that Grinberg's term has rarely been used in Britain and that in American usage Grinberg's definition has usually been altered to mean what in Britain would be called the analyst's responses to the patient's projection.

American views on projective identification have been profuse, complex, and varied. I have attempted to simplify their description by dividing them into three sets. In the first set are those whose main concern is to use the concept in clinical work: I call this set the **adopters**. In the second set are those who define the term and relate it to other concepts but do not make very much use of it clinically: I call this set **partial adopters**. In the third set are those who focus on the definition of the term, usually in order to disagree with it or dismiss it: I call this set the **definers and doubters**. There is also, of course, a very large fourth set: those who have not written about the concept and so are presumably indifferent or negative about it. I assume that many orthodox ego-psychologists would consider themselves to belong to this fourth set.

The adopters

The best known and most prolific analysts of this group are James Grotstein, Thomas Ogden and Otto Kernberg, although by now (2010) there are many others.

James Grotstein (Grotstein, 1981, 1982, 1994a, 1994b, 1995, 1997, 2001, 2002, 2005; Malin and Grotstein, 1966)
James Grotstein is one of the first American analysts to write about projective identification and it has continued to be a cornerstone of his psychoanalytic thinking. He has written a great many papers in which the concept is central, more than ten, and he has been concerned to develop a theory of mind and of the analytic relationship in which projective identification plays an important part.

Grotstein's first paper on projective identification was written in 1966 with Arthur Malin (Malin and Grotstein, 1966, reprinted in Chapter 16 of this book). They give Segal's (1964) version of Klein's definition of the concept and go on to say that 'the external object now receives the projected parts, and then this alloy – external object plus newly arrived projected part – is reintrojected to complete the cycle' (Malin and Grotstein, 1966, p. 26). They do not quite make clear the fact that in Klein's view this procedure is an unconscious phantasy, not an interpersonal process. They cite Robert Knight's 1940 paper 'Introjection, projection and identification' as an anticipation of Klein's and their own view (Knight, 1940). They also describe Harold Searles' (1963) paper as an exemplification of projective identification, although Searles himself makes it clear in his paper that he thought of what he was describing as 'symbiotic relatedness' rather than projective identification.

Malin and Grotstein refer to Rosenfeld's and Bion's papers, which use the idea of projective identification in analysing psychotic patients. They do not quite in my view recognise the extent to which Bion's approach led to an idea of projective identification as a basic preverbal process of communication or the extent to which he emphasises the way in which the recipient is likely to be affected by the projection, in contrast to Klein's more exclusive emphasis on projective identification as the individual's phantasy.

Malin and Grotstein stress that projective identification is a normal process and that it is 'the way in which the human organism grows psychically, nurtured by his environment' (Malin and Grotstein, 1966, p. 28). 'Transference phenomena', they say, 'are obviously very closely related to projective identification' and they stress that there is no difference between projection and projective identification. 'A projection', they say, 'of itself seems meaningless unless the individual can retain some contact with what is projected' (Malin and Grotstein, 1966, pp. 28 and 27). Finally, they think that projective identification is a normal process existing from birth, though it can also become pathological and defensive.

These attributes of projective identification have continued to be essential in Grotstein's later work. In his book *Splitting and Projective Identification* (Grotstein, 1981) written fifteen years after his paper with Malin, Grotstein emphasises the varied motives for projective identification much in the fashion of Rosenfeld (1971): fusion, control of the object, evacuation and disavowal of aspects of the self, communication to other aspects of the self. He does not, however, emphasise the projection of good aspects of the self, which was important in Klein's thinking. Once again he asserts that there is no difference between projection and projective identification. He now emphasises much more than before the concept of splitting, which is an essential aspect of Klein's view of projective identification. He emphasises the difference between intrapsychic and interpersonal projective identification more than before, but he does not discuss the importance of evocative behaviour. Indeed, he thinks that we do not actually project into external objects, but into 'our images of them'. In other words, projective identification is intrapsychic, although, as Dorpat (1983) points out, Grotstein's usage is inconsistent for at some points he regards projective identification as interactional. Dorpat thinks, and I agree, that 'the unconscious phantasy is actualised through verbal and non-verbal communications unconsciously designed to provoke in another person various emotions and attitudes' (Dorpat, 1983, p. 119).

In his many later papers that use the concept of projective identi-fication, Grotstein relates it to other concepts of object–relations theory and to ideas of his own to form a somewhat new and complex conceptual system in which projective identification is central (Grotstein, 1981, 1982, 1994a, 1994b, 1995, 1997, 2001, 2002). He also stresses that the concept of projective identification was abso-lutely central in Klein's thinking. In my view this is an exaggeration. To Klein and to contemporary Kleinians, projective identification is important clinically, but its importance as a theoretical concept derives from its place in the rest of Klein's conceptual system, most especially the ideas of the paranoid-schizoid and depressive positions.

Thomas Ogden (Ogden, 1978a, 1978b, 1979, 1982, 1986, 1994a, 1994b, 1994c, 2004)
As Roy Schafer describes in Chapter 14, Ogden's work, including his work on projective identification, is well known and frequently cited in the literature. In understanding projective identification and then in developing his own conceptualisation of the mind and of the analyst–patient relation, Ogden builds on the ideas of Klein and Bion on the one hand and of Winnicott on the other. He has also been influenced by Rosenfeld, Balint, Searles, Langs, and by his friends James Grotstein and Bryce Boyer, and, inevitably, by the intensity of his work with severely disturbed patients, the sort of patient with whom an understanding of projective identification is particularly important. He also spent some time at the Tavistock Clinic in the 1970s, which I surmise was an important introduction to the thinking of British object–relations theorists.

His first paper discussing projective identification was 'A develop-mental view of identification resulting from maternal impingements' (Ogden, 1978a). This paper was followed in 1979 by 'On projective identification' (reproduced in Chapter 17), and then by the book *Projective Identification and Psychoanalytic Technique* (Ogden, 1982). In 'On projective identification' Ogden (1979) describes projective identification as a process in which the first step consists of a phantasy in which the patient wishes to rid himself of unwanted aspects of the self into another person. The second part of the process consists of the projector unconsciously putting pressure on the recipient to think and behave in a manner congruent with the projection. The third part of the process consists of the recipient processing the

251

projected feelings so that they can be re-internalised by the projector. He does not make clear that in Klein's view the whole process of projective identification takes place in the projector's phantasy and that it was Bion who added the interpersonal communicative element and the containing function described in the third part of Ogden's view of the process. One gets the impression that Ogden is not particularly concerned about academic niceties concerning attribution. His aim is to develop a workable interpretation of the processes involved.

In his 1979 paper 'On projective identification' Ogden, unlike Grotstein, distinguishes projection from projective identification. He thinks that in projection an aspect of the self is in phantasy expelled, disavowed and attributed to the recipient whom the projector often experiences as foreign, strange and frightening. In projective identification the link with what has been projected and attributed to the recipient is to some extent retained. In practice I have found this distinction difficult to maintain for it has been on the occasions when a patient has found me foreign, strange, frightening, hateful even, that the patient has had the most intense although denied relationship with what he has located and evoked in me. The difficulty, as always, is to metabolise the experience sufficiently to be able to use it constructively and to express one's understanding of it in attitudes and words that the patient can at least partially begin to take in.

In his book *Projective Identification and Psychotherapeutic Technique* Ogden (1982) explains how he uses the related concepts of externalisation, introjection and introjective identification. He also explains his own technique in more detail, contrasting it with that of other psychoanalytic traditions, and he describes his work with hospital in-patients and seriously disturbed schizophrenic patients.

Ogden's later work builds on these early formulations and experiences, leading to an integration of it with the work of Klein, Winnicott, Esther Bick, Donald Meltzer, Frances Tustin and others: see Chapter 6 of *The Matrix of the Mind* (Ogden, 1986) and Chapters 6 and 10 of *Subjects of Analysis* (Ogden, 1994c). Projective identification continues to play a part in his later formulation of the 'dialectical' relationship between the 'autistic–contiguous', the paranoid–schizoid and the depressive positions, and also in the dialectical relationship of the two subjectivities of the analyst and the patient and their intersubjectivity, which Ogden calls the 'analytic third' (Ogden, 1994a, 1994c [especially Chapter 5], 2004).

It is clear that projective identification has been a central organising concept for Ogden, as for Grotstein and others, because of its inter-personal dimension. He has used it extensively in the development of his conceptual system, which takes some ideas from Klein herself and from other Kleinians and object-relations theorists, but he weaves these ideas together into a new and rather different synthesis. Both Grotstein and Ogden have had considerable personal contact with Kleinian and Independent analysts, which supports Helmut Hinz's thesis that such contact encourages adoption of new concepts (see Hinz's Chapter 11 in the present book). But both Ogden and Grotstein have not just adopted some aspects of the Kleinian and object-relations traditions, they have used parts of these traditions, including the idea of projective identification, in developing new syntheses.

Otto Kernberg (Kernberg, 1975, p. 56; 1980, pp. 27, 45; 1984, pp. 16–17, 113–115; 1989, pp. 6, 24; 1992, especially Chapter 10)
Like Grotstein, Ogden, and others, Otto Kernberg is particularly interested in severely ill and borderline patients and it is mainly (though not exclusively) in the context of their treatment that he uses the concept of projective identification (Kernberg, 1986, 1987).

Kernberg defines projective identification as a more primitive defence than projection (Kernberg, 1986; 1987; 1989, pp. 6, 24). He thinks it consists of three processes: first, projection of badness into the object (he does not say anything about the projection of good-ness); second, maintaining empathy with what has been projected; and third, inducing the object to experience what has been projected.

He regards projection as a more mature defence in which unac-ceptable experience is repressed and then projected into the object. Empathy is not maintained with what has been projected (Kernberg, 1986, 1987). This is not a definition that I think other American or British authors have proposed.

In psychosis, Kernberg says, there is a loss of ego boundaries accompanied by regression to an abnormal symbiotic phase bringing about an obliteration of the self and destruction of the object world 'under the influence of projective identification'. He does not advo-cate interpreting projective identification to psychotic patients because he thinks that such interpretations would exacerbate the loss of ego boundaries, a finding which has not, to my knowledge, been emphasised by other analysts who use the concept of projective identification in the analysis of psychotic patients.

He thinks, on the contrary, that it is useful to interpret projective identification to borderline and narcissistic patients, and that in the case of neurotic patients projective identification is less important and one would find oneself interpreting projection.

In 'Projection and projective identification: developmental and clinical aspects', Kernberg (1987) illustrates his formulations by three clinical cases: first, an hysterical woman who Kernberg thought did not use either projective identification or projection; second, a narcissistic woman who used projective identification; and third, a paranoid borderline man who also used projective identification.

One gets the impression that although Kernberg is familiar with British Kleinian theory, he focuses especially on clear definition of its concepts more than its own practitioners do, and in a form that they would probably not use, particularly in the distinction he makes between projection and projective identification and in his classification of patients for whom interpretation of projective identification is or is not appropriate. Perhaps some of this focus on precise definition and application comes about because of the importance of Kernberg's role in the United States in communicating psychoanalytic ideas to psychiatrists and psychologists as well as to psychoanalysts.

Although Ogden, Grotstein and Kernberg have made the main contributions in this field, there have been contributions by many others: Bryce Boyer (1978, 1986, 1989, 1990a, 1990b); Lucy La Farge (1989); Harold Boris (1993, 1994a, 1994b); Albert Mason (a current paper is included as Chapter 18 in the present book); Robert Caper (1988, 1999); Dan Gilhooley (1998); Louis Brunet and Diane Casoni (Brunet and Casoni, 1996, 2001); Judith Mitrani (2001); Roger Karlsson (2004); Jeffrey Eaton (2005); Stephen Purcell (2006); Henry Smith (2000; 2006).

Bryce Boyer (1978, 1986, 1989, 1990a, 1990b)
Bryce Boyer, like Ogden and Grotstein, but in his own unique way, integrates the theory of British object relations with that of ego-psychology and, like Grotstein and Ogden, his chief area of clinical work has been with psychotic and seriously disturbed borderline patients (Boyer, 1978, 1986, 1989, 1990a, 1990b). He uses the concept of projective identification but he is less concerned than Grotstein and Ogden with formulating it conceptually and using it to develop a conceptual system. He also discusses countertransference, especially the contributions of Racker, Heimann, Rosenfeld and

Balint. But it is as a talented clinician that his writings are most memorable.

Lucy La Farge (1989)
Lucy La Farge's contribution to projective identification is briefer than those discussed so far, but is of the same general type. She uses the idea, along with other concepts, to analyse the way severely ill borderline patients create empty states to ward off regression to states of fragmentation or pathological fusion.

Harold Boris (1993, 1994a, 1994b)
Harold Boris is in a special category for he was not an analyst but he became a skilled analytic clinician at a time when non-medical people were not allowed to be formally trained analytically in the United States. He is one of the few American practitioners who took in the whole ethos of Klein's and Bion's thinking as if he had known it emotionally in himself all along. His conceptualisation of it, however, is all his own. Unlike most other American authors he does not define projective identification or try formally to relate it to other concepts. His concern is to use it clinically especially in trying to understand envy, hope as a defence, anorexia and bulimia (Boris, 1993, 1994a, 1994b). His most intensive discussion of projective identification is to be found towards the end of his paper 'Torment of the object: a contribution to the study of bulimia' (Boris, 1988). In a later paper (Boris, 1994a) he gives an engaging description of projective identification and envy in a four-year-old girl. Boris is not particularly concerned to make conceptual definitions of projective identification. He explains the concept by example rather than by formal definition, and he uses the idea as a tool in understanding both normal and 'difficult' patients.

Albert Mason (his current paper is included as Chapter 18 in the present book)
Albert Mason is an English Kleinian analyst who went to the United States (Los Angeles) in 1957. He has written several unpublished papers about projective identification, one of which, 'Vicissitudes of projective identification', is published in Chapter 18 in the present book for the first time. In it Mason describes Klein's use of the term and he gives many examples of his own use of it in clinical practice.

255

Robert Caper (1988, 1999)

Caper has not written specific papers on projective identification although he discusses the concept in his two books, *Immaterial Facts* (1988) and *A Mind of One's Own* (1999). He is familiar with the work of Klein, Bion, Mason, Grotstein and contemporary Kleinian authors generally. Caper's discussions of projective identification are distinguished by particularly detailed and evocative clinical examples. He is especially interested in the role of projective identification in developing relations with internal objects. 'The most prominent of the internal objects with which the child must learn to live', he says, 'is the superego, an unconscious melding of his or her external objects and impulses toward them brought about by projective identification' (Caper, 1988, p. 236). He also describes the role of projective identification in developing a differentiation between identification in the paranoid–schizoid position ('narcissistic identification') and in the depressive position ('depressive identification') (Caper, 1999, pp. 5–6, 96–104).

Dan Gilhooley (1998)

Dan Gilhooley describes several episodes in the life of a three-year-old boy which he then analyses in terms of his views on projection, which he defines as intrapsychic, and projective identification, which he defines as interpersonal.

Louis Brunet and **Diane Casoni** (Brunet and Casoni, 1996, 2001)

Brunet and Casoni describe the symbolisation, projective identification and use of the analyst by a schizophrenic adolescent boy. In this analytic experience of projective identification the analyst was able to act as a container for the patient's actions and thoughts in such a way that he could symbolise the patient's archaic and overwhelming thoughts and feelings in a way that the patient could take in.

Judith Mitrani (2001)

Judith Mitrani describes several episodes of clinical material illustrating the way the analyst needs to be fully open to feeling the patient's emotional experience. Only such meaningful containment of emotionally charged projective identifications can hope to develop emotional understanding and a potential for psychic change. Intellectual understanding is not enough, and projective identification is an important aspect of emotional communication.

Roger Karlsson (2004)

Roger Karlsson thinks that in some cases the analyst needs to be able to experience prolonged tolerance of the patient's projecting intolerable aspects of himself into the analyst before the patient is able to progress from an experience of 'oneness' to an experience of 'twoness'. Experience of 'twoness', of separateness, was feared by the particular patient he describes because it involved recognition of the analyst's and the mother's imperfections, which threatened the patient's defence of idealisation.

Stephen Purcell (2006) and Henry Smith (2000, 2006)

Both Purcell and Smith describe in clinical papers how they used understanding of their patients' particular projective identifications. In all three papers it was evident that the authors were taking it for granted that the reader would understand that they were using the concept of projective identification implicitly even when they were not formally defining it or, in Smith's case, hardly using it by name. Projective identification was not the theme of these papers – the focus of the papers was the particular clinical problem of each patient-analyst pair.

The partial adopters

The analysts of this group have made use of the concept of projective identification, but usually in comparative isolation from the other concepts and the general ethos of the Kleinian tradition, and their clinical use of the concept is less intensive than that of the first set of analysts described above.

Robert Langs (1978a, 1978b, 1978c, 1979)

In the Preface to his book *Technique in Transition* (Langs, 1978c) Langs says that he encountered the idea of projective identification in the 1960s when 'looking for a language that could help me to conceptualize my observations in the interactional sphere'. He thought that the Kleinian literature was interactional although not in quite the way he had in mind. It was not until he read a paper by Madeline and Willi Baranger (1966) with their concept of the bi-personal field and the role of projective identification in it that Langs fully realised the immense significance that the two concepts could have in his work. For Langs his developing interest in this theme was the essence of his shift from a 'classical' to a 'neo-classical' approach.

Like many American analysts, Langs describes projection as an intrapersonal concept and projective identification as interactional. Projection he defines as

> an intrapsychic mechanism through which the patient unconsciously attributes his own inner contents and impulses to another individual without actual interactional efforts to place those contents into the other person and to have the other person experience and deal with them. Projective identification is specifically interactional in that it is unconsciously designed to create an intrapsychic effect within the recipient.
>
> (Langs, 1978c, p. 317)

Langs describes his understanding and use of projective identification by describing how, through observations of patients and analysts, combined with much reading of Bion, Khan and Winnicott, he delineated three sub-types of bi-personal field. Langs illustrates the three sub-types of bi-personal field in the work of his supervisees, and in the description of the three fields he finds the concept of projective identification useful, though I do not think his main purpose is to develop or expand upon the concept of projective identification in itself.

Walter Burke and Michael Tansey (Burke and Tansey, 1985; Tansey and Burke, 1985, 1989)

Burke and Tansey explore the relationship of projective identification to empathy and countertransference, all three concepts being important for them in linking intrapsychic and interpersonal experiences. They maintain, rightly I think, that Heinrich Racker is mistaken in thinking that empathy is likely to accompany what Racker calls 'concordant' countertransference and that lack of empathy and projective identification are likely to accompany what he calls 'complementary' countertransference (see Racker, 1957). Burke and Tansey think that projective identification and complementary countertransference may lead to empathy; concordant countertransference may lead to discord. Projective identification, the authors say, can be defensive, adaptive or communicative – and perhaps all three at the same time, although they do not go quite so far as to say that.

Burke and Tansey seem to make a tacit assumption that where empathy is, understanding will follow. Judging from their case material, I think it is often the other way around. Once one understands what is going on between analyst and patient, one is more likely to feel empathy.

Tansey and Burke have developed a very complex set of categories for analysing progress or lack of progress in analytic empathy and understanding. The first phase of such understanding they categorise as 'reception', the second as 'internal processing' and the third as 'communication'. Within each of these phases, at least in their first exposition of them, there are three sub-phases. At first I thought this scheme unnecessarily elaborate and ponderous – how could one use it in a session? Apparently I am not alone, for in a review of Tansey and Burke's (1989) book *Understanding Countertransference: From Projective Identification to Empathy*, James Frosch says, 'The clinical examples lack the richness, depth and individuality that we are accustomed to in analytic case reports' (Frosch, 1990). But on reading their papers and the book again, I thought Frosch's judgement was a little harsh. Although their system is too cumbersome to be used in the heat of a session, it does give a means for examining what has gone wrong after it is over, and once one knows what has gone wrong, one is half way towards putting it right.

Jill Savage Scharff (1992)

In her book *Projective and Introjective Identification and the Use of the Therapist's Self* (Scharff, 1992), Jill Savage Scharff reviews a great many definitions and uses of the concepts of projection, projective identification, introjection and introjective identification in both Britain and the United States, and illustrates her own usages extensively in work with individuals, couples, and families. She considers too the usefulness of these ideas in understanding art and culture. In spite of its comprehensiveness, her work is somewhat piecemeal; she does not attempt to choose among the many definitions or to develop an integrated approach in which the various definitions of identification would be related to one another, and in her clinical applications she gives the impression of using whatever particular definition or aspect of a definition seemed to make sense to her on that occasion.

Morris N. Eagle (2000)

Eagle disapproves of facile assertions by analysts, perhaps especially facile assertions about projective identification in transference and

countertransference as a response to it. His view is that in the process
of correcting the idea of the analyst as a 'blank screen', the misleading
idea has developed that everything that the analyst thinks and feels
about his patient, all his countertransference reactions, can be seen as
a virtually unerring guide to the patient's mental contents. He is
equally critical of Racker's belief that when the analyst feels resentful
about a patient's critical attacks on him this means that the analyst is
in a state of 'complementary identification' with one of the patient's
internal objects (Racker, 1957). Nor does Eagle agree with those
analysts who explain their thoughts about their patients by asserting
that the thoughts have been 'put into' them by the patient. He
expects more rigorous attention and thinking from the analyst:
'explicit and specific knowledge of the other, theoretical knowledge,
explicitly searching for patterns and cues, examination of evidence,
and clinical reasoning and inference based on the patient's productions'. His paper is reminiscent of Joseph Sandler's paper 'On
communication from patient to analyst: not everything is projective
identification' (Sandler, 1993).

Ely Garfinkle (2005)

Garfinkle gives a careful review of American and British uses of the
concept of projective identification and concludes that it has been
confusing to extend the definition of the concept to include interpersonal as well as intrapersonal components. He rejects Ogden's
definition because it includes interpersonal components, and he
rejects the definitions of the British analysts Priscilla Roth (1999,
pp. 4–5) and Ronald Britton (1998a, pp. 4–5) because they require
familiarity with Kleinian concepts. He suggests that projective
identification should be defined as follows:

> Projective identification is to be defined strictly as an unconscious
> phantasy in which split off parts of the self are disowned, projected,
> and attributed to someone else. In addition, a conclusion by
> the analyst based on clinical evidence, that an unconscious
> motive in the unconscious phantasy of the analysand is to control
> and/or to influence the thinking, feeling and/or action of the
> object, would be a sufficient (though not necessarily exclusive)
> criterion to define such an unconscious phantasy as a projective
> identification.
>
> (Garfinkle, 2005, pp. 202–203)

He also defines the term 'projection', as follows:

> In order to distinguish projective identification from simple projection, I would also propose that we define simple projection in the following manner: that the term projection reflect a situation in which the subject perceives the object in accordance with the subject's internal reality without an unconscious intent to affect the mind of the object.
>
> (Garfinkle, 2005, pp. 203–204)

I do not know whether other analysts have adopted Garfinkle's definitions, but I suspect that the inclusion of interpersonal components in American usage, especially by Ogden, has become too well accepted for it to be abandoned. Further, deductions about a patient's thoughts and feelings are necessarily made through the perceptions of the analyst, fallible though they may be, so that some sort of interpersonal component is inevitably part of the perceiving and defining process.

The researchers
Within the set I have called 'partial adopters' is a sub-set who have used the concept of projective identification in psychological and psychosocial research in ways that required conceptual understanding and application of the concept, although without very extensive clinical use of it. There have been three such projects, reported by John Zinner and Roger Shapiro (Zinner and Shapiro, 1972), Roy Muir (1982, 1990) and Paolo Migone (1995).

In summary, the analysts of the set I have called 'partial adopters' tend to define and to some extent to use the concept of projective identification, but they stress its formal aspects rather than its clinical usefulness.

The definers and doubters

Almost all the large group of authors of this group have written just one paper on projective identification. Most complain in one way or another about a lack of clarity in the concept which many try to remedy by giving their own definition. Some authors are neutral in their views (Carveth, 1992; Crisp, 1986; Goldman, 1988; Hamilton,

1986, 1990; Issacharoff and Hunt, 1994; Jaffe, 1968). Two authors (Adler, 1989; Feinsilver, 1983) have tried to translate projective identification into a Winnicottian framework. The remaining authors variously find the concept 'mysterious', 'confusing', 'jargon', 'imprecise', 'obfuscating', 'psychobabble', or part of 'Klein's fantastic metapsychology' (Blechner, 1994; Finell, 1986; Meissner, 1980, 1987; Ornston, 1978; Pantone, 1994; Porder, 1987; Whipple, 1986). Not surprisingly, these authors do not use the concept of projective identification clinically, and, with the exception of an occasional expression of interest in the work of Winnicott, they do not express any interest in other aspects of the Kleinian or object-relations traditions.

Considering their generally negative attitude, it is surprising that the members of this group have written even one paper on the topic of projective identification. It seems possible that they have done so because they thought at first that the concept might be relevant to an interpersonal view of the analyst–patient relationship and other relationships more generally. The fact that other well-known analysts were writing about projective identification may also have stimulated their interest.

Conclusion

This examination of American responses to the concept of projective identification provides an interesting and perhaps unusual example of the spread of a concept from one analytic school of thought to another. I have described three sorts of response: adoption, partial adoption, defining but doubting. There is of course the fourth response, that of simply ignoring the 'new' concept entirely. The fact that so much notice has been taken of the concept, even though the noticing is negative as well as positive, suggests that there is something about the idea that intrigues analysts. I think the 'something' is its potential for helping to understand the relationship of analyst and patient from a slightly new and unfamiliar angle.

There has also been a gradual change over time in the types of paper written by the 'adopters'. There is less attention to definitions of projective identification, and more tacit use of the idea in analytic work on particular clinical problems; sometimes the actual term is used in such papers, sometimes it is hardly mentioned. Perhaps, in addition to projective identification coming to be taken more for granted, there is some reluctance to use the term by name in case readers might assume that the writer was too 'Kleinian', for Kleinian ideas have for many years been regarded in the United States as quite ridiculous, and have only recently acquired a certain respectability in some quarters.

Projective identification in the therapeutic process[44]

Arthur Malin and James S. Grotstein

Recent articles by Loewald (1960) and Searles (1963) having to do with certain aspects of the therapeutic process have stimulated us to investigate what we believe may be the basis of the therapeutic effect in psycho–analysis. In our view the concept of projective identification can be fruitfully applied to an understanding of the therapeutic process. We shall attempt to describe the concept of projective identification and then discuss the relevance of this idea to normal and pathological development with a view toward clarifying the therapeutic process in light of it.

The term projective identification was first used by Melanie Klein (1946) and was meant to indicate a process in which parts of the self are split off and projected into an external object or part object. Hanna Segal (1964) states:

> Projective identification is the result of the projection of parts of the self into an object. It may result in the object's being perceived as having acquired the characteristics of the projected part of the self, but it can also result in the self becoming identified with the object of its projection.

---

44 This chapter reproduces the text of Malin, A. and Grotstein, J. S. (1966). Projective identification in the therapeutic process. *International Journal of Psychoanalysis*, 47, 26–31.

This idea was developed from Klein's (1932b; 1935) earlier concept of object relations existing from the start of extrauterine life. Klein had indicated that the relation to the first object, the breast, is through introjection. She also demonstrated that object relations from the beginning depend for their development on projective and introjective mechanisms. Klein (1946) suggested that these mechanisms are seen in the earliest period of normal development, which she described as the paranoid-schizoid position. She stated further that these mechanisms are also a type of defence found particularly in schizophrenic patients.

We wish to emphasize at this point that projective identification to us has come to mean many different things and embraces many concepts. Our paper is an attempt both to clarify and to expand on it, and to place it in its proper perspective in psycho-analytic theory and practice.

First, we should like to say why we use the term projective identification and not projection. Projection alone is a mechanism for dealing with instinctual drives, akin to incorporation. It is an instinctual mode. We feel, as does Fairbairn (1952), that all intra-physic and inter-personal relations are transacted on the basis of object relationships, rather than on the basis of instinctual drives alone. The object is the irreducible vehicle in human interaction.

Once we make this assumption, we then conceive of the psychic apparatus as a dynamic structure composed of internalized objects (and part-objects) with drive charges inseparably attached to them. We feel that these charged parts of self (or identifications) are projected outward and that the status of the identification changes by virtue of the projection, thus enabling the ego to discharge, for instance, unwanted or disclaimed parts of the self (purified pleasure ego of Freud, 1915a). The external object now receives the projected parts, and then this alloy – external object plus newly arrived projected part – is re-introjected to complete the cycle.

In the preceding paragraph, we have dealt with the defensive nature of projective identification. We wish to emphasize that it is also, at the same time, a way of relating to objects. As Freud (1921) has stated, the infant relates by identification prior to making anaclitic object choices. We agree with this and go two steps further; first, we believe that all identification includes projection, as we hope to show; and second, that projective identification is also a normal, as well as abnormal, way of relating which persists into mature adulthood.

We hope to develop the reasons why these burdensome emendations of theory are necessary, especially since the advent of object-relations theory has imposed this task upon us.

An article by Knight (1940) appears to anticipate the concept of projective identification although it is not described directly by that name. In this short article Knight attempts to describe the different ways in which identification may be used and defined. Knight states, 'Identification is never an irreducible process or state of affairs, but is always based on a subtle interaction of both introjective and projective mechanisms.' Knight makes a point that Bibring's term, 'altruistic surrender', involves a projection of one's own desires for pleasure and gratification into another person with whom one then identifies. Knight goes further and states,

> The awareness of how we would feel under similar circumstances enables us to project our own needs and wishes on to the object and then to experience his feelings as if they were ours through the resultant temporary identification with him. Even though this vicarious experience would appear to be an instantaneous process, it seems to me valuable to reduce it to its constituent mechanisms of projection and possibly also introjection.

It is obvious that Knight is referring to identification with whole objects rather than part objects as emphasized by Klein, but Knight's ideas are certainly compatible with the concept of projective identification.

In line with Knight's thinking, we want to emphasize what seems obvious in the concept of identification, namely, that all identification includes projection, and all projection includes identification.[45] Before we are ready to internalize (take in psychically, incorporate), we must be in some state of readiness for this process. That is, we must tentatively project out a part of our inner psychic contents in order to be receptive to the object for introjection and subsequently

---

45 We define introjection as a psychic phenomenon in which the object is taken into the psychic apparatus but is kept separate from the self; in other words, it is within the ego but unassimilated, much like a foreign body. Following introjection, identification may take place by the object's becoming assimilated into the ego or self. See Greenson (1954).

to form an identification with it. When we start with the projection it is necessary that there be some process of identification or internalization in general, or else we can never be aware of the projection. That is, what is projected would be lost like a satellite rocketed out of the gravitational pull of the earth. Eventually all contact with the satellite will be lost. Although the satellite has left Earth, it must remain under the influence of Earth's gravitational pull to remain in orbit in order for it to maintain some contact with Earth. A projection, of itself, seems meaningless unless the individual can retain some contact with what is projected. That contact is a type of internalization, or, loosely, an identification. We want to show that Klein's concept of projective identification can be broadened greatly in order to understand many phenomena in psychic life both normal and pathological, and to enhance our knowledge of identification itself.

Rosenfeld (1952a, 1952b, 1954) and Bion (1955b, 1956) have applied the concept of projective identification to the understanding and treatment of the psychotic patient. They state that when a patient splits off a part of himself and projects it into the object, such as the analyst, he has a feeling of relatedness to the analyst but with some corresponding feelings of inner impoverishment. Very often the patient feels that the split–off part, now in the external object, is a persecutor. They emphasize the importance of projective identification in understanding delusional transference material.

Searles (1963) describes very similar phenomena. He relates much of his material to the Kleinian concept of projective identification, but he does emphasize some important differences between his ideas and Klein's. In a more broadly defined manner, however, we would view Searles's ideas on transference psychosis as being another aspect of projective identification. Searles makes an important point, for instance, of the schizophrenic patient's need to project a part of himself into the therapist. The therapist must provide, according to Searles, a suitable and receptive object in himself to receive this projection from the patient. Searles suggests,

Moreover, it is my experience that he [the chronic schizophrenic patient] actively needs a degree of symbiotic relatedness in the transference, which would be interfered with were the analyst to try, recurrently, to establish with him the validity of verbalized transference interpretations.

Searles suggests here that the projective identification from the patient to the analyst must first be accepted by the analyst before verbal interpretations will be of any help.

Loewald (1960) writes of therapeutic change as involving structural change in the ego. In speaking of the patient's reaction to the analyst, Loewald states, 'A higher stage of organization, of both himself and his environment, is thus reached, by way of the organizing understanding which the analyst provides.'

Loewald emphasizes throughout his article the importance of higher levels of ego integration which the patient can achieve through the analytic treatment. We suggest that projective identification helps explain the development of these higher levels of ego integration.

Transference phenomena are obviously very closely related to projective identification. Transference implies the projection of inner attitudes which came from earlier object relationships into the figure of the analyst during the analysis. A much broader concept of transference would state that all subsequent relationships are modified on the basis of the earliest object relationship of the individual which is now established in the inner psychic life. This view very closely approximates the concept of primary objects which was advanced by Balint (1937). If we accept a broad view of transference to include all object relations, internal and external, after the primary relationship with the breast–mother which is now internalized, then we are stating that all object relations and all transference phenomena are examples, at least in part, of projective identification. This implies that there must be a projection from within the psychic apparatus into the external object. We emphasize that this includes parts of self as well as internal object representations. To go back to Klein's ideas for a moment, some of her lack of emphasis on the environment in human development can be understood in terms of projective identification. It can be understood in the sense that the early instinctual representations, including the death instinct, are projected into the breast–mother, and then the bad breast–mother is introjected on the basis of the earlier projection and not so much on the basis of the actual environmental situation of that breast–mother. We should like to modify this idea, however, with the suggestion that it is just the fact that the inner psychic contents related to earliest object relations are projected into the external objects that makes for the tremendous influence of the environment. It seems to us that it is only upon perceiving how the external object receives our projection and deals with our projection that we now introject back into the psychic apparatus the original projection, but now modified and on a newer level. Hopefully, the mother has helped the infant by allowing this projection to be met with a response of understanding, care, and love. It is the mother who cannot do this, and who sees the child's projections as destructive and frightening, who will confirm the infant's fears of his own bad destructive self.[46] We suggest, moreover, that this method of projecting one's inner psychic contents into external objects and then perceiving the response of these external objects and introjecting this response on a new level of integration is the way in which the human organism grows psychically, nurtured by his environment. The environment must meet the needs of these projections and be able to reinterpret for the developing individual the inner workings of their psychic apparatus and to demonstrate that these are not destructive, 'bad' parts. The external object must confirm those constructive and 'good' aspects of the developing individual and thus facilitate higher ego integration which will mitigate the effect of the destructive components of the self.

We propose that these concepts are of crucial importance in understanding the earliest experiences of the infant, the further growth and development of children and adults, and to a great extent the therapeutic effect of psycho–analysis. We have all observed how patients must project into the analyst their inner psychic contents. These consist of objects and part objects with associated feelings and attitudes. It is mainly through his perception of the manner in which the analyst handles these projections that the patient can find a new level of integration. As Searles (1963) emphasizes, what is important is a receptiveness without an encouragement of these projections, and an attempt at understanding their meaning without the fear that these projections will destroy the analyst.

The essence of the therapeutic process is through modification of internal object relationships within the ego, and this is largely brought about by projective identification. Correct interpretations can be seen as an important way in which the patient can observe how his projections have been received and acknowledged by the analyst. If this does not take place the patient is left with futility, despair, and doubt in regard to his inner self worth.

---

46 Erikson (1959) has shown that the mother also projects her needs and feelings into the infant and responds to the child's perception of these needs.

One of the most common defences of the schizophrenic border-line patient, as well as of many neurotics, is the need to preserve the analyst as a good object by maintaining a distance which paradoxically is not very helpful to developing understanding. Much of this is related to what seems to be a negative therapeutic reaction. It would appear that these patients are trying to preserve the analyst by avoiding closeness to him, i.e. not projecting any of their bad parts into the analyst which they feel will destroy the analyst and therefore their only hope for survival. For example, a borderline patient could rarely speak of any positive feelings toward the analyst, but would occasionally, with great disappointment, point out what he felt was an error on the part of the analyst. It was learned in the analysis that in this way the patient would demonstrate his great reliance and positive attitude toward the analyst, but only through this method of expressing disappointment. To speak directly of his concern and closeness to the analyst would be forbidden because the patient felt that any closeness and trust would mean that the analyst would have to handle the patient's destructiveness and would therefore be destroyed. Therefore, to keep some distance from the analyst was to preserve him. Conversely, a patient may often keep his distance because he has already projected bad objects into the analyst and therefore sees the analyst as a persecutor.

The following case history will illustrate some of the above ideas:

A 23-year-old civil engineer came into analysis because of increasing anxiety over his loneliness. He found himself very aloof from his fellow office workers toward whom he felt a mixture of fear and contempt and did not dare, as a consequence, get close to them. His sexual life, other than masturbation, consisted of a few contacts with prostitutes and one contact with a girl toward whom he had begun to develop feelings. Subsequent sexual attempts with her resulted in humiliating impotent failures, however, so he abruptly terminated the relationship with her. His life otherwise was characterized by a lonely, stark impoverishment in which he spent most of his spare time in his apartment, drinking, playing the guitar, or reading.

He is the second eldest of four children, having an older sister and a younger brother and sister respectively. His father was described as an angry, loud, drunk, martinet of a man who once was a prize-fighter. His mother was a willowy, soft-spoken, subtly patronizing martyr of a woman who was frequently beaten by the father while the children watched in paralyzed horror. When the patient was 12, the mother 'escaped' from the father and encouraged her children to come with her. Only the oldest child obliged, however; the others remained with the father. Immediately thereafter the father moved them away from New York to a small town in California where he forced them to use assumed names so that the mother could not trace them and have them brought back to New York.

Life with father consisted of hearing his insults and temper fits, subjecting oneself to Spartan discipline (the father enforced regular calisthenics upon them as if they were in training), and consistently being reminded of what a better parent he was than their mother who, he claimed, wanted them sent to an orphan's home. After graduating from high school the patient left home against his father's will and used his savings to enter college to become an engineer.

His initial behaviour in analysis was cold, formal, and detached. He would describe a very lonely, impoverished life with an eerie detachment. He did not seem to be involved with his own life. Provocative gestures at work, such as frequently arriving late, allowing himself to be seen idle, and arguments with the supervisor, changed into transference phenomena of professing mild to enormous contempt and ridicule toward the analyst, whose weaknesses and deficiencies almost invariably bore a striking resemblance to the patient's own shortcomings, in addition to shortcomings of both parents. Examples of some of the projections are as follows: frequently he would accuse the analyst of being weak and poorly integrated and possibly suffering from a huge inner impoverishment. Along with this he would state that he felt the analyst also had a hidden homosexual problem. These all were projections of his weak self-concept. On other occasions he would berate the analyst as being too rigid and demanding, and he would freely express how he hated pleasing him – that would be like giving in. This perception of the analyst as rigid, autocratic, and hard to please, represented a projection of the father identification. On still other occasions he would perceive the analyst as supercilious, polite, ingratiating, insincere, and martyr-like. All these qualities belonged to his mother identification.

The projections were accepted by the analyst for their psychic validity, and then interpreted as his need to put bad parts of himself, including bad objects and part objects, into the analyst in order to rid his ego of these bad contents. In addition he was symbolically entering the analyst through these projections, to take control of him by weakening his self-esteem through consistent criticism and denigration. Not only was he repeating with the analyst what he had experienced with his father and mother, but he was also taking possession, in fantasy, of the analyst from within to guarantee total possession of the object. In his life history there was no precedent for him to assume he could have any relationship with anyone without total control or total subjugation. Without this guarantee, as it were, there existed no relationship for him.

The projection of bad parts of himself (and bad objects and part objects) had still another purpose which closely dovetailed with the mechanisms described. This patient was so trapped in his schizoid world that he could not trust his good, positive love feelings to be truly good. He had the conviction that his very love was bad and would be rejected; thus he related with his overtly bad self in order to establish a relationship and, paradoxically, protect the external object and himself from destruction. Moreover, he got a particular delight if he felt the analyst was hurt by his tirades of abuse. As long as the analyst was hurt (i.e. affected), then he as an individual was having some effect on another person and was therefore asserting his identity and was at the same time dealing with his deep envy of the analyst's immutability.

Consistent interpretations of all of these mechanisms wherever they occurred considerably lessened the negative transference, and the patient was subsequently able to recognize that he was warding off his deep feelings of dependency on the analyst. Changes occurred by virtue of analysing the projections rather than by the analyst's unconsciously or consciously responding as if they were objectively valid. In other words, this was a new experience for the patient which allowed him to integrate the previously projected parts, now reintegrated into the ego, so that a higher level of functioning could occur. This is an example of transference, but it is also something more than is ordinarily conveyed by that term. The patient was not merely displacing from the past; he was projecting from within himself bad contents into the analyst. By permitting the patient to project into the analyst, that is, to accept the psychic validity of the projection, a way of establishing a relationship with the patient was developed which allowed successful interpretation and resolution of this archaic way of relating. It also anticipated and precluded a negative therapeutic reaction and aided the patient to heal his ego fragments.

In the light of all the above material we should like to offer some speculative ideas in regard to the general concept of identification.

We suggest the possibility that there is an early primary identification with the breast-mother and that in a sense no further real identification takes place. Instead, there is a constant modifying and integrating of this earliest identification. This might explain the contradiction that appears in the literature in regard to identification at one point appearing as a normal process of development and at another point as a pathological defence mechanism. It would seem that normal identification refers to the primary identification and that any further identification later on in life would be of a more pathological defensive nature more likely on the level of introjection, that is, an unassimilated foreign-body reaction in the psychic apparatus. However, normal development does include identification, but of a far more transient nature than originally assumed, which really has to do with further structuring, integrating, and synthesizing of the earliest primary identification. What is commonly thought of as good identifications can be seen to be growth of the self through these mechanisms. It may be stated that we can never change the facts of what has happened to the patient in his life. What we hope to do, however, is to help the patient integrate his experiences in a new way so that he may have a choice in the way he relates to the world.[47]

Fairbairn (1952) has made an interesting contribution to the concept of identification. He feels that primary identification takes place with the pre-ambivalent object, which is then split into good and bad objects. All future identifications are made solely with the bad objects. The good objects, he states, do not need to be identified with. There is a different kind of internalizing of the good objects, but this is transitory and is given up as one matures. In other words, the good objects are loosely held as a scaffolding, as it were, for ego growth and differentiation. As this takes place, the scaffolding is removed.

To summarize, we are suggesting that projective identification is a normal process existing from birth. It is one of the most important mechanisms by which growth and development take place through object relations. This mechanism can be described as one in which objects and associated affects are re-experienced on a new integrative level so that further synthesis and development will take place within the ego.

47 See Lichtenstein's (1961) concept of 'identity theme'.

273

We have taken Klein's concept of projective identification and have attempted to show how this idea can be greatly broadened to increase our understanding of normal and pathological development and the therapeutic process. In our view projective identification seems to be the way in which human beings are able to test their own inner psychic life by projecting psychic contents out into the environment and perceiving the environment's reaction to these projected parts of oneself. This process gives rise to newer psychic integrations leading to normal growth and development, and is, moreover, of crucial importance in the therapeutic process.

On projective identification[48]

Thomas H. Ogden

I. Introduction

It is a continuing task of psychoanalytic thinking to attempt to generate concepts and consistent language that are helpful in understanding the interplay between phenomena in an intrapsychic sphere (e.g. thoughts and feelings) and phenomena in the sphere of external reality and interpersonal relations (e.g. the reality of the other person in an object relationship as opposed to the psychological representation of that person). Psychoanalytic theory suffers from a paucity of concepts and language that help to bridge these areas. Since projective identification can be understood as representing one such bridging formulation, it is to the detriment of psychoanalytic thinking that this concept remains one of the most loosely defined and incompletely understood of psychoanalytic conceptualizations.

   This paper attempts to make some steps towards a wider understanding of projective identification, as well as towards an increased precision of definition in this area. The concept of projective identification will be located in relation to other related psychoanalytic concepts, such as projection, introjection, identification, internalization, and externalization. In addition, there is an effort to arrive at a more precise understanding of the nature and function of fantasy in projective identification, and the relation of that fantasy component to external reality and to real object relations, specifically how

48 This chapter reproduces the text of Ogden, T. (1979). On projective identification. *International Journal of Psychoanalysis*, *60*, 357–373.

projective fantasies (intrapsychic phenomena) abut with real, external objects. Further, the paper attempts to specify more clearly the experiential referents of projective identification. Once what is meant by projective identification has been clarified, a brief historical overview of the concept is offered. Finally, on the basis of the understanding of projective identification arrived at earlier in the paper, there is a discussion of the resulting implications for psychotherapeutic technique and for clinical theory. This will include an examination of sources of problems in the handling of projective identifications and a view of the role of interpretation in a therapeutic interaction characterized by projective identifications.

II. Projective identification as fantasy and object relationship

Projective identification is a term that was introduced by Melanie Klein in 1946. Since then, there has been considerable lack of clarity about what is meant when the term is used, how it differs from projection on the one hand and from identification on the other, and its relation to fantasy. The term has been used to refer to a type of projection wherein the person projecting feels 'at one with' the object of the projection (Schafer, personal communication, 1974). The term is also commonly used to refer to a class of fantasy wherein a part of the self is felt to be located in another person (Segal, 1964). Without going further into the different usages of the term, it will suffice at this point to say that the term 'projective identification' has been used to refer to a variety of different, but often complementary, conceptualizations. The definition of projective identification that will be presented in this paper represents a synthesis of, and extension of, contributions made by a number of analysts.

Projective identification will be used in this paper to refer to a group of fantasies and accompanying object relations having to do with the ridding of the self of unwanted aspects of the self; the depositing of those unwanted 'parts' into another person; and finally, with the 'recovery' of a modified version of what was extruded.

Projective identification will be discussed as if it were composed of a sequence of three parts, phases, or steps (Malin and Grotstein, 1966). However, the idea of there being three aspects of a single psychological event better conveys the sense of simultaneity and

interdependence that befits the three aspects of projective identification that will be discussed. In a schematic way, one can think of
projective identification as a process involving the following
sequence: first, there is the fantasy of projecting[49] a part of oneself
into another person and of that part taking over the person from
within; then there is pressure exerted via the interpersonal interaction such that the 'recipient' of the projection experiences pressure
to think, feel, and behave in a manner congruent with the projection; finally, the projected feelings, after being 'psychologically
processed' by the recipient, are reinternalized by the projector.

The first step of projective identification must be understood in
terms of wishes to rid oneself of a part of the self either because that
part threatens to destroy the self from within, or because one feels
that the part is in danger of attack by other aspects of the self and
must be safeguarded by being held inside a protective person. This
latter psychological use of projective identification was prominent in
a schizophrenic adolescent who vehemently insisted that he opposed
psychiatric treatment and was only coming to his sessions because his
parents and the therapist were forcing him to do so. In reality, this
18-year-old could have resisted far more energetically than he did
and had it well within his power to sabotage any treatment attempt.
However, it was important for him to maintain the fantasy that all of
his wishes for treatment and for recovery were located in his parents
and in the therapist so that these wishes would not be endangered by
the parts of himself that he felt were powerfully destructive and intent
on the annihilation of himself.

The type of projective identification involving the fantasy of
getting rid of an unwanted, 'bad' part of the self by putting it into
another person is exemplified by a psychotic obsessional patient who
frequently talked about wishing to put his 'sick brain' into the therapist, who would then have to add up obsessively the numbers on
every licence plate that he saw and be tormented by fears that every
time he touched something that was not his, people would accuse

49 The term 'projection' will be used to refer to the fantasy of expelling a part of the self
  that is involved in the first phase of projective identification even though it is understood
  that this is not the same as a projection that occurs outside of the context of a projective
  identification. The nature of the difference between projection as an independent
  process and projection as a part of projective identification will be discussed later in this
  paper.

him of trying to steal it. This patient made it clear that his fantasy was not one of simply ridding himself of something; it was equally a fantasy of inhabiting another person and controlling him from within. His 'sick brain' would in fantasy torment the therapist from within in a way that it was currently felt to be tormenting the patient. This type of fantasy is based on a primitive idea that feelings and ideas are concrete objects with lives of their own. These 'objects' are felt to be located inside oneself, but it is also felt that they can sometimes be removed from one's insides and placed into another person, thereby relieving the self of the effects of containing such entities. The obsessional patient just described would often in the course of a therapy hour turn his head violently to the side in an effort to 'shake loose' a given worry.

The fantasy of putting a part of oneself into another person and controlling them from within reflects a central aspect of projective identification: the person involved in such a process is operating at least in part at a developmental level wherein there is profound blurring of boundaries between self and object representations. The projector feels that the recipient experiences his feeling, not merely a feeling like his own, but his own feeling that has been transplanted into the recipient. The person projecting feels 'at one with' (Schafer, personal communication, 1974) the person into whom he has projected an aspect of himself. This is where projective identification differs from projection. In projection, the projector feels estranged from, threatened by, bewildered by, or out of touch with, the object of the projection. The person involved in projection might ask, 'Why would anyone act in such an angry way when there is nothing to be angry about? There's something the matter with him.' In projection, one feels psychological distance from the object; in projective identification, one feels profoundly connected with the object. Of course, the contrasting processes are rarely found in pure form; instead, one regularly finds a mixture of the two, with greater or lesser preponderance of feelings of oneness or of feelings of estrangement.

In the second phase of projective identification (more accurately, a second aspect of a single unit), there is a pressure exerted by the projector on the recipient of the projection to experience himself and behave in a way congruent with the projective fantasy. This is not an imaginary pressure. This is real pressure exerted by means of a multitude of interactions between the projector and the recipient.

Projective identification does not exist where there is no interaction between projector and object. A 12-year-old in-patient, who as an infant had been violently intruded upon psychologically and physically, highlights this aspect of projective identification. The patient said and did almost nothing on the ward, but made her presence powerfully felt by perpetually jostling and bumping into people, especially her therapist. This was generally experienced as infuriating by other patients and by the staff. In the therapy hours (often a play therapy), her therapist said that he felt as if there were no space in the room for him. Everywhere he stood seemed to be her spot. This form of interaction represents a form of object relationship wherein the patient puts pressure on the therapist to experience himself as inescapably intruded upon. This interpersonal interaction constitutes the 'induction phase' of this patient's projective identification.

The psychotic obsessional patient mentioned earlier consistently generated a type of therapeutic interaction that illuminated the induction phase of projective identification. This 14-year-old patient was born with pyloric stenosis and suffered from severe projectile vomiting for the entire first month of his life, before the condition was diagnosed and surgically corrected. His psychological experience since then has been continuous in the sense that he has imagined himself to be inhabited by attacking presences: scolding parents, burning stomach pains, tormenting worries, and powerful rage over which he feels little or no control. The initial phases of his therapy consisted almost exclusively of his attempt to torment the therapist by kicking the therapist's furniture, repeatedly ringing the waiting room buzzer, and by ruminating without pause in a high-pitched whine. All of this invited retaliatory anger on the part of the therapist, and it was to the extent that the therapist experienced feelings of extreme tension and helpless rage that the patient felt momentarily calmed. The patient was fully conscious of both his attempts to get the therapist to feel angry, as well as the calming and soothing effect that that had on him. I would understand this therapeutic interaction as an enactment of the patient's fantasy that anger and tension are noxious agents within him that he attempted to get rid of by placing them in the therapist. However, as with his projectile vomiting, a solution is not simple: the noxious agents within that he wishes to rid himself of (anger/food/parents) are also essential for life. Projective identification offers a compromise solution wherein the patient could in fantasy rid himself of the noxious, but life-giving, objects within

279

himself while at the same time keeping them alive inside a partially separate object. This solution would be merely a fantasy without the accompanying object relationship in which the patient exerted terrific pressure on the therapist to conform to the projective fantasy. When there was evidence of verification of the projection (i.e. when the therapist showed evidence of tension and anger), the patient experienced a sense of relief since that offered confirmation that the noxious/life-giving agents had been both extruded and preserved.

I would like to mention very briefly a third clinical example in which the induction phase of projective identification will be focused upon. T. A. Tähkä of Finland (Tähkä, 1977) has reported that a profound lack of concern for a patient on the part of the therapist often immediately precedes the patient's suicide. Although Dr Tähkä does not approach this phenomenon from the point of view of projective identification, his observations can be understood as reflecting the patient's attempt to induce in the therapist his own state of total lack of caring for himself or for his life. This could be viewed as an attempt on the part of the patient to: (1) Rid himself of this malignant absence of concern for life. (2) Make himself understood by the therapist by inducing the feeling in him. The process of this 'induction' of feelings constitutes the second stage of projective identification.

Warren Brodey (1965), from a family observational viewpoint, has studied one mode of interaction that serves to generate pressure to comply to a projective fantasy. He describes very vividly the way one member of a family may manipulate reality in an effort to coerce another member into 'verifying' a projection. Reality that is not useful in confirming a projection is treated as if it did not exist. This manipulation of reality and the resultant undermining of reality testing is but one technique in the generation of pressure for compliance with a projective fantasy.

One further point that needs to be made with regard to the induction of a projective identification is the 'or else' that looms behind the pressure to comply with a projective identification. I have described elsewhere (Ogden, 1976, 1978a) the pressure on an infant to behave in a manner congruent with the mother's pathology, and the ever-present threat that if the infant were to fail to comply, he would become non-existent for the mother. This threat is the 'muscle' behind the demand for compliance: 'If you are not what I need you to be, you don't exist for me,' or in other language, 'I can only see in you what I put there, and so if I don't see that in you,

I see nothing.' In the therapeutic interaction, the therapist is made to feel the force of the fear of becoming non-existent for the patient if he were to cease to behave in compliance with the patient's projective identification. (See Ogden, 1978a for a detailed discussion of a therapy revolving around this issue.)

So far, I have talked about two aspects of projective identification: the first involves a fantasy of ridding oneself of an aspect of the self and of the entry of that part into another person in a way that controls the other person from within. The second aspect of projective identification that has been discussed is the interpersonal interaction that supports the fantasy of inhabiting and controlling another person. Through the projector's interaction with the object, two aspects of the fantasy are verified: (1) The idea that the object has the characteristics of the projected aspects of the self. (2) That the object is being controlled by the person projecting. In fact, the 'influence' is real, but it is not the imagined absolute control by means of transplanted aspects of the self inhabiting the object; rather, it is an external pressure exerted by means of interpersonal interaction. This brings us to the third phase of projective identification, which involves the 'psychological processing' of the projection by the recipient, and the re-internalization of the modified projection by the projector. In this phase of projective identification, the recipient of the projection experiences himself in part as he is pictured in the projective fantasy. The reality is that the recipient's experience is a new set of feelings experienced by a person different from the projector. The recipient's feelings may be close to those of the projector, but those feelings are not transplanted feelings. The recipient is the author of his own feelings albeit feelings elicited under a very specific kind of pressure from the projector. The elicited feelings are the product of a different personality system with different strengths and weaknesses. This fact opens the door to the possibility that the projected feelings (more accurately, the congruent set of feelings elicited in the recipient) will be handled differently from the manner in which the projector has been able to handle them. A different set of defences and other psychological processes may be employed by the recipient so that the feelings are 'processed', 'metabolized' (Langs, 1976), 'contained' (Bion, 1961), or managed differently. The fact that the projector is employing projective identification indicates that he is dealing with a given aspect of himself by attempting to rid himself of the unwanted feelings and representations. Alternative psychological processes that could potentially be employed by the recipient to handle the same set of feelings would include attempts at integration with other aspects of the personality, attempts at mastery through understanding, and sublimation. These methods of dealing with feelings contrast with projective identification in that they are not basically efforts to avoid, get rid of, deny, or forget feelings and ideas; rather, they represent different types of attempts to live with, or contain, an aspect of oneself without disavowal. If the recipient of the projection can deal with the feelings projected 'into' him in a way that differs from the projector's method, a new set of feelings is generated which can be viewed as a 'processed' version of the original projected feelings. The new set of feelings might involve the sense that the projected feelings, thoughts and representations can be lived with, without damaging other aspects of the self or of one's valued external or internal objects (cf. Little, 1966). The new experience (or amalgam of the projected feelings plus aspects of the recipient) could even include the sense that the feelings in question can be valued and at times enjoyed. It must be kept in mind that the idea of 'successful' processing is a relative one and that all processing will be incomplete and contaminated to an extent by the pathology of the recipient.

This 'digested' projection is available through the recipient's interactions with the projector for internalization by the projector. The nature of this internalization (actually a re-internalization) depends upon the maturational level of the projector and would range from primitive types of introjection to mature types of identification (cf. Schafer, 1968). Whatever the form of the re-internalization process, the internalization of the metabolized projection offers the projector the potential for attaining new ways of handling a set of feelings that he could only wish to get rid of in the past. To the extent that the projection is successfully processed and re-internalized, genuine psychological growth has occurred. (The consequences of inadequate reception of, or processing of, projective identifications are discussed later in this paper.)

The following is an example of projective identification involving a recipient more integrated and mature than the projector. Mr J had been a patient in analysis for about a year and the treatment seemed to both patient and analyst to be bogging down. The patient repetitively questioned whether he was 'getting anything out of it', 'maybe it's a waste of time' etc. Mr J had always grudgingly paid his bills, but gradually they were being paid later and later, leaving the analyst to wonder whether the bill was going to be paid at all. The analyst found himself questioning whether the patient might drop out of treatment, leaving that month's and the previous month's bills unpaid. Also, as the sessions dragged on, the analyst thought about colleagues who held fifty minute sessions instead of fifty-five minute ones, and charged the same fee as this analyst. Just before the beginning of one session, the analyst considered shortening the 'hour' by making the patient wait a couple of minutes before letting him into the office. All of this occurred without attention being focused on it either by the patient or the analyst. Gradually, the analyst found himself having difficulty ending the sessions on time because of an intensely guilty feeling that he was not giving the patient 'his money's worth'. After this difficulty with time repeated itself again and again over several months, the analyst was gradually able to begin to understand his trouble in maintaining the ground rules of the analysis. It began to be apparent to the analyst that he had been feeling greedy for expecting to be paid for his 'worthless' work and was defending himself against such feelings by being so generous with his time that no one could accuse him of greed. With this understanding of the feelings that were being engendered in him by the patient, the analyst was able to take a fresh look at the patient's material. Mr J's father had deserted him and his mother when the patient was 15 months old. His mother, without ever explicitly saying so, had held the patient responsible for this. The unspoken, shared feeling was that it was the patient's greediness for the mother's time, energy and affection that had resulted in the father's desertion. The patient developed an intense need to disown and deny feelings of greed. He could not tell the analyst that he wished to meet more frequently because he experienced this wish as greediness that would result in abandonment by the (transference) father and in attack by the (transference) mother that he saw in the analyst. Instead, the patient insisted that the analysis and the analyst were totally undesirable and worthless. The interaction with the analyst subtly engendered in the analyst intense feelings of a type of greed that was felt to be so unacceptable to the analyst that the analyst at first also made an attempt to deny and disown it. For the analyst, the first step in integration of the feeling of greediness was the ability to register a perception of himself experiencing guilt and defending himself against his feelings of greed. He could then mobilize an aspect of himself that was interested in understanding his greedy and guilty feelings, rather than trying to deny, disguise, displace or project them.

Essential for this aspect of psychological work was the analyst's feeling that he could have greedy and guilty feelings without being damaged by them. It was not the analyst's greedy feelings that were interfering with his therapeutic work; rather, it was his need to disavow such feelings by denying them and by putting them into defensive activity. As the analyst became aware of, and was able to live with, this aspect of himself and of his patient, he became better able to handle the financial and time boundaries of the therapy. He no longer felt that he had to hide the fact that he was glad to receive money given in payment for his work. After some time, the patient commented as he handed the analyst a cheque (on time), that the analyst seemed happy to get 'a big, fat cheque' and that that wasn't very becoming to a psychiatrist. The analyst chuckled and said that it is nice to receive money. During this interchange, the analyst's acceptance of his hungry, greedy, devouring feelings, together with his ability to integrate those feelings with other feelings of healthy self-interest and self-worth was made available for internalization by the patient. The analyst at this point chose not to interpret the patient's fear of his own greed and his defensive, projective fantasy. Instead, the therapy consisted of the digesting of the projection and the process of making it available for re-internalization through the therapeutic interaction.

In the light of the above discussion, it is worth considering whether this kind of understanding of projective identification may not bear directly on the question of the means by which psychotherapy and psychoanalysis contribute to psychological growth. It may be that the essence of what is therapeutic for the patient lies in the process of the therapist or analyst making himself available to receive the patient's projections, utilizing facets of his more mature personality system in the processing of the projection, and then making available the digested projection for re-internalization through the therapeutic interaction (Langs, 1976; Malin and Grotstein, 1966; Searles, 1963).

To summarize, projective identification is a set of fantasies and object relations that can be schematically conceptualized as occurring in three phases: first, the fantasy of ridding oneself of an unwanted part of oneself and of putting that part into another person in a controlling way; then the induction of feelings in the recipient that are congruent with the projective fantasy by means of an interpersonal interaction; and finally, the processing of the projection by the recipient, followed by the re-internalization by the projector of the 'metabolized projection'.

III. The early developmental setting

Projective identification, as described in the previous section, is a psychological process that is simultaneously a type of defence, a mode of communication, a primitive form of object relationship, and a pathway for psychological change. As a defence, projective identification serves to create a sense of psychological distance from unwanted (often frightening) aspects of the self; as a mode of communication, projective identification is a process by which feelings congruent with one's own are induced in another person, thereby creating a sense of being understood by or of being 'at one with' the other person. As a type of object relationship, projective identification constitutes a way of being with and relating to a partially separate object; and finally, as a pathway for psychological change, projective identification is a process by which feelings like those that one is struggling with, are psychologically processed by another person and made available for re-internalization in an altered form.

Each of these functions of projective identification evolves in the context of the infant's early attempts to perceive, organize, and manage his internal and external experience and to communicate with his environment. The infant is faced with an extremely complicated, confusing, and frightening barrage of stimuli. With the help of a 'good enough' mother (Winnicott, 1952), the infant can begin to organize his experience. In this effort towards organization, the infant discovers the value of keeping dangerous, painful, frightening experiences separate from comforting, soothing, calming ones (Freud, 1920). This kind of 'splitting' becomes established as a basic part of the early psychological modes of organization and of defence (Jacobson, 1964; Kernberg, 1976). As an elaboration of, and support for, this mode of organization, the infant utilizes fantasies of ridding himself of aspects of himself (projective fantasies) and fantasies of taking into himself aspects of others (introjective fantasies). These modes of thought help the infant to keep what is valued psychologically separate from, and in fantasy safe from, what is felt to be dangerous and destructive.

These attempts at psychological organization and stability occur within the context of the mother–infant dyad. Spitz (1965) describes the earliest 'quasi-telepathic' communication between mother and infant as being of a 'conesthetic type' wherein sensing is visceral and stimuli are 'received' as opposed to being 'perceived'. The mother's affective state is 'received' by the infant and is registered in the form of emotions. The mother also utilizes a conesthetic mode of communication. Winnicott beautifully describes the state of heightened maternal receptivity that is seen in the mother of a newborn:

> I do not believe it is possible to understand the functioning of the mother at the very beginning of the infant's life without seeing that she must be able to reach this state of heightened sensitivity, almost an illness, and then recover from it. . . . Only if a mother is sensitized in the way I am describing can she feel herself into the infant's place, and so meet the infant's needs.
>
> (Winnicott, 1956)

It is in this developmental setting that the infant develops the process of projective identification as a mode of fantasy with accompanying object relations that serve both defensive and communicative functions. Projective identification is an adjunct to the infant's efforts at keeping what is felt to be good at a safe distance from what is felt to be bad and dangerous. Aspects of the infant can in fantasy be deposited in another person in such a way that the infant does not feel that he has lost contact either with that part of himself or with the other person. In terms of communication, projective identification is a means by which the infant can feel that he is feeling. The infant cannot describe his feelings in words for the mother; instead, he induces those feelings in her. In addition to serving as a mode of interpersonal communication, projective identification constitutes a primitive type of object relationship, a basic way of being with an object that is only partially separate psychologically. It is a transitional form of object relationship that lies between the stage of the subjective object and that of true object relatedness.

This brings us to the fourth function of projective identification, that of a pathway for psychological change. The following hypothetical interaction will be presented in an attempt to describe the place of this aspect of projective identification in early development. Let us imagine that a child is frightened by his wish to destroy and annihilate anyone who frustrates or opposes him. One way of his handling these feelings would be to project unconsciously his destructive wishes in fantasy into his mother, and through the real interaction with her, engender feelings in her that she is a ruthless, selfish person who wishes to demolish anything standing in the way of the satisfaction of her aims and wishes. One way a child could engender this feeling in his mother would be through persistently stubborn behaviour in many areas of daily activity, e.g. by making a major battle out of his eating, his toileting, his dressing, getting him to sleep at night and up in the morning, leaving him with another caretaker, etc. The mother might unrealistically begin to feel that she perpetually storms around the house in a frenzy of frustrated rage ready to kill those that stand between her and what she desires. A mother who had not adequately resolved her own conflicts around such destructive wishes and impulses would find it difficult to live with the heightening of these feelings. She might attempt to deal with such feelings by withdrawing from the child and never touching him. Or she might become hostile or assaultive toward him or dangerously careless with him. In order to keep the child from becoming the target, the mother might displace or project her feelings on to her husband, parents, employer, or friends. Alternatively, the mother may feel so guilty about, or frightened of, these frustrated, destructive feelings that she might become overprotective of the child, never allowing him out of her sight and never allowing him to be adventurous for fear that he might get hurt. This type of 'closeness' may become highly sexualized, e.g. by the mother constantly caressing the child in an effort to demonstrate to herself that she is not harming him with her touch. Any of these modes of dealing with the engendered feelings would result in the confirmation for the child of his feeling that angry wishes for the demolition of frustrating objects are dangerous to himself and to his valued objects. What would be internalized from the mother in this case would be an even stronger conviction than he had held before that he must get rid of such feelings. In addition, the child could internalize aspects of the mother's pathological methods of handling of this type of feeling (e.g. excessive projection, splitting, denial, or violent enactment as a mode of tension relief or as a mode of expression of feeling). On the other hand, 'good enough' handling of the projected feelings might involve the mother's ability to integrate the engendered feelings with other aspects of herself, e.g. her healthy self-interest, her acceptance of her right to her anger and resentment at her child for standing in the way of what she wants, her confidence that she can contain such feelings without acting on them with excessive withdrawal or retaliatory attack. None of this need be available to the mother's conscious awareness. This act of psychological integration constitutes the processing phase of projective identification. Through the mother's interactions with the child, the processed projection (which involves the sense of the mother's mastery of her frustrated feelings and destructive, retaliatory wishes) would be available to the child for re-internalization.

It can be seen from this developmental perspective that the concept of projective identification is entirely separable from a Kleinian theoretical or developmental framework, and for that matter, from that of any other school of psychoanalytic thought. In particular, there is no necessary tie between projective identification and the death instinct, the concept of envy, the concept of constitutional aggression, or any other facet of specifically Kleinian clinical theory or metapsychology. Moreover, there is nothing to tie the concept of projective identification to any given developmental timetable. The concept of projective identification requires only that: (1) The projector (infant, child or adult) be capable of projective fantasy (albeit often very primitive in its mode of symbolization) and specific types of object-relatedness that are involved in the induction and re-internalization phases of projective identification. (2) That the object of the projection be capable of the type of object-relatedness that is involved in 'receiving' a projection in addition to being capable of some form of 'processing' of the projection. At some point in development, the infant becomes capable of these psychological tasks and it is only at that point that the concept of projective identification would become applicable. It is unfortunate that the discussion of projective identification so often becomes ensnared in a debate over the Kleinian developmental timetable which is in no way inherent to the concept of projective identification.

IV. An historical perspective

Before discussing the technical and theoretical implications of the above discussion, it will be useful to present a brief historical overview of the important contributions to the development and application of the concept of projective identification. The concept and term 'projective identification' were introduced by Melanie Klein in 'Notes on Some Schizoid Mechanisms' (Klein, 1946). In this paper, Mrs Klein applies the term 'projective identification' to a psychological process arising in the paranoid-schizoid phase of development, wherein 'bad' parts of the self are split off and projected 'into' another person in an effort to rid the self of one's 'bad objects', which threaten to destroy oneself from within. These bad objects (psychological representations of the death instinct) are projected in an effort to 'control and take possession of the object'. The only other paper in which Mrs Klein discusses projective identification at any length is 'On Identification' (Klein, 1955). In that paper, Mrs Klein, by means of a discussion of a story by Julian Green ('If I Were You') offers a vivid account of the subjective experience involved in the process of projective identification. In Green's story, the devil grants the hero the power to leave his own body and enter and take over the body and life of anyone he chooses. Mrs Klein's description of the hero's experience in projecting himself into another person captures the sense of what it is like to inhabit someone else, control them, and yet not totally lose the sense of who one really is. It is the sense of being a visitor in the other person, but also of being changed by the experience in a way that will make one forever different from the way one was before. In addition, this account brings home an important aspect of Mrs Klein's view of projective identification: the process of projective identification is a psychologically depleting one that leaves the projector impoverished until the projected part is successfully re-internalized. The attempt to control another person and have them act in congruence with one's fantasies requires tremendous vigilance and a very great expenditure of psychological energy that leaves a person psychologically weakened.

Wilfred Bion (1959, 1961) has made important steps in elaborating upon and applying the concept of projective identification. He views projective identification as the single most important form of interaction between patient and therapist in individual therapy, as well as in groups of all types. Bion's strongly clinical perspective is helpful in emphasizing an aspect of this process that is very little elucidated by Mrs Klein: 'The analyst feels that he is being manipulated so as to be playing a part, no matter how difficult to recognize, in somebody else's phantasy' (Bion, 1961). Bion is consistently aware that in addition to projective identification's being a fantasy, it is also a manipulation of one person by another, i.e. an interpersonal interaction. Bion's work also manages to capture some of the strangeness and mystery that characterize the experience of being involved as the container (i.e. the recipient) of a projective identification. He likens the experience to the idea of 'a thought without a thinker' (Bion,

1977). In a sense, being the recipient of a projective identification is like having a thought that is not one's own. A further point that Bion makes is the idea that there is a severely destructive impact of a parent (or therapist) who cannot allow himself to receive the projective identifications of the child (or patient): 'The environment . . . at its worst denied to the patient the use of the mechanisms of splitting and projective identification' (Bion, 1959). An essential part of normal development is the child's experience of his parents as people who can safely and securely be relied upon to act as containers for his projective identifications.

Herbert Rosenfeld contributed several important early papers (Rosenfeld, 1952b, 1954) on the clinical applications of projective identification theory to the understanding and treatment of schizophrenia. In particular, he used the concept of projective identification to trace the genetic origins of depersonalization and confusional states.

The development and application of the concept of projective identification has not been limited to the work done by Melanie Klein and her followers. Even though the term projective identification is not always used by members of other schools of analytic thought, the work of non-Kleinians has been a fundamental part of the development of the concept. For example, Donald Winnicott rarely used the term projective identification in his writing, but I would view a great deal of his work as a study of the role of maternal projective identifications in early development and of the implications of that form of object relatedness for both normal and pathological development, e.g. his concepts of impingement and mirroring (Winnicott, 1952, 1967).

Michael Balint's accounts (Balint, 1952, 1968) of his handling of therapeutic repression (especially in the phase of treatment that he calls the 'new beginning') focuses very closely on technical considerations which have direct bearing on the handling of projective identifications. Balint cautions us against having to interpret or in other ways having to act on the feelings the patient elicits; instead, the therapist must 'accept', 'feel with the patient', 'tolerate', 'bear with' the patient and the feelings he is struggling with and asking the therapist to recognize.

The analyst [when successfully handling the patient's regression] is not so keen on 'understanding' everything immediately, and in particular, on 'organizing' and changing everything undesirable by his correct interpretations; in fact, he is more tolerant towards the patient's sufferings and is capable of bearing with them – i.e. of admitting his relative impotence – instead of being at pains to 'analyse' them away in order to prove his therapeutic omnipotence.

(Balint, 1968, p. 184)

I would view this in part as an eloquent statement on the analyst's task of keeping himself open to receiving the patient's projective identifications without having to act on these feelings.

Harold Searles enriches the language that we have for talking about the way a therapist (or parent) must attempt to make himself open to receiving the projective identifications of the patient (or child). In his 1963 paper on 'Transference Psychosis in the Psychotherapy of Chronic Schizophrenia', Searles discusses the importance of the therapist's refraining from rigidly defending himself against the experiencing of aspects of the patient's feelings: 'The patient develops ego-strengths . . . via identification with the therapist who can endure, and integrate into his own larger self, the kind of subjectively non-human part-object relatedness which the patient fosters in and needs from him'. And later in the same paper, Searles adds,

> The extent to which the therapist feels a genuine sense of deep participation in the patient's 'delusional transference' relatedness to him during the phase of therapeutic symbiosis . . . is difficult to convey in words; it is essential that the therapist come to know that such a degree of feeling-participation is not evidence of 'counter-transference psychosis' but rather is the essence of what the patient needs from him at this crucial phase of the treatment.

Searles is here presenting a view that therapy, at least in certain phases of regression, can progress only to the extent that the therapist can allow himself to feel (with diminished intensity) what the patient is feeling, or in the terminology of projective identification, to allow himself to be open to receiving the patient's projections. This 'feeling-participation' is not equivalent to becoming as sick as the patient because the therapist, in addition to receiving the projection, must process it and integrate it into his own 'larger' personality, and make this integrated experience available to the patient for re-internalization. In his recent article, 'The Patient as Therapist to the Analyst' (Searles, 1975), Searles describes in detail the opportunity for growth in the analyst that is inherent in his struggle to make himself open to his patient's projective identifications.

There has been a growing body of literature that has attempted to clarify the concept of projective identification and has made efforts to integrate the concept into a non-Kleinian psychoanalytic framework. Malin and Grotstein (1966) present a clinical formulation of projective identification in which they help make this very bulky concept more manageable by discussing it in terms of three elements: the projection, the creation of an 'alloy' of external object plus projected self, and re-internalization. These authors present the view that therapy consists of the modification of the patient's internal objects by the process of projective identification. Interpretation is seen as a way in which the patient can be helped to observe 'how his projections have been received and acknowledged by the analyst'.

Finally, I would like to mention the work of Robert Langs (1975, 1976) who is currently involved in the task of developing an adaptational-interactional framework of psychotherapy and psychoanalysis. His efforts represent a growing sense of the importance and usefulness of the concept of projective identification as a means of understanding the therapeutic process (see also Kernberg, 1968, 1976; Nadelson, 1976). Langs contends that it is necessary for analytic theory to shift from viewing the analyst as a screen to viewing him as a 'container for the patient's pathological contents who is fully participating in the analytic interaction' (Langs, 1976). By making such a shift, we clarify the nature of the therapist's response to the patient's transference and non-transference material and are in a better position to do the self-analytic work necessary for the treatment of the patient, in particular for the correction of errors in technique. For Langs, projective identification is the basic unit of study within an interactional frame of reference.

V. Implications for technique and for clinical theory

I would like now to move to a discussion of several technical and theoretical implications of the view of projective identification presented above.

1. A question that immediately arises is, 'What does a therapist "do" when he observes that he is experiencing himself in a way that is congruent with his patient's projective fantasy, i.e. when he is

aware that he is the recipient of his patient's projective identification?' One answer is that the therapist 'does' nothing; instead, he attempts to live with the feelings engendered in him without denying his feelings or in other ways trying to rid himself of the feelings. This is what is meant by 'making oneself open to receiving a projection'. It is the task of the therapist to contain the patient's feelings. For example, when the patient is feeling that he is hopelessly unmotherable, unloveable, and untreatable, the therapist must be able to bear the feeling that the therapist and the therapy are worthless for this hopeless patient, and yet at the same time not to act on the feelings by terminating the therapy (cf. Nadelson, 1976). The 'truth' about himself that the patient is presenting must be treated as a type of transitional phenomenon (Winnicott, 1953) wherein the question of whether the patient's 'truth' is reality or fantasy is never an issue. As with any transitional phenomenon, it is both reality and fantasy, subjective and objective at the same time. In this light, the question 'If the patient can never get better, why should the therapy continue?' never needs to be acted upon. Instead, the therapist attempts to live with the feeling that he is involved in a hopeless therapy with a hopeless patient and is, himself, a hopeless therapist. This of course is a partial truth that the patient experiences as a total truth. The 'truth' of the patient's feelings must be experienced by the therapist as emotionally true just as the good-enough mother must be able to share the truth in her child's feelings about the comforting and life-giving powers of his piece of satin.

There are several further aspects of the question raised about the handling of projective identification that need to be considered. The first is that the therapist is not simply an empty receptacle into which the patient can 'put' projective identifications. The therapist is a human being with his own past, his own repressed unconscious, his own conflicts, his own fears, his own psychological difficulties. The feelings that patients are struggling with are, by their nature, highly charged, painful, conflict-laden areas of human experience for the therapist as well as for the patient. Hopefully, the therapist, through the benefit of greater integration in the course of his own developmental experience and in the course of his analysis, is less frightened of, and less prone to run from, these feelings than is the patient. However, we are not dealing with an 'all or nothing' phenomenon here, and the handling of the feelings projected by the patient require considerable effort, skill, and 'strain' (Winnicott, 1960) on the part of the therapist. One major tool at the disposal of the therapist in his efforts at containing his patient's projective identifications is his ability to bring understanding to what he is feeling and to what is occurring between himself and his patient. The therapist's theoretical training, his personal analysis, his experience, his psychological-mindedness, and his psychological language can all be brought to bear on the experience he is attempting to understand and to contain.

The question now arises, 'How much of the therapist's effort at understanding the patient's projective identification is put to the patient in the form of interpretations?' The therapist's ability not only to understand but also to formulate clearly and precisely his understanding in words is basic to his therapeutic effectiveness (Freud, 1914; Glover, 1931). In the case of working with projective identifications, this is so not only because such verbal understandings may be of value to the patient in the form of well-timed clarifications and interpretations, but equally because these understandings are an essential part of the therapist's effort to contain the feelings engendered in him. The therapist's understanding may constitute a correct interpretation for the therapist, but may not be at all well-timed for the patient. In this case, the interpretation should remain 'a silent one' (Spotnitz, 1969), i.e. it is formulated in words in the therapist's mind, but not verbalized to the patient. Another aspect of the importance of the silent interpretation is that it can contain a much heavier weight of self-analytic material than one would include in an interpretation offered to the patient. Continued self-analysis in this way is invaluable in a therapist's attempts to struggle with, contain, and grow from the feelings his patients are eliciting in him.

The other side of this must also be mentioned. There is a danger that the therapist in his handling of projective identifications may be tempted to use the patient's therapy exclusively as an arena in which to find help with his own psychological problems. This can result in a repetition for the patient of an early pathogenic interaction (frequently reported in the childhood of pathologically narcissistic patients) wherein the needs of the mother were the almost exclusive focus of the mother–child relationship. (See Ogden, 1974, 1976, 1978a for further discussion of this form of mother–child interaction.)

2. The subject of the recognition of errors in the handling of projective identifications and the corrective steps that can be taken has been addressed in various places in the above discussion. Errors in technique very often reflect a failure on the part of the therapist to

process adequately the patient's projective identification. Either through an identification with the patient's methods of handling the projected feelings, or through reliance on his own customary defences, the therapist may come to rely excessively on denial, splitting, projection, projective identification, or enactment in his efforts to defend against the engendered feelings. This basically defensive stance can result in 'therapeutic misalliances' (Langs, 1975) wherein the patient and therapist 'seek gratification and defensive reinforcements in their relationship'. In order to support his own defences, the therapist may introduce deviations in technique, and may even violate the basic ground rules and framework of psychotherapy and psychoanalysis, e.g. by extending the relationship into social contexts, by giving gifts to the patient or by encouraging the patient to give him gifts, by breaches of confidentiality, etc. A therapist's failure adequately to process a projective identification is reflected in one of two ways: either by his rigidly defending himself against awareness of the feelings engendered, or by allowing the feeling or the defence against it to be translated into action. The consequences of either type of failure to contain a projective identification are that the patient re-internalizes his own projected feelings combined with the therapist's fears about, and inadequate handling of, those feelings. The patient's fears and pathological defences are reinforced and expanded. In addition, the patient may despair about the prospect of being helped by a therapist who shares significant aspects of his pathology.

3. The patient is not the only person in the therapeutic dyad who employs projective identification. Just as the patient can apply pressure to the therapist to comply with his projective identifications, the therapist similarly can put pressure on the patient to validate his own projective identifications. Therapists have an intricately overdetermined wish for their patients to 'get better' and this is often the basis for an omnipotent fantasy that the therapist has turned the patient into the wished-for patient. Very often, the therapist, through the therapeutic interaction, can exert pressure on the patient to behave as if he were that wished for, 'cured' patient. A relatively healthy patient can often become aware of this pressure and alert the therapist to it by saying something like, 'I'm not going to let you turn me into another of your "successes".' This kind of statement, however over-determined, should alert the therapist to the possibility that he may be engaged in projective identification and that the

patient has successfully processed his projections. It is far more damaging to the patient and to the therapy when the patient is unable to process a projective identification in this way and has either to comply with the pressure (by becoming the 'ideal' patient) or rebel against the pressure (by an upsurge of resistance or by termination of therapy).

Winnicott (1949) also reminds us that therapists' and parents' wishes for their patients and children are not exclusively for cure and growth. There are also hateful wishes to attack, kill or annihilate the patient or child. A stalemated therapy, a perpetually silent patient, a flurry of self-destructive or violent activity on the part of the patient, may all be signs of the patient's efforts to comply with a therapist's projective identification that involves an attack upon or the annihilation of the patient. As Winnicott suggests, it is imperative that a parent or therapist be able to integrate his or her anger and murderous wishes toward their children and patients without enacting these feelings or having to get rid of them through denial and projection. Persistent and unchanging projective identifications on the part of the therapist should, if recognized, alert the therapist to a need to examine seriously his own psychological state and possibly to seek further analysis.

4. In the light of the understanding of projective identification outlined in this paper, I would like to clarify the relationship of projective identification to a group of related psychological processes: projection, introjection, identification, and externalization. As mentioned earlier, projection in a broad sense is a mode of thought in which one experiences oneself as having expelled an aspect of oneself. A distinction has to be drawn between the projective mode of thought involved in projective identification and projection as an independent process. In the former, the individual employs a projective mode of thought in his fantasy of ridding himself of a part of himself and inhabiting another person with that part. The subjective experience is one of being at one with the other person with regard to the expelled feeling, idea, self-representation, etc. In contrast, in projection as an independent process, the aspect of oneself that is expelled is disavowed and is attributed to the object of the projection. The projector does not feel kinship with the object and, on the contrary, often experiences the object as foreign, strange, and frightening. In projective identification, the projective mode of thought is but one aspect of a dynamic interplay between projection and internalization. However, it must be borne in

mind that the distinction between projection and projective identification is not an all–or–nothing affair. As Knight (1940) pointed out, every projective process involves an interaction with an introjective one and vice versa. Projection and projective identification should be viewed as two ends of a gradient in which there is increasing preponderance of interplay between the projective and introjective processes as one moves toward the projective identification end of the gradient.

Just as a projective mode of thought, as opposed to projection, can be seen as underlying the first phase of projective identification, one can understand the third phase as being based on an introjective mode as opposed to introjection. In the final phase of projective identification, the individual imagines himself to be repossessing an aspect of himself that has been 'reposing' (Bion, 1959) in another person. In conjunction with this fantasy is a process of internalization wherein the object's method of handling the projective identification is perceived and there is an effort to make this aspect of the object a part of oneself. Following the schema outlined by Schafer (1968), introjection and identification are seen as types of internalization processes. Depending upon the projector's maturational level, the type of internalization process he employs may range from primitive introjection to mature types of identification. In introjection, the internalized aspect of the object is poorly integrated into the remainder of the personality system and is experienced as a foreign element ('a presence') inside oneself. In identification, there is a modification of motives, behaviour patterns, and self-representations in such a way that the individual feels that he has become 'like' or 'the same as' the object with regard to a given aspect of that person. So the terms introjection and identification refer to types of internalization processes that can operate largely in isolation from projective processes or as a phase of projective identification.

To expand briefly upon what has been said earlier, the concept of externalization (as discussed by Brodey, 1965) would be used narrowly to refer to a specific type of projective identification wherein there is a manipulation of reality in the service of pressuring the object to comply with the projective fantasy. However, in a broader sense, there is 'externalization' in every projective identification in that one's projective fantasy is moved from the internal arena of psychological representations, thoughts and feelings, to the external arena of other human beings and one's interactions with them. Rather than simply altering the psychological representations of an external object, in projective identification one attempts to, and often succeeds in, effecting specific alterations in the feeling state and self-representations of another person.

5. Finally, I would like to attempt briefly to locate projective identification in relation to projective transference, counter-transference and projective counter-identification. Transference involves the attribution to the therapist of qualities, feelings and ideas that originated in relation to an earlier object. Transference projection is a type of transference wherein aspects of the self are attributed to the therapist. When projective identification is an aspect of the transference relationship, it would be differentiated from transference projection in that a transference projection is largely an intrapsychic defensive phenomenon. In contrast, projective identification not only involves an intrapsychic event (a projective fantasy) but also involves an interpersonal interaction in which the object is pressured to become the way he or she is represented in the projection. Also, as with other forms of projection, the term projective transference would imply a greater weight of disavowal of an aspect of the self than is involved in projective identification, and would entail less of the feeling of being at one with the object than is encountered in projective identification.

Counter-transference has been defined in a number of different ways. It has been viewed by some as the set of feelings of the therapist elicited by the patient which reflect the therapist's unanalysed pathology. Such feelings interfere with his ability to respond therapeutically to his patient. Others have viewed counter-transference as the totality of the response of the therapist to the patient. Still others refer to that portion of the counter-transference that represents the therapist's mature, empathic response to the patient's transference, as the 'objective counter-transference' (Winnicott, 1949). This aspect of the therapist's response to the patient is viewed as the complement to the aspect of the earlier relationship portrayed by the patient in the transference. The remainder of the counter-transference would then be seen as a reflection of the therapist's pathology. I find Winnicott's view to be the most useful in clarifying the role of a therapist's feelings in the successful handling of a patient's projective identifications. As an object of the patient's projective identifications, it is the task of the therapist both to experience and process the feelings involved in the projection. The therapist allows himself to participate to an extent in an object relationship that the patient has constructed on the basis of an earlier relationship. In so doing, the therapist has the opportunity to observe the qualities of the previously internalized object relationship and, over time, process the feelings involved in such a way that the patient is not merely repeating an old relationship in the therapy. In Winnicott's terminology, this aspect of the therapist's work would represent the observation of and therapeutic use of the objective counter-transference. A failure on the part of the therapist in his handling of the patient's projective identifications is often a reflection of the fact that instead of his therapeutically making use of the objective counter-transference data, he is involved in what Grinberg (1962) calls 'projective counter-identification'. In this latter form of counter-transference, the therapist, without consciously being aware of it, fully experiences himself as he is portrayed in the patient's projective identification. He feels unable to prevent himself from being what the patient unconsciously wants him to be. This would differ from therapeutically 'being open to' a patient's projective identification, because in the latter case, the therapist is aware of the process and only partially, and with diminished intensity, shares in the feelings that the patient is unconsciously asking him to experience. The successful handling of projective identification is a matter of balance – the therapist must be sufficiently open to receive the patient's projective identification, and yet maintain sufficient psychological distance from the process to allow for effective analysis of the therapeutic interaction.

Summary

This paper presents a clarification of the concept of projective identification through a delineation of the relation of fantasy to object relations that is entailed in this psychological-interpersonal process. Projective identification is viewed as a group of fantasies and accompanying object relations involving three phases which together make up a single psychological unit. In the initial phase, the projector fantasies ridding himself of an aspect of himself and putting that aspect into another person in a controlling way. Secondly, via the interpersonal interaction, the projector exerts pressure on the recipient of the projection to experience feelings that are congruent with the projection. Finally, the recipient psychologically processes the projection and makes a modified version of it available for re-internalization by the projector.

Projective identification, as formulated here, is a process that serves as: (1) A type of defence by which one can distance oneself from an unwanted or internally endangered part of the self, while in fantasy keeping that aspect of oneself 'alive' in another. (2) A mode of communication by which one makes oneself understood by exerting pressure on another person to experience a set of feelings similar to one's own. (3) A type of object relatedness in which the projector experiences the recipient of the projection as separate enough to serve as a receptacle for parts of the self, but sufficiently un-differentiated to maintain the illusion that one is literally sharing a given feeling with another person. (4) A pathway for psychological change by which feelings similar to those with which one is struggling are processed by another person, following which the projector may identify with the recipient's handling of the engendered feelings.

Projection and projective identification are viewed as representing two poles of a continuum of types of fantasies of expulsion of aspects of the self with the former being seen as predominantly a one–person phenomenon involving a shift in self- and object-representations; in contrast, the latter requires that one's projective fantasies impinge upon real external objects in a sequence of externalization and internalization.

18

Vicissitudes of projective identification

Albert Mason

In 1946 Melanie Klein published one of her most important works entitled 'Notes on some schizoid mechanisms.' In this paper Klein described the psychic processes occurring in the first three months of life; she delineated the characteristics of the early ego as well as the form and nature of its object relations and anxieties. Klein described schizoid states including idealization, ego disintegration, and projective processes connected with splitting for which she introduced the term 'projective identification'. For Klein, splitting was the key concept of this stage of development and state of mind.

Klein (1921) had also examined splitting processes in her first published paper and continued her investigation of splitting throughout the 1930s, from the pathological to the more normal forms. She suggested that the ego's first defence against anxiety was not repression, wherein the anxiety, although unconscious, remained attached to the self, but expulsion, a violent form of splitting that relieved the ego of pain, distress, and anxiety. Since Klein believed that the phantasy of expulsion was also object related, any split-off part of the self would go into the object. Just as introjection, like feeding, is always from an object, so projection, like evacuation, is always onto or into an object. Feeding (or introjection) can be gentle, loving, voracious, greedy, biting, tearing or violent; and projection can be invasive, fragmenting, erotic, possessive, or a host of other qualities which depend upon the particular phantasies of the projector at any given moment. It is precisely the same with projective identification, which is a combination of expulsion and acquisition.

To continue the analogy between projective identification and the gastrointestinal tract, one could describe two methods of feeding or acquiring what one needs. One method entails feeding from an object repeatedly, digesting the food (that is, working internally and thinking), and assessing what one retains so that one may eventually become like the nourishing object if one chooses to do so. In this system the anxieties attendant on the awareness of the separateness of self and object, or mouth and breast, are essentially tolerated. This is in contrast to devouring the nourisher (breast) whole in order to become the nourishing object in as little time and with as little work as possible, thereby eschewing the painful awareness of separateness altogether. Acquiring and becoming the envied object or breast by projective identification and acquiring and becoming it by greedy devouring are two omnipotent phantasies producing many complex consequences.

A second main stream of Klein's ideas took shape in a paper entitled 'Early stages of the Oedipus conflict (Klein, 1928) and was concerned with phantasies of intrusion into the mother's body. This intrusion had many motives. The motives could stem from any affective state including love, hate, sadness, sadism, possessiveness, or the desire for fusion. Klein saw the infant as having an internal world (itself) and an external world that was equated with the mother's body. The boundaries between these two worlds were frequently missing or porous because of the continual processes of introjection and projection which often blurred the distinction between self and object.

These earlier ideas all formed part of the broader concept of projective identification, which is an overall term for a number of distinct yet related processes connected to splitting and projection. Klein believed that projective identification was the leading defence against anxiety in the paranoid schizoid position, and that it constructed the narcissistic object relations characteristic of this period, in which objects became equated with the split-off and projected parts of the self. Simultaneous with the projection was an introjection and an identification for the purpose of acquiring the desired and envied qualities and capacities of the object. Klein also described how the ego became impoverished due to the excessive use of projective identification. For example, weak functioning of the ego would occur as a consequence of projecting away hostile, aggressive parts of oneself, thereby losing the strength that these qualities could impart to the ego were they retained.

Projective identification has been confused with projection from the outset, and both terms have been used in overlapping ways historically to describe phenomena that are not completely distinguished. Freud described projection as one person's ideas being attributed to someone else, creating a state of paranoia. His concept of projection seemed to be largely limited to the projection of impulses and feelings into the object. Abraham seemed much more concerned with projection into the external world of an internal object. Klein developed these ideas and elaborated them in terms of projecting split-off parts of the ego. She would postulate, for example, that it was not simply anger that was being projected into an object, but, say, an angry baby part of the personality that was jealous of a mother's attention to a sibling.

An example of projective identification occurred before a holiday break in a patient who historically had had temper tantrums at the birth of his baby sister and subsequently could not be separated from his bottle. He had the following dream on his sister's birthday thirty years later: his mother and father were searching for his sister who was lost. When they returned, his mother had a white moustache which the patient thought was due to her having snorted cocaine. His father was driving his car out of control, and the patient felt he now had to take care of them both. When he tried to leave them, his parents pleaded with him to stay and became very angry when he could not. We can see in this dream that the parents who were exhibiting loss of control, jealousy, and anger were containing the projections of the baby part of the patient who felt both angry and jealous when his sister was born. The patient's early addiction to milk (his inability to part from his bottle) was now projected into his mother who had a white moustache, and the patient had become both the caretaking parent as well as the parent whose attention was elsewhere, producing jealousy in the left-out child. In the transference I later became the left-out parent containing the patient's left-out child part of himself when he pre-empted my vacation with a break of his own.

Klein also pointed out that parts of the ego which are projected are often connected to an internal object. Since both the ego and its internal objects are constructed from mixtures and integrations of the self and the external world, the whole process is extremely complex. What is important to understand is that Klein added depth and complexity to Freud's concept of projection by emphasizing that one cannot project impulses without simultaneously projecting parts of the ego that are associated to these impulses. Hence, a split in the ego occurs. The aspect or aspects of the self that are projected go into the object and consequently distort the appearance of the object. In addition, the perception of the self is altered due to the impoverishment which occurs as a result of splitting and projecting parts of the self.

This projection of parts of the self often produces a deep sense of connection and responsibility on the part of the projector towards the recipient of the projection – whether this be mother and child or child and mother – and can occur in therapists who may compulsively look after very disturbed patients, or very poor people who may unconsciously represent hated or disowned aspects of the therapist him/herself. Such compulsive care of a particular population may also be connected to the exculpation of unconscious guilt, as though the therapist were somehow responsible for their plight. A dentist, for example, removed his patients' teeth at the slightest provocation, claiming this to be a necessary operation in each case. The dentist, in fact, had had his own teeth removed at the age of thirty-six. He had frequent dreams of being pursued by packs of wolves – animals with prominent teeth. As might be anticipated, the dentist's own appetites, both oral and genital, were voracious and felt to be dangerously destructive to his objects. The teeth extraction was both a punishment for and a prevention of his destructive phantasies.

One can see that the differences between projective identification and the simpler mechanism of projection are due to the consequences of the immensely varied phantasies connected to projective identification. These may include paranoia, a result of the projection into others of threatening parts of the self. Claustrophobia can be the result of identification with the part of the self that is felt to be lodged inside the object. This consequence contrasts with identification with the object that contains the projected part of the self. The reintrojection of a hostile projection meant to damage the object can cause hypochondriasis when the introject is located somatically, whereas the reintrojection of a damaged object into the mind can be experienced as a damaged or dead internal object, which is a frequent cause of depression. Internalized objects, containing projections, become complex superegos that can be experienced as internal persecutors capable of depriving one of all pleasure and good experiences. An idealized object, when introjected and identified with, produces manic states of mind or obsessional perfectionism, in contrast to the depressive consequence of the introjection of the devalued or damaged object.

Hostile projections due to envy and jealousy damage and distort the child's view of the parents' pleasure or creativity, and psycho-sexual disorders can frequently be due to an identification with these damaged views of parental genitality. Money-Kyrle (1968) has described how the patient produces a misconception of parental intercourse by his/her projections, concluding that 'every conceivable representation of it (parental intercourse) seems to proliferate in the unconscious except the right one' (p. 417). Attacks on parental intercourse can be directed at any form of intercourse including the parents' speech or their emotional involvement with each other as well as at their genital activity. These phantasies commonly have the aim of splitting the parents away from each other, thus diminishing the envy and jealousy that the child feels as a consequence of recognizing that he/she lacks the capacity to take part in the parents' intercourse at any level. Damaged or separated parents, when intro-jected and identified with, can produce any disorder of articulation including sexual disorders, speech disorders, emotional disorders, and/or thought disorders. Thinking itself, or the process of putting thoughts together, may be equated to the parents' intercourse. This finding of Klein was later amplified by Bion (1959) in his paper entitled 'Attacks on Linking'. The ideas set forth in Bion's paper have proven invaluable in the understanding and treatment of thought disorders.

A patient with a thought disorder had a dream of connecting an electric wire with a water-pipe to form a 'jagger'. When asked what a jagger was, the patient responded that he didn't know. So in phan-tasy he was connecting two things that were incompatible to make something which was unknown and probably dangerous. These symbols stood for the patient's envious and jealous devaluation of his parents' intercourse, and the consequence of identification with the devalued parental introjects was the destruction of his own capacity to think and create. Flattening and shallowness of affect is a conse-quence of the identification with parental intercourse that has been enviously drained of all pleasure and enjoyment. It is also created when projective identification produces phantasies of fusion with an object, as affect depends to a large degree upon separateness. Perception, phantasy, and thinking develop in the gap between self and object and are a result of separateness. Consequently, the more massive the projective identification, the more the individual's capacity for perception, phantasy, and thinking will be impaired.

The projection of the aggressive parts of one's personality linked to hating, biting, excreting, mocking, or devaluing produce various versions of paranoia so that the paranoid object will be seen to be either hating, biting, mocking, or devaluing oneself, depending upon which part of the self is projected. Projections into animals or insects will result in typical animal or insect phobias. Similarly, feelings of violence fragmented and projected into the world around one can produce fear of every earthquake tremor, every shadow, every virus, every sneeze – all depending upon the quality and phantasy of the actual projection.

A patient literally saw his father's stern face (an internal object) in the middle of a mountain when he was leaving town. Frightened, he turned his car around and headed for the safety of his home, which was, in phantasy, his mother's body. There seems to be no limit to the persecutory phantasies produced by projecting into the outside world. For example, one can project one's demanding nature into work, traffic, one's wife, or one's children. One then experiences a persecutory pressure coming from these various situations or people which appear to pursue one with relentless expectations, turning life into a series of burdens rather than satisfying effort.

Part-objects can also become the subject of projective identification, wherein a part of the self (a part of the mind or the body) is projected and confused with a part of the object. An easily recognizable version of this is the thumb sucking or tongue thrusting of the infant and the adult versions of this such as cigarette or pipe smoking, or nail biting. Freud felt that 'the thumb-sucking child was involved in auto-erotic stimulation, gratifying or soothing itself through sensuous pleasure to avoid a painful state of mind'. Kleinians would see the thumb sucking as part-object projective identification in which the infant in phantasy takes into its thumb the nipple of the mother or the penis of the father depending upon the source of the gratification needed. This defence against dependency, and the anger or anxiety experienced because of the absence of the nipple would be dealt with in Klein's view by the child's phantasised possession of a nipple with which it can feed itself. Such an example of part-object projective identification was given by Susan Isaacs (1952) in the case of a young boy who watched his mother breast-feed her new baby. He pointed to her breast and exclaimed, 'That's what you bit me with' (p. 88). The little boy was clearly projecting his hostile, greedy, biting mouth into the breast which had now become a biting persecutor, rather than an envied or jealousy-producing source of nourishment.

A patient during analysis was revealing envy of me as a paternal object. Her material also led me to interpret that she was particularly envious of what she felt to be the magical quality of the erect penis – how it drew attention to itself, how it excited others who observed it (both herself and other women), and how it was felt to be superior to her own genital, which was, in her eyes, just a little hole. When I pointed this out to her and linked her feelings of inadequacy to her idealized views of the penis, she came to her next session wearing a pointed hat, standing erect on high heels, and carrying a string bag containing two cabbages that she had bought on the way. She wore a tight-fitting, shiny yellow slicker which matched the hat. The patient felt this to be an eye-catching and exciting outfit, having observed many women on the subway watching her. It seemed clear that she felt herself to be a penis, stimulating admiration and excitement, originally in Mommy. The interpretation of her phantasised erect penile state produced a rather rapid collapse of this patient on to the couch.

In his paper 'A psychoanalyst looks at a hypnotist: a study of *folie à deux*' (1994), Mason has described a patient who projected both loving and hating parts of herself into her objects. Her loving aspects were meant to repair a damaged sister, and her hating aspects were aimed at stealing and possessing envied qualities of her objects. Eve had persistent fears of being raped, which were explicated using dream and transference material. She felt and feared she could not resist rape because she herself wished and, in fact, believed that she could magically invade her objects – her sister, mother, and the analyst in the transference. Being raped was the persecutory mirror image of her own invasive phantasies. Her fear of rape was also experienced as a terror of many situations including visits to her doctor or dentist. The patient dreamt that she was in a room with seven other women. A man came in and raped everyone, one after the other, and there was nothing anyone could do. Her association to the dream was that the rapist had hypnotized everyone with his baby-blue eyes (which were, by association, the same colour as the patient's). This patient had come for treatment because she awakened one morning with her legs paralysed – a condition which lasted several weeks. The paralysis had developed the morning after she had had her first sexual experience. She remembered how wonderful this experience had felt, and at the same time she had had the thought that her sister would never ever know what it felt like to be made love to. This sister, who was four years older than Eve, had been institutionalized since the age of four with spastic diplegic paralysis. Following Eve's sexual encounter, she had a dream about two fir trees standing side by side. One tree was alive and the other was dead. The dead tree sprouted a few leaves, and the patient said that she now knew that the live tree would die.

Eve had been extremely jealous of her older sister who was often held up to her by her parents as a saint. She felt that her parents loved this sister more than herself. It seemed that Eve's unconscious guilt following her sexual triumph over the sister led to her identification with the sister's paralysis. This identification with a damaged object seemed to be a defence against guilt, as suffering the same damage as the object was felt to exculpate the crime. In addition, the dream of the fir tree suggested that the identification was an unconscious attempt to omnipotently repair the damaged sister by the sacrifice of her own life. In her mind and in her body through her symptom of paralysis, the repair had been achieved by the projection of Eve's healthy legs and life into the 'dead sister tree legs'.

One could also infer that this patient's fear of rape was a projection into men of her own omnipotent, intrusive powers that she would be helpless to resist. The baby blue eyes of the rapist in her dream were her own eyes which she felt had the power to invade, possess and control whomever she looked at. This patient had many conscious voyeuristic fantasies of 'knowing all about people'; the knowing – like the Biblical knowing – implying taking possession of. She also displayed ongoing wishes and attempts to get into my private life through her questions and fantasies. Eve's projected omnipotence and consequent feelings of helplessness toward the imagined power of the rapist were potent factors in the production of her terror. The analysis of her intrusive omnipotent phantasies gradually led to the disappearance of her phobias and to her marriage several years later.

A striking example of part-object projective identification was demonstrated by a forty-six-year-old lawyer who sought treatment for depression and difficulty in her relationships with men. Janet had had several relationships which lasted a few years, after which time she would find something wrong with her partners, lose interest in them sexually, and end the relationship. She had been engaged twice but never married. Janet had been hospitalized at the age of two for polio and had been isolated from her parents for four months. During this period she could only see them through her hospital window and speak to them by telephone. One day, through the window, her parents showed her their new baby. After that visit, the patient smeared faeces continuously during her hospitalization.

This patient masturbated frequently, often several times before coming to her session. An unusual feature of the masturbation was that she came to orgasm by contracting her levator ani muscles on a hard stool held in her rectum. Janet had been doing this as long as she could remember; she particularly recalled masturbating in this way in elementary school before a class bell would ring. She would try to achieve orgasm before she had to change rooms for a new class.

I believe that the masturbation was a defence against depression and jealousy; the stool with which she masturbated sometimes stood for Daddy's penis and at times became Mommy's nipple, swallowed and possessed. This part-object projective identification was also meant to project her jealousy and left-out feelings into her objects while she enacted the phantasy of sexual intercourse in her anus. The masturbating activities became more frequent prior to breaks in treatment and, like the masturbation in class, the excitation took her mind away from loss and depression. The trapped and idealized stool was sometimes equated with God who was always with Janet, unlike the breast that at times went away, fed her baby brother, and was unavailable to soothe her persecutory anxieties.

When Freud said of the Wolf Man, 'There is a wish to be back in a situation in which one was in the mother's genitals; and in this connection the man is identifying himself with his own penis and is using it to represent himself' (Freud, 1918, p. 102), he was anticipating the findings of Klein and her followers in the understanding of a vast number of somatic and hypochondriacal disorders. A man or woman can identify not only with his penis or her vagina, but also with his/her stools, urine, flatus, breath – in fact with any part of the body or body products and/or the body of the object. Meltzer wrote about a patient who 'functioned in a state of projective identification with a father's penis, alive but detached as a part-object from the rest of the dead father' (Meltzer, 1968, p. 70).

The use of projective identification for the purpose of elevating one's status can also be achieved by identifying with one's car (a Bentley), one's football team (when it wins), one's child (my son the doctor), one's diamond ring, one's fur coat (sable, my dear), or even, like Charles De Gaulle, one's country: 'La France, c'est moi!' These examples demonstrate one's phantasy of acquiring the power, prestige, or the 'goodness' of the selected thing, and that, in a similar fashion, one can also project one's own badness into hated objects or things, which is the principle of scapegoating. In his paper 'Megalomania', Money-Kyrle has written about projecting into clothing for the purpose of acquiring the emperor's power and prestige (Money-Kyrle, 1965). Mason has described projection into parts of one's own body in his paper 'The suffocating superego: psychotic break and claustrophobia' (Mason, 1981).

Angela, a woman of twenty-three, was referred for treatment because her parents could not stand her keeping glasses of her urine in their refrigerator which she would drink daily. The patient said that drinking urine was healthy – since this was a tradition practiced in India – and that she could not understand her parents' concern. Angela's biological parents had divorced when she was eleven. After a brief period of living with her mother, she and her younger sister had moved in with her father and step-mother, who had had four more daughters in the next eight years. Angela described her step-mother as looking like a witch and said that she hated the woman. But she herself felt no need for therapy and came only because her father and step-mother insisted.

On the surface, she did not seem worried about the fact that she had had only one menstrual period at age sixteen and none since. Nor was she upset that she had no breast development and needed continuous enemas and suppositories for normal defecation. Her abdomen protruded like a six-month pregnancy. The patient had never masturbated nor had she had sexual intercourse. She thought that sex was 'dirty'. When asked if her lack of periods concerned her, she responded by recounting a dream she had had the night before: 'I lived in Communist Russia and was married to a monster who sewed up a pregnant woman's vagina.' She had no idea what the dream might mean.

I interpreted that living in Communist Russia reflected a state of mind in which there were no aristocrats or peasants – all people were equal. It was as though she wanted babies to be equal to mommies. This state of mind also hated her grown-up step-mother's breasts and pregnant belly and sewed up her vagina to kill any babies and to prevent intercourse with her father. She took this sewn-up mother into herself and so she became sewn up – with no periods, no sex, and no baby. She had no doubt lost her own breasts in a similar way, identifying with a step-mother whose breasts were enviously destroyed. Drinking her own urine was Angela's way of showing she could produce food and feed herself just as well as her step-mother could produce milk and feed babies. Her shit-filled abdomen was like the dead baby she felt she had caused in the step-mother by her monstrous, envious wishes. Upon hearing all this Angela changed her mind and decided to come for two sessions a week which she kept for two years, lying on the couch the opposite way round. Her periods began after three months as did her breast development, and her bowel function eventually became normal. She married a year later and now has two children and a thriving business. Angela's rather rapid improvement was unusual and somewhat inexplicable. Perhaps it was related to her youth and perhaps to the fact that the major trauma in this patient's life – the envy and jealousy of the step-mother and her babies – developed when she was a child of eleven rather than an infant. But whatever the reasons, Angela has maintained her therapeutic gains to the present time.

William was a young man of twenty-five who came to treatment complaining of severe and persistent depression and an inability to work and concentrate. He was lonely and shy, and reported an incapacity to make friends and a strong feeling of being stared at and laughed at in the streets. He also suffered from claustrophobia, the analysis of which occupied the first stage of his treatment. Following the initial period of claustrophobia and its resolution, there was a period in which material emerged slowly – sometimes with great difficulty or pain – which I equated with constipation. The patient revealed that he was indeed literally constipated and had been severely so all his life. He remembered and recounted having written an essay at school in which he advocated constipation as a solution for the world's starving people. He had thought that if the people were constipated and therefore had their bellies full, they would not feel hunger.

A long portion of the analysis dealt with William's confused phantasies concerning the function of his anus and the nature of his own faeces, which were commonly equated with food. He used faecal equivalents in place of food to fill himself up, turning frequently to the use of alcohol, barbiturates, cigarettes, snuff, and junk food which he would eat in enormous quantities. Eating these 'bad foods' was his phantasized effort to deny and replace his need for an external living object. Concurrent with his idealization of faeces were scathing and contemptuous attacks on breasts – actual breasts as well as their derivatives and function. Interpretations or food for thought were treated equally badly except for past interpretations which became the equivalent of faeces. The patient would ruminate about them, play around with them, and elaborate on them. He would make notes on his sessions, or secretly tape the sessions, and re-read the notes or replay the tapes continuously, particularly at times when he felt ill, as he believed they would help him. It was only after much painful working through that he began to accept that the interpretations of yesterday were only meaningful in a particular context, and might have no relevance to today's analysis.

William's phantasies about stools were accompanied by all sorts of manipulations of his anus. Suppositories were used, there was frequent and prolonged cleansing with water and ointments, and also bouts of pruritis and piles. I felt that these activities were thinly disguised masturbation seen (together with his phantasies about his stools) as a support of a projective identification process with his mother's body, particularly her breast. The patient dreamed that he mocked a female statue and bit off pieces of it, which he swallowed. He then allowed his penis to be sucked by little boys who were trussed up like chickens (William was swaddled as an infant). By swallowing the breast, he became the breast and could identify with this envied part-object by projective phantasies or introjective cannibalistic phantasies.

Another dream at this time illustrated a similar dynamic. In reality there existed in the patient's country of origin a tribe who believed that their dead must be buried in a certain district to achieve paradise. Often these people had to save for half their lives to acquire enough money for this purpose and until that time, the bodies were entrusted to a certain group for safe-keeping. In the dream the people who were keeping the bodies turned out to be gangsters who buried the bodies without correct preservation. When an effort was made to recover them, it was discovered that the bodies had disintegrated and been washed out to sea by the rains.

This dream could be interpreted as his own waste of life and energy by idealizing and worshipping dead and useless stools; that is to say, a material remnant and representation of something like the breast, once alive and loved. This dream and the extensive working through

312

of its meaning marked a turning point in William's analysis as he gradually relinquished his need to record and concretely retain specific interpretations.

Following the analysis of his anal masturbation and idealization of faeces, there emerged a severe and persistent delusion that stemmed imperceptibly from the preceding material. At first it made itself felt as a constant consciousness of his anus. This consciousness grew in intensity until it became what he described as a tormenting mental irritation. Finally, the depression and persecution produced by his symptoms became so acute that William almost broke down. He had frequent suicidal thoughts during this episode and was sure that he was going mad. The final form that the delusion took was William's conviction that his anus was a vagina. He became constantly preoccupied with fears, wishes, and phantasies of being penetrated and felt that penises were jumping at him and into him in the street. Frequently he felt that my penis was being taken out and was going to jump into him. Sometimes he even felt that I looked like a penis and that everything I said went into him and produced excitation or pain. An aspect of the analysis demonstrated that his delusion was a part–object state of projective identification with his mother's body to escape the pains of being the dependent child. He also had many complex phantasies related to his father and his envy of his mother's 'power and control' over the father. In contrast, most of his conscious fantasies were heterosexual.

It should be noted that in addition to the phenomenon of identifying with an idealized part-object, one may also identify with a devalued part-object. An example of this phenomenon occurs in the anorectic girl who feels her body to be ugly if she gains a pound or two. Her envious hatred of the beauty and fecundity of her mother's breasts and body causes damaging attacks on them which then become a source of self-hatred when these damaged maternal qualities are introjected and identified with.

It seems clear that projective identification exists along the whole continuum of human development – that it is both healthy and, indeed, necessary as well as pathological – and can be used as a defence against all anxieties. 'I am the object' defends against loss of the object either by separation (separation anxiety), to another person (jealousy), or through envy, as one now possesses the object's envied qualities or capacities. It must also follow if one accepts Klein's model of development from paranoid-schizoid states (unintegrated) to

depressive states (separate, realistic, integrated), that projective identification will occur with both integrated whole objects and unintegrated part-objects. The transsexual who in phantasy 'becomes' a
woman or the boy who 'becomes' his father (whole object) is quite
different from the baby's sucked thumb which becomes, in phantasy,
a nipple (part-object). Perhaps identification with a whole object is
most often a depressive defence against loss of the object, while identification with a part-object is most often a defence against paranoid
anxieties. Klein frequently stated that the breast is a source of protection against persecutors as well as a source of nourishment.

A particular consequence of projective identification occurs when
the identification with the envied object is a mixture of the feelings
of love and hate experienced simultaneously. Love stimulates a faith-
fully preserved or even an idealized identification, and hate produces
a parodied or debased identification. For example, a fifty-two-year-
old patient who described himself as a 'flaming fag' seems to have
identified with his beautiful baby sister (three years his junior) whom
he believed was his father's favourite child. His envy and jealousy of
her produced an admiring identification but also a devalued identification as the envy stirred up both admiring and hating (mocking)
feelings. The resultant identification was a parodied version of femi-
ninity that caused the patient's 'swishy' behaviour to be laughed at
and mocked rather than admired.

One important characteristic of projective identification is its
unconscious use as a method of communication. This property of
projective identification is a significant factor in the production of
countertransference responses during analysis. This phenomenon was
originally described by Heimann, Racker, Money-Kyrle, and Bion
and has been elaborated by many analysts since. Projective identification is an important contributor to non-verbal communication, a
property which is particularly important for non-verbal infants. I
believe when we 'intuit' some aspect of our patient's psychic state we
are responding to the patient's projective identification. In fact, intuition could be called a countertransference response. An example of
this function was told to me by a supervisee, whose patient was a
borderline female. When this analyst opened her waiting room door,
the patient was standing with her ear pressed against the door which
separated the waiting room from the consulting room. The patient
entered the consulting room muttering quietly and intensely to
herself. The analyst responded by asking, 'What did you say?'

Here we see how the patient successfully projected into the analyst her frustrated curiosity at detecting a couple in the adjoining room whom she had not understood or heard clearly. This enactment was probably a replay of the young patient's exclusion from her parents' bedroom and the projection of this frustrated curiosity into the analyst. It was also a repetition of the many secret, forbidden activities that the patient had indulged in throughout her childhood and had phantasized would make her parents feel left out and envious.

Following his treatment of some one hundred and fifty patients by hypnosis and extensive research into the outcomes of other hypnosis practitioners, Mason (1994) suggested that:

> the most dramatic and powerful effects of projective identification are produced when it exists in its most primitive, i.e., magical or omnipotent, form in a patient, and when the patient meets a therapist in whom this phantasy is also powerfully present. Then 'I wish to possess' and the corollary and mirror image of this wish, i.e., 'I can be possessed,' has found a practitioner who also wishes and believes he or she can possess another human being. A duet such as this is what I believe to be the basis of the hypnotic state. This highly charged folie à deux takes many forms in medicine, religion, and politics, for messiahs will always find devoted disciples. I believe that some phantasies of invasive possessiveness are universal and part of normal development, but when phantasies are extreme and are colluded with by a parent with similar phantasies, then a folie à deux can result.

This phenomenon can be observed when the entitled 'prince' and 'princess' wishes of children are met by the parents' own omnipotent phantasies about these children. Meltzer wrote, 'Where a child and an adult form a stable acting out collaboration, the folie à deux, so refractory to analysis, arises' (Meltzer, 1967, pp. 5–6).

In his paper 'Quick Otto and slow leopard: The Freud–Fliess Relationship' (Mason, 1997), Mason described a dramatic folie à deux that developed in the years 1895–1905 between Freud and his colleague Fliess. At this time Freud suffered from severe depressions as well as the physical symptoms of migraine, nasal difficulties, cardiac pain, arrhythmia, and dyspnoea. He obtained relief from these symptoms with the use of cocaine, nicotine (twenty cigars daily), and nasal cauterization performed by Fliess. These physical 'cures' accompanied and were clearly supported by Freud's manic episodes connected to his love of Fliess and his belief in Fliess's delusional theory concerning numbers (number twenty-three and number twenty-eight stood for the male and female periods) which were seen as determining human growth stages, the dates of illness, and each individual's date of death. Freud believed his own death would occur at the age of fifty-one which was the sum of twenty-three and twenty-eight. Fliess thought that his numbers theory applied not only to human beings but also to animals and all living organisms. Additionally, Fliess developed a 'nasal reflex neurosis' theory which was meant to explain almost all physical illness. Not only did Freud have Fliess operate on his own nose and on several patients' noses, but he referred to Fliess as 'The Kepler of Biology' and 'The Messiah'. Freud supported the irrational neurological connections made by Fliess despite his own neurological training and a classical paper Freud (1898) wrote differentiating hysterical from organic paralysis.

The view that a folie à deux existed between Freud and Fliess was stated originally by Strachey (1951) who communicated to Jones about Freud's letters to Fliess. In a letter to Jones, Strachey stated, 'It's really a complete instance of folie à deux with Freud in the unexpected role of a hysterical partner to a paranoiac.' Mason also described a folie à deux between Freud and Fliess concerning the denial of the forgotten gauze left in his patient's nose post-operatively by Fliess. Freud went to great lengths to exculpate Fliess's serious oversight and later became 'amnesic' himself concerning the cause of the patient's haemorrhages. Freud's life-long physician Max Schur observed that even after his break with Fliess '. . . Freud still needed to cling to the fiction that Fliess's speculations about periodicity were valid, . . . he did not totally overcome this conviction for decades, if indeed he ever did' (Schur, 1972, p. 47).

The formation of the superego was first described by Freud (1923) who called it the heir to the Oedipus complex. He theorized that a child between the age of three and five, faced with the impossibility of his Oedipal wishes – because of his love for his parents and his fear of punishment – permanently incorporates and installs these parental figures inside his/her mind. These internal parents now become internal objects controlling the child's dangerous and destructive impulses.

Klein (1932a) continued Freud's investigation into the nature of the superego and the processes of introjection and projection as well as her understanding of the nature of projective identification, which is, in effect, a combination of both these processes. It was Klein's idea that many pathological superegos (harsh, cruel, envious, perfectionist) were due not just to external reality but to the child's own primitive impulses projected into the external parents and then reintrojected. The formation of the pathological superego also gave us a tool for the possible modification of this structure which is the source of so much distress and mental illness. The tool was, of course, the observation of the mechanisms of projective identification that occur in the transference and, through this, the possibility of showing the patient his/her transference distortions. The patient's understanding of his projective processes through interpretation hopefully enables him to reclaim what has been projected. This, in turn, gives the patient a truer view of himself and his objects present and past and is a major aspect of the therapeutic value of psychoanalysis. It is the understanding of projective identification with the analyst and its consequences now and with parents in the past that comprise a great deal of the therapeutic value of psychoanalysis.

The formation of a pathological superego was illustrated by a thirty-six-year-old man who sought treatment because of relationship difficulties and obsessive procrastination. He dreamt that he parked his car outside a market and went in to shop. He returned to find a dent in his fender and, upon inspecting the dent, noticed that it contained a piece of mirror. He could also see his own eye reflected in the mirror. This patient's associations were that he had seen me driving and that my car had large side-view mirrors which stuck out a long way (an accurate observation). He surmised that I had dented his car.

I could interpret his view of me as violently intruding into him and mirroring him back to himself. However, my view of him contained a part of himself – his eye that looked back at him. This patient was, in fact, a voyeur who spied on people to triumph over them and feel superior by 'knowing their dirty secrets'. This was the me he took into himself; a me looking at him with his own eye. The introjection of this view of me became a very persecuting internal object which looked at him critically and harshly – noticing all his flaws – and was primarily the cause of the inhibition of all his activities. He feared being judged severely and mocked by cruel eyes.

As previously stated, the conflict between advocates of the difference between projective identification and projection no longer generates much interest among Kleinians. There does, however, seem to be a present-day disagreement between those who believe projective identification to be a purely intrapsychic phenomenon and those who regard it as an interpersonal phenomenon. Klein's original view was that projective identification was an omnipotent phantasy – that is, purely in the mind of the projector who is projecting into an internal object and changing his perception of himself and the object. This can occur in the presence or the absence of the object in question.

It is now also widely accepted that the phantasies of the projector can at times be conveyed in some way to the object who is present. The countertransference response of the analyst would be one way of detecting this. Another noticeable effect of projection would be some kind of overt response from the recipient that would be described an enactment. What part of any response is due to unanalysed targets in the recipient of the projections is certainly food for much investigation and speculation. However, I believe that a good case can be made for seeing our countertransference responses or 'intuitions' as benign or empathic, temporary folies à deux. Unlike the psychotic folie à deux, the folie à deux described here is benign because the projection on the part of the patient is to communicate and the projection on the part of the analyst is to understand. The mechanism involved is mutual rather than one way. It also appears that this dynamic is the essential basis of the phenomenon we call containment, in which there is a shared desire for and attempt at understanding. It does seem clear that both intrapsychic and interpersonal phenomena occur with the complex and fascinating mental mechanism that Klein brought to our awareness, and that it will take much work and evidence to flesh out all the implications of this universal human phenomenon.

Summary

In this paper projective identification has been described and contrasted with Freud's view of projection. Various motives for projective identification and some of the consequences of these motives are discussed. A dream illustrating projective identification is recounted, followed by a brief description of attacks on linkage by projective identification and the consequences of identification with the damaged links. An example of the production of a thought disorder following a patient's phantasized attack on the parental intercourse is discussed.

Part-object projective identification is demonstrated with examples of breast-mouth confusion due to jealousy and the phantasy of the body as a part-object due to envious identification. Projective identification as a method of communication is illustrated with a clinical vignette. Various examples of projective identification – both whole-object and part-object – are elucidated, and the phenomenon of folie à deux due to mutual projective identification is discussed as related to the state of hypnosis and to the relationship of Freud and Fliess from 1895 to 1905. A link between intuition, countertransference, containment, and benign, temporary folie à deux, is suggested. Finally, there is a discussion of the role of projective identification in the formation of the superego and a mention of the present speculations about intersubjective and interpersonal aspects of projective identification.

SECTION 4

Latin America

Introduction

Luiz Meyer

The papers that make up the South American contribution to this book are informative about the way that psychoanalysis has developed and matured in the three countries which are represented: Argentina, Chile and Brazil.

Argentina is the Latin American country in which psychoanalysis has gained the greatest preeminence, 'socialized' and disseminated itself. It is also the one whose psychoanalysts had, and still have, the greatest participation at an international level (although still less than they deserve). This is likely to result from the association of a privileged economic setting, characterized by the presence of a large middle class, with a high level of education among the population. This has enabled Gustavo Jarast, author of the paper about Argentina, to choose an authorial approach to study the concepts of projective identification most used in that country.

His study discusses the contribution of four important authors: Heinrich Racker, León Grinberg, and Willy and Madeleine Baranger. It is worth emphasizing not only the cosmopolitan nature of this group but also the type of training they had. Willy Baranger is of French origin, studied philosophy and it was as a philosophy professor that he went to Buenos Aires. Racker was born in Poland but graduated in philosophy in Vienna, having migrated to Argentina due to the war. There was certainly a mutual fertilization between the receptive environment they encountered in Buenos Aires and the European cultural experience/background they were able to offer.

Juan Francesco Jordan-Moore, author of the paper about Chile, centres his presentation on a conceptual discussion: is projective

identification a solipsistic concept? What is the weight of intersubjectivity? He describes how this question has gained relevance in the
Chilean psychoanalytic *milieu*, lists the psychoanalysts that have
discussed it, and presents the arguments they have used, supported
either by 'classical' authors (such as Rosenfeld and Bion), by the
already mentioned Argentinean authors, or by contemporary authors
(such as Ogden), as well as Ignacio Matte-Blanco, the Chilean
psychoanalyst whose work is best known internationally. His presentation can be read as an article that addresses questions relevant to
the understanding of the functioning of the concept of projective
identification.

Marina Massi, in order to write her article about Brazil, used a
different methodology from the previous authors. Basing herself on
publications about the history of psychoanalysis in Brazil and on
bibliographic research, she sent a questionnaire to various analysts in
the country. Brazil is a country of continental proportions. It is the
only country in Latin America in which the language is Portuguese,
and not Spanish. This results in a certain amount of isolation when
compared to the intense psychoanalytic interchange that takes place
among Spanish-speaking countries. Furthermore, Brazil was not
aided by the migration of intellectuals who already had undergone/
undertaken psychoanalytic training or that would be interested in it
upon arrival in the country. Massi's article implicitly makes the point
that, if in the case of Argentina we can refer to a 'socialization' of
psychoanalysis, in the case of Brazil we should talk about its popularization: today the country has twelve societies and eleven nuclei of
psychoanalysis spread through its entire territory. This implies a
certain pulverization of theoretical concepts, reflected in the article.
Massi presents the work of various authors who have approached the
subject of projective identification and tried to offer a personal interpretation. However, none achieved an authorial dimension, as was
the case in Argentina, neither did a burning question arise, as was the
case in Chile, capable of stimulating a fruitful debate regarding the
subject of projective identification. There is, however, a rich and
continuous contact with the most varied international schools of
psychoanalytic thinking. Numerous foreign analysts visit Brazil,
establishing contact with its members and their production. It is
certainly a way to enrich, to make known, and to discuss the different
concepts of projective identification.

---

19 ---

Projective identification

The concept in Argentina

Gustavo Jarast

The Kleinian movement in Latin America was at its peak between the 1950s and the 1970s. During this time Melanie Klein's own contributions, as well as the contributions of the Kleinians and post-Kleinians, were fruitfully taken up by the various psychoanalytical groups that were gradually forming. Argentina's Psychoanalytical Association (APA) was founded in 1942, and articles by Klein, Susan Isaacs and Joan Riviere were published in the first issues of its *Revista de Psicoanálisis*.

In 1952 Enrique Pichon-Rivière published an important contribution on working with projective identifications in the context of the psychoanalytic process in the *Revue Française de Psychanalyse*.

Authors such as Heinrich Racker, León Grinberg, Willy and Madeleine Baranger, David Liberman and José Bleger, among others, were able to see the richness of these new theories, and how they shed light on other areas of clinical research. Of all the above, it was probably Grinberg who developed the most explicitly Kleinian train of thought. First Racker and then the Barangers also contributed to the theory of Kleinian psychoanalytical technique, although in Racker's case the links are not made explicit. The Barangers made a creative contribution with their concept of the 'psychoanalytic field'. This concept actually includes the mechanism of projective identification in its configuration.

In the years following the founding of the APA, Kleinian thought circulated in a familiar way through the regular publication of papers

325

in which these ideas became common language. These papers laid the foundations for clinical practice and the theoretical development of authors such as Arminda Aberastury (child psychoanalysis), and of Enrique Pichon-Rivière (the treatment of psychotic patients). These authors were considered pioneers in the field. Even in groups who were not wedded to Kleinian theory, theoretical and technical debate took place mainly through a central reference to Kleinian thought.

In 1956 Liberman published 'Identificación proyectiva y conflicto matrimonial', in the *Revista de Psicoanálisis* (Liberman, 1956).

In 1966, Emilio Rodrigué wrote 'Relación entre descubrimiento e identificación proyectiva', in his book written with his wife Genevieve, *El contexto del proceso analítico* (Rodrigué, 1966).

In 1967 José Bleger published his very important book *Simbiosis y ambigüedad*, but he did not draw attention to his use of the concept of projective identification. He made a more explicit contribution in 'Psicoanálisis del encuadre psicoanalítico', published in 1967 in the *Revista de Psicoanálisis* (Bleger, 1967a, 1967b).

After the 1970s, debate grew more complex, taking on board recent French thinking, including Lacanian theory. The contributions of 'post-Kleinian' authors such as Bion, Rosenfeld, and Meltzer were also regarded as invaluable, and helped strengthen Kleinian thought. There is no doubt that Klein's concept of projective identification has been one of the contributions which laid the groundwork for the theoretical, clinical and technical development of psychoanalytical practice. 'Notes on some schizoid mechanisms' was published in Spanish in 1947 in the *Revista de Psicoanálisis*, and from that time onwards there was regular theoretical and clinical debate on this topic.

Contributions, developments, problems

Heinrich Racker

Melanie Klein was never keen on extending the concept of projective identification to apply to the countertransference. Despite her disagreement, the idea of countertransference as a response to the patient's projective identification was widely used from Paula Heimann onwards – in Argentina, initially by Heinrich Racker. Racker has made a clear distinction between two sorts of countertransference based on the two types of identifications suggested by Helene Deutsch. He speaks of 'concordant countertransference', where the analyst identifies parts of himself with the corresponding psychological part in his patient (ego, id, superego), in an empathic tendency to understand his own emotional experience, together with that of the patient. The patient's transference encourages the analyst's emotional psychological processes, in which the latter responds with a sublimated positive countertransference. Racker wrote that

> Concordant identification is based on introjection and projection, or, in other words, on the resonance of the exterior in the interior, on recognition of what belongs to another as one's own ('this part of you is I') and of the equation of what is one's own with what belongs to another ('this part of me is you').
>
> (Racker, 1957, p. 312)

When the analyst identifies himself with the patient's internal objects, feels treated like them, and experiences them as his own, he is experiencing a 'complementary countertransference', in which the patient now represents an internal object belonging to the analyst. This countertransference reaction implies that the analyst's neurotic remnants are activated by the projection of the patient's objects. Racker (1957, p. 312) said, 'The complementary identifications are produced by the fact that the patient treats the analyst as an internal (projected) object, and in consequence the analyst feels treated as such; that is, he identifies himself with this object'. In very few cases does Racker *explicitly* use the phrase projective identification to refer to this identificatory process:

> For instance, the analyst perceives the analysand's intense rejection of his own libidinous feelings towards the analyst (which may be caused by feelings of guilt, paranoid angst, rivalry, masochism, an internal object's boycott, etc.); he perceives the insistent annulment of his interpretations, which might have enabled this rejection to be overcome, and he reacts with anxiety, which communicates to his conscience as tension. But the perception of exterior danger – of the analysand's resistance – is just one of two factors, and countertransferential anxiety is the result. Another factor is the analyst's unconscious perception of interior danger, for example, danger of

327

being frustrated by an internal object of his own, of being a victim of his own masochism or counter-resistances.

Whatever the proportions between the subjective and the objective factors (that is to say, between 'the danger' from the analyst or the analysand's interior or between the death instinct of either analyst or analysand), these factors cause the 'tension'. If the analyst is aware of this tension, it may serve as a sign enabling him to discover that part of the analysand's internal object, which is opposed to the libidinous relationship to the analyst. Violent irruptions of countertransferential anxiety occur at times – as was already mentioned – as a consequence of the analyst's identification with abruptly threatened internal objects of his own, or as a consequence of his identification with parts of the analysand's ego, which have been intensely dissociated by the analysand and projected on to the analyst. Often it is the analysand's difficulty in tolerating excessive feelings of guilt which underlies these intense projections on to the analyst – in this case, projection of a part of the ego experienced as guilty.

It has been observed on a number of occasions that the analyst feels compelled to return the dissociated part to the analysand as soon as possible. This is because the analyst has trouble tolerating the guilt deposited in him. This fact can serve to remind us of how much harder it is likely to be for the analysand (whose ego is usually weaker than the analyst's) to accept this dissociated part as belonging to his ego. The anxiety the analyst has experienced once again indicates what is going on within the analysand and what he is fighting against; the intensity of this countertransferential anxiety can help the analyst to gauge the appropriate dose of interpretation of this conflict. I would like to add that the analysand's defence mechanism mentioned above (the 'projective identification') usually achieves its goal. In our example: the analyst feels guilty, and this not only implies (as it has sometimes been said) that 'the analysand expects the analyst to feel guilty' or that the analysand 'supposes that the analyst is sad and depressed'. The analyst's identification with the object with which the analysand identifies him is – I repeat – the normal countertransferential process.

(Racker, 1968, pp. 65–66)

For some authors this omission (of the phrase 'projective identification') is due to a desire to use Freudian terminology, and to the fact that Racker's main therapeutic ideal was 'to remember', rather than a belief in 'mechanisms', implying essentially the idea of 'reliving', and that this explains his reluctance to use the expression 'projective identification' explicitly (Lichtman, 1979). But the fact is that he uses the concepts in a clearly 'Kleinian' way: a part of the patient's ego that refuses a 'good' or a 'persecutory' content, and projects it on the analyst, so that the analyst becomes identified with it. The analyst must be unaware of having received the projected part, e.g. of the patient's ego, *and for that reason* he cannot interpret it.

For some authors, it was Klein's seminal 1946 paper that allowed further studies of the countertransference to flourish. In 1948 both Paula Heimann and Heinrich Racker, without knowing each other, began their studies of countertransference, using the concept of projective identification as an *instrument* for understanding it, as well as for interpreting it. Racker presented his first work on the subject in APA in that year: 'La neurosis de contratransferencia', published in the *International Journal of Psychoanalysis* in 1953 as 'A contribution to the problem of countertransference'. These two presentations of countertransference phenomena are closely interdependent, and enable the analyst to be more aware of the complex effects of the persistent, strong forces of the patient's projections. This awareness is not only useful to the analyst in understanding more of his own unsolved childhood neurosis, but also helps him to avoid the danger of a defensive fixation of a countertransferential position, and enables him to explore the patient's objects with which he originally is partially identified. The conceptualization of projective identification and its effects on the object allows the analyst to re-evaluate his experiences and opens up new areas of discovery. A deeper awareness of the strong presence of projective identification, and the splitting processes of massive characterological pathologies in very disturbed patients, have enabled new work with the countertransference technique to be done using the idea of the analyst's countertransference as a source of information about the patient, although Klein never made her peace with the term being used in this way, as described above.

Racker's work had a deep impact on psychoanalytic technique in Latin America; the most well-known analysts of the time went on to reflect upon these ideas in their work, and to develop them.

329

León Grinberg

As noted above, Grinberg was one of the analysts who used Kleinian theory most directly in his theoretical writing. He coined the term 'projective counteridentification' in 1956 to refer to a kind of countertransferential reaction brought about when a patient makes particularly *intense* use of the mechanism of projective identification. He presented this idea in a paper published later as 'Sobre Aspectos mágicos en la transferencia y en la contratransferencia. Sus implicancias técnicas. Identificación y "contraidentificación" proyectivas', in the Argentinean *Revista de Psicoanálisis*. He explained that this mechanism eventually leads the analyst passively to enact what the patient unconsciously wants him to. He was thinking of a particular response of the analyst in reaction to the patient's projections and introjections, which would be *independent* of the analyst's own emotions.

Grinberg emphasizes that this reaction should be attributed to the extreme violence of the patient's projective identification, which is related to traumatic childhood experiences, and is a result of violent projective identifications that the patient himself has received from others. The counteridentification reaction shows the analyst's inability to tolerate the projection or to be aware of what is going on: he only suffers the impact of the material projected by the analysand, and reacts to it in a 'real and concrete way', acquiring and assimilating it. The analyst may feel that he can no longer manage his own feelings, and that he is bewildered. He may rationalize this state of affairs, but he cannot become aware that he has become an object of the analysand, or a part of him (e.g., the id, the ego).

Grinberg gives detailed description and analysis in order to differentiate his concept from Racker's complementary countertransference. As described above, Racker's description refers to a kind of object relationship in which the patient becomes an internal object of the analyst because of the analyst's own infantile neurotic remnants, reactivated by the anxieties and projections resulting from the patient's conflicts. The patient's internal objects may be experienced as the analyst's own. Thus, different analysts might react in different ways to the same situation posed by a patient, depending on the type and nature of their own conflicts. In projective counteridentification Grinberg's hypothetical patient's projective identification would provoke the *same* countertransferential response in different analysts. This is because the quality, the intensity and the force of the projection will no longer permit a critical threshold in an analyst's perception, and the extra-verbal pressure on him will produce a particular reaction.

Grinberg uses the following clinical vignette as an example:

A male patient began his session in the following way: 'I feel very nervous today. I don't know how to describe it, but it is absolutely necessary that I do. I would like to tell you what I have discovered or what has been revealed to me.' [With great emotion]: 'It was so surprising the other day when the diarrhoea stopped as a result of what you said to me . . . Besides I remember that something else you said gave me a physical stitch. Diarrhoea is a physical process . . . Since you spoke, these words seem to produce a physico-chemical reaction in some or other of my nerve cells; but before that, when you think, there is also a transformation in other cells to the point where the voice comes from the lungs, lips, tongue, etc., and a string of words which are now sound, vibrations, comes out. At this moment the receptive process begins in my ear, through various means until it becomes conscious listening. I ask myself if all those words, instead of being spoken by you, came from someone else, would they have the same therapeutic meaning? I think not. It is extremely important for me that those words came from Dr. Grinberg and no one else.'

All this material was said with force and with a resounding voice which surprised me. It was not common for him to express himself like that and therefore I felt particularly attracted, as much by what was said as by the way it was said. Using my impressions as a guide, I interpreted that he was trying to produce in me the same effect that he said I had had on him, and to show me that it was his voice and no one else's which produced this special effect on me. That is to say that my interpretation was made showing his positive transference. I did not yet realize that it was only a defence against his deepest paranoid situation.

The patient went on to say: 'Now that we are talking about sound and listening, I would like to talk about music: it is divided into three basic parts, rhythm, melody and harmony which are indissociably joined together. I play jazz; in that we see rhythm and the harmony of the song we are playing. The melody is impro-vised. In modern jazz, the rhythm and the harmony are also impro-vised. I can improvise for hours in melodies with rhythm but I find it difficult to carry on a specific harmony. A melody in 8/4 time in the chord of A for four beats and the other four in A sharp is impossible for me. The same happens with written music; I cannot give the timing correctly to each note. On the other hand, when my music teacher played one of the pieces I was studying, I could play it afterwards exactly by ear. In the session, for example, I find it difficult to adapt to the reality of time. I don't even know what time it is. It is as if I made my own time, which is different from your time. I can compare it to my inhibition in music; this specific harmony which we improvise is the kind which allows people who don't know each other to improvise a jam session.'

While he was telling me all this, I did not fully understand what was happening. I felt quite uneasy. I felt sorry that I did not understand sufficiently the theory and the technique of music which I have always loved. I admired and envied his knowledge and the apparent precision with which he described and explained it . . . with its technical jargon, the relationship between rhythm, melody, and harmony. I felt the need to interpret it in his own words; it was a way of showing him that I could also play in the same field as him and which he knew so well. My interpretation was that I represented the chord of A major and he the chord of A minor, but that between our beats there was no harmony and we needed to find a rhythm and a timing between the two of us which would harmonize so that we could improvise (free association) together in a common melody. The interpretation was now spoiled; it only demonstrated a partial aspect and deviated from what was essential. The important thing would have been to show him his envy and that he was really interested in discovering which was my timing and which was my rhythm.

The meaning of his deepest phantasy began to dawn on me and I paid attention to the following material. The patient went on: 'I don't know why I thought that one could do all kinds of tests on a patient; encephalograms, BMR's, a tape recording, a thermometer to take temperature with, an oscilloscope to record sound waves; anyway the use of all those appliances so that you would have a better knowledge of the patient, both inside and out.' While I was listening to him I surprised myself with a parallel and simultaneous phantasy of having a metronome to regulate, control, and direct the time on him, that is to say, to have something which I already knew was lacking in him. I realized exactly at that moment the full

play of his unconscious phantasy, contained in his intense projective identification, and also how I 'counteridentified' myself
projectively with a partial aspect of him, full of envy and anxiety.
One of the major effects of my 'projective counteridentification'
was a blind spot towards the paranoid content of his attitude and
my having stressed instead the positive aspect of the transference.
The patient used this in a defensive way to pacify the persecutor,
which I represented. But that was only his defence because of his
anxiety and panic due to the power he attributed to me.

My words not only cured him of his diarrhoea but also gave
him a physical stitch. I was in possession of a secret which he
envied and feared because I could do what I wanted with him. He
wanted to take this over so that he could limit its danger and so
that he could dominate me at the same time. For this he needed
both to know me and to control me. It was for this that he 'took'
me into his own field, acoustics and music. He made me feel,
projectively, what he had felt, with me. My feeling of dislike
corresponded to his feeling of anxiety. My admiration and envy
reflected similar feelings which he had felt, and my need to use his
terminology and concepts was the equivalent of his desire to take
onto himself my special terminology and concepts. My fantasy
of the metronome formed the response to his desire to use all
kinds of medical apparatus so as to get to know me completely,
that is to say, to control me. As a last resort, and as a transactional
solution, he offered me his beat and timing in exchange for
knowing mine.

(Grinberg, 1979, pp. 180–183, author's translation)

To summarize, Grinberg thought that the analyst's reaction to the
patient's projections is essentially independent of the analyst's
conflicts. What he refers to as a pathological projective identification,
he saw as a further development of Melanie Klein's projective identification, as an omnipotent phantasy. He thought of it as a kind of
projection that produced real effects on the analyst as a receptor, so
that he became dominated by it. Hence his view that all analysts,
regardless of their character and abilities, would have the same
'projective counteridentification'. Grinberg found support for his
ideas in Bion's theory of thinking processes: the concept of the beta
screen in the psychotic patient, through which the patient's projections of beta elements go beyond the analyst's countertransference,

333

leading to the possibility of understanding, and transforming them into thinkable or 'alpha' elements.

Horacio Etchegoyen questioned Grinberg's affirmation, suggesting that when these processes have this kind of impact, it is only because the analyst is under the influence of his 'countertransferential neurosis' (Etchegoyen, 1986). In 1982 Grinberg modified his original position, asserting that projective counteridentification enables the analyst to feel a kind of emotion that, when understood and sublimated, would convert into a very useful tool for keeping in touch with the most profound levels of a patient's conflicts (Grinberg, 1982). For this to happen, the analyst must be prepared to receive and contain the patient's projections.

Madeleine and Willy Baranger

At the beginning of the 1960s Madeleine and Willy Baranger introduced one of Latin America's most fruitful contributions to psychoanalysis with their concept of the 'psychoanalytic field'. They published a paper in the *Revista Uruguaya de Psicoanálisis* entitled 'La situación analítica como campo dinámico' (Baranger and Baranger, 1961–1962). In this paper they presented an original idea of the psychoanalytic field as a dynamic and bipersonal one, made up of the unconscious phantasies of both members of the therapeutic couple during the analytic process, thus developing the concept of unconscious phantasy as described by Melanie Klein and Susan Isaacs. The idea of a dynamic field was founded on the concepts of Gestalt theory and on Merleau-Ponty's phenomenology. It was Etchegoyen who said that the Barangers, and Latin American analysts in general, place the psychoanalytic process not in the patient, but *'in between'* the analyst and the patient (Etchegoyen, 1986). The Barangers thought that in the regressive situation of analysis, a bipersonal phantasy is formed, different from that of either the patient or the analyst, considered individually. This phantasy underlies the dynamic of the analytic field. It can be seen not as a sum of the unconscious phantasies of each member of the couple, but as something created between them, enabled by the unity created during the session.

Central to this phantasy are the mechanisms of projective and introjective identification, and projective counteridentifications. The Barangers thought that the patient's and the analyst's bodily experiences and phantasies were involved in this dynamic. The use of projective identification in the present reactivates patterns of past experience, which have not up until that moment been crystallized. In the process of countertransference exploration, the analyst may realize that he is identified with split-off aspects of the patient's internal world, and he can then interpret this phenomenon. In such situations projective identification is limited, so that the analyst's regression is partial. But in other situations these processes are much more active, so that the transference–countertransference neurosis may paralyse the analytic process, through the constitution of a 'bastion', a structure which immobilizes the process.

In the 1970s, French thinking gained increasing influence among Latin American psychoanalysts, and this had some impact on the Barangers' conception of the psychoanalytic field. They continued thinking of their original structure as before, but they included the conception of 'intersubjectivity' in response to Lacanian criticism of the idea of the analytic field as a 'specular' (mirror-like) relationship. Lacan accented the idea of a 'third', which established a difference in the 'specular couple'.

However, the most fertile element of the Barangers' theory of the psychoanalytic dynamic comes from their exploration of counter-transference phenomena, for instance through their definition and analysis of the bastion. As mentioned earlier, the bastion is a patho-logical structure which immobilizes the dynamic analytic process, as a consequence of the patient's resistance and the analyst's counter-resistance. It may become chronic, leading to an analytic impasse, or a negative therapeutic reaction. In their prepublished presentation in the Thirty-third International Congress of Madrid in 1983, the Barangers offered several clinical vignettes which illustrated what they conceived of as the bastion: 'a neo-formation set up around a shared phantasy assembly which involves important areas of the personal history of both participants and attributes a stereotyped imaginary role to each' (Baranger, Baranger, and Mom, 1983, p. 2).

Here are some of the brief examples which they presented to illustrate the concept of a bastion.

A. A manifestly perverse patient. He behaves like a 'good patient', complies with the formal aspects of the pact, manifests no resis-tances, does not progress. The sessions, over a certain period, seem to be a condensed version of the whole of 'Psychopathia Sexualis' by Krafft-Ebing (1886). The analyst 'has never seen anyone with so many perversions'. The bastion here is set up between an exhibitionist analysand and a fascinated-horrified analyst, the forced 'voyeur', complacent with regard to the perverse display.

B. *An analysand, veteran of a number of analytic treatments.* Apparently, each session bears the fruit of some 'discovery'; in reality, nothing is happening. The analyst is delighted by the subtlety of the analysand's descriptions of his internal states, enjoying his own Talmudism. Until he realizes that, while they are toying with their disquisitions, the analysand is monthly placing the analyst's fees at interest, speculating with his delay in paying. The analysis of this bastion reveals a shared fantasy set-up: the analysand's old, surreptitious vengeance on his stingy father and the analyst's guilt-ridden compulsion to set himself up as the cheated father.

C. *Example of a bastion which has invaded the field.* A seriously psychopathic patient. The analyst is terrified, fearing the analysand's physical, homicidal aggression without being able either to suspend or to carry the treatment forward. The nodular fantasy of this bastion is the patient's as torturer in a concentration camp, and the analyst's as tortured, powerless victim. With the conscious formulation of this manoeuvre, the analyst's terror disappears. The two individual histories converge in the creation of this pathological field.

(Baranger et al., 1983, p. 2)

In the first vignette the fascinated analyst cannot separate himself from his exhibitionistic patient. In the second, the guilty identification of the analyst combines with the vengeance of the analysand. In the third, the combination is between the sadomasochistic aspects of patient and analyst, expressed through the phantasy of victim and torturer. In each case a shared unconscious phantasy is the result of mutual projective identifications, coming from the infantile histories of each participant. This situation converges in the formation of a bastion structure, which requires a special 'second look' at the immobilized situation. The Barangers concluded:

Each of us possesses, explicitly or not, a kind of countertransferential dictionary (bodily experiences, movement phantasies, appearance of certain images, etc.) which indicates the moments in which one abandons one's attitude of 'suspended attention' and proceeds to the second look, questioning oneself as to what is happening in the analytic situation . . . This structure (the bastion) never appears directly in the consciousness of either participant, showing up only through indirect effects: it arises, in unconsciousness and in silence, out of a complicity between the two protagonists to protect an attachment which must not be uncovered. This leads to a partial crystallization of the field, to a neoformation set up around a shared phantasy assembly, which implicates important areas in the personal history of both participants and attributes a stereotyped imaginary role to each. Sometimes the bastion remains as a static foreign object while the process apparently goes forward. In other situations, it completely invades the field and removes all functional capacity from the process, transforming the entire field into a pathological field.

(Baranger et al., 1983, p. 2)

When 'things go well', the analyst's second look may create timely interpretations which will help to undo the bastion and enable the patient to gain insight into the projective identifications which have been active. According to the Barangers, 'Projective identifications of the analyst toward the analysand and his reactions to the projective identifications of the latter [. . .] provoke pathological structuring of the field, require a second look toward it, also demand priority in interpretive management' (Baranger et al., 1983, p. 5). The breaking of a bastion implies returning to the analysand the aspects which were placed in the analyst by projective identification. Extreme forms of bastion crystallizations in a psychoanalytic field may become stagnations, in which the analyst may feel 'as though he were "inhabited" by the analysand, a prisoner of worry which goes beyond the sessions' (through fear of a self-destructive or criminal act of the analysand, of the imminence of a psychotic 'outbreak', or of other, less dramatic situations). 'These parasitic situations (equivalent to micropsychoses in the analytic field) tend to lead either to a violent rupture of the analytic situation or to its re-channelling by reducing splitting and by returning the projective identifications to the analysand' (Baranger et al., 1983, p. 9).

The Barangers believed that the pioneering papers of Heimann and Racker showed that countertransference was not only a universal phenomenon, but an instrument of analytic technique as well. They also thought that Melanie Klein's discovery of projective identification demanded profound modifications in transference theory. For them the concept of projective identification was overextended, to the point that finally transference became quite synonymous with 'a continually active projective identification', and that 'this led her to define the movement of the analytic session as a succession of projective and introjective identifications, resulting from the analyst's interpretive activity'. Later they circumscribed the transference by projective identification as follows: 'This type of transference is distinguishable from the others thanks to the very well-defined countertransferential expressions accompanying it, and intervenes determinatively in the constitution of the pathology of the field' (Baranger et al., 1983, pp. 3 and 4).

Authors such as Beatriz de Leon de Bernardi use the concept in line with the Barangers, at the Uruguayan Psychoanalytic Association.

Conclusion

The authors discussed in this chapter are the Latin Americans who have most richly used and extended the concept of projective identification. They pioneered new possibilities in therapeutic practice, allowing analysts to get in touch with the more regressive aspects and defended parts of their patients. In that sense these authors can be clearly located in the tradition of post-Kleinian thinking which has done so much to benefit the most disturbed patients, from Bion to Rosenfeld. Moreover, they are dignified heirs to the intuitions and conquest of Kleinian research.

In this short enumeration and narration, I have discussed what I consider to be the most important and fruitful contemporary contributions of these authors, and only mentioned some others whose contributions have not influenced today's debates on technique to the same degree as, for example, the Barangers' contributions. Researchers like Joseph Aguayo are working hard at the heart of the concept in order to uncover the controversial roots of Klein's rich concept.

Projective identification

Brazilian variations of the concept[50]

Marina Massi

The aim of this paper is to present the use, or different uses, of the concept of projective identification within the scope of analysts belonging to the IPA in Brazil. A brief summary of the historical facts can help us to understand and contextualize some of the characteristics of this psychoanalytic production.

The psychoanalytic movement in Brazil has its origins in the mid 1920s through the pioneering figure of Durval Bellegarde Marcondes, through whose efforts the IPA-qualified training analyst Dr Adelheid Koch arrived in Brazil, in 1936, giving rise to the education of a group of candidates. After years of intense educational and institutional organizational efforts, in 1951, the first Society of Psychoanalysis was founded, gaining IPA recognition, in Brazil.

English analyst Mark Burke, member of the British Psychoanalytical Society, arrived in Rio de Janeiro in 1948, and began the analysis of candidates. In 1949, German psychoanalyst Werner Kemper

50 This is a condensed version of a research study conducted by the author. I would like to thank Luiz Meyer for the valuable discussions during the writing of this paper; my colleagues who undertook interviews for the research, including Aloísio de Abreu, Alírio Dantas Jr., Gley P. Costa, José Carlos Zanin, Maria Elena Salles, Maria Inês E. Carneiro, Marilza Taffarel, Nelson José de Nazaré Rocha, Paulo Marchon, Sergio Leukowics and Sonia Azambuja; Aurea Rampazzo and Greice Klem for help with the text; and Henrik Carbonnier, who translated it into English.

(considered a member of the Nazi party through documentation unearthed by Riccardo Steiner) also began the analysis of other candidates as part of their education. Due to a misunderstanding between these two groups, a third group of candidates was formed, seeking education in Argentina, and thus becoming known as the 'Argentine group'. In the 1950s, some analysts such as Décio Soares de Souza and Henrique Mendes, who became a member of the British Society, returned to Brazil (Sagawa, 1980, 1992).

In Rio Grande do Sul, due to its proximity to Argentina, psycho-analytic activities were influenced by the APA (Argentine Psychoanalytic Association). Thus, in 1963, the Porto Alegre Psychoanalytical Society was recognized (Sagawa, 1980, 1992).

The influence of the Kleinian school of thought in Brazil was introduced during the 1950s, when the first generation of Brazilian psychoanalysts went to London to come into contact with Klein and her followers. The point of entry of the concept of projective iden-tification into Brazil was through the direct influence of seminars and clinical supervisions experienced by Brazilian analysts with members of the Kleinian group in London, or through visits by foreign psychoanalysts.

However, as opposed to other countries, it seems that Brazil was not widely regarded as a destination by foreign psychoanalysts[51] with a solid theoretical background. Nor has Brazil had pioneering analysts with an organizing power of influence – in the theoretical or clinical fields – that nurtured an original psychoanalytical production.

The *Revista Brasileira de Psicanálise* (Brazilian Psychoanalysis Journal) featured Melanie Klein on the cover and a reproduction of the letter she sent to Durval Marcondes, on 1 October 1956, in which she writes: 'It makes me happy knowing that my work has been both stimulating and useful to the Society of São Paulo.' This was, in fact, a truthful assessment.

The Kleinian school of thought prevailed during the 1960s, concurrently with growing interest in the thinking of Wilfred Bion. Virgínia Bicudo and Frank Philips played important roles in the introduction of Bion's ideas to São Paulo. The first translation of Bion's work – *Os Elementos da Psicanálise* (Elements of Psychoanalysis) – was published in 1966.

---

51 Heinrich Racker and Marie Langer.

Frank Philips, a controversial psychoanalyst, went to London in 1940 and underwent analysis with Melanie Klein and then with Bion, during which period he maintained contact with Brazil through supervisions and a few lectures. He returned to Brazil in 1968, establishing a new frontier of psychoanalysis at the SBPSP (Brazilian Society of Psychoanalysis of São Paulo).

According to Sagawa's historical studies, Philips had a decisive influence on the implantation of Bion at the SBPSP, 'which based itself on the presentation of a new focus of Psychoanalysis, to the point that, in the 1970s and 1980s, it became common to oppose a classic psychoanalysis with a new one and it was even designated the "real" Psychoanalysis.'[52] Philips was the analyst for the re-analysis of many of the SBPSP's training analysts (Oliveira, 2005, p. 266).

The 1990s saw a different scenario. The participation of new generations of training analysts within the Societies introduced new ideas and opened the door to restlessness regarding what constitutes Brazilian psychoanalysis. The return of analysts seeking education in London contributed to the debate on Brazil's theoretical and clinical psychoanalytical productions (Perestrello, 1992, p. 176).

The various theories and schools of thought seem to be better represented within Brazil's Societies, even though the English School still predominates. Brazilian psychoanalysts now have a greater interest in dialogue between schools and this could well represent one of the important characteristics of contemporary psychoanalysis in Brazil.

Contributions to the use of the concept

When discussing the contributions of psychoanalysts to the use of the concept of projective identification, in some ways, we are seeking the origin and structure of the universality of certain psychoanalytical concepts.

The creation of a concept or the formulation of a change to a concept involves specific contributions that come from daily clinical thought, refined by the parameters of the theory and the technique.

---

52 Sagawa, R. Y. (n.d.). *Um recorte da História da Psicanálise no Brasil* [An Extract of the History of Psychoanalysis in Brazil], p. 9, www.cocsite.coc.fiocruz.br/psi/pdf/artigos1.pdf.

That which is original is born out of that which is known and transformed.

Luiz Meyer, in a piercing reflection on the universality of psychoanalytical production, said:

> it is not built as an absorption or dilution resulting in a placid and aseptic whole. On the contrary, it is formed by specific contributions of a remarkable character – a bumpy terrain – each of which have an organic quality that confers its coherence. What marks a school, what gives it consequence is not merely originality. Originality sustains itself in the weave of the thinking, in the fruit of the transformation effected on what is already known.
>
> (Meyer, 1989, p. 364)

Although the problem is not one of originality, what needs to be faced in this paper is the fact that Brazil lacks a psychoanalyst with international recognition as an expressive collaborator to some aspect or use of this concept.

I am not proposing to ignore Brazil's contributions, but attempting to identify a specific reality that, once recognized, needs a strategy to be approached.

Brazil currently has twelve societies and eleven nuclei of psychoanalysis over a vast national territory, which implies a wide variety of social contexts and a production that is spread out and not always known and discussed by the country's analysts. Faced with this context, I sought to create a tool – a questionnaire – to enable a mapping of the main theoretical influences used by Brazilian analysts.

What can be seen is that Klein and her followers have had the greatest influence regarding the concept of projective identification among Brazilian psychoanalysts, with special mention of Herbert Rosenfeld, Betty Joseph, Heinrich Racker, Paula Heimann, Meltzer, Joseph Sandler and Grinberg (through his concept of projective counter-identification). Recently, Thomas Ogden, Antonino Ferro and James S. Grotstein have contributed with the concept of *transidentification*.

However, Bion is considered the follower who most expanded the use of the concept when he described it as a means of communication, re-evaluating the importance of projective identification in the analytic relationship, as well as human relationships.

Based on the history of psychoanalysis in Brazil, bibliographic research and the questionnaire replies from psychoanalysts belonging to various societies in the country, it was possible to obtain some information about the authors who have developed a different use of the concept of projective identification, and I have tried to convey this below.

Mario Pacheco de Almeida Prado (1917–1991)

Mario Pacheco de Almeida Prado was the founding member of the Brazilian Society of Psychoanalysis of Rio de Janeiro (SBPRJ). He was the Director of the Institute and President of the Society. He underwent analysis with the English psychoanalyst Mark Burke, responsible for his Kleinian influence.

In his book *Identificação Projetiva no Processo Analítico* [Projective Identification in the Analytical Process], the author writes that the use of projective identification happens 'as a vehicle of perception; that is, conceiving perception as an identification resulting from a projective identification of something that is separated and placed outside the ego or self' (Almeida Prado, 1979, p. 32). Perception and identification are possible only as a reintrojection of projective identification.

In a paper about the work of Almeida Prado, José Carlos Zanin (2004) summarizes his ideas, affirming that:

> we verify that, due to the use of projective identification before perception, what is perceived is not the totality, the authenticity of the lost object, but a mixture of that which belongs to the object and that which the observer inserts from within into the perceived object.
>
> (Zanin, 2004, p. 318)

That which is *mainly inserted* can be love (life instinct) or hate (death instinct), according to the conception developed by the author.

Through his study on projective identification, Almeida Prado (1979) formulated, in an original manner, the concepts of *states of ingrainment* and the *ingrained object*.

In analysis, the *state of ingrainment* can be understood as a phenomenon unconsciously lived by the patient, of feeling undifferentiated or intermingled with the analyst, which the patient constructs through projective identification and the reintrojection of the figure of the analyst into the patient.

Therefore, the interference of the destructive impulses in the appearance and maintenance of the self leads to the consequent *state of ingrainment* of the subject within its objects.

Isaías Melsohn (1921–)

Isaías Melsohn, a psychoanalyst of the SBPSP, critically situates the concept of projective identification in the scope of the phenomenology of Max Scheler, the empirical research of Klages, Kurt Goldenstein, Köhler and Kofka and, finally, in the concept of expressive perception of Ernest Cassirer.

Based on these authors, Melsohn locates the concept of the schizoid position as a state of consciousness in which there is an absolute split. There are no connections. It relates to a purely expressive moment of the consciousness, which may reappear later in, for example, psychosis. These expressive experiences are not only persecutory. The child may be captivated by fascination, tranquillity, pleasure, grimness, fright, etc. This is where Melsohn disagrees with Klein regarding the denomination of the paranoid-schizoid position (Sister and Taffarel, 1996).

In his book, *A Psicanálise em nova Chave* [Psychoanalysis in a New Key], Melsohn (2000) relates his concept of *expressive perception* to projective identification, the paranoid-schizoid position and the *perception of 'you'*, as described by Max Scheler.

The author believes that the roots of the perceptive process in children are not syntheses of sensorial 'elements', but understandings of totalities. They are 'original, primitive and immediate expressive characters' (Melsohn, 2002, p. 250). For Melsohn, the infant's perceptive experiences are expressive experiences, as described by the psychology of form, and revisited by Max Scheler and Cassirer.

Melsohn insists on clarifying two points: there is no understanding of isolated sensory content that is then synthesized; and there is no 'objective' perception that is deformed by emotions.

According to the author, expressive perception, as a unit and fusion of the external-internal, is the notion that corresponds to Klein's projective identification. 'It is not just the subjective projected externally, nor a copy of the exterior; both aspects determine each other as objectifying is only possible in contact with suitable significant forms.' (Melsohn, 2002, p. 252).

Walter Trinca (1938–)

Walter Trinca's work on *intrapsychic projective identification* departs from Klein's view of projective identification and moves on to Bion's so-called normal projective identification. For Trinca, projective identification is processed in object relationships and the same process can be considered to take place inside the actual self. In intrapsychic projective identification, the subject unconsciously splits the self, projecting one of the resulting parts inside another, equally split part. The part that contains the aspects placed within tends to be taken as the identification of the whole self, becoming dominant, while the part whose aspects were relocated becomes empty and poor.

Trinca's first studies date back to 1991 (Trinca, 1991),[53] when he took the self as the representation of the whole person. It is precisely this self that, through intrapsychic projective identification, divides, constituting a nucleus that Trinca calls the self's sensory system. This system occupies the self to varying degrees, occasionally taking it over entirely. Instead of occurring only in object relationships, the projective identification takes place between the parts of the self.

Trinca considers it necessary to delimit a sensory system within the self in order to account for the nature of sensory experiences. The part of the self that contains the sensory system tends to be taken as the whole of the self. When this happens, the non-sensory and immaterial part of the self becomes impoverished, leading the person to become mentally and spiritually compromised.

Trinca wrote a paper for *Free Associations*, published in London, where he separated the interior being from the self (Trinca, 1992). For Trinca, the interior being and the self form distinct entities, albeit ones that communicate between themselves.

His book, *O ser interior na psicanálise* [The Interior Being in Psychoanalysis] (Trinca, 2007), shows us that while the self is an entity of conflicts and turbulence, the interior being is in itself

---

53 Trinca, W. (1991). *A etérea leveza da experiência* [*The Ethereal Lightness of Experience*]. São Paulo: Siciliano, p. 100. In 2006, Vetor Editora published the second revised and updated edition, under the title *Psicanálise e transfiguração: a etérea leveza da experiência* [Psychoanalysis and Transfiguration: The Ethereal Lightness of Experience]. See also Trinca, W. (1991). Notas para um estudo da sensorialidade da mente [Notes for a study of the mind's sensory sensitivity]. *Revista Insight Psicoterapia*, *12* (2), 20–23.

harmonious and non-sensory. A greater or lesser influence can result in diversifying psychic disturbances.

Instead of a psychoanalysis of elements, the author describes a psychoanalysis of factors that are, basically:

1 a constellation of the internal enemy
2 a distancing of contact with the interior being
3 a fragility of the self
4 the sensory ability
5 an unconscious structuring
6 self dissipation anxiety.

As projective identification plays the role of an active and mobilizing element within the psychic apparatus, it continues to exercise a function of internal communication, whether between the entities or between the factors. It only specializes in this function of communication.

Trinca believes that projective identification in the self plays a role in the constitution of the psychic entities we call the id and superego.

Trinca affirms that projective identification assists the operating of factors and the moving of systems (pertaining to a comprehensive psychoanalysis). Its function is made relative and not absolute, because it constitutes an element instead of a psychic factor.

Trinca believes that its use reflects more on what he calls the closing state, related to psychotic personalities (Bion). Therefore, the communication exercised by projective identification under these conditions consists not of a bonding function, but instead of a depositing of the products of one or several parts into another or others, as in anxiety defence, although conserving the original characteristic proposed by Klein.

Projective identifications in phobias and panic are related to the difficulties in what Bion calls normal projective identifications, responsible for the emptying of the self, the precarious position of the basic confidence matrix and the instability of the internal support centre.

As for the uses of Bion's normal projective identification, Trinca employs them in relation to the phobic personality. He starts from the principle common to psychoanalysis that the infant, experiencing mental situations of 'unimaginable anguish', requires special conditions of psychic 'metabolization' that should be assumed by the mother or caregiver. If there are no configuring resonances from the mother's responses to the infant, the infant's emotions tend to remain turbulent and he will have difficulties in representing himself. The failure of the primary container results in the maintenance of the feelings of threat regarding life.

For Trinca, projective identifications in intuitive images are an individual's direct or symbolic representations of the meaning of the deep emotional states of another or other individuals. Beyond the nature and intelligible meaning of the patient's oral communication, and apparently without any clear relationship with it, intuitive images appear spontaneously in the mind of the professional. These images lead to non-verbal communication through the medium of Bion's normal projective identification.

Luiz Carlos U. Junqueira Filho (1943–)

For some years, Junqueira has worked on the importance of specular phenomena in emotional development, trying to elaborate the concept of specular identification as part of a broader investigation regarding the essence of metapsychology.

The material presented below comes from the author himself, who has generously provided sections of a chapter soon to be published in book form.

> Psychoanalysts are convinced that the human mind is the stage par excellence where the drama of emotional transformations is played out. Consider, for example, two commonly used characters, Narcissus and Echo, often seen as each other's opposites: indeed, Narcissus is unknowingly deprived of a partner with whom he can identify or into whose interior he can project his excluded parts; Echo, in turn, represents a clandestine second self to exercise these functions. [. . .]
>
> The double is, at heart, an illusory resource used by the subject when his tolerance for reality runs out: in creating a second character that steals the scene, the subject diverts his attention from the painful focus, but, at the same time, sets a trap for himself. This is what happened with Oedipus who, under the illusion at the cross-roads that his fight with Laius was no more than an incident of

mere 'road rage', could not be conscious that he was fulfilling the oracle's prophecy. The perception of the subject under the illusion thus becomes split in two: a theoretical aspect (theoréin, meaning 'that which is seen') emancipating itself from the practical aspect (i.e. 'that which is done').

With this backdrop of the 'multiplication of personalities', we can and should now reconsider projective identification in strictly psychoanalytical terms, trying to map the variation of its meaning.

It seems clear that the Freudian and Kleinian subject uses it to defend himself from the vicissitudes of his own personality or from external traumas [. . .]. However, from the point of view of Lacanian, Winnicottian and Bionian subjects, its power is used to develop the identity of the self, to introduce the subject to the field of culture and to establish the bases of human communication and thinking.

Some analysts, such as Grotstein [. . .] and Ogden [. . .] have offered interesting developments of the theories of Klein, Bion and Meltzer. Grotstein admits that when the image of the mother-as-object is internalized by the infant, child or adult, this image is altered by the fantasized effect of subsequent projective identifications. To understand the installation of that which he called 'psychic presences', and which in my opinion correspond to 'relational ghosts', into the self, Grotstein posited the immanent subject (the one recognized as the 'I' in conscious terms) and an ineffable subject of the unconscious.

In Ogden's vision, the ineffable subject of the unconscious communicates to the immanent subject the individual's anonymous pains through symptoms, dreams, actings and so on; in the opposite manner, the conflicts of daily life are transmitted to the ineffable subject of the unconscious, which processes them through unconscious dreaming. Thus, an internal process of projective identifications is created, through which emotional experience can be thought and so transmitted to oneself and others.

As a consequence of this situation, Grotstein proposes the idea of 'autoctonia', the fantasy of auto-creation through which we 'personalize' the world by imagining it as a reflection of who we are [. . .].

In my experience, to better understand the constitutive dynamic between the ideal I and the I's Ideal, I propose 'mirroring' as a term to denominate the process of reception on the part of the parents of the infant's projections and communications in an atmosphere of reception and comprehension: in this case, the parents' response is always constructive, collaborating in the elaboration of the infant's anxieties or its success in communicating. It would be something very akin to the notion of reverie proposed by Bion. The term 'reflectment', I reserve to designate to parental insensitivity that returns, unmodified, to the infant, everything that it authentically produces in its efforts to face the reality of life.

Thus, it would be expected that the healthy infant could count on a positive response from its parents as regards the 'consultation' directed to them when the infant aims to validate its ideal I: when this takes place, the infant feels that its parents legitimate that which belongs to it, independent of any judgement of value.

Should reflectment prevail, under the terms described above, there is the risk that, in addition to not having its anxieties comforted, the infant may receive a package of parental judgements and values in return, which implicitly disqualify it as a subject. From the metapsychological point of view, in this last case everything would happen as if the infant had sent its ideal I for validation and in return received it dressed in the I's Ideal: of course, the doors for the constitution of a false self would be open under these conditions.

Junqueira's concept of specular identification deals with the importance of specular phenomena in the constitutive dynamic between the ideal I and the I's ideal. The *mirroring* and *reflectment* are different receptive processes by the parents of the infant's projective identifications.

Elizabeth Lima da Rocha Barros (1948–   ) and Elias Mallet da Rocha Barros (1946–   )

Elizabeth and Elias Rocha Barros have presented works on projective identification in which they discuss how the splits and subsequent projective identifications appear differently in the paranoid–schizoid and depressive positions, as the introduction of verbalization in the projective processes impacts on various issues in the area of how communication takes place between patient and analyst, mother and infant, etc.

349

The authors affirm that the process involved is highly complex and cannot be encompassed by a single term without specifying its evolution. They view projective identification as a difficult concept to be understood in its phenomenology and inherent processes, in addition to being intrinsically linked to the issue of the production/construction of symbols, countertransference and its expression in an evocative–expressive plane belonging to affections and emotions.

In other works, these authors have discussed the operation of projective identification as a basis for a kind of special empathy, a way of getting to know the other in that it allows us to place ourselves 'in the other's place', albeit with the addition of a new 'metaphorizing' function – the authors believe that the projection needs to allow for the capturing of meanings and their elaboration.

For the authors, projective identification produces evocations, invitations for the construction of a mental representation coloured by emotion. Thus, the evocation is a manner of non-discursive expression, even if permeated by the patient's verbalized discourse, thus allowing connections other than those belonging to discursive logic and mediated by words to appear, and in this manner expanding the forms of representation of emotional relationships.

Influenced by Susanne Langer, they came to work on the issue of the nature of symbolic communication and how it presents itself in the processes of projective identification.

From the clinical point of view, the authors point to the fact that the transmission of communication through projective identification is influenced by the actual structure of the symbol, which in turn, can be deformed or limited by attacks aimed at its own structure. In other words, the capacity for symbolic expression present in projective identification can still be affected during the actual process of symbolic production. These attacks thus limit the field of meaning present in the symbolic structure.

Roosevelt M.S. Cassorla (1945–   )

Roosevelt M. S. Cassorla has developed the theme of *crossed projective identifications* since 1997. This refers to group occurrences (including the group formed by the patient and analyst) in which each of the members impacts the other with mass projective identifications and is, in turn, also impacted by similar phenomena originating from the other.

According to the author, crossed projective identifications are also the basis for 'enactment'. Cassorla studies and extends this concept,[54] describing it as situations in which the analytical dyad produce an obstructive plot thanks to projective identifications taking place in a double sense between the patient and analyst. This plot, which is not perceived by the members of the pair, is termed a 'chronic enactment' or 'paired-non-dream' by the author. The projective identifications are understood, based on a Bionian reference, as 'non-dreams'; that is, as undigested facts (beta elements) that neither the patient nor the analyst is able to dream or turn into dreams through alpha-functions. When this plot is unravelled, a very noticeable event, called an 'acute enactment' by the author, takes place. Cassorla's 'acute enactment' is what is described by other authors as 'enactment', but Cassorla considers such enactments to be the fruit of recapturing the pair's capacity for thought which unravels the 'chronic enactment'. The author demonstrates that the 'acute enactment' is created in the revival of archaic traumatic situations that have been implicitly elaborated (implicit alpha-function) during the 'chronic enactment'. Cassorla believes that mutual suggestion, a fact that is part of any analytic process, is the fruit of crossed projective identifications between the members of the pair. The analyst's art would be to allow himself to be influenced in a first instance (to experience at-one-ment with the patient and what he experiences) and simultaneously (or subsequently) to 'dream' this fact, permitting his entry into the symbolic network of thought.

There is no doubt that other authors also describe crossed projective identifications, but Cassorla calls attention, in a decisive manner, to the fact that crossed projective identifications are the basis for enactment. The author promotes the relationship between the use of the concept of projective identification and enactment in an original way.

---

54 Cassorla highlights the importance of several authors who dissected the importance of countertransference as an instrument (Racker, Heimann, Betty Joseph and Money-Kyrle), and those who followed the Barangers (and their concept of Field) stimulating the intersubjective view (of whom Cassorla believes Ogden and Ferro to be the most important).

Final considerations

The main objective of this article was to track the different uses of the concept of projective identification in Brazil. As previously stated, there is no single psychoanalyst who has made an original contribution in the consensus of the psychoanalytical community. Hence the need for a bibliographic survey and the adoption of a questionnaire as a means to find out which authors have been influential within the psychoanalytical community through their original uses of the concept of projective identification.

What can be noted, then, is that there are at least two branches: the first the more frequent use of the concept based on the contributions of the English school of thought; while the second relates to some original contributions by Brazilian analysts who are not particularly widely known, either in Brazil or abroad.

As the English School's influence over the various psychoanalytic societies in Brazil is significant, we can state that the most frequent use of the concept is founded on Klein and Bion, as well as authors such as Rosenfeld, Meltzer, Joseph, Grinberg and, more recently, Ogden, Grotstein and Antonino Ferro. Both the bibliographic survey and the questionnaire results point to these authors as having the greatest influence on the use of the concept of projective identification in Brazil.

The second branch includes the seven Brazilian authors presented who have made original contributions using different approaches.

Almeida Prado describes the *state of ingrainment* and the *ingrained object* as phenomena derived from projective identification.

Melsohn, in turn, through his studies on *expressive perception* and the *representative function*, presents a different manner of understanding the relationship between the perception and the perceived object. It is possible to say that, in this case, the author tries to restrict the definition of projective identification in order to clarify the concept. There is a criticism of the concrete manner of thinking that projects itself into the object and what actually belongs to the object (its content).

Elizabeth and Elias Rocha Barros propose the presence of a 'metaphorizing' and metabolizing function within the concept.

Trinca (*intrapsychic*) and Junqueira (*specular*) seek to specify different uses of the concept. In other words, we could say that these authors describe the actual concept of projective identification in a diverse manner.

Cassorla attributes a special relevance to projective identification by promoting an original relationship between the concept of crossed projective identification and enactment.

This research has made it clear that there is a need to further the discussion regarding Brazil's production. I believe we still lack the productive experience of what I would term as 'Brazilian controversies', a deep and intense debate on theoretical and clinical experience that does, in fact, deserve to constitute a common ground for us all.

Projective identification and the weight of intersubjectivity

Juan Francisco Jordan-Moore

Introduction

To recount the history of projective identification in Chile I will use the publications that have addressed the concept in my country. There are not many of them but they give a fair picture of its development. After an initially uncritical reception the concept has been challenged on the grounds that it is based in a monadic conception of the mind that diminishes the contribution of the analyst to the interactive nature of the psychoanalytic process. However, the acknowledgment of the analyst's contribution to projective identification in a dyadic conception of the analytic process may not suffice to give a full account of projective identification as an intersubjective phenomenon.

Development of the concept

Edy Herrera (2000) describes the progressive interpersonalization of the concept and its development from a pathological defense mechanism to its consideration as a normal process of psychic life. Projective identification was at first considered to be an intrapsychic pathological aggressive phantasy and its effect on the recipient was not taken into account. Later, it was linked to a deepening of the theory of object relations and the connection between transference and countertransference. Projective identification is thus linked to the analyst's countertransference. Hererra highlights León Grinberg's (1985) concept of projective counteridentification. Grinberg distinguishes between the latter and complementary countertransference as defined by Racker. The analyst's neurotic residues are activated by the patient's conflicts in complementary countertransference, whereas in counter-projective identification, the analyst's response is mainly the consequence of the intensity and unconscious intention of the patient's projective identification.

Finally Herrera discusses Bion's contribution to the theory of projective identification through the link he makes between projective identification and the model of the container-contained. Projective identification is considered as a mode of communication of primitive mental states that affect the container. Depending on the containing capacity of the latter, this process may result in psychic growth or in intolerable anxiety and psychic depletion. This is the most interactive definition of projective identification, yet, it seems that there is an assumption concerning the original unconscious intention of PI in the projector. Is the intention communicative or is it destructive?

Polemical stances regarding projective identification

Ayuy et al. (1997), commenting on clinical material presented at the Trans Andean Meetings, are concerned with the clinical problem presented when a patient who is feeling persecuted by the analyst due to massive projective identification violently rejects his interpretation. This refusal is described as 'an acute rejection situation', to stress a complex experience that is not simply a consequence of a negation of the meaning of the interpretation. The main problem is the fragmentation it suffers, hence losing almost all significance. They present a thorough investigation of the different strategies found in the publications of Kleinian authors to confront this problem. John Steiner's recommendation to formulate analyst-centred interpretations; Betty Joseph's emphasis on the need to focus interpretation on the formal aspects of the patient's communication; Priscilla Roth's interpretations that address what is enacted in the relationship. They emphasize the analyst's unavoidable enactments, described by Irma Brenman, Elizabeth Bott Spillius, Edna O'Shaughnessy and Denis Carpy, as well as the need for close scrutiny of these. This allows the analyst to become aware of subtle pressures, coming from the patient, that induce the analyst to act. This pressure can then be interpreted. Yet all these strategies, designed to contain the patient's projection, and finally formulate a verbal interpretation, may not be enough. They distinguish two stances concerning the problem of containment of the patient's projective identification. One conceives an initial unconscious intention in the patient, communicative or evacuative. The latter is related to the rejection of reality by the psychotic part of personality. This intention can overflow the containment capacity of the object. The other conceives projective identification as a dyadic phenomenon. In this frame, meaning cannot be discerned from the beginning, it is not a priori. It depends on the quality of the analyst–analysand interaction. Thus, the intention of projective identification is defined a posteriori. Ayuy et al. (1997) subscribe to the idea that there is an unconscious initial meaning of projective identification in the patient that can determine a fateful analytic process, independently of the perturbation in the analyst's counter-transference.

Juan Pablo Jimenez (1992) argues that the analyst's contribution to projective identification has not been given due significance. He makes the point that the communicative, or evacuative and destructive intention of projective identification, is a meaning that depends on the analyst's capacity to contain the patient's projections. If the analyst fails, projection is signified as destructive, if he succeeds, projection is connoted as communicative. He criticizes León Grinberg's (1985) phenomenology of different a priori meanings (communicative, destructive, evacuative, reparative, controlling) of projective identification. He recognizes that Bion and Rosenfeld tried to go beyond a monadic conception of projective identification, attributing to the analyst, as the patient's object, an active function as a subject who tries to put an end to the vicious circle of projections and reintrojections. Yet, from the point of view of a dyadic communication theory, this concept still implies a monadic conception of mind. Projective identification is described as almost always coming from the patient to the analyst as the container. The reverse of the contained–container metaphor, the patient as the container of the analyst, should also be considered. In Jimenez' view, the theory of projective identification emerges in the analyst as an explanation for emotionally intense countertransference experiences. Edy Herrera (2000) notices that this arises frequently with psychotic and borderline patients. She thinks that the value of the concept becomes manifest in working with these patients.

Juan Pablo Jimenez (1992) illustrates his thesis with two vignettes. One of them, Veronica, seems to be a demanding borderline patient. For three years the analyst had to manage intense acting out in the session, till finally, as a result of an interpretation of a dream, the intense acting out subsided. She was then able to continue her analysis fruitfully. The patient's projective processes were thus understood to be communicative projective identification. During the period of intense acting out the analyst experienced intense countertransference feelings, such as anger, which he took home with him. He had to confront the patient repeatedly, sometimes very forcefully. Frequently he had feelings of triumph over the patient, sensing that he could control and defeat her. He understood these troubling feelings as a dim awareness that he was 'projecting' himself into the patient with more or less violence, with the hope of being introjected by her with his analytical function. The analyst recognized that this process took place in the structure of a sado–masochist relationship, stating that the latter was determined by the patient's psychopathology.

It is noteworthy that although Jimenez states that the contribution of the analyst is underestimated in the theory of projective identification, he ends by assigning the determination of their relationship as sado–masochistic to the patient. There is no acknowledgement of the analyst's contribution to the patient's massive projective identification prior to the interpretation of the dream, and no attention is paid to the possibility of the analyst's own masochistic and sadistic aspects contributing to the sado-masochistic structure of the relationship. This discussion can be expected in an intersubjective frame that gives a full account of the influence of the psychoanalyst.

Josefina Figueroa (1997), in her summary of the group discussions at the above mentioned meeting, reports a consensus that what transpires in the analytic dyad is two minds interacting closely and mutually influencing each other. The analyst is emotionally involved with his patient. 'Living through' this experience is the main way to know disavowed aspects of the patient. There was also consensus that the concept of projective identification had developed to encompass an interactive notion of the analytic situation. Enactment by the analyst is inevitable and, perhaps, the only way to make a valid interpretation, through the careful analysis of countertransference. Priscilla

Roth's suggestion of interpretations that include the analyst's involvement in the enactment was valued as an alternative to classical technique, although the need clearly to distinguish this kind of intervention from a countertransference confession was enhanced. Others considered that any change in technique could dilute the analyst's identity, and should be considered psychoanalytic psychotherapy. Figueroa concludes that the concept of projective identification has evolved from Melanie Klein's original understanding to one that takes into account the 'ever-growing weight of the inter-subjective aspect of the analytic couple'.

Jaime Coloma (2002) understands the psychoanalytic session as determined by a theory that includes projective identification and a preponderance of oneiric thought in both participants. The coupling of PI and oneiric thought is considered the main way of dealing with emotions. Based on Matte-Blanco, he thinks that every emotion connects with a symmetrical mode of being, and thus, with an existential dimension that is lost if psychoanalysis is defined as a positivist science. Starting from this definition of a psychoanalytic session, he posits that the technique and setting are not defined in terms of expected behavior of the analyst, but, instead, as different possible interventions that emerge from an analytical understanding of what happens in the session, taking into account the therapeutic benefit for the patient. In the same vein as J.P. Jimenez, he thinks that the meaning of the analyst's interventions is defined a posteriori, i.e. it becomes clear only retrospectively whether it is an acting-out by the psychoanalyst, or a proper understanding of the total existential situation of the patient in which his emotional experience is included. From this definition of the session other kinds of analytic interventions may emerge, not restricted to verbal interpretations, as in the case of interpretative actions (Casaula et al., 1994). The issue of the interactive nature of projective identification is not addressed. Yet an interactive approach seems to be implicit when Coloma posits the analytic session as structured by projective identification and oneiric thought in both participants. This can be interpreted as meaning that the patient also functions as the analyst's container. Coloma does not address the patient's participation in defining whether the meaning of the analyst's intervention is or is not acting out. It seems that the analyst should be able to decide on his own which is the case.

The above summary of these papers enables us to identify two polemical issues regarding the theory of projective identification in

Chile. One is the question of how the meaning of projective identification is determined; the other, the question of what modifications are acceptable to classical analytic technique in order to deal with the inevitable enactments linked to projective identification.

Discussion: the weight of intersubjectivity

Josefina Figueroa's final commentary that stresses the 'ever-growing weight of intersubjectivity' in the analytic situation seems an apt place to begin to discuss the first issue. In what sense is intersubjectivity a weight? Perhaps it presents difficulties for a theory and practice that understands mind as generating unconscious and conscious meaning mainly as an intrapsychic phenomenon. The intrapsychic model seems to have given way under the weight of accumulated clinical evidence, leading to an understanding of mind as engendering meaning in an intersubjective field and its associated dialogue.

Recognition of the participation of the analyst in a dyadic model of communication does not necessarily take us all the way to intersubjectivity, as can be seen in the incongruence between the theoretical importance assigned to the analyst's influence, and what is reported in clinical vignettes. Every so often it seems that what is written with one hand is erased by the other. A dyad may still be two monads communicating their emotions through windows in the monads. Take for example the following description of projective identification by Thomas Ogden (1994c, p. 105): 'The projector and the recipient of a projective identification are unwitting, unconscious allies in the project of using the resources of their individual subjectivities and their intersubjectivity to escape the solipsism of their own separate existences'. This is a striking affirmation about existence considering that through his conceptualization of PI as manifestation of the subjugating intersubjective third, Ogden has given one of the fullest account of projective identification in terms of intersubjectivity, and thus of the primeval being-with-other in our existence.

I have posited (Jordan, 2005) that the difficulty for an intersubjective theory of projective identification lies in positing projective identification as a mechanism that is independent from the meanings that are negotiated in the relationship. The Barangers (Baranger and Baranger, 1961–1962) first thought of their concept of a bi-personal field as structured by projective identifications and introjections from patient to analyst and vice versa.[55] In this first version of their field theory, their clinical vignettes also present the analyst as the rather passive receptor of the patient's projective identification, as when they state, for example, that the patient's desperate projective identification ultimately creates a tranference-countertransference psychosis in the session. In this conceptualization of their field theory, constituted by crossed projections and introjections, from which unconscious phantasy emerges as a bi-personal phenomenon, no attention is paid to the fact that projective identification is also a phantasy and, as such, should also be considered as a bi-personal phantasy, i.e. 'the processes that are postulated as structuring the unconscious bi-personal phantasies of the field are themselves an unconscious phantasy' (Baranger and Baranger, 1961–1962, p. 162).

Later on, Madeleine Baranger (1993, 2005) posits that the concepts of projective and counterprojective identification may be attempts to elude the need to acknowledge the participation of the analyst in the events of the field. If the analyst fails he can easily slide into viewing the patient as 'guilty' and as taking the initiative in projective identification. Applying Bion's idea about 'basic assumption' group phenomena to the analytic couple,[56] they defined a 'basic unconscious phantasy' created by the same field situation. One basic phantasy might be the solipsistic existence of two human beings desiring to migrate into one another in order to escape from their desperate isolation.

I proposed (Jordan, 2005) to understand the field as isomorphic with Matte-Blanco's (1998) notion of a basic matrix of projection and introjection. In this region of the 'deep unconscious, things – including those that regarded from outside appear as projection and introjection – do not occur, they simply are' (Jordan, 2005, p. 194). At this level events do not exist, no inside or outside can be discerned, there is a simple manifestation of being. This is not an easy matter to understand, we are in the region of ontology, of being as such. Perhaps Thomas Ogden's description of the experience of projective identification may help us to understand (Ogden, 1994c). He says:

55 When thinking interactively projective identification as going from patient to analyst and vice versa it is always stressed that it is desirable that the intensity of this kind of exchange is more intense and frequent from patient to analyst than vice-versa. This is due to the asymmetry of the analytic situation.

56 Bion (1961) specifies that the 'basic assumption' of the group should be sought in the matrix of the group and not in the individuals that conform the group.

'The recipient is not simply identifying with an other (the projector); he *is becoming an other* and experiencing himself through the subjectivity of a newly created other/third/self' (Ogden, 1994c, p. 102, my italics). Projective identification is a matter of 'being-the-other' and the other 'being-myself' because, 'In part, . . . there is never a recipient who is not simultaneously a projector in a projective identificatory experience' (Ogden, 1994c, p. 102). This kind of experience can be expressed succinctly as: *I am* yourself; *you are* myself; *we are* together. I think that what has been called communicative projective identification can be included today in a theory that posits an indivisible system of self-regulation and mutually regulated affects (Beebe and Lachmann, 2005). When this system fails, affects become dysregulated, and a phantasy of projective identification may emerge as a desire and a need to find an other who can help in the regulation of distressing emotions like anxiety, shame, envy, depressive affect, rage, etc., that threaten to disintegrate the self. Projective identification can function, in a given interaction, as a self-regulating phantasy in a subject that experiences himself as emotionally isolated, expecting to trust someone and, thus, to use the opportunity for successful mutual regulation, in order to ease the burden of self-regulation at the expense of frail mutual regulation.

Perhaps the difficulty of developing projective identification into a fully intersubjective concept lies in the fact that at its inception it was linked with drive theory. In this frame, meaning is generated endogenously from the drives. Anxiety, for example, is originally understood as the consequence of the impact of the death drive on the ego. In this theoretical imaginary first moment, a solipsistic subject without a world is posited. The world is a creation of the subject. A persecutory object comes into being through projection to protect the ego from annihilation. A good object is created afterwards by the libido, to protect the ego from the bad object.

If we substitute affect or emotion for drive,[57] we start with a different picture. Affects, as currently understood, are, from the very beginning, regulated in an intersubjective field. They are inherently communicative. There is not first an emotion and then the intention to communicate it. Affects open up a meaningful world from which

---

57 Affect and emotion are used as synonymous. Some authors use affect to indicate the description from the point of view of an observer and emotion to connote the subjective experience.

we are not separated. This world is with-the-other by whom we are affected and whom we affect in many ways. The stuff of the basic matrix of projection and introjection are affects which, 'on the deepest level . . . are often transpersonal . . . [they] are evoked inter-personally through dense resonances between people, without regard for who, specifically, is feeling what' (Mitchell, 2000, p. 61).

Bion's conclusion in his paper 'On arrogance' (Bion, 1957b) states:

> the denial to the patient of a normal employment of projective identification precipitates a disaster through the destruction of an important link. Inherent in this disaster is the establishment of a primitive superego which denies the use of projective identification.
>
> (Bion, 1957b, p. 92)

A premature superego implies an internalization of an object and consequently a premature caesura of inside and outside, coupled with a premature knowledge of the other and self as objects. This implies there is an untimely isolation of the self, a solipsistic subject, deprived of emotional contact with another subject, a denial of intersubjectivity. This psychic state can precipitate the need and desire to invade another in search of the intersubjective experience that has been denied. The phantasy of projective identification can be understood as emerging, a posteriori, from a failure in the mutuality of affect regulation, i.e. 'the normal employment of projective identification'. If mutual affect regulation is going ahead smoothly there is no need to represent the process in phantasy, because emotions are inherently communicative and transpersonal. This emotional experience is embedded in the matrix of projection and introjection, in which what comes to light is a continuity of being.

The same may apply to the clinical situation. As stated above, Juan Pablo Jimenez suggests that the theory of projective identification may emerge in the analyst as an explanation for emotionally intense countertransference experiences or dysregulated emotions. The same can be said of the patient when going through emotionally intense transference experiences. In my view, the emergent theory of projective identification in the analyst is linked to a mutually elaborate unconscious phantasy, of introducing one's own intolerable emotions into the other, who thus becomes myself, perhaps searching for an opportunity to restore a lost sense of being-with-other.

The other controversial question concerns the interventions used to handle events in which projective identification and impasses appear on the scene. In a previous paper (Casaula et al., 1994) we noted that interpretation in psychoanalysis has been restricted to the analyst's verbal utterances. Following Heidegger (1927) we proposed an extension of the psychoanalytic notion of interpretation to include the assignation of meaning through actions performed by the analyst. We put forward the concept of interpretative action. Joan's case is presented in the paper. The analyst recalls the confused countertransference with a child in analysis. In a climax of confusion and desperation on the part of the analyst, with the child in a fragmented manic state in a session in which she experienced herself as being in many places at the same time, the analyst, starting to think from her desperation and confusion, decides to reflect Joan's image on the back of the lid of a round tin pencil box, interpreted jointly, in that moment, as a mirror. The child, anticipating the analyst's intention, screams: 'Don't do it Leito, don't do it'. The analyst insists forcefully in her act. The child, seeing her reflection, dramatically calms down in an experience that the analyst understands as an integration of the patient and herself.

In the same year, Thomas Ogden (1994b) published a paper with the same concept of interpretative action. He explores new ways of transmitting meaning in analytic processes that are experienced as futile. This should not surprise us given that affective regulation is based on pre-verbal exchanges in adults as well. After all, projective identification is based on actions that transmit emotions in consonance with the origin of the word, i.e. to move.

Interpretative actions convey meaning, in a direct and holistic way. They are what Susanne Langer described as non-discursive or presentational symbols. This kind of 'symbol has an immediate, idiosyncratic sensory reference' (quoted in Rayner, 1995, p. 16). For example, bang, standing for the noise of a pistol. Interpretative actions seem to have the capacity to restore to language the proper function it loses when it is used to conceal meaning instead of disclosing it.

It is for analysts of the future to decide what interventions are properly analytic and how projective identification may be conceptualized most appropriately. In the meantime it is still a useful concept in clinical practice. Our controversies may be our best means of bringing the future of the concept to the fore.

Final commentary: news from the past

Edy Herrera (2000), trying to untangle the mystery of how projective identification manages to bring on psychic states in the analyst, thinks that it functions by inducing something akin to an hypnotic state in the analyst. It is surprising to discover a reversal in the history of psychoanalysis. From a psychoanalyst that hypnotizes his patients we have reached a situation in which the patient is considered to hypnotize the analyst. This may be a consequence of the need to negate the analyst's influence on the process. The whole truth may be that the analytic couple is frequently on the threshold of mutual hypnosis. Freud (1921) called this latter situation a 'mass of two'.

Afterword

Elizabeth Spillius and Edna O'Shaughnessy

The idea of projective identification, of which there were forerunners in the writings of Freud and others, emerged as a distinct concept within the language of psychoanalysis in Melanie Klein's paper 'Notes on some schizoid mechanisms' in 1946 (see Chapter 2). In this book we chart the further evolution of the concept in the work of British Kleinians, and also its acceptance, rejection and alteration by analysts of different psychoanalytic persuasions in Britain, Europe, and in North and South America.

So widespread an interest in a new concept is unusual. It is due, we think, to the illumination projective identification can offer of central features of the clinical situation in the formation of transference and countertransference between patient and analyst. In the future it will be interesting to see what becomes of the concept as psychoanalysis develops further in Eastern Europe and Russia, Africa, Southeast Asia and the Far East.

In our view, the concept of projective identification is not particular to the clinical situation but a universal of human communication, one that Freud was questing for. In 1915 in his paper 'The Unconscious', he writes: 'It is a very remarkable thing that the Ucs. of one human being can react upon that of another, without passing through the Cs. This deserves closer investigation' (Freud, 1915b, p. 194). And later, in 1933, he again describes this process.

There is, for example, the phenomenon of thought-transference [. . .] It claims that mental processes in one person – ideas, emotional states, conative impulses – can be transferred to another person through empty space without employing the familiar methods of communication by means of words and signs.

(Freud, 1933, p. 39)

We think that the concept of projective identification gives a name to, and a clarification of, the dynamics of direct communication and the phenomena of transference and countertransference that are universal among humankind.

References

Abraham, K. (1908). Psycho-sexual differences between hysteria and Dementia Praecox. In Abraham (1927). *Selected Papers on Psycho-Analysis*. London: Hogarth Press.

Adler, G. (1989). Transitional phenomena, projective identification, and the essential ambiguity of the psychoanalytic situation. *Psychoanalytic Quarterly*, *58*, 81–104.

Almeida Prado, M. P. (1979). *Identificação projetiva no processo analítico* [Projective Identification in the Analytical Process]. Rio de Janeiro: José Fagundes do Amaral.

Amati Mehler, J. (2003). Identificazione proiettiva: fondamenti teorici [Projective identification: theoretical foundations]. *Psicoanalisi*, 7(1), 48–83.

Ayuy, C., Feuerhake, O., Pola, A. and Rowe, J. (1997). Material teórico. Contención, comunicación y resistencia en la transferencia: el abordaje desde la teoría de la identificación proyectiva [Containment, Communication and Resistance in the Transference: The Approach from the Theory of Projective Identification]. *Revista Chilena de Psicoanalisis*, *14*(2), 57–65.

Balint, M. (1937). Early developmental stages of the ego: primary object love. In Balint (1965). *Primary Love and Psychoanalytic Technique*. London: Tavistock, pp. 90–108.

Balint, M. (1950). Changing therapeutical aims and techniques in psychoanalysis. *International Journal of Psychoanalysis*, *31*, 117–124.

Balint, M. (1952). *Primary Love and Psychoanalytic Technique*. New York: Liveright (1965).

Balint, M. (1968). *The Basic Fault*. London: Tavistock.

Baranger, M. (1993). The mind of the analyst: from listening to interpretation. *International Journal of Psychoanalysis*, *74*, 15–24.

Baranger, M. (2005). Field theory. In S. Lewkowicz and S. Flechner (Eds.), *Truth, Reality, and the Psychoanalyst: Latin American Contributions to Psychoanalysis*. London: IPA International Psychoanalysis Library.

Baranger, M. and Baranger, W. (1961–1962). La situación analítica como campo dinámico [The analytic situation as a dynamic field]. *Revista Uruguaya de Psicoanálisis, 4*(1), 3–54.

Baranger, W. and Baranger, M. (1966). Insight and the analytic situation. In R. Litman (Ed.), *Psychoanalysis in the Americas.* New York: International Universities Press, pp. 56–72.

Baranger, W., Baranger, M. and Mom, J. (1983). Process and non process in analytic work. *International Journal of Psychoanalysis, 64*, 1–15.

Bayle, G. (1996). Les clivages. *Revue Française de Psychanalyse, 60*, 1303–1547.

Beebe, B. and Lachmann, F. (2005). *Infant Research and Adult Treatment: Co-constructing Interactions.* Hillsdale, NJ: Analytic Press.

Beland, H. (1992). Die zweifache Wurzel des Gefühls [The twofold root of emotions]. In *Jahrbuch der Psychoanalyse, 29.* Stuttgart-Bad Cannstatt: Frommann-holzboog, pp. 63–91.

Bell, D. (2001). Projective identification. In C. Bronstein (Ed.), *Kleinian Theory: A Contemporary Perspective.* London: Whurr.

Bernardi, R. (2002). The need for true controversies in psychoanalysis. *International Journal of Psychoanalysis, 83*, 851–873.

Bick, E. (1968). The experience of the skin in early object–relations. *International Journal of Psychoanalysis, 49*, 484–486.

Bion, W. R. (1955a). Group dynamics: a review. In M. Klein, P. Heimann and R. Money-Kyrle (Eds.), *New Directions in Psycho-Analysis.* London: Tavistock, pp. 440–477. Also in Bion (1961). *Experiences in Groups and Other Papers,* London: Tavistock, pp. 141–191.

Bion, W. R. (1955b). Language and the schizophrenic. In M. Klein, P. Heimann and R. Money-Kyrle (Eds.), *New Directions in Psycho-Analysis.* London: Tavistock, pp. 220–239.

Bion, W. R. (1956). Development of schizophrenic thought. *International Journal of Psychoanalysis, 37*, 344–346.

Bion, W. R. (1957a). Differentiation of the psychotic from the non-psychotic personalities. *International Journal of Psychoanalysis, 38*(3–4), 266–275.

Bion, W. R. (1957b). On arrogance. In Bion (1967). *Second Thoughts.* New York: Jason Aronson, pp. 86–92.

Bion, W. R. (1958). On hallucination. In Bion (1967). *Second Thoughts.* New York: Jason Aronson, pp. 65–85.

Bion, W. R. (1959). Attacks on linking. *International Journal of Psychoanalysis, 40*, 308–315. Also in Bion (1967). *Second Thoughts.* London: Heinemann, pp. 93–109. Also published in E. B. Spillius (Ed.) (1988). *Melanie Klein Today: Developments in Theory and Practice.* Volume 1: *Mainly Theory.* London: Routledge, pp. 87–101.

Bion, W. R. (1961). *Experiences in Groups.* London: Tavistock.

Bion, W. R. (1962a). *Learning from Experience.* London: Heinemann.

Bion, W. R. (1962b). A theory of thinking. In Bion (1967). *Second Thoughts*. New York: Jason Aronson, pp. 110–119.

Bion, W. R. (1963). *Elements of Psychoanalysis*. London: Heinemann.

Bion, W. R. (1965). *Transformations*. London: Heinemann.

Bion, W. R. (1967). *Second Thoughts*. New York: Jason Aronson.

Bion, W. R. (1970). *Attention and Interpretation*. London: Tavistock.

Bion, W. R. (1977). Unpublished children's hospital presentation. San Francisco, CA.

Birksted-Breen, D. (2003). Time and the après-coup. *International Journal of Psychoanalysis*, *84*, 1501–1515.

Blechner, M. (1994). Projective identification, countertransference, and the 'Maybe-me'. *Contemporary Psychoanalysis*, *30*, 619–630.

Bleger, J. (1967a). Psicoanálisis del encuadre psicoanalítico [Psychoanalysis of the psychoanalytic setting]. *Revista de Psicoanálisis*, *24*, 241–258.

Bleger, J. (1967b). *Simbiosis y ambigüedad* [Symbiosis and Ambiguity]. Buenos Aires: Paidós.

Bollas, C. (1987). *The Shadow of the Object: Psychoanalysis of the Unthought Known*. London: Free Association Books.

Bonnard, A. (1961). Über pathologische Funktionsweisen aus der Vorstufe des Körper-Ichs [On pathological functioning of the precursor of the body-ego psychology]. *Psyche: Zeitschrift für Psychoanalyse und ihre Anwendungen*, *15*, 274–297.

Boris, H. (1988). Torment of the object: a contribution to the study of bulimia. In H. J. Schwartz (Ed.), *Bulimia: Psychoanalytic Treatment and Theory*. Madison, CT: International Universities Press, pp. 89–110. Reprinted in Boris (1994). *Sleights of Mind: One and Multiples of One*. Northvale, NJ: Jason Aronson, pp. 187–205.

Boris, H. (1993). *Passions of the Mind: Unheard Melodies – A Third Principle of Mental Functioning*. New York: New York University Press.

Boris, H. (1994a). *Envy*. Northvale, NJ: Jason Aronson.

Boris, H. (1994b). *Sleights of Mind: One and Multiples of One*. Northvale, NJ: Jason Aronson.

Boyer, L. B. (1978). Countertransference experiences with severely regressed patients. *Contemporary Psychoanalysis*, *14*, 48–71.

Boyer, L. B. (1986). Technical aspects of treating the regressed patient. *Contemporary Psychoanalysis*, *22*, 25–44.

Boyer, L. B. (1989). Countertransference and technique in working with the regressed patient: further remarks. *International Journal of Psychoanalysis*, *70*, 701–714.

Boyer, L. B. (1990a). Countertransference and technique. In L. B. Boyer and P. Giovacchini (Eds.), *Master Clinicians on Treating the Regressed Patient*. Northvale, NJ: Jason Aronson, pp. 303–324.

Boyer, L. B. (1990b). Psychoanalytic intervention in treating the regressed patient. In L. B. Boyer and P. Giovacchini (Eds.), *Master Clinicians on Treating the Regressed Patient*. Northvale, NJ: Jason Aronson, pp. 1–32.

Brenman-Pick, I. (1985). Working through in the counter-transference. *International Journal of Psychoanalysis, 66*, 157–166.

Brierley, M. (1945). Further notes on the implications of psycho-analysis: metapsychology and personology. *International Journal of Psychoanalysis, 26*, 89–114.

Brierley, M. (1947). Notes on psycho-analysis and integrative living. *International Journal of Psychoanalysis, 28*, 57–105.

Britton, R. (1998a). *Belief and Imagination: Explorations in Psychoanalysis*. London: Routledge.

Britton, R. (1998b). Introduction. In Britton, *Belief and Imagination: Explorations in Psychoanalysis*. London: Routledge, pp. 1–7.

Brodey, W. (1965). On the dynamics of narcissism. I: Externalization and early ego development. *Psychoanalytic Study of the Child, 20*, 165–193.

Brunet, L. and Casoni, D. (1996). A review of the concepts of symbolization and projective identification in regards [*sic*] to the patient's use of the analyst. *Canadian Journal of Psychoanalysis, 4*, 109–127.

Brunet, L. and Casoni, D. (2001). A necessary illusion: projective identification and containing function. *Canadian Journal of Psychoanalysis, 9*(2), 137–163.

Burke, W. and Tansey, M. (1985). Projective identification and countertransference turmoil: disruptions in the empathic process. *Contemporary Psychoanalysis, 21*, 372–402.

Canestri, J. (1989). *La Babel de l'inconscient: Langue maternelle, mangues étrangères et psychanalyse*. Paris: Presses Universitaires de France (PUF) [translated 1993 as *Babel of the Unconscious: Mother Tongue and Foreign Languages in the Psychoanalytic Dimension*. Madison, CT: International Universities Press].

Canestri, J. (2002). Projective identification: the fate of the concept in Italy and Spain. *Psychoanalysis in Europe, Bulletin 56*, 130–139.

Caper, R. (1988). *Immaterial Facts*. New York: Jason Aronson.

Caper, R. (1999). *A Mind of One's Own*. London: Routledge.

Carloni, G. (1983). Con Melanie Klein e Anna Freud. *Rivista Psicoanalisis, 29*, 429–434.

Carpy, D. V. (1989). Tolerating the countertransference: a mutative process. *International Journal of Psychoanalysis, 70*, 287–294.

Carveth, D. (1992). Dead end kids: projective identification and sacrifice in *Orphans* [a play and film]. *International Review of Psychoanalysis, 19*, 217–227.

Casaula, E., Coloma, J., Colzani, F. and Jordan, J. F. (1994). La bilógica de la interpretación. *Revista Chilena de Psicoanálisis*.

Coloma, J. (2002). Bilógica, identificación proyectiva y pensamiento onírico [Biological relevance, projective identification and dream thought]. *Gradiva, 3*(1), 9–18.

Corti, A. (1983). Melanie Klein e Anna Freud: riunione commemorativa nell'ambito del Convegno a Seminari multipli, Bologna 22.5.83. *Rivista di Psicoanalisi*, *29*(4).

Crisp, P. (1986). Projective identification: an attempt at clarification. *Journal of the Melanie Klein Society*, *4*(1), 47–76.

Cycon, R. (1995). *Vorwort zur Gesamtausgabe der Werke von Melanie Klein* [Foreword to the Complete Works of Melanie Klein]. Stuttgart: Frommann-holzboog.

Danckwardt, J. F. (2001). Die Hilflosigkeit des Unbewussten und die Prozessidentifizierungen als Arbeitsebene bei schweren Konflikten. In W. Bohlheber and S. Drews (Eds.), *Die Gegenwart der Psychoanalyse – die Psychoanalyse der Gegenwart* [The Presence of Psychoanalysis – Psychoanalysis of the Present]. Stuttgart: Klett-Cotta, pp. 409–423.

Dantlgraber, J. (1982). Bemerkungen zur subjektiven Indikation für Psychoanalyse [Comments on the subjective indication for psychoanalysis]. *Psyche: Zeitschrift für Psychoanalyse und ihre Anwendungen*, *36*, 193–225.

de M'Uzan, M. (1994). *La Bouche de l'inconscient* [The Mouth of the Unconscious]. Paris: Gallimard.

de Saussure, R. (1929). Les fixations homosexuelles chez les femmes névrosées [Homosexual fixations in neurotic women]. *Revue Française de Psychanalyse*, *3*, 50–91.

Diatkine, G. (1997). *Jacques Lacan*. Paris: Presses Universitaires de France (PUF).

Di Chiara, G. (1983). La fiaba della mano verde o dell'identificazione proiettiva [The tale of the green hand or projective identification]. *Rivista di Psicoanalisi*, *29*(4), 459–475.

Di Chiara, G. and Flegenheimer, F. (1985). Identificazione proiettiva, Nota Storico-Critica. *Rivista di Psicoanalisi*, *31*(2), 233–243.

Dornes, M. (1993). Psychoanalyse und Kleinkindforschung [Psychoanalysis and infant research]. *Psyche: Zeitschrift für Psychoanalyse und ihre Anwendungen* *12*, 1116–1152.

Dorpat, T. (1983). Review of 'Splitting and Projective Identification', by J. Grotstein. *International Journal of Psychoanalysis*, *64*, 116–119.

Duparc, F. (2001). The countertransference scene in France. *International Journal of Psychoanalysis*, *81*, 151–169.

Eagle, M. N. (2000). A critical evaluation of current conceptions of transference and countertransference. *Psychoanalytic Psychology*, *17*, 24–37.

Eaton, J. (2005). The obstructive object. *Psychoanalytic Review*, *92*, 355–372.

Eiguer, A. (1989). *Le Pervers narcissique et son complice* [The Narcissistic Pervert and his Accomplice]. Paris: Dunod.

Erikson, E. H. (1959). *Identity and the Life Cycle*. New York: International Universities Press.

Eskelinen de Folch, T. (1987). The obstacles to the analytic cure: comments on 'Analysis Terminable and Interminable'. In J. Sandler (Ed.), *On Freud's*

371

'*Analysis Terminable and Interminable*'. New Haven, CT: Yale University Press, pp. 111–126.

Etchegoyen, R. H. (1986). *The Fundamentals of Psychoanalytic Technique.* London: Karnac.

Fain, M. (1984). De l'identification hystérique et de l'identification projective [On hysterical identification and projective identification]. *Revue Française de Psychanalyse, 48,* 784.

Fairbairn, W. R. D. (1941). A revised psychopathology of the psychoses and neuroses. *International Journal of Psychoanalysis, 22,* 250–279.

Fairbairn, W. R. D. (1944). Endopsychic structure considered in terms of object-relationships. *International Journal of Psychoanalysis, 27,* 70–93.

Fairbairn, W. R. D. (1946). Object-relationships and dynamic structure. *International Journal of Psychoanalysis, 27,* 30–37.

Fairbairn, W. R. D. (1952). *Psychoanalytic Studies of the Personality.* London: Tavistock Also published as Fairbairn (1954). *An Object-Relations Theory of the Personality.* New York: Basic Books.

Fairbairn, W. R. D. (1958). On the nature and aims of psychoanalytical treatment. *International Journal of Psychoanalysis, 39,* 374–385.

Feinsilver, D. (1983). Reality, transitional relatedness and containment in the borderline. *Contemporary Psychoanalysis, 19,* 537–569.

Feldman, M. (1992). Splitting and projective identification. In R. Anderson (Ed.), *Clinical Lectures on Klein and Bion.* London: Routledge, pp. 74–88.

Feldman, M. (1994). Projective identification in phantasy and enactment. *Psychoanalytic Inquiry, 14,* 423–440.

Feldman, M. (1997). Projective identification: the analyst's involvement. *International Journal of Psycho-Analysis, 78,* 227–241.

Ferenczi, S. (1909). Introjection and transference. In Ferenczi, *Contributions to Psychoanalysis.* Boston, MA: R. G. Badger.

Ferenczi, S. (1930). Notes and fragments, II. In Ferenczi (1994). *Final Contributions to the Problems and Methods of Psycho-Analysis.* London: Karnac, pp. 219–231.

Ferro, A. (1987). Il mondo alla rovescia: l'inversione di flusso delle identificazioni proiettive [The world turned upside down: inversion of the flow of projective identification]. *Rivista di Psicoanalisi, 33*(1), 59–77.

Figueroa, J. (1997). Resumen de los grupos de discusión del material teórico. *Revista Chilena de Psicoanalisis, 14*(2), 66–67.

Finell, J. S. (1986). The merits and problems with the concept of projective identification. *Psychoanalytic Review, 73,* 103–128.

Fonagy, P. (1991). Thinking about thinking: some clinical and theoretical considerations in the treatment of a borderline patient. *International Journal of Psycho-Analysis, 72,* 1–18.

Frank, C. (2001). Vorlesungsreihe zur projektiven Identifizierung, bisher unveröffentlichtes [Lectures about projective identification]. Unpublished manuscript.

Frank, C. (2002). Identified with the bombing and dangerous Hitler-father (M. Klein, 1945, p. 377) Zu Melanie Kleins zeitgenössischer Bezugnahme auf Hitler in Ihren Behandlungen. Unpublished manuscript.

Freud, A. (1936). *The Ego and the Mechanisms of Defence.* London: Hogarth Press (1987).

Freud, A. (1967). About losing and being lost. *Psychoanalytic Study of the Child, 8,* 9–19.

Freud, S. (1898). Die infantile Cerebrallähmung. *Jahrbuch Leist. Neurol, 1,* 613 [translated 1968 as *Infantile Cerebral Paralysis.* Coral Gables, FL: University of Miami Press].

Freud, S. (1900). *The Interpretation of Dreams.* In J. Strachey (Ed.), *The Standard Edition of the Complete Psychological Works of Sigmund Freud.* London: Hogarth Press: *S.E. 4–5.*

Freud, S. (1910). The future prospects of psycho-analytic therapy. In *S.E. 9,* pp. 144–145.

Freud, S. (1911). Psycho-analytic notes on an autobiographical account of a case of paranoia (Dementia Paranoides). *S.E.* 12: 1–79.

Freud, S. (1914). Remembering, repeating, and working through. In *S.E. 12,* pp. 145–156.

Freud, S. (1915a). Instincts and their vicissitudes. In *S.E. 14,* pp. 109–140.

Freud, S. (1915b). The unconscious. In *S.E. 14,* pp. 159–215.

Freud, S. (1917). Mourning and melancholia. In *S.E. 14,* pp. 237–259.

Freud, S. (1918). From the history of an infantile neurosis. In *S.E. 17,* pp. 3–122.

Freud, S. (1920). Beyond the pleasure principle. In *S.E. 18,* pp. 3–64.

Freud, S. (1921). Group psychology and the analysis of the ego. In *S.E. 18,* pp. 67–143.

Freud, S. (1923). The Ego and the Id. In *S.E. 19,* pp. 12–66.

Freud, S. (1933). *New Introductory Lectures on Psychoanalysis.* In *S.E. 22,* pp. 1–182.

Frosch, J. P. (1990). Review of Michael Tansey and Walter Burke, 'Understanding Countertransference: From Projective Identification to Empathy', 1989, Hillsdale, New Jersey: The Analytic Press. *International Journal of Psychoanalysis, 71,* 351–354.

Gabbard, G. (1995). Countertransference: the emerging common ground. *International Journal of Psychoanalysis, 76,* 475–485.

Gammill, J. (1989). Some personal reflections on Melanie Klein. *Melanie Klein and Object Relations, 7*(2), 1–15.

Garfinkle, E. (2005). Towards clarity in the concept of projective identification: a review and a proposal (Part 1). Defining projective identification as an intrapsychic unconscious phantasy. *Canadian Journal of Psychoanalysis, 13,* 202–229.

Gibeault, A. (2000a). De la projection et de l'identification projective [Projection and projective identification]. *Revue Française de Psychanalyse, 64,* 723–742.

Gibeault, A. (2000b). In response to Otto F. Kernberg's 'Psychoanalysis, psychoanalytic psychotherapy and supportive psychotherapy: contemporary controversies'. *International Journal of Psychoanalysis, 81*, 379–383.

Gilhooley, D. (1998). Projection and projective identification in a three-year-old boy. *Psychoanalytic Review, 92*, 355–372.

Glover, E. (1931). The therapeutic effect of inexact interpretation. *International Journal of Psychoanalysis, 12*, 397–411.

Goldman, H. A. (1988). Paradise destroyed, the crime of being born: a psycho-analytic study of the experience of evil. *Contemporary Psychoanalysis, 24*, 420–450.

Green, A. (1980). La mère morte. In Green (1983). *Narcissisme de vie, narcissisme de mort*. Paris: Minuit [translated 1986 as The dead mother. In Green, *On Private Madness*. London: Hogarth, reprinted 1997 by Karnac, pp. 142–173].

Green, A. (1990). *La Folie privée*. Paris: Gallimard.

Greenson, R. R. (1954). The struggle against identification. *Journal of American Psychoanalytic Association, 2*, 200–217.

Grinberg, L. (1958). As pectos mágicos en la transferencia y en la contratrans-ferencia. *Revista de Psicoanálisis, 15*, 15–26.

Grinberg, L. (1962). On a specific aspect of countertransference due to the patient's projective identification. *International Journal of Psychoanalysis, 43*, 436–440.

Grinberg, L. (1979). Countertransference and projective counteridentification. In L. Epstein and A. H. Feiner (Eds.), *Countertransference*. New York: Jason Aronson, pp. 169–191.

Grinberg, L. (1982). Los afectos en la contratransferencia: Más allá de la contra-identificación proyectiva. *XIV Congreso de FEPAL. Actas*, 258–259.

Grinberg, L. (1985). *Teoría de la Identificación* [Identification Theory]. Madrid: Tecnipublicaciones.

Grinberg, L., Sor, D. and de Bianchedi, E. T. (1977). *Introduction to the Work of Bion*. New York: Jason Aronson.

Grotstein, J. S. (1981). *Splitting and Projective Identification*. New York: Jason Aronson.

Grotstein, J. S. (1982). Newer perspectives in object relations theory. *Contemporary Psychoanalysis, 18*, 43–91.

Grotstein, J. S. (1994a). Projective identification and countertransference: a brief commentary on their relationship. *Contemporary Psychoanalysis, 30*, 578–592.

Grotstein, J. S. (1994b). Projective identification re-appraised. Part 1: Projective identification, introjective identification, the transference/countertransfer-ence neurosis/psychosis, and their consummate expression in the crucifixion, the Pietà, and 'therapeutic exorcism'. *Contemporary Psychoanalysis, 30*, 708–746.

Grotstein, J. S. (1995). Projective identification re-appraised. Part II: The countertransference complex. *Contemporary Psychoanalysis*, *31*, 479–511.

Grotstein, J. S. (1997). Integrating one-person and two-person psychologies: autochthony and alterity in counterpoint. *Psychoanalytic Quarterly*, *66*, 403–430.

Grotstein, J. S. (2001). A rationale for the psychoanalytically informed psycho-therapy of schizophrenia and other psychoses: towards the concept of 'reha-bilitative psychoanalysis'. In P. Williams (Ed.), *A Language for Psychosis*. London: Whurr.

Grotstein, J. S. (2002). Projective identification and its relationship to infant development. In S. Alhanati (Ed.), *Primitive Mental States*, Volume 2: *Psychobiological and Psychoanalytic Perspectives on Early Transference and Personality Development*. London: Karnac, pp. 67–98.

Grotstein, J. S. (2005). 'Projective *trans*identification': an extension of the concept of projective identification. *International Journal of Psychoanalysis*, *86*, 1051–1069.

Guignard, F. (1984). Identification hystérique et identification projective [Hysterical identification and projective identification]. *Revue Française de Psychanalyse*, *48*, 515–527.

Guignard, F. (1996). Un trouble de la pensée sur la métapsychologie [Disturbance of thought on metapsychology]. *Revue Française de Psychanalyse*, *60*, 1551–1571.

Guignard, F. (1997). *Épître à l'objet* [Epistle to the Object]. Paris: Presses Universitaires de France (PUF).

Gutwinski-Jeggle, J. (1995). Zum Verhältnis von Gegenübertragung und projek-tiver Identifizierung [On the relationship between counter-transference and projective identification]. *Luzifer-Amor: Zeitschrift zur Geschichte der Psychoanalyse* [*Journal of the History of Psychoanalysis*], *15*, 61–83.

Haber, M. and Godfrind-Haber, J. (2002). L'expérience agie partagée [The shared enacted experience]. *Revue Française de Psychanalyse*, *66*, 1417–1460.

Hamilton, N. G. (1986). Positive projective identification. *International Journal of Psychoanalysis*, *67*, 489–496.

Hamilton, N. G. (1990). The containing function and the analyst's projective identification. *International Journal of Psychoanalysis*, *71*, 445–453.

Heidegger, M. (1927). *Being and Time*, translated by Macquarrie, J. and Robinson, E. Oxford: Blackwell (1962).

Heimann, P. (1942). A contribution to the problem of sublimation and its rela-tion to the processes of internalization. *International Journal of Psychoanalysis*, *23*, 8–17.

Heimann, P. (1950). On countertransference. *International Journal of Psycho-Analysis*, *31*, 81–84.

Heimann, P. (1966). Comment on Dr Kernberg's paper 'Structural derivatives of object relationships'. *International Journal of Psycho-Analysis*, *47*, 254–260. Also published in M. Tonnesmann (Ed.) (1989). *About Children and*

Children-No-Longer: Collected Papers of Paula Heimann, 1942–80. London: Routledge, pp. 218–230.

Heimann, P. (1969). Postscript to 'Dynamics of transference interpretation' (1955/6). In M. Tonnesmann (Ed.) (1989). *About Children and Children-No-Longer: Collected Papers of Paula Heimann, 1942–80*. London: Routledge, pp. 252–261.

Herrera, E. (2000). Identificación proyectiva: el desarrollo de un concepto [Projective identification: development of a concept]. *Revista Chilena de Psicoanalisis*, *17*(1), 32–41.

Hinshelwood, R. D. (1991). Entry on 'Projective identification'. In Hinshelwood, *A Dictionary of Kleinian Thought*, 2nd edn. London: Free Association Books, pp. 179–208.

Hinshelwood, R. D. (1999). Countertransference. *International Journal of Psychoanalysis*, *80*, 797–818.

Hinshelwood, R. D. (2000). *Dictionnaire de la pensée kleinienne* [Dictionary of Kleinian Thought]. Paris: Presses Universitaires de France (PUF).

Hinz, H. (1989). Projektive Identifizierung und psychoanalytischer Dialog [Projective identification and psychoanalytical dialogue]. *Psyche: Zeitschrift für Psychoanalyse und ihre Anwendungen*, *43*, 609–631.

Hinz, H. (2002a). Projective identification: the fate of the concept in Germany. *Psychoanalysis in Europe, Bulletin 56*, 118–129.

Hinz, H. (2002b). Wer nicht verwickelt wird, spielt keine Rolle. Zu Money-Kyrle: 'Normale Gegenübertragung und mögliche Abweichungen [Who is not involved does not matter. To Money-Kyrle: 'Normal countertransference and possible deviations']. In C. Frank, L. Hermanns and H. Hinz (Eds.), *Jahrbuch der Psychoanalyse 44*. Stuttgart-Bad Cannstat: Frommann-holzboog, pp. 197–223.

Hoffman, I. Z. (1983). The patient as interpreter of the analyst's experience. *Contemporary Psychoanalysis*, *19*, 389–422.

Isaacs, S. (1948). Un caso de ansiedad psicótica aguda en un niño de 4 años [An acute psychotic anxiety occurring in a boy of four years, originally published in English in 1938]. *Revista de Psicoanálisis*, *6*, 433–483.

Isaacs, S. (1949). Naturaleza y función de la fantasía [The nature and function of phantasy, originally published in English in 1943]. *Revista de Psicoanálisis*, *7*, 555–609.

Isaacs, S. (1952). The nature and function of phantasy. In M. Klein, P. Heimann, S. Isaacs and J. Riviere (Eds.), *Developments in Psychoanalysis*. London: Hogarth Press, pp. 68–121.

Issacharoff, A. and Hunt, W. (1994). Transference and projective identification. *Contemporary Psychoanalysis*, *30*, 593–603.

Jackson, M. and Williams, P. (1994). *Unimaginable Storms: A Search for Meaning in Psychosis*. London: Karnac.

Jacobson, E. (1954). Contribution to the metapsychology of psychotic identifications. *Journal of the American Psychoanalytical Association*, 2, 239–262.

Jacobson, E. (1964). *The Self and the Object World*. New York: International Universities Press.

Jacobson, E. (1967). *Psychotic Conflict and Reality*. New York: International Universities Press.

Jaffe, D. (1968). The mechanism of projection: its dual role in object relations. *International Journal of Psychoanalysis*, 49, 662–677.

Jiménez, J. P. (1992). La contribución del analista en los procesos de identificación proyectiva [The contribution of the analyst to processes of projective identification]. *Revista Chilena de Psicoanalisis*, 9(2), 54–66.

Jiménez, J. P. (1995). Sobre identificatión proyectiva. *Revista de Psicoanálisis de Madrid*, 5, 111–123.

Jordan, J. F. (2005). External reality/internal reality: a real dichotomy? In S. Lewkowicz and S. Flechner (Eds.), *Truth, Reality, and the Psychoanalyst: Latin American Contributions to Psychoanalysis*. London: IPA International Psychoanalysis Library.

Joseph, B. (1961). Über einige Persönlichkeitsmerkmale des Psychopathen [Some characteristics of the psychopathic personality]. *Psyche: Zeitschrift für Psychoanalyse und ihre Anwendungen*, 15, 132–141.

Joseph, B. (1978). Different types of anxiety and their handling in the analytic situation. In M. Feldman and E. Spillius (Eds.) (1989). *Psychic Equilibrium and Psychic Change: Selected Papers of Betty Joseph*. London: Routledge, pp. 105–114.

Joseph, B. (1987). Projective identification: some clinical aspects. In J. Sandler (Ed.), *Projection, Identification, Projective Identification*. London: Karnac, pp. 65–76. Also published in E. Spillius (Ed.) (1988). *Melanie Klein Today: Developments in Theory and Practice*. Volume 1: *Mainly Theory*. London: Routledge, pp. 138–150. Also published in M. Feldman and E. Spillius (Eds.) (1989). *Psychic Equilibrium and Psychic Change: Selected Papers of Betty Joseph*. London: Routledge, pp. 169–180.

Joseph, B. (1988). Object relations in clinical practice. *Psychoanalytic Quarterly*, 57, 626–642. Also published in M. Feldman and E. Spillius (Eds.) (1989). *Psychic Equilibrium and Psychic Change: Selected Papers of Betty Joseph*. London: Routledge, pp. 203–214.

Joseph, B. (1989a). Psychic change and the psychoanalytic process. In M. Feldman and E. B. Spillius (Eds.), *Psychic Equilibrium and Psychic Change: Selected Papers of Betty Joseph*. London: Routledge, pp. 192–202.

Joseph, B. (1989b). *Psychic Equilibrium and Psychic Change: Selected Papers of Betty Joseph*, edited by M. Feldman and E. B. Spillius. London: Routledge.

Joseph, B. (2001). Zur Übertragungsliebe: Aktuelle Überlegungen [About transference-love: recent reflections]. In *Freud heute: Wendepunkte und*

Streitfragen, Band 3: *Über Freuds, Bemerkungen über die Übertragungsliebe* [Freud Today: Turning Points and Controversies, Volume 3: On Freud's 'Observations on Transference-Love']. Stuttgart-Bad Cannstatt: Frommann-holzboog, pp. 129–148.

Karlsson, R. (2004). Collusion as interactive resistances and possible stepping-stones out of impasses. *Psychoanalytic Psychology*, *21*, 567–579.

Kennedy, R. (1993). *Freedom to Relate*. London: Free Association Books.

Kernberg, O. F. (1968). The treatment of patients with borderline personality organization. *International Journal of Psychoanalysis*, *49*, 600–619.

Kernberg, O. F. (1975). *Borderline Conditions and Pathological Narcissism*. New York: Jason Aronson.

Kernberg, O. F. (1976). Normal and pathological development. In Kernberg, *Object-Relations Theory and Clinical Psychoanalysis*. New York: Jason Aronson.

Kernberg, O. F. (1980). *Internal World and External Reality*. New York: Jason Aronson.

Kernberg, O. F. (1984). *Severe Personality Disorders: Psychotherapeutic Strategies*. New Haven, CT: Yale University Press.

Kernberg, O. F. (1986). Identification and its vicissitudes as observed in psychosis. *International Journal of Psycho-Analysis*, *67*, 147–158.

Kernberg, O. F. (1987). Projective identification: developmental and clinical aspects. In J. Sandler (Ed.), *Projection, Identification, Projective Identification*. Madison, CT: International Universities Press, pp. 93–115. Also published in 1988, London: Karnac. Also published in 1987 in *Journal of the American Psychoanalytic Association*, *35*, 795–819.

Kernberg, O. F. (1989). *Psychodynamic Psychotherapy of Borderline Patients*. New York: Basic Books.

Kernberg, O. F. (1992). *Aggression in Personality Disorders and Perversions*. New Haven, CT: Yale University Press.

King, P. (1974). On a patient's unconscious need to have 'bad parents'. In King, *Time Present and Time Past: Selected Papers of Pearl King*. London: Karnac.

King, P. (1978). Affective response of the analyst to the patient's communications. *International Journal of Psychoanalysis*, *59*, 329–334.

King, P. (2004). What has happened to psychoanalysis in the British Society? In A. Casement (Ed.), *Who Owns Psychoanalysis?* London: Karnac.

King, P. and Steiner, R. (1991). *The Freud-Klein Controversies: 1941–45*. London: Routledge.

Klein, M.

Note. In 1975 Klein's writings were brought together as *The Writings of Melanie Klein*, divided into four volumes: Volume 1, (1975) *Love, Guilt and Reparation and Other Works, 1921–1945*; Volume 2, (1975) (Originally published in 1932) *The Psycho-Analysis of Children*; Volume 3, (1975) *Envy and Gratitude and Other Works, 1946–1963*; Volume 4, (1980) *Narrative of a Child Analysis*. All 4 volumes were published by The Hogarth Press and The Institute of Psycho–Analysis, London. The Klein References in the present book are all to be found in Volumes 1, 2, and 3. Because the general contents of Vols 1, 2, and 3 are listed in this note, the specific content of each Klein reference will be noted below in the title of the reference, but the general content of the volume cited can be seen by checking its description in this note.

Klein, M. (1921) The development of a child. In *Writings* (1975), Volume 1, pp. 1–53.

Klein, M. (1928) Early stages of the Oedipus conflict. *International Journal of Psycho-Analysis, 9*, 167–180. Also in Klein, M. *Writings* (1975) Vol. 1, pp. 186–198.

Klein, M. (1932) *The Psycho-Analysis of Children, Writings* (1975) Vol. 2.

Klein, M. (1933) The early development of conscience in the child. In *Writings*, (1975) Vol. 1, pp. 248–257.

Klein, M. (1935) A contribution to the psychogenesis of manic-depressive states. In *Writings* (1975) Vol. 1, pp. 262–289.

Klein, M. (1940) Mourning and its relation to manic-depressive states. In *Writings* (1975) Vol. 1, pp. 344–369.

Klein, M. (1943). Primeros estadios del conflicto de Edipo y de la formación del superyó [Early stages of the Oedipus conflict, originally published in English in 1928]. *Revista de Psicoanálisis, 1*(1), 83–110.

Klein, M. (1945) The Oedipus complex in the light of early anxieties. *Writings*, (1975) Vol. 1, 370–419.

Klein, M. (1946) Notes on some schizoid mechanisms. *International Journal of Psycho-Analysis, 27*: 99–110. Also published in 1952a in Klein, M. *Writings*, (1975) Vol. 3, 1–24.

Klein, M. (1947a). Contribución a la psicogénesis de los estados maníaco-depresivos [A contribution to the psychogenesis of manic-depressive states, originally published in English in 1935]. *Revista de Psicoanálisis, 4*(3), 508–539.

Klein, M. (1947b). El papel de la escuela en el desarrollo libidinoso del niño [The role of the school in the libidinal development of the child, originally published in English in 1923]. *Revista de Psicoanálisis, 5*(2), 480–500.

Klein, M. (1948a) A contribution to the theory of anxiety and guilt, *International Journal of Psycho-Analysis, 29*, 114–123. Also in *Writings* (1975) Vol. 3, as On the theory of anxiety and guilt, pp. 25–43.

Klein, M. (1948b). Notas sobre algunos mecanismos esquizoides [Notes on some schizoid mechanisms, originally published in English in 1946]. *Revista de Psicoanálisis, 6*(1), 82–113.

Klein, M. (1949). El duelo y su relación con los estados maníaco-depresivos [Mourning and its relation to manic-depressive states, originally published in English in 1940]. *Revista de Psicoanálisis, 7*(3), 415–449.

Klein, M. (1952a) Notes on some schizoid mechanisms. In Klein, M. Writings, (1975) Vol. 3, pp. 1–24. (Already noted above under Klein, M. 1946.)

Klein, M. (1952b) The origins of transference. In Klein, M. *Writings*, (1975) Vol. 3, pp. 48–56.

Klein, M. (1952c) Theoretische Betrachtungen Uber das Gefuhlsleben des Sauglings (Some theorectical conclusions regarding the life of the infant. In R. Cycon and H. Erb (Eds*.) Gesammelte schriften Melanie Klein 1995–2002).* Volume III*: Das Seelenleben des Kleinkindes.* (The Mental Life of the Infant.) Stuttgart: Klett-Cotta.

Klein, M. (1955) On identification. In Klein, M. *Writings*, (1975) Vol. 3, pp. 141–175.

Klein, M,. (1957) Envy and Gratitude. In Klein, M. Writings,(1975) Vol. 3, pp. 176–235.

Klein, M., Heimann, P., Isaacs, S. and Riviere, J. (1952) Edited by Joan Riviere. *Developments in Psycho-Analysis,* London: The Hogarth Press and The Institute of Psychoanalysis.

Klüwer, R. (1995). Agieren und Mitagieren – zehn Jahre später [Acting and co-acting – ten years later]. *Zeitschrift für Psychoanalytische Theorie und Praxis, 10,* 45–70.

Knight, R. P. (1940). Introjection, projection and identification. *Psychoanalytic Quarterly, 9,* 334–341.

Kohon, G. (1986). *The British School of Psychoanalysis: The Independent Tradition.* London: Free Association Books.

Krafft-Ebing, R. von (1886). *Psychopathia sexualis: Eine klinisch-forensische Studie* [Aberrations of Sexual Life]. Stuttgart: Ferdinand Enke.

La Farge, L. (1989). Emptiness as defense in severe regressed states. *Journal of the American Psychoanalytic Association, 37,* 965–995.

Langs, R. (1975). Therapeutic misalliances. *International Journal of Psychoanalysis, 45,* 77–105.

Langs, R. (1976). *The Therapeutic Interaction.* New York: Jason Aronson.

Langs, R. (1978a). The adaptational-interactional dimension of counter-transference. *Contemporary Psychoanalysis, 14,* 502–533.

Langs, R. (1978b). Some communicative properties of the bipersonal field. *International Journal of Psychoanalytic Psychotherapy, 7,* 89–161. Also published in Grotstein, J. (Ed.) (1981). *Do I Dare Disturb the Universe: A Memorial to Wilfred R. Bion.* Beverly Hills, CA: Caesura Press, pp. 441–487.

Langs, R. (1978c). *Technique in Transition.* New York: Jason Aronson.

Langs, R. (1979). Interventions in the bipersonal field. *Contemporary Psychoanalysis, 15,* 1–54.

Laplanche, J. (1992). Faut-il brûler Melanie Klein? In Laplanche, *La Révolution Copernicienne inachevée* [The Unfinished Copernican Revolution]. Paris: Aubier, pp. 213–226.

Laplanche, J. and Pontalis, J.-B. (1973). *The Language of Psychoanalysis.* London: Hogarth Press.

Liberman, D. (1956). Identificación proyectiva y conflicto matrimonial [Projective identification and matrimonial conflict]. *Revista de Psicoanálisis*, *13*, 1–20.

Lichtenstein, H. (1961). Identity and sexuality: a study of their interrelationship in man. *Journal of the American Psychoanalytic Association*, *9*, 179–260.

Lichtman, A. (1979). Consideraciones acerca de la transferencia y los mecanismos psicóticos en Freud y Melanie Klein. *Revista de Psicoanálisis*, *1*, 55–68.

Little, M. (1966). Transference in borderline states. *International Journal of Psychoanalysis*, *47*, 476–485.

Loch, W. (1962). Anmerkungen zur Pathogenese und Metapsychologie einer schizophrenen Psychose [Remarks on the pathogenesis and metapsychology of a schizophrenic psychosis]. *Psyche: Zeitschrift für Psychoanalyse und ihre Anwendungen*, *15*, 684–720.

Loch, W. (1965). *Voraussetzungen, Mechanismen und Grenzen des psychoanalytischen Prozesses* [Preconditions, Mechanisms and Limits of the Psychoanalytical Process]. Stuttgart: Klett-Cotta.

Loch, W. (2001). *Mit Freud über Freud hinaus: Ausgewählte Vorlesungen zur Psychoanalyse* [With Freud and Beyond Freud: Selected Lectures on Psychoanalysis], edited by J. Dantlgraber and W. Damson. Tübingen: Diskord.

Loewald, H. W. (1960). On the therapeutic action of psycho-analysis. *International Journal of Psychoanalysis*, *41*, 16–33.

Mahler, M. S. (1952). On child psychosis and schizophrenia: autistic and symbiotic infantile psychoses. *Psychoanalytic Study of the Child*, *7*, 286–305.

Mahler, M. S. (1967). On human symbiosis and the vicissitudes of individuation. *Journal of the American Psychoanalytical Association*, *15*(4), 740–763.

Malin, A. and Grotstein, J. S. (1966). Projective identification in the therapeutic process. *International Journal of Psychoanalysis*, *47*, 26–31.

Mancia, M. (1996). Imitazione, rappresentazione, identificazione: loro ruolo nello sviluppo e nel transfert [Imitation, representation, identification: their role in the development and transfer]. *Rivista di Psicoanalisi*, *42*(2), 225–247.

Manfredi Turilazzi, S. (1974). Dalle interpretazioni mutative di Strachey alle interpretazioni delle relazioni tra gli oggetti interni [Strachey's mutative interpretations from interpretations of the relationship between internal objects]. *Rivista di Psicoanalisi*, *20*, 127–143.

Manfredi Turilazzi, S. (1984a). L'Unicorno: saggio sulla fantasia e l'oggetto nel concetto di identificazione proiettiva. *Rivista di Psicoanalisi*, *31*(4), 462–477.

Manfredi Turilazzi, S. (1984b). Sull'identificazione proiettiva: uno studio preliminare. *Letto al Centro Milanese di Psicoanalisi*.

Manzano, J. and Palacio Espasa, F. (1986). *Etude sur la psychose infantile* [Study of Infantile Psychosis]. Lyon: Simed.

Manzano, J., Palacio Espasa, F. and Zilkha, N. (1999). *Les Scénarios narcissiques de la parentalité* [Narcissistic Scenarios of Parenthood]. Paris: Presses Universitaires de France (PUF).

Martindale, B. (2001). New discoveries concerning psychoses and their organizational fate. In P. Williams (Ed.), *A Language for Psychosis*. London: Whurr, pp. 27–36.

Mason, A. (1981). The suffocating superego: psychotic break and claustrophobia. In J. Grotstein (Ed.), *Do I Dare Disturb the Universe?* London: Karnac, pp. 139–166.

Mason, A. (1994). A psychoanalyst looks at a hypnotist: a study of *folie à deux*. *Psychoanalytic Quarterly, 63*, 641–679.

Mason, A. (1997). Quick Otto and slow leopard: the Freud–Fliess relationship. Paper presented to the Fortieth International Psychoanalytic Congress, Barcelona, Spain.

Massidda, G. B. (1999). Shall we ever know the whole truth about projective identification? *International Journal of Psychoanalysis, 80*, 365–367.

Matte-Blanco, I. (1998). *Thinking, Feeling and Being: Clinical Reflections of the Fundamental Antinomy of Human Beings and World*. London: Routledge.

Meissner, W. W. (1980). A note on projective identification. *Journal of the American Psychoanalytic Association, 28*, 43–66.

Meissner, W. W. (1987). Projection and projective identification. In J. Sandler (Ed.), *Projection, Identification, Projective Identification*. Madison, CT: International Universities Press, pp. 27–49.

Melsohn, I. (2002). *A psicanálise em nova chave* [Psychoanalysis in a New Key]. São Paulo: Perspectiva.

Meltzer, D. (1966). The relation of anal masturbation to projective identification. *International Journal of Psychoanalysis, 47*, 335–342.

Meltzer, D. (1967). *The Psycho-Analytical Process*. London: Heinemann.

Meltzer, D. (1968). The introjective basis of polymorphous tendencies in adult sexuality. In *Sexual States of Mind* (pp. 64–73). Strath Tay: Clunie Press.

Meyer, L. (1989). Editorial. *Revista Brasileira de Psicanálise, 23*(3), 364.

Migone, P. (1995). Expressed emotion and projective identification: a bridge between psychiatric and psychoanalytic concepts? *Contemporary Psychoanalysis, 31*, 617–640.

Milton, J., Polmear, C. and Fabricius, J. (2004). *A Short Introduction to Psychoanalysis*. London: Sage.

Mitchell, S. (2000). *Relationality: From Attachment to Intersubjectivity*. Hillsdale, NJ: Analytic Press.

Mitrani, J. (2001). Taking the transference: some technical implications in three papers by Bion. *International Journal of Psychoanalysis, 82*, 1085–1104.

Money-Kyrle, R. (1956). Normal counter-transference and some of its deviations. *International Journal of Psycho-Analysis, 37*, 360–366. Also published in D. Meltzer with E. O'Shaughnessy (Eds.) (1978). *Collected Papers of Roger Money-Kyrle*. Strath Tay: Clunie Press, pp. 330–342.

Money-Kyrle, R. (1965). Megalomania. *American Imago, 22*(1–2), 142–154.

Money-Kyrle, R. (1968). Cognitive development. *International Journal of Psychoanalysis, 49,* 691–698. Also published in D. Meltzer with E. O'Shaughnessy (Eds.) (1978). *Collected Papers of Roger Money-Kyrle.* Strath Tay: Clunie Press, pp. 416–433.

Money-Kyrle, R. (1991). Normale Gegenübertragung und mögliche Abweichungen [Normal countertransference and possible deviations]. In E. B. Spillius (Ed.), *Melanie Klein Heute: Entwicklungen in Theorie und Praxis.* Band 2: *Anwendungen* [Melanie Klein Today: Developments in Theory and Practice. Volume 2: Mainly Practice]. Stuttgart: Klett-Cotta, pp. 29–44.

Muir, R. (1982). The family, the group, transpersonal processes and the individual. *International Review of Psychoanalysis, 9,* 317–326.

Muir, R. (1990). Transpersonal processes: a bridge between object relations and attachment theory in normal and psychopathological development. *British Journal of Medical Psychology, 68,* 243–257.

Nadelson, T. (1976). Victim, victimizer: interaction in the psychotherapy of borderline patients. *International Journal of Psychoanalysis, 50,* 115–129.

Nissim Momigliano, L. (1974). Come si originano le interpretazioni nello psicoanalista [As they originate in the psychoanalyst's interpretations]. *Rivista di Psicoanalisi, 20,* 144–165.

Nissim Momigliano, L. (1984). '. . . Due persone che parlano in una stanza . . .' (Una ricerca sul dialogo analitico) ['. . . Two people talking in a room . . .' (Research on the analytic dialogue). *Rivista di Psicoanalisi, 30*(1), 1–17.

Nissim Momigliano, L. (1991). Il tè nel deserto: ulteriori considerazioni a proposito de 'Lo psicoanalista allo specchio' [The sheltering sky: further considerations on 'The psychoanalyst in the mirror']. *Rivista di Psicoanalisi, 37*(4), 772–819.

Ogden, T. (1974). A psychoanalytic psychotherapy of a patient with cerebral palsy: the relation of aggression to self and body representations. *International Journal of Psychoanalysis, 53,* 419–433.

Ogden, T. (1976). Psychological unevenness in the academically successful student. *International Journal of Psychoanalysis, 55,* 437–448.

Ogden, T. (1978a). A developmental view of identifications resulting from maternal impingements. *International Journal of Psycho-Analytic Psychotherapy, 7,* 486–587.

Ogden, T. (1978b). A reply to Dr Orston's discussion of 'A developmental view of identifications resulting from maternal impingements'. *International Journal of Psycho-Analytic Psychotherapy, 7,* 528–532.

Ogden, T. (1979). On projective identification. *International Journal of Psychoanalysis, 60,* 357–373.

Ogden, T. (1982). *Projective Identification and Psychotherapeutic Technique.* New York: Jason Aronson.

Ogden, T. (1986). *The Matrix of the Mind: Object Relations and the Psychoanalytic Dialogue*. Northvale, NJ: Jason Aronson.

Ogden, T. (1994a). The analytic mind: working with intersubjective clinical facts. *International Journal of Psychoanalysis*, *75*, 3–20.

Ogden, T. (1994b). The concept of interpretative action. *Psychoanalytic Quarterly*, *63*(2), 219–245.

Ogden, T. (1994c). *Subjects of Analysis*. Northvale, NJ: Jason Aronson.

Ogden, T. (2004). The analytic third: implications for psychoanalytic theory and technique. *Psychoanalytic Quarterly*, *73*, 167–195.

Oliveira, C. L. M. V. (2005). *História da psicanálise – São Paulo (1920–1969)* [History of Psychoanalysis – São Paulo (1920–1969)]. São Paulo: Escuta.

Ornston, D. (1978). Projective identification and maternal impingement. *International Journal of Psychoanalytic Psychotherapy*, *7*, 508–528.

O'Shaughnessy, E. (1975). Explanatory notes. In M. Klein (1975). *Envy and Gratitude and Other Works 1947–1963*. London: Hogarth Press, pp. 324–336.

O'Shaughnessy, E. (1992). Enclaves and excursions. *International Journal of Psychoanalysis*, *73*, 603–611.

Pantone, P. J. (1994). Projective identification: affective aspects. *Contemporary Psychoanalysis*, *30*, 604–618.

Parsons, M. (2000). *The Dove that Returns, the Dove that Vanishes: Paradox and Creativity in Psychoanalysis*. London: Routledge.

Pasche, F. (1982). A propos de l'identification projective [About projective identification]. *Revue Française de Psychanalyse*, *46*, 408–411.

Perestrello, M. (1992). *A Psicanálise no Brasil. Encontros: psicanálise*. Rio de Janeiro: Imago.

Pérez-Sánchez, A. (1997). *Análisis terminable: estudio de la terminación del proceso psicoanalítico* [Terminable Analysis: A Study of the Termination of the Psychoanalytic Process]. Valencia, Spain: Promolibro.

Pichon-Rivière, E. (1952). Quelques observations sur le transfert chez des patients psychotiques. *Revue française de psych analyse*, *16*, 252–262.

Pierrakos, M. (2003). *La 'tapeuse' de Lacan: souvenirs d'une sténotypiste fâchée, réflexions d'une psychanalyste navrée*. Paris: L'Harmattan.

Porder, M. (1987). Projective identification: an alternative hypothesis. *Psychoanalytic Quarterly*, *56*, 431–451.

Purcell, S. (2006). The analyst's excitement in the analysis of perversion. *International Journal of Psychoanalysis*, *87*, 105–123.

Quinodoz, D. (1989). Les 'interprétations dans la projection'. *Revue Française de Psychanalyse*, *53*, 103–110 [translated 1994 as 'Interpretations in projection'. *International Journal of Psychoanalysis*, *75*, 755–762].

Quinodoz, D. (2002). *Les Mots qui touchent: une psychanalyste apprend à parler*. Paris: Presses Universitaires de France (PUF) [translated 2003 as *Words that Touch: Psychoanalyst Learns to Speak*. London: Karnac].

Quinodoz, J.-M. (1992). *La Solitude apprivoisée: l'angoisse de séparation en Psychanalyse*. Paris: Presses Universitaires de France (PUF) [translated 1993 as *The Taming of Solitude: Separation Anxiety in Psychoanalysis*. London: Routledge].

Quinodoz, J.-M. (2000). Mélancolie maniaque: quelle issue? [The outcome of manic melancholia]. *Revue Française de Psychanalyse*, *64*, 1825–1835.

Quinodoz, J.-M. (2001). *Les Rêves qui tournent une page* [The Dreams that Turn a Page]. Paris: Presses Universitaires de France (PUF).

Quinodoz, J.-M. (2002a). L'identification projective: qu'en pensent les psychanalystes de langue française? *Bulletin de la Fondation Européene pour la Psychanalyse*, *56*, 148–156. Also published as Projective identification: what do French-speaking psychoanalysts think? *Psychoanalysis in Europe, Bulletin 56*, 139–147.

Quinodoz, J.-M. (2002b). Suisse romande (histoire de la psychanalyse). In A. de Mijolla (Ed.), *Dictionnaire de la psychanalyse* [Dictionary of Psychoanalysis]. Paris: Calmann-Lévy.

Racamier, P. C. (1992). *Le Génie des origines: psychanalyse et psychoses* [The Genius of Origins: Psychoanalysis and Psychoses]. Paris: Payot.

Racker, H. (1953). A contribution to the problem of counter-transference. *International Journal of Psycho-Analysis*, *34*, 313–324.

Racker, H. (1957). The meaning and uses of counter transference. *Psychoanalytic Quarterly*, *26*, 303–357.

Racker, H. (1958a). Classical and present technique in psycho-analysis. In H. Racker (Ed.) (1968). *Transference and Countertransference*. London: Hogarth Press, pp. 23–70.

Racker, H. (1958b). Counterresistance and interpretation. *International Journal of Psycho-Analysis*, *6*, 215–221.

Racker, H. (1968). *Transference and Countertransference*. New York: International Universities Press.

Rayner, E. (1990). *The Independent Mind in British Psychoanalysis*. London: Free Association Books.

Rayner, E. (1992). Matching attunement and the psychoanalytic dialogue. *International Journal of Psychoanalysis*, *73*, 39–54.

Rayner, E. (1995). *Unconscious Logic: An Introduction to Matte Blanco's Bi-logic and its Uses*. London: Routledge.

Ribas, D. (1992). *Un cri obscur: l'énigme des enfants autistes*. Paris: Calmann-Lévy.

Riesenberg Malcolm, R. (1970). El espejo: una fantasia sexual perversa en una mujer, vista como defensa contra un derrumbe psicótico. *Revista Psicoanalisis*, *27*, 793–826. Also published as 'The mirror: a perverse sexual phantasy in a woman seen as a defense against a psychiatric breakdown', in E. Spillius (Ed.) (1988). *Melanie Klein Today*. Volume 2: *Mainly Practice*. London: Routledge, pp. 1115–1137.

Rivière, J. (1949). Contribución al análisis de la reacción tarepéutica negativa [A contribution to the analysis of the negative therapeutic reaction, originally published in English in 1936]. *Revista de Psicoanálisis*, 7, 121–142.

Rivière, J. (Unpublished). Paranoid attitudes seen in everyday life and in analysis. Paper read before the British Psycho-Analytical Society in 1948.

Rodrigué, E. (1966). Relación entre descubrimiento e identificación proyectiva. In Rodrigué, *El contexto del proceso analítico* [The Context of the Analytical Process]. Buenos Aires: Paidós.

Rosenfeld, H. A. (1947). Analysis of a schizophrenic state with depersonalization. In Rosenfeld (1965). *Psychotic States: A Psycho-Analytical Approach.* London: Hogarth Press and Institute of Psycho-Analysis, pp. 13–33.

Rosenfeld, H. A. (1949). Remarks on the relation of male homosexuality to paranoia, paranoid anxiety and narcissism. In Rosenfeld (1965). *Psychotic States: A Psycho-Analytical Approach.* London: Hogarth Press and Institute of Psycho-Analysis, pp. 34–51.

Rosenfeld, H. A. (1950). Note on the psychopathology of confusional states in chronic schizophrenias. *International Journal of Psychoanalysis*, *31*, 132–137.

Rosenfeld, H. A. (1952a). Notes on the psychoanalysis of the superego conflict in an acute schizophrenic patient. *International Journal of Psychoanalysis*, *33*, 111–131.

Rosenfeld, H. A. (1952b). Transference-phenomena and transference-analysis in an acute catatonic schizophrenic patient. *International Journal of Psychoanalysis*, *33*, 457–464.

Rosenfeld, H. A. (1954). Considerations regarding the psycho-analytic approach to acute and chronic schizophrenia. In Rosenfeld (1965). *Psychotic States: A Psycho-Analytical Approach.* London: Hogarth Press and Institute of Psycho-Analysis, pp. 117–127.

Rosenfeld, H. A. (1964a). Object relations of an acute schizophrenic patient in the transference situation. In P. Solomon and B. C. Glueck (Eds.), *Recent Research on Schizophrenia: Psychiatric Research Reports of the American Psychiatric Association.* Washington, DC: American Psychiatric Association.

Rosenfeld, H. A. (1964b). On the psychopathology of narcissism: a clinical approach. *International Journal of Psycho-Analysis*, *45*, 332–337. Also published in Rosenfeld (1965). *Psychotic States: A Psycho-Analytical Approach.* London: Hogarth Press and Institute of Psycho-Analysis, pp. 1169–1179.

Rosenfeld, H. A. (1965). *Psychotic States: A Psycho-Analytical Approach.* London: Hogarth Press and Institute of Psycho-Analysis.

Rosenfeld, H. A. (1969). The negative therapeutic reaction. In P. Giovacchini (Ed.) (1975). *Tactics and Techniques in Psychoanalytic Theory*, Volume 2. New York: Jason Aronson.

Rosenfeld, H. A. (1971). Contribution to the psychopathology of psychotic states: the importance of projective identification in the ego structure and object relations of the psychotic patient. In P. Doucet and C. Laurin (Eds.),

Problems of Psychosis, Volume 1. The Hague: Excerpta Medica, pp. 115–128. Also published in E. Spillius (Ed.) (1988). *Melanie Klein Today: Developments in Theory and Practice.* Volume 1: *Mainly Theory.* London: Routledge, pp. 117–137.

Rosenfeld, H. A. (1983). Primitive object relations and mechanisms. *International Journal of Psycho-Analysis, 64,* 261–267.

Rosenfeld, H. A. (1987a). *Impasse and Interpretation.* London: Routledge.

Rosenfeld, H. A. (1987b). The influence of projective identification on the analyst's task. In Rosenfeld, *Impasse and Interpretation.* London: Routledge, pp. 157–264.

Rosenfeld, H. A. (1987c). Projective identification in clinical practice. In Rosenfeld, *Impasse and Interpretation.* London: Routledge, pp. 157–189.

Rosenman, S. (2003). Assaultive projective identification and the plundering of the victim's identity. *Journal of the American Academy of Psychoanalysis, 31,* 521–540.

Roth, P. (1999). General introduction. In R. Riesenberg Malcolm and P. Roth (Eds.), *On bearing unbearable states of mind.* London: Routledge, pp. 1–7.

Roudinesco, E. and Plon, M. (1997). *Dictionnaire de la psychanalyse.* Paris: Fayard.

Roussillon, R. (1999). *Agonie, clivages et symbolisation* [Agony, Splitting and Symbolization]. Paris: Presses Universitaires de France (PUF).

Sagawa, R. Y. (1980). *Durval Marcondes e o início do movimento psicanalítico brasileiro* [Durval Marcondes and the Beginning of the Psychoanalytic Movement in Brazil]. São Paulo: Cortez, Cadernos Freud/Lacan.

Sagawa, R. Y. (1992). *Redescobrir as psicanálises* [Rediscovering Psychoanalysis]. São Paulo: Lemos.

Sandler, J. (1960). Identification in children, parents and doctors. In R. MacKeith and J. Sandler (Eds.), *Psychosomatic Aspects of Paediatrics.* London: Pergamon.

Sandler, J. (1976a). Countertransference and role–responsiveness. *International Review of Psychoanalysis, 3,* 43–48.

Sandler, J. (1976b). Dreams, unconscious fantasies and 'identity of perception'. *International Review of Psycho-Analysis, 3,* 33–42.

Sandler, J. (1983). Reflections on some relations between psychoanalytic concepts and psychoanalytic practice. *International Journal of Psychoanalysis, 64,* 35–45.

Sandler, J. (1987a). The concept of projective identification. In J. Sandler (Ed.), *Projection, Identification, Projective Identification.* Madison, CT: International Universities Press, pp. 13–26. Also published as Sandler (1987). The concept of projective identification. *Bulletin of the Anna Freud Centre, 10,* 33–49.

Sandler, J. (Ed.) (1987b). *Projection, Identification, Projective Identification.* Madison, CT: International Universities Press.

Sandler, J. (1990). On internal object relations. *Journal of the American Psychoanalytic Association, 38,* 859–880.

Sandler, J. (1993). On communication from patient to analyst: Not everything is projective identification. Thirty-eighth International Psychoanalytical Congress Presidential Address: From Listening to Interpretation (1993, Amsterdam, Netherlands). *International Journal of Psycho-Analysis*, 74(6), 1097–1107.

Sandler, J. and Dreher, A. U. (1996). *What Do Psychoanalysts Want?* London: Routledge.

Sandler, J. and Joffe, W. G. (1967). The tendency to persistence in psychological function and development, with special reference to fixation and regression. *Bulletin of the Menninger Clinic*, *31*, 257–271.

Sandler, J. and Rosenblatt, B. (1962). The concept of the representational world. *Psychoanalytic Study of the Child*, *17*, 128–162.

Sandler, J. and Sandler, A.-M. (1978). On the development of object relationships and affects. *International Journal of Psychoanalysis*, *59*, 285–296.

Sandler, J. and Sandler, A.-M. (1984). The past unconscious, the present unconscious and interpretation of the transference. *Psychoanalytic Inquiry*, *4*, 367–399.

Sandler, J., Dare, C. and Holder, A. (1973). *The Patient and the Analyst: The Basis of the Psychoanalytic Process*. New York: International Universities Press.

Schafer, R. (1968). *Aspects of Internalization*. New York: International Universities Press.

Scharff, J. S. (1992). *Projective and Introjective Identification and the Use of the Therapist's Self*. New York: Jason Aronson.

Schur, M. (1972). *Freud: Living and Dying*. New York: International University Press.

Searles, H. F. (1962). The differentiation between concrete and metaphorical thinking in the recovering schizophrenic patient. *Journal of the American Psychoanalytic Association*, *10*, 22–49.

Searles, H. F. (1963). Transference psychosis in the psychotherapy of chronic schizophrenia. *International Journal of Psycho-Analysis*, *44*, 249–281. Also in Searles (1965). *Collected Papers on Schizophrenia and Related Subjects*. London: Maresfield Library, pp. 654–716.

Searles, H. F. (1975). The patient as therapist to the analyst. In P. Giovacchini (Ed.), *Tactics and Techniques in Psychoanalytic Theory*, Volume 2. New York Jason Aronson.

Segal, H. (1950). Some aspects of the analysis of a schizophrenic. *International Journal of Psychoanalysis*, *31*, 268–278.

Segal, H. (1957). Notes on symbol formation. *International Journal of Psycho-Analysis*, *38*, 391–397.

Segal, H. (1962). The curative factors in psycho-analysis. *International Journal of Psycho-Analysis*, *43*, 212–227.

Segal, H. (1964). *Introduction to the Work of Melanie Klein*. London: Heinemann.

Segal, H. (1973). *Introduction to the Work of Melanie Klein*, new enlarged edn. London: Hogarth Press and Institute of Psycho-Analysis.

Segal, H. (1981). Countertransference. In Segal, *The Work of Hanna Segal: A Kleinian Approach to Clinical Practice*. New York: Jason Aronson, pp. 81–88.

Sinason, M. (1993). Who is the mad voice inside? *Psychoanalytic Psychotherapy*, 7, 207–221.

Sinason, M. (1999). How can you keep your hair on? In P. Williams (Ed.), *Psychosis (Madness)*. London: Karnac.

Sister, B. M. and Taffarel, M. (1996). *Isaías Melsohn, A psicanálise e a vida: setenta anos de histórias paulistanas e a formação de um pensamento renovador na psicanálise*. São Paulo: Escuta.

Smith, H. F. (2000). Countertransference, conflictual listening and the analytic object relationship. *Journal of the American Psychoanalytic Association*, 48, 95–128.

Smith, H. F. (2002). Creating the psychoanalytical process, incorporating three panel reports: opening the process, being in the process and closing the process. *International Journal of Psychoanalysis*, 83, 211–227.

Smith, H. F. (2006). Analyzing disavowed action: the fundamental resistance of analysis. *Journal of the American Psychoanalytic Association*, 54, 713–737.

Sodré, I. (2004). Who's who? Notes on pathological identifications. In E. Hargreaves and A. Varchevker (Eds.), *In Pursuit of Psychic Change: The Betty Joseph Workshop*. London: Brunner-Routledge, pp. 53–68.

Sohn, L. (1985). Narcissistic organisation, projective identification and the formation of the identificate. *International Journal of Psychoanalysis*, 66, 201–214.

Speziale-Bagliacca, R. (1983). *Introduction to Grotstein J.J., Scissione e identificazione proiettiva*. Rome: Armando.

Spillius, E. B. (1988a). Introduction to 'projective identification'. In Spillius (Ed.), *Melanie Klein Today: Developments in Theory and Practice*. Volume 1: *Mainly Theory*. London: Routledge, pp. 81–86.

Spillius, E. B. (Ed.) (1988b). *Melanie Klein Today: Developments in Theory and Practice*. Volume 1: *Mainly Theory*. London: Routledge.

Spillius, E. B. (Ed.) (1990). *Melanie Klein Heute: Entwicklungen in Theorie und Praxis*. Band 1: *Beiträge zur Theorie* [Melanie Klein Today: Developments in Theory and Practice. Volume 1: Mainly Theory]. Stuttgart: Klett-Cotta.

Spillius, E. B. (1992). Clinical experiences of projective identification. In R. Anderson (Ed.), *Clinical Lectures on Klein and Bion*. London: Routledge, pp. 59–73.

Spillius, E. B. (1994). Developments in Kleinian thought: overview and personal view. *Psychoanalytic Inquiry*, 14, 324–364.

Spillius, E. B. (2002). A brief introduction to the concept of projective identification. *Psychoanalysis in Europe, Bulletin 56*, 115–117.

Spillius, E. B. (2007). *Encounters with Melanie Klein*, edited by Priscilla Roth and Richard Rusbridger. London: Routledge.

Spira, M. (1985). *Créativité et liberté psychique* [Creativity and Psychic Freedom]. Lyon: Césura.

Spitz, R. (1965). *The First Year of Life*. New York: International Universities Press.

Spotnitz, H. (1969). *Modern Psychoanalysis of the Schizophrenic Patient*. New York: Grune & Stratton.

Steffens, W. (1999). Bemerkungen über Verfolgung, Verzweiflung und Wiedergutmachung [Remarks on persecution, despair and reparation]. In C. Frank (Ed.), *Stillstand, Veränderung und die Angst vor einer Katastrophe. Perspektiven Kleinianischer Psychoanalyse* [Standstill, Change and the Anxiety of a Catastrophe. Perspectives in Kleinian Psychoanalysis]. Tübingen: Diskord, pp. 61–84.

Steiner, J. (1993). *Psychic Retreats: Pathological Organisations in Psychotic, Neurotic and Borderline Patients*. London: Routledge.

Steiner, R. (1985). Some thoughts about tradition and change arising from an examination of the British Psychoanalytical Society's Controversial Discussions (1943–1944). *International Review of Psychoanalysis, 12*, 27–71.

Steiner, R. (1999). Who influenced whom? And how? *International Journal of Psychoanalysis, 80*, 349–375.

Strachey, J. (1934). The nature of the therapeutic action of psychoanalysis. *International Journal of Psychoanalysis, 15*, 127–159.

Strachey, J. (1951). Letter from Strachey to Jones, October 24, 1951. Strachey Archives, Institute of Psychoanalysis, London.

Tähkä, T. A. (1977). Presentation at the Sixth World Congress of Psychiatry, Honolulu, Hawaii.

Tansey, M. and Burke, W. (1985). Projective identification and the empathic process: interactional communications. *Contemporary Psychoanalysis, 21*, 42–69.

Tansey, M. and Burke, W. (1989). *Understanding Countertransference: From Projective Identification to Empathy*. Hillsdale, NJ: Analytic Press.

Thomä, H. and Kächele, H. (1985). *Lehrbuch der Psychoanalytischen Therapie* [Textbook of Psychoanalytical Therapy], Volumes 1 and 2. Berlin: Springer.

Thorner, H. A. (1963). Ursache, Grund und Motiv. Ein psychoanalytischer Beitrag zum Verständnis psychosomatischer Phänomene [Cause, Reason and Motive: A Psychoanalytical Contribution to Understanding Psychosomatic Phenomena]. *Psyche: Zeitschrift für Psychoanalyse und ihre Anwendungen, 16*, 670–685.

Tonnesmann, M. (1989). Editor's Introduction. In Tonnesmann (Ed.), *About Children and Children-No-Longer: Collected Papers of Paula Heimann, 1942–80*. London: Routledge.

Trinca, W. (1991). *A etérea leveza da experiência* [The Ethereal Lightness of Experience]. São Paulo: Siciliano.

Trinca, W. (1992). Dreams, psychic mobility and inner being. *Free Associations, 8*(4), 562–575.

Trinca, W. (2007). *O ser interior na psicanálise: fundamentos, modelos e processos* [The Interior Being in Psychoanalysis]. São Paulo: Vetor.

Tuckett, D. (1997). Mutual enactment in the psychoanalytic situation. In J. L. Ahumada, J. Olagaray, A. K. Richards and A. D.Richards (Eds.), *The Perverse Transference and Other Matters: Essays in Honor of R. Horacio Etchegoyen*. Northvale, NJ: Jason Aronson.

Tuckett, D. (2005). Does anything go? Towards a framework for the more transparent assessment of psychoanalytic competence. *International Journal of Psychoanalysis, 86*, 31–49.

Wallerstein, R. (1988). One psychoanalysis or many? *International Journal of Psycho-Analysis, 69*, 5–21.

Weiss, E. (1925). Über eine noch nicht beschriebene Phase der Entwicklung zur heterosexuellen Liebe. *Internationale Zeitschrift für Psychoanalyse, 11*, 429–443.

Whipple, D. (1986). Discussion of 'The merits and problems with the concept of projective identification' by Janet Finell. *Psychoanalytic Review, 73*, 121–128.

Widlöcher, D. (2003). L'avenir de la psychanalyse: débat entre Daniel Widlöcher et Jacques-Alain Miller [The future of psychoanalysis: debate between Daniel Widlöcher and Jacques-Alain Miller]. *Psychiatrie, Sciences Humaines, Neurosciences, 1*(1), 10–18.

Winnicott, D. W. (1945). Primitive emotional development. *International Journal of Psychoanalysis, 26*, 137–143.

Winnicott, D. W. (1949). Hate in the countertransference. *International Journal of Psycho-Analysis, 30*, 69–75.

Winnicott, D. W. (1952). Psychoses and childcare. In Winnicott (1975). *Through Paediatrics to Psycho-Analysis*. New York: Basic Books.

Winnicott, D. W. (1953). Transitional objects and transitional phenomena. *International Journal of Psycho-Analysis, 34*, 1–9.

Winnicott, D. W. (1956). Primary maternal preoccupation. In Winnicott (Ed.) (1958). *Collected Papers: Through Paediatrics to Psycho-analysis*. London: Tavistock, pp. 300–305.

Winnicott, D. W. (1958). *Collected Papers*. London: Tavistock.

Winnicott, D. W. (1960). Countertransference. In Winnicott (1965). *The Maturational Processes and the Facilitating Environment*. New York: International Universities Press.

Winnicott, D. W. (1967). Mirror-role of the mother and family in child development. In P. Lomas (Ed.), *The Predicament of the Family: A Psycho-Analytical Symposium*. London: Hogarth Press, pp. 26–33.

Winnicott, D. W. (1971). *Playing and Reality*. London: Tavistock.

Wisdom, J. O. (1962). Ein methodologischer Versuch zum Hysterieproblem [A methodological approach to the problem of hysteria]. *Psyche: Zeitschrift für Psychoanalyse und ihre Anwendungen, 15*, 561–587.

Zanin, J. C. (2004). Uma época fértil e evolutiva da Psicanálise no Rio de Janeiro. In P. Marchon (Ed.), *A psicanálise no Rio de Janeiro e sua difusão pelo Brasil*. São Paulo: CNPQ, Coleção Memória do Saber.

Zinner, J. and Shapiro, R. (1972). Projective identification as a mode of perception and behaviour in families of adolescents. *International Journal of Psychoanalysis, 53*, 523–530.

Zwiebel, R. (1985). Das Konzept der projektiven Identifizierung. Bericht über die Tagung 'Projektion, Identifikation, projektive Identifizierung' (Jerusalem, 27–29 May 1984). [The concept of projective identification. Report on the conference 'Screening, Identification, Projective Identification']. *Psyche: Zeitschrift für Psychoanalyse und ihre Anwendungen, 39*, 456–468.

Zwiebel, R. (1988). Einige klinische Anmerkungen zur Theorie der Projektiven Identifizierung [Some clinical remarks about the theory of projective identification]. *Zeitschrift für Psychoanalytische Theorie und Praxis, 3*(2), 165–186.

Index